Springer Series in Cognitive Development

Series Editor
Charles J. Brainerd

Springer Series in Cognitive Development
Series Editor: Charles J. Brainerd
(recent titles)

Adult Cognition: An Experimental Psychology of Human Aging
Timothy A. Salthouse

Recent Advances in Cognitive-Developmental Theory: Progress in Cognitive Development Research
Charles J. Brainerd (Ed.)

Learning in Children: Progress in Cognitive Development Research
Jeffrey Bisanz/Gay L. Bisanz/Robert Kail (Eds.)

Cognitive Strategy Research: Psychological Foundations
Michael Pressley/Joel R. Levin (Eds.)

Cognitive Strategy Research: Educational Applications
Michael Pressley/Joel R. Levin (Eds.)

Equilibrium in the Balance: A Study of Psychological Explanation
Sophie Haroutunian

Crib Speech and Language Play
Stan A. Kuczaj, II

Discourse Development: Progress in Cognitive Development Research
Stan A. Kuczaj, II (Ed.)

Cognitive Development in Atypical Children: Progress in Cognitive Development Research
Linda S. Siegel/Frederick J. Morrison (Eds.)

Basic Processes in Memory Development: Progress in Cognitive Development Research
Charles J. Brainerd/Michael Pressley (Eds.)

Cognitive Learning and Memory in Children: Progress in Cognitive Development Research
Michael Pressley/Charles J. Brainerd (Eds.)

The Development of Word Meaning
Stan A. Kuczaj, II/Martyn D. Barrett (Eds.)

The Development of Word Meaning

Progress in Cognitive Development Research

Edited by
Stan A. Kuczaj, II and Martyn D. Barrett

Springer-Verlag
New York Berlin Heidelberg Tokyo

Stan A. Kuczaj, II
Department of Psychology
Southern Methodist University
Dallas, Texas 75275
U.S.A.

Martyn D. Barrett
Department of Psychology
Roehampton Institute
Digby Stuart College
London SW15 5PH
U.K.

Series Editor
Charles J. Brainerd
Department of Psychology
University of Alberta
Edmonton, Alberta
Canada T6G 2E9

With 21 Figures

Library of Congress Cataloging-in-Publication Data
Main entry under title:
The development of word meaning.
(Springer series in cognitive development)
  Bibliography: p.
  Includes index.
  1. Cognition in children.   2. Semantics.
3. Language acquisition.   I. Kuczaj, Stan A.
II. Barrett, Martyn D.   III. Title.   IV. Series.
BF723.C5D493   1985   155.4′13   85-17276

© 1986 by Springer-Verlag New York Inc.
All rights reserved. No part of this book may be translated or reproduced in any form without written permission from Springer-Verlag, 175 Fifth Avenue, New York, New York 10010, U.S.A.
The use of general descriptive names, trade names, trademarks, etc., in this publication, even if the former are not especially identified, is not to be taken as a sign that such names, as understood by the Trade Marks and Merchandise Marks Act, may accordingly be used freely by anyone.

Typeset by Publishers Service, Bozeman, Montana.
Printed and bound by R.R. Donnelley & Sons, Harrisonburg, Virginia.
Printed in the United States of America.

9 8 7 6 5 4 3 2 1

ISBN 0-387-96152-6 Springer-Verlag New York Berlin Heidelberg Tokyo
ISBN 3-540-96152-6 Springer-Verlag Berlin Heidelberg New York Tokyo

*This book is dedicated to
transatlantic conferences, cooperation, and dances
(not necessarily in that order)*

Series Preface

For some time now, the study of cognitive development has been far and away the most active discipline within developmental psychology. Although there would be much disagreement as to the exact proportion of papers published in developmental journals that could be considered cognitive, 50% seems like a conservative estimate. Hence, a series of scholarly books devoted to work in cognitive development is especially appropriate at this time.

The *Springer Series in Cognitive Development* contains two basic types of books, namely, edited collections of original chapters by several authors, and original volumes written by one author or a small group of authors. The flagship for the Springer Series is a serial publication of the "advances" types, carrying the subtitle *Progress in Cognitive Development Research*. Each volume in the *Progress* sequence is strongly thematic, in that it is limited to some well-defined domain of cognitive-developmental research (e.g., logical and mathematical development, development of learning). All *Progress* volumes will be edited collections. Editors of such collections, upon consultation with the Series Editor, may elect to have their books published either as contributions to the *Progress* sequence or as separate volumes. All books written by one author or a small group of authors are being published as separate volumes within the series.

A fairly broad definition of cognitive development is being used in the selection of books for this series. The classic topics of concept development, children's thinking and reasoning, the development of learning, language development, and memory development will, of course, be included. So, however, will newer areas such as social-cognitive development, educational applications, formal modeling, and philosophical implications of cognitive–developmental theory. Although it is anticipated that most books in the series will be empirical in orientation, theoretical and philosophical works are also welcome. With books of the latter sort, heterogeneity of theoretical perspective is encouraged, and no attempt will be made to foster some specific theoretical perspective at the expense of others (e.g., Piagetian versus behavioral or behavioral versus information processing).

C. J. Brainerd

Preface

Parents, scholars, and scholar-parents (or parent-scholars) have long been fascinated with young children's acquisition of word meaning. Interest in this topic was largely anecdotal until the 1970s, during which time the theories of Eve Clark (Clark, 1973) and Katherine Nelson (Nelson, 1974) provided the impetus for many scholars to search for reliable empirical techniques that would provide both accurate descriptions of word-meaning acquisition and reasonable bases from which to evaluate theories of word-meaning acquisition. The resulting investigations have broadened our understanding of the relation between word-meaning acquisition and developmental period, at least insofar as descriptions of word-meaning acquisition are concerned.

There seem to be three general phases of word-meaning acquisition. The first phase begins somewhere around 10–12 months of age and lasts until approximately 16–18 months of age. During this phase, children produce idiosyncratic sounds and/or words which do not appear to be used in a true referential manner. Instead, they are used in a specific contextualized fashion (Barrett, 1985; Bates, Benigni, Bretherton, Camaioni, & Volterra, 1979; Halliday, 1975). In addition, vocabulary growth is quite slow—children adding one to three words per month to their primitive lexicon (Nelson, 1973). The event-bound words discussed by Barrett (Chapter 2, this volume) and the social-personal words discussed by Gopnik and Meltzoff (Chapter 8, this volume) first appear during this initial period of word-meaning acquisition.

The second phase begins when children start to use words in a referential manner: Children begin to *name* objects, actions, states, and attributes. These names are no longer idiosyncratic as they were in the first phase, but instead are the conventional names used by the speakers in the children's language-learning environment. Although children learn conventional names quickly during this phase (20–50 new words per month; Halliday, 1975; Nelson, 1973), they make many errors in the use of such words, demonstrating that word-meaning acquisition involves both the learning of conventional labels and the determination of the appropriate meaning of these labels. Knowing a word does not necessitate that the child (or adult, for that matter) also knows the particular meaning to which the word should be attached. In fact, much of the work concerned with this and the next phase of lexical-meaning acquisition has focused on the manner in which children determine the appropriate meanings of conventional labels (e.g., see Barrett, 1978; Kuczaj, 1975, 1982). In this book, the chapters by Anglin, Barrett, Edwards and Goodwin, Gopnik and Meltzoff, and Kuczaj (Chapters 4, 2, 10, 8, and 5, respectively) consider different aspects of the developments of the lexicon that occur during these phases.

The third phase of word-meaning acquisition begins sometime during the third year of life, with vocabulary growth continuing to proceed at the rate of 50 or more new words per month (Smith, 1926; Templin, 1957). The main characteristic of this phase is the addition to the lexicon of many new *types* of words, including a variety of logical connectives. The chapters by Dockrell and Campbell, French, and McShane, Whittaker, and Dockrell (Chapters 6, 12, and 11, respectively) in this book consider various aspects of word-meaning acquisition that occur within this third phase.

Although this description of the three phases of word-meaning acquisition suggests that we have learned a great deal about the general course of word-meaning acquisition, it is important to note that it is in fact only a description of word-meaning acquisition, not an explanation of the processes involved in such acquisition. Despite the advances made in the descriptive level in the past decade, explanations of word-meaning acquisition have lagged. At present, it seems safest to say that we can ask questions, but are unable to provide answers. These questions fall into four main categories.

Question Category 1. What are the similarities and differences between the three general developmental phases? The above description of these phases has highlighted certain of the differences between them, but it is possible that the phases reflect different manifestations of the same symbolic processes, the apparent differences masking the continuity of the underlying processes. Or the differences between the three phases may result from different symbolic processes, more primitive ones being used in the earliest phase and more advanced ones being used in subsequent phases. Obviously, in order to resolve these issues, it will be necessary to focus more on the nature of the symbolic processes than on the description of similarities and differences of the phases. Thus, we need more reasonable speculations as well as additional reliable and valid descriptions.

Question Category 2. How do children acquire the meanings of words? At first blush, this would appear to be the only question that might be asked of word-meaning acquisition. However, the questions that fall within this general category recognize the richness and diversity that characterize word-meaning acquisition. On the one hand, we might ask what phenomena characterize the acquisition of the meanings of object names, action names, nouns, verbs, logical connectives, and so on. On the other hand, we must consider the similarities and differences that characterize the acquisition of these different types of words, as well as similarities and differences in production and comprehension (see Chapter 4 by Anglin and Chapter 5 by Kuczaj, this volume, for discussions of these issues). Answers to these questions will depend on our ability to accurately specify: (a) the nature of semantic representations that are acquired during the course of word-meaning acquisition, and (b) the cognitive processes that are involved in the acquisition of these representations. Although it may be possible to account for word-meaning acquisition in terms of one overarching theory, at present we are faced with a wide range of specific accounts of specific acquisitions (see Chapter 1 by Merriman, this volume, for a discussion of the problems facing the most ambitious theories to date, namely those of Clark and Nelson). The different chapters in this book reflect the diversified nature of lexical development (e.g., compare Chapters 6, 12, and 8, this volume, by Dockrell & Campbell, French, and Gopnik & Meltzoff). Nonetheless, there appears to be some consensus emerging in one area, namely the acquisition of object words. A variety of theorists have suggested that object word meaning may be related to prototype-based concepts (see Chapters 7, 4, 2, 5, and 3, this volume, by Adams & Bullock; Anglin; Barrett; Kuczaj; and Tager-Flusberg). Whether or not this consensus holds, and whether a similar consensus can be reached for action names, state names, logical connectives, and so on remains to be seen. Hopefully, the chapters in this book will stimulate additional work on all types of word-meaning acquisition and eventually help to answer these basic theoretical issues.

Question Category 3. What are the factors that influence the course of lexical development? For example, how do children's developing cognitive capabilities influence, constrain, or facilitate word-meaning acquisition? Newly acquired words might map directly onto well-established cognitive categories. Alternatively, the acquisition of lexical knowledge might facilitate cognitive-developmental changes. Or the relationship between cognitive and lexical development might consist of a two-way interdependence (see Chapter 8 by Gopnik & Meltzoff, this volume, for a discussion of these issues). Other factors that might influence lexical development concern linguistic input and communicative needs. Characteristics of the input to children may help to explain why young children acquire many more object names than any other type of word (see Chapter 9, this volume, by Bridges) and why children acquire some types of object names before others (see Chapter 7 by Adams & Bullock). Similarly, the communicative needs of young children may influence the meanings that children attach to action names (see Chapter 10 by Edwards & Goodwin).

Question Category 4. How is syntactic and morphological information related to lexical development? It seems likely that considerable syntactic and morphological information is stored in the lexicon (Lyons, 1977). This information depends on the formation of form-classes and as such may affect the structure and organization of the lexicon. Although there has been precious little work on this topic, Chapter 11 by McShane, Whittaker, and Dockrell in this book examines the possibility that the acquisition of verb inflections to encode aspect and tense reveals considerable information about the internal structure of the verb lexicon (see Maratsos, 1983, for further discussion of these issues).

The above set of questions, albeit not mutually exclusive, strike us as critical ones insofar as the eventual evolution of a comprehensive theory of word-meaning acquisition is concerned. Until such a theory is advanced, evaluated, reformulated, and accepted, we shall have to struggle along trying to fit the pieces of the puzzle together. It is a formidable task in that we lack many of the pieces, but we must continue to add pieces until we have the complete puzzle. Of course, once we have all of the pieces, we will still have to put them together. It is our hope that the wide range of issues and concerns expressed by the contributors to this book will help accomplish these goals.

References

Barrett, M. D. (1978). Lexical development and overextension in child language. *Journal of Child Language*, 5, 205-219.

Barrett, M. D. (Ed.) (1985). *Children's single-word speech*. New York: John Wiley & Sons.

Bates, E., Benigni, L., Bretherton, I., Camaioni, L., & Volterra, V. (1979). *The emergence of symbols: Cognition and communication in infancy*. New York: Academic Press.

Clark, E. V. (1973). What's in a word? On the child's acquisition of semantics in his first language. In T. E. Moore (Ed.), *Cognitive development and the acquisition of language*. New York: Academic Press.

Halliday, M. A. K. (1975). *Learning how to mean: Explorations in the development of language*. London: Edward Arnold.

Kuczaj, S. A. (1975). On the acquisition of a semantic system. *Journal of Verbal Learning and Verbal Behavior*, 14, 340-358.

Kuczaj, S. A. (1982). The acquisition of word meaning in the context of the development of the semantic system. In C. Brainerd & M. Pressley (Eds.), *Verbal processes in children*. New York: Springer-Verlag.

Lyons, J. (1977). *Semantics, Vol. 2*. New York: Cambridge University Press.

Maratsos, M. P. (1983). Some current issues in the study of the acquisition of grammar. In P. H. Mussen (Eds.), *Handbook of Child Psychology, 4th Ed.: Vol. 3. Cognitive development*. New York: John Wiley & Sons.

Nelson, K. (1973). Structure and strategy in learning to talk. *Monographs of the Society for Research in Child Development*, 38, (serial No. 149).

Nelson, K. (1974). Concept, word, and sentence: Interrelations in acquisition and development. *Psychological Review*, 81, 267-285.

Smith, M. E. (1926). An investigation of the development of the sentence and the extent of vocabulary in young children. *University of Iowa Studies in Child Welfare*, 3, No. 5.

Templin, M. C. (1957). Certain language skills in children: Their development and interrelationships. *University of Minnesota Institute of Child Welfare Monograph*, 26.

London
July, 1985

Stan A. Kuczaj, II
Martyn D. Barrett

Contents

Chapter 1	**How Children Learn the Reference of Concrete Nouns: A Critique of Current Hypotheses** .... *William E. Merriman*	1
	The Original Hypotheses of Clark and Nelson	1
	Subsequent Developments	11
	Revisions and Extensions	19
	Conclusions and Some Suggestions for Future Research	32
Chapter 2	**Early Semantic Representations and Early Word-Usage** .... *Martyn D. Barrett*	39
	The Principal Phenomena Characterizing Early Word-Usage ..	39
	The Development of Semantic Representations: A Summary of the Proposed Model	58
	Conclusions	64
Chapter 3	**Constraints on the Representation of Word Meaning: Evidence From Autistic and Mentally Retarded Children** ... *Helen Tager-Flusberg*	69
	The Study	71
	Results	72
	Discussion	78

Contents

Chapter 4 Semantic and Conceptual Knowledge Underlying the
Child's Words 83
Jeremy M. Anglin

Extensional Studies 84
Interview Studies 89
Conclusion 94

Chapter 5 Thoughts on the Intensional Basis of Early Object
Word Extension: Evidence From Comprehension
and Production 99
Stan A. Kuczaj, II

Object Word Meaning 99
Children's Extension Errors 100
The Comprehension/Production Issue 101
The Notion of Prototypes and Its Implications for the
Comprehension/Production Issue 103
Conclusions and Speculations 114
An Unembarrassed Return to the Notion of Prototype-Based
Word Meaning 115

Chapter 6 Lexical Acquisition Strategies in the Preschool Child 121
Julie Dockrell and Robin Campbell

What's in a Word? 122
Data Bases and Strategies 124
The Input 131
Experimental Evidence 135
Conclusion 148

Chapter 7 Apprenticeship in Word Use: Social Convergence
Processes in Learning Categorically Related Nouns 155
Alison K. Adams and Daniel Bullock

The Vygotsky-Wittgenstein Legacy 156
Some Clarifications and Implications 160
The Framework Applied to Maternal Labeling Research ... 163
Factors Affecting Parent-Child Reference Patterns 165
An Illustrative Study 171
Conclusion 191

Contents xv

Chapter 8   Words, Plans, Things, and Locations: Interactions Between Semantic and Cognitive Development in the One-Word Stage 199
Alison Gopnik and Andrew N. Meltzoff

Meaning in the One-Word Stage 200
Words About Things 200
Words About Plans 204
Words About Locations 206
Other Early Words and Meanings 207
Changes in the Meanings of Early Words 208
Summary 209
Conceptual Development and Early Meaning 210
Theories of Semantic Development in the One-Word Stage 216
An Alternative Hypothesis 218

Chapter 9   Actions and Things: What Adults Talk About to 1-Year-Olds 225
Allayne Bridges

Speech Input Characteristics 229
What Is the Topic of Conversation: Action or Object? 231
Mother Speech Styles 235
Conversational Demands and Child-Directed Speech 237
Descriptive Comments About Objects and Actions 238
Directing Visual Attention 242
Directing Actions 244
Promoting Verbal Responses 246
Conclusion 249

Chapter 10 Action Words and Pragmatic Function in Early Language 257
Derek Edwards and Roger Goodwin

Action Words: Classes and Contexts 258
Data: Actions and State Changes 261
The Pragmatics of Early Action Words 269
Mental Process Verbs 271
Conclusions 272

Chapter 11 Verbs and Time 275
John McShane, Stephen Whittaker, and Julie Dockrell

Cutting Up Verbs 275
Time Talk 278
The Category *Verb* 293
Conclusion 299

Chapter 12 Acquiring and Using Words to Express Logical Relationships 303
Lucia A. French

Selective Review of the Literature Concerning Children's Understanding of the Terms *Before*, *After*, *Because*, *So*, *If*, *But*, and *Or* 306
Production and Comprehension Measures 313
Content as a Context for Comprehending Relational Terms... 320
Conclusions... 331
Summary 332

Author Index 339
Subject Index 347

Contributors

Alison K. Adams Department of Psychology, University of Hawaii, Honolulu, Hawaii 96822, U.S.A.

Jeremy M. Anglin Department of Psychology, University of Waterloo, Waterloo, Ontario N2L 3G1, Canada.

Martyn D. Barrett Department of Psychology, Roehampton Institute, Digby Stuart College, London SW15 5PH, U.K.

Allayne Bridges Department of Psychology, University of Birmingham, Birmingham B15 2TT, U.K.

Daniel Bullock Department of Psychology, University of Denver, Denver, Colorado 80208, U.S.A.

Robin Campbell Department of Psychology, University of Stirling, Stirling FK9 4LA, Scotland.

Julie Dockrell The Royal National Throat, Nose, and Ear Hospital, Nuffield Speech and Hearing Centre, London WC1, U.K.

Derek Edwards Department of Social Sciences, Loughborough University, Loughborough, Leicestershire LE11 3TU, U.K.

Lucia A. French Center for the Study of Psychological Development, Graduate School of Education and Human Development, University of Rochester, Rochester, New York 14627, U.S.A.

Roger Goodwin   Psychology Subject Group, University of Sussex, Brighton, U.K.

Alison Gopnik   Department of Linguistics and Psychology, Scarborough College, University of Toronto, Toronto, Ontario M5S 1A1, Canada.

Stan A. Kuczaj, II   Department of Psychology, Southern Methodist University, Dallas, Texas 75275, U.S.A.

John McShane   Department of Psychology, London School of Economics, London WC2A 2AE, U.K.

Andrew N. Meltzoff   Department of Psychology, University of Washington, Seattle, Washington 98195, U.S.A.

William E. Merriman   Institute of Child Development, University of Minnesota, Minneapolis, Minnesota 55455, U.S.A.

Helen Tager-Flusberg   Department of Psychology, University of Massachusetts, Boston, Massachusetts 02125, U.S.A.

Stephen Whittaker   Department of Psychology, London School of Economics, London WC2A 2AE, U.K.

1. How Children Learn the Reference of Concrete Nouns: A Critique of Current Hypotheses

William E. Merriman

This chapter will trace the historical development of several recent hypotheses about the acquisition of concrete noun reference. This history will begin with the many hypotheses proposed in the seminal papers of Clark (1973a) and Nelson (1974), since much attention over the last 10 years has focused on these hypotheses. Clark and Nelson have responded to developments subsequent to the publication of their hypotheses by revising, extending, and, in some cases, abandoning them as well as by contributing new hypotheses. Four avenues will be taken in critiquing the hypotheses of Clark and Nelson: (a) the hypotheses will be assessed for how well they account for the data they were designed to explain; (b) alternative explanations of these data will be sought; (c) the logical consistency of the hypotheses will be examined; and (d) research in which implications of the hypotheses have been confirmed or disconfirmed will be analyzed. The chapter will dwell on the inadequacies of the hypotheses of Clark and Nelson with the goal of developing a more accurate and more complete account of how children learn the reference of concrete nouns.

The Original Hypotheses of Clark and Nelson

Semantic Feature Acquisition

Clark's hypotheses. Clark (1973a) proposed several hypotheses about lexical development within the framework of a componential theory of word meaning (Postal, 1966; Bierwisch, 1970). In this theory, a set of semantic features constitutes a word's intension—the criterion for using a word to refer to a thing, property, relation, or event. According to Bierwisch (1970), semantic features are symbols for the mental processes by which attributes and relations in the world are perceived and conceptualized.

Clark proposed that when a young child first learns a word, the child derives a small set of semantic features as the word's intension. This set is usually only a subset of the features that make up the adult intension of the word. Clark stressed the incompleteness of the child's set of features over the inappropriateness of any feature. The features the child identifies as criterial are usually criterial for the adult as well.

The empirical basis for Clark's claim of the incompleteness of early word intensions was the reports in several diary studies of children's *overextensions*. An overextension is the use of a term to refer to something outside of the term's extension or set of acceptable referents. For example, calling a squirrel a "kitty" is an overextension of "kitty." Diary studies indicated that overextensions were common errors of children from the time they first started to talk until they were about 2½ years old. According to Clark, overextensions reflect the incompleteness of children's word intensions. For example, a child's intension for "kitty" might consist of the features (four-legged) (furry) and (small). This intension would allow for the overextension of "kitty" to things that are not kitties, but are small, furry, and four-legged. Clark proposed that with development, the child adds features to the intensions of words so that the extensions of the words narrow until they eventually match the adult extensions. For example, the child might add (has whiskers) and (meows) to the intension of "kitty." These features would overrule application of the word to inappropriate animals.

Clark claimed that the *feature addition process* is affected by both cognitive/perceptual development and linguistic input. Cognitive/perceptual development causes new, more complex semantic features to become available for addition to intensions. Linguistic input provides the child with information about the correctness of his or her intensions. The child may be told that he or she has used the right or wrong name. Less directly, new words occurring in input may compel the child to change the intension of old words to accommodate new words. If a new word is applicable to some things to which an old word is applicable, the child may posit a contrastive feature which partitions the extensions of the new and old words. For example, once the child learns that a rabbit is a "bunny"—despite the fact that a rabbit manifests all of the features specified by the intension of "kitty"—the child might attempt to represent a distinction between bunnies and kitties by adding the feature (slinks) to the intension of "kitty" and by taking (hops) plus the previous set of features for "kitty" as the intension of "bunny." Two pieces of evidence that this process occurs are the indications in the diary studies that the end of a particular overextension error often coincides with the acquisition of an appropriate word for a referent (Barrett, 1978) and that the end of the general period of overextensions coincides with a rather abrupt increase in the child's vocabulary (Clark, 1973a).

Clark noted that the referents of an overextended term usually share only features of form and movement, although some share only features of sound, size, taste, texture, or use. These observations prompted Clark to claim that all initial word intensions consist of features derived directly from children's perception of word referents and that only later in development are more abstract features added. For example, relational features such as (is a parent of X) are added to kin terms relatively late. Clark also proposed that general features are added before more specific features. This hypothesis was corroborated by the general pattern, revealed in the diary studies, of initially broad extensions which became narrower with development. If specific features were added early, then early extensions would be narrow. Clark's generalizations rested on the critical assumption that the sample of utterances presented in the diary studies was representative of all utterances of the child. Many have argued that in the sample, overextensions are overrepresented (Nelson, 1974; Anglin, 1977; Rescorla, 1980).

Clark's General-Before-Specific Feature Hypothesis (GBSH) had other sources of empirical support. Clark (1971) found that children's comprehension of "before" and "after" followed the pattern predicted by GBSH. Children initially learned that both words had to do with time, then that both referred to a sequential rather than a simultaneous aspect of time, and, finally, that "before" referred to one temporal ordering and "after" to the reverse ordering. A corollary of GBSH is that terms with several general features in common should be treated as synonyms until more specific differentiating features are added to each. This hypothesis was supported by the results of early investigations of developmental change in children's understanding of pairs of words such as "before" and "after" (Clark, 1971), "more" and "less" (Donaldson & Balfour, 1968), "same" and "different" (Donaldson & Wales, 1970), "ask" and "tell" (Chomsky, 1969), "sister" and "girl," and "brother" and "boy" (Piaget, 1928). More recent investigations have challenged whether children actually treat any of these pairs as synonyms and have shown that certain biases in children's responses to questions with unfamiliar words (Eilers, Oller, & Ellington, 1974; Carey, 1982) or with unfamiliar uses of words (Glucksberg, Hay, & Danks, 1976) could have produced the results of the early investigations. Excellent reviews of the evidence concerning the validity of Clark's hypotheses for parts of speech other than nouns have been written by Richards (1979), Carey (1982), and Blewitt (1982). Also, there is an inconsistency between the view that the child should treat some terms as synonyms until differentiating features are added and the view that the child is predisposed to contrast new terms with known terms.

Feature subtraction and its implications. One of the first amendments made by Clark (1973b) and Clark and Clark (1977) to her original proposals was to allow for the subtraction of features. This process was necessitated by evidence that children occasionally abstract an erroneous feature. For example, many children consider (not an adult) to be a feature of "brother" (Piaget, 1928). This feature must be subtracted if these children are ever to learn the reference of "brother." The investigations of Bloom (1973), Reich (1976), and Anglin (1977) revealed many instances of *underextension*, that is, failure to accept a term for some of its appropriate referents. Underextensions indicate that the intension of a word contains feature(s) that inappropriately restrict its extension. These features must be subtracted.

The GBSH is affected by the admission of *feature subtraction*. Since some child word intensions contain unnecessary features, it is likely that some of these are unnecessary because they are too specific. Of course, an underextension can result from an inappropriate general feature, for example, (not an adult) in the intension of "brother." However, some of the examples reported by investigators suggest the incorporation of inappropriate specific features, for example, Dale (1976) reported that (contains blueberries) was a feature of "muffin" for his child.

The possibility that early intensions contain very specific features also indicates that some word pairs such as "brother" and "boy," which share general features, may never be treated as synonyms during development. For example, before the child has acquired the relational features that distinguish "brother" from "boy," the child may have attached very specific features such as (lives in the same house as X) to "brother," thus distinguishing it from "boy." Clark (1973a) claimed that social or functional features such as (lives in the same house as X) are added only after more general, perceptually derived features such as (male) and (not an adult). This claim is based on the features mentioned in the definitions which children of different ages give for "brother" and on children's replies to questions such as, "Is every boy a brother?" (Piaget, 1928; Danziger, 1957; Haviland & Clark, 1974). However, these test situations put excessive demands on children's ability to think about words in the absence of their referents and to put those thoughts into words. Anglin (1977) has demonstrated that the features children mention in their definitions of words are not always adhered to in their comprehension and production of those words. Also, Chambers and Tavuchis (1976) found that 6-year-olds who were shown a picture of a family could correctly respond to, "If these two boys (in the picture) each have different parents, are they still brothers to each other?" Six-year-olds do not mention the necessity of having the same parents in their definitions of "brother" (Danziger, 1957). Whether the order of changes in the features of kinship terms suggested by changes in definitions is the same as that suggested by earlier changes in the comprehension and production of such terms remains for future research to determine.

The issue of whether children attach specific features to intensions is also relevant to the acquisition of proper names. If early intensions consist of small sets of general features, children ought to overextend proper names since a small set of general features could not sufficiently differentiate the single referent of a proper name from all similar nonreferents. If children attached specific features to proper names, such as a peculiar smell to "Daddy" or an idiosyncratic mannerism to "Mommy," overextensions of proper names would be less likely. There is evidence that overextensions of "Mommy" and "Daddy" occur (Clark, 1973a; Thompson & Chapman, 1977), but it is difficult to assess how widespread this phenomenon is. Questions about the proportion of a child's terms that are overextended or underextended or about the proportion of children overextending or underextending a certain word often cannot be answered without making questionable assumptions about the representativeness of the few words, children, or contexts sampled in most investigations. Studies of spontaneous productions are biased against the detection of portions of the true extension not included in a child's extention (Anglin, 1977). If a child does not use a term in reference to an appropriate example, one cannot be sure whether the child has rejected this example as a referent of the term or just happens not to name it. Even in cases in which a child uses the wrong name for something, it is still possible that the child considers the correct name to be appropriate as well. For example, just because a child calls a squirrel a "kitty" even though "squirrel" is a term in her vocabulary, does not rule out the possibility that the child considers the squirrel also to be a "squirrel." Overextension may also be underestimated by production data since there is a considerable chance that an inappropriate referent meeting the child's erroneous criterion just does not happen along while the child is being observed, or if it does happen along, the child just happens not to name it. Despite these tendencies toward underestimation, Rescorla's (1980) analysis of six mothers' diaries of their children's early productions revealed substantial overextension of proper names. At least four of the children overextended "Dada" and at least three overextended "Mommy." This finding confirms a prediction of the GBSH. However, Rescorla found that only 33% of the children's words were observed to be overextended. Despite the potential for underestimation of overextension inherent in Rescorla's method, 33% is hardly a large enough percentage to support the claim that *all* of children's early intensions consist of small sets of general features.

Miller and Johnson-Laird (1976) have argued that children initially learn "brother" and "sister" as proper names for their siblings and incorporate very specific features in the intensions of these terms. Consistent with these claims is the observation that some children think their siblings are called "brothers" or "sisters," but they themselves are not. Research is needed to determine how narrow the early extensions of proper names and kin terms are. We do not know whether children ever think "brother" is just a popular proper name for boys, akin to "Bill" or "Jim," or how children reconcile differences in the syntactic privileges of proper names versus kin terms such as occurrence in determiner + X or possessive + X phrases. The fact that this syntactic distinction is blurred for parental kin terms, that is, "a Mommy," "my Mommy," and "Mommy" are all acceptable, may contribute to a delay in the acquisition of the kin term/proper name distinction.

Katz, Baker, and MacNamara (1974) documented the sensitivity of 17-month-old girls to the implications of the absence versus presence of articles before novel names for the extension of those names. A child who heard "This is zav" when introduced to a new doll reserved "zav" for that doll and tended to use only that doll when asked to dress or feed zav. A child who heard "This is a zav" did not. The boys in the study did not demonstrate this sensitivity, even at 24 months of age. Even the girls' interpretation of the absence versus presence of articles interacted with the nature of the thing named. Children hearing "This is zav" in reference to a block did not treat "zav" as a proper name. If it is true that some children as young as 17 months old understand that certain names have only one referent, that these names are more likely to apply to one kind of referent than to another, and that the absence of an article indicates the occurrence of such a name, then it is likely that, contrary to the GBSH, some very young children attach specific features to the intensions of proper names so as to be able to differentiate their true referents from similar nonreferents. The findings of Katz et al. are also important because they identify other sources of information in linguistic input which the child may use in constructing word intensions.

Functional Core Construction and Tagging—Nelson's Hypotheses

The hypotheses of Nelson and Clark spring from different empirical bases. Clark's hypotheses accounted for observed patterns in children's overextensions and in the development of the comprehension and definition of terms from certain lexical domains. Nelson's hypotheses, on the other hand, account for the observations that most of the first terms of reference refer to objects which are highly functional, that children occasionally invent words, and that several kinds of child-adult extension correspondences, not just overextension, occur.

Nelson (1974) hypothesized that the very young child will not form a concept of an object which has no salient function. An object has a salient function if it is the ready object of one of the child's motor behaviors or if the object is very active. The very first names the child acquires will be those that name things of which the child has concepts. The child is not likely to learn the names of things that do not move and are not easily moved, such as tables, walls, and statues. Nelson proposed that a 12-month-old child's concept formation involves associating representations of things sharing similar functional relations or associating representations of the many functional relations of one thing. Only after a concept of the first type is formed will the common static perceptual features, such as shape, smell, or texture, of the instances of a concept be abstracted. These features can then be used to identify new instances of the concept. Nelson asserted that the abstraction of features from a set grouped according to a common function, rather than according to a common label, and the use of abstracted features in instance identification usually take place *before* names are attached to such concepts. Thus, the first use of a name by a child could be an overextension based on a static perceptual features since the child is already recognizing instances on the basis of static perceptual features.

According to Nelson, the 12-month-old child simply sets out to assimilate names to well-formed concepts. The child is motivated to attach names to concepts. This motivation accounts for the observation that children occasionally invent names for concepts. Only later in lexical development can naming draw attention to objects in such a way that the child looks for features common to objects given the same name.

One criticism concerning the implications of children's name inventions is that the great majority of children's words for objects are attempts to reproduce a sound pattern heard in association with an object or event (Lewis, 1951). Children's sensitivity to recurring associations between sound patterns and world features is the very basis of the label-based feature abstraction process Nelson argues against. Also, because of the phonological constraints on what sounds children can produce, it may seem that a name has been "invented." For example, Lewis (1951) reported that his child called many animals "tee." This name seems to have little similarity to adult names for animals. However, Lewis observed that "tee" was first used to refer to a cat. "Tee" was probably an attempt to say "kitty." Many of children's "invented" words have an onomatopoeic quality (Werner & Kaplan, 1964), for example, "tick-tock" for clock or "bow-wow" for dog. Whether these expressions are first introduced by an adult or by the child, their use reflects the child's sensitivity to recurring sound pattern—world feature associations. Also, since adults sometimes use baby words such as "tick-tock" in speaking to children (Snow, 1977), the possibility of a label-based feature abstraction process influencing the construction of the intension of these words cannot be ruled out.

Nelson proposed that a concept must be formed before a child attaches a name to it. It is not clear how well formed a concept must be, however. A child's concept of bird, for example, is not exhaustive before the child learns to use "bird." The child will acquire more functional and formal information about birds, for example, that not all birds fly or that some birds have fan-like plumage. The acquisition of this information should change both the functional core and the static periphery of the child's concept of bird. The weaker stipulation—that a child must have a certain amount of functional information about a class of objects before acquiring its name—may be justifiable, but more precision would be required of such a stipulation before it became useful.

Nelson's proposals lack a justification for the loss of static perceptual information in the transition from a concept based on the many functions of one thing to a concept based on the common function of many things. In the first type of concept, the only way an infant can recognize that it is the same object exhibiting a variety of functions is by means of a representation of identifying features of the object. There is an arbitrariness to the claim that these represented identifying features should be lost when the concept is generalized. The identifying features of the concept-defining object have no special weight in the later determination of the identifying features of the generalized concept, which seems counterintuitive.

Nelson argued that after the child has abstracted the many functions of a single object, such as a particular ball, the child observes which of these functions characterize other objects and which do not. The child retains only the former functions in the object concept. One problem with this proposal is that there is no means by which object concepts are prevented from growing ever more general.

According to Nelson, even after abstracting static attributes, the child will not consider this information to be as reliable as functional information. Only functional information is defining. Nelson's (1973b) experiment allegedly corroborates this claim. Fifteen- to twenty-month-old children were given nine ball-like objects and what adults judged to be a prototypical child's ball. According to the adult judges, three of the objects resembled the prototype in function, but not in form; three resembled the prototype in form, but not in function; and three were unlike the prototype in both form and function. When asked to choose a "ball," the children's first five choices were as likely to be of the formally similar as the functionally similar objects. After playing with the objects for 10 minutes, the children had a greater tendency to choose the functionally similar objects when asked to choose a "ball." Once children were able to ascertain how much like a ball each object functioned, they changed their minds about which should be called "balls" accordingly.

It is difficult to explain why more of the children's initial choices were not of the formally similar objects. The children had no functional information to influence their initial choices, except what could be inferred from formal information. The explanation may lie in Nelson's method of having adults determine how similar in form and function each object is to a presumably prototypical round rubber ball.

There is no evidence that a round rubber ball is prototypical *for toddlers*. Andersen (1975) found that three-year-old children show little agreement among themselves or with adults when asked to choose the best example of a cup from a set of cups and glasses. Consistency within an age group increased from 3 to 12 years of age in the names chosen for different drinking vessels and in selection of a prototype. Until children have experience with a wide range of referents of a term, it is not likely that there is a consensus prototype. For some toddlers, the prototypical ball may be a round rubber ball, but for others it may be a plastic football. Two of the three objects in the functionally similar group of Nelson's experiment were footballs. Thus, initial choices were as likely to be of functionally similar as formally similar objects perhaps because the functionally similar objects were equal to the formally similar objects in their formal similarity to toddlers' varied prototypes.

More importantly, the finding that children alter their acceptance of a name for an object after gaining functional information about it need not imply that static features are any less defining than functional features. Both types of features may have the same diagnosticity, that is, the same probability that an object having a certain feature has a certain name. Suppose the child's intension for "ball" consists of the two necessary features (spherical) and (rolls), but the child considers sphericality to be a better diagnostic. Upon seeing a sphere and not knowing whether it rolls, the child may have great confidence that it is a ball. But should the child discover that the object does not roll, it will no longer be considered a ball since (rolls) is a necessary, though less diagnostic, feature. A feature can be necessary, but lack diagnosticity, for example, (born of humans) is a necessary feature of *Bill Merriman*, but hardly a good predictor of whether something *is* Bill Merriman. Conversely, a child might know an object rolls and not know whether it is spherical. In this case, the child is somewhat less certain that the object is a ball since (rolls) is less diagnostic than (spherical). Should the child discover the object is not spherical, the object will no longer be considered a ball. The point is that necessity should be distinguished from diagnositicity and that Nelson's experiment tests neither the necessity nor comparative diagnositicity of formal and functional features.

The behavior of the toddlers in Nelson's (1973b) experiment is consistent with a state of affairs in which functional and formal features are each necessary, but have varying diagnositicity. However, the results are consistent with other states of affairs as well. Suppose the children considered several functional and formal features to each be perfectly diagnostic, that is, sufficient. The children would have considered most objects in the functionally and formally similar groups to be balls since it is likely that these objects possessed at least one of the sufficient features of "ball." Also, the number of objects considered to be balls should have increased from test to retest since it is likely that sufficient functional features of objects would have been discovered in play. At least all objects accepted as balls before play should be accepted as balls after play. Since children were not asked whether each object was a ball or not, it cannot be determined whether features were treated as sufficient, or necessary, or probabilistic.

Nelson's (1973b) experiment does show that children will change their minds about the appropriateness of a name for an object after obtaining functional information about that object. Children also may change their minds after obtaining more formal information about objects, however. Nelson's experiment did not test for this. It may be that the chief difference between formal and functional features does not involve the necessity or diagnosticity of these features, but the manner in which the features are verified. Formal information is usually immediately apparent in the perception of an object, but reception of functional information may require extended viewing or manipulation. If children were only allowed to touch but not see a set of ball-like objects, or only shown the fronts of the objects, asked to decide which were balls, and *then* were allowed to see the set (or were shown the backs), it is likely that the children would change their decisions after acquiring this additional formal information.

Nelson (1974) proposed that concept instances will be first named only in the context of one of their definitionally specified actions or relations. This proposal is incompatible with her hypothesis that names are attached to concepts usually after several objects have been recognized as concept instances on the basis of common function and after instances can be recognized on the basis of static perceptual features. Nelson claimed that only after the functional core is separated from other relations in the concept will children name objects outside of the context of their defining relations. Also, a child's first namings imply functional cores and no more. "Ball" uttered by a child means that the thing referred to can roll, bounce, and be thrown. The child's other statements specify which of the optional attributes hold for a particular instance. The child may say "Ball gone," "Daddy ball," or "Ball chair." The child will never say "Ball roll" because this would be redundant since "ball" implies the functional core. It is not obvious why the child cannot say "Ball roll" to convey the proposition that what rolls, bounces, and can be thrown is now rolling. According to Nelson, the child will not say "Ball round" because this is uninteresting information to the child. Of course, of Nelson permitted static information in concept cores, "Ball round" would be ruled out for being redundant. Nelson does not offer reasons why "Ball round" is uninteresting to the child.

Comparison of the Original Hypotheses

Both Clark and Nelson characterize lexical development in terms of features being abstracted, added, and subtracted. Both give developmental priority to one kind of feature over another, but differ concerning how features are to be classified and which features have priority. Only Nelson makes distinctions between the necessity of different kinds of features. The period of development prior to and during the acquisition of the first 50 words occupies more of Nelson's theoretical attention than Clark's. Only Nelson offers a description of the object concept formation process during this period. Only Nelson asserts that cognitive development and nonlinguistic experience with objects has a greater role than experience with language in determining the intensions of these first words. Both Nelson and Clark concur that after this period children's attention to linguistic input will also affect their word intensions. Only Clark addresses the later acquisition of more complex distinctions underlying the meanings of words other than concrete nouns.

Since Nelson does not accept Clark's claim that defining or identifying features are general and few, no prediction follows from Nelson's views about the correspondence between the extensions of any of the child's first words and the adult extensions of those words. Nevertheless, the case of proper names does highlight the concept generality problem in Nelson's account. Nelson's version of the toddler concept formation process does not allow for the maintenance of concepts of single objects or persons since once a second object is observed to enter into one relation found in the core of an existing single object concept, that concept becomes a concept of at least two objects. More generally, it is not clear in either Clark's or Nelson's account how the child maintains concepts of overlapping extension and how the child, when hearing an instance from more than one concept named, decides which concept to tag with the name. It is reasonable to suppose that before producing any words, the child has a concept of *mommy, adult, person*, and *physical entity*. How these relate to one another and how one concept is chosen over the others to be associated with "Mommy" is not well-specified.

Nelson has criticized Clark's GBSH for vagueness concerning the manner of determining the comparative generality of perceptually derived features. Nelson's theory has a similar disadvantage in that there are only rough ways of identifying functionally salient objects and no ways of comparing the salience of functions. Nelson (1979a) has reported the preliminary results of a study showing that the number of specific action schemes each of five complex objects elicited from 20-month-olds corresponded perfectly to the order in which the children learned artificial names for these objects. This results supports Nelson's claim that the more salient functions an object has for a child the more likely it is that the child will learn its name. Further support for Nelson's functional core hypothesis would be provided if it could be demonstrated that children generalize object names in a fashion consistent with observed similarities and differences in the action schemes children address to objects. Also, since spontaneous movements are functions just as action schemes are, Nelson's measure is limited to predicting the order of acquisition of names for inanimate objects.

Whitehurst, Kedesdy, and White (1982) have offered similiar criticisms of the predictive power of Nelson's hypotheses. They have pointed out that there is no way of comparing the salience of different functions. Is the edibility of a cheeseburger more salient than the flight pattern of a frisbee or the uses of a shoe? Whitehurst et al. propose that the *value* of an object, which may or may not coincide with its functionality, is a better predictor of whether a child will learn an object's name. Whitehurst et al. carried out a study nearly identical to Nelson's (1979). They found that the more time a child spent playing with a novel toy, the more likely the child was to learn that toy's name in a later training session. The number of action schemes each toy elicited was not measured, so a comparison of the predictive power of Nelson's versus Whitehurst et al.'s measures cannot be made. If some preference measure could be shown to predict the order of acquisition of names for things children cannot manipulate—such as large animals or depicted objects—this would be evidence for the greater scope of Whitehurst et al.'s value hypothesis over Nelson's number-of-functions hypothesis. Whitehurst et al. also suggest that further support for the value hypothesis would be provided if it could be shown that some experimental manipulation which changed the value of an object for a child also changed the probability of the child learning its name.

It is important to note that the proposal that children are more likely to learn the names of things with salient functions does not logically entail that functional information has primacy in the structure of the intensions of these names. These are two independent claims. Nelson makes both of these claims, but only provides evidence for the first claim.

Subsequent Developments

Many observations have been reported which directly challenge the hypotheses of Clark and Nelson. Several investigations have reported a lack of correspondence between children's productive and receptive word extensions. This asymmetry is predicted by neither Clark's nor Nelson's hypotheses, which were induced chiefly from patterns of production. Secondly, children have been observed to extend words in a complex manner which is inconsistent with the model of word intension assumed in the accounts of Clark and Nelson. Thirdly, contrary to Nelson's hypotheses, children have been observed to extend names to novel objects which are formally similar, but functionally dissimilar to correct referents known to the children. Finally, Nelson's prediction that children initially use a name only in definitionally specified contexts has not been confirmed. In addition to the empirical findings, several theoretical advances have been made in models of the structure of natural categories which are relevant to any account of how children learn the reference of concrete nouns. These theoretical advances have centered around three notions: (a) feature interdependence; (b) typicality; and (c) the basic level of object categorization.

Asymmetry Between Comprehension and Production

Some children overextend certain words in production, but not in comprehension. Labov and Labov (1974) observed this asymmetry in their daughter's early use and comprehension of "Mommy." The child called several family members "Mommy," but when asked "Where is Mommy?" the child always sought out her mother. Huttenlocher (1974) observed four children for 6 months from the age of 10 or 11 months onward and found overextensions only in production.

Although there is considerable disagreement concerning the extent of the asymmetry between production and comprehension (cf. Rescorla, 1982; Thompson & Chapman, 1977; Fremgen & Fay, 1980; Kuczaj, 1982; Kay & Anglin, 1982), neither Clark's nor Nelson's original hypothesis predicted any asymmetry at all. The incidence of overextensions in production, but not comprehension, suggests that, contrary to Clark's assumption, not all productive overextensions indicate deficiencies in word intensions.

Another kind of asymmetry between comprehension and production also has been explored recently. The size of early vocabulary has been known to be larger in comprehension than in production for some time (McCarthy, 1954). Goldin-Meadow, Seligman, and Gelman (1976) found that the four children with the smallest vocabularies of twelve children between 14 and 26 months of age comprehended roughly three or more times as many nouns as they produced. These four children produced no verbs, but comprehended from nine to twenty-two of thirty verbs tested. The remaining children comprehended only a few more nouns than they produced, but comprehended about twice as many verbs as they produced. The experimenters proposed that by the time a child is 2-years-old, the size of productive vocabulary approaches that of receptive vocabulary. They argued that the appearance and the gradual disappearance of this vocabulary asymmetry was due, only in part, to changes in articulation abilities. They did not suggest other causal mechanisms, however. Benedict (1978, 1979) reported a similar developmental trend from a longitudinal diary study. I have some doubts about the claim of Goldin-Meadow et al. that productive vocabulary size come to match that of receptive vocabulary. Even adults find that often they cannot produce synonyms for other words, although they can recognize synonyms. Name recognition is easier than name recall in most cases at all ages.

The finding of early word comprehension has implications for Nelson's hypotheses about concept formation processes that must occur *before* a concept is tagged with a label. These processes must start early and proceed rapidly if labels are to be attached to some concepts by the time the child is 11 months old.

Complexive Word Use

Bowerman (1978a) has noted that *complexive word use*, a phenomenon emphasized by early theorists of semantic development (Werner, 1948; Vygotsky, 1962; Brown, 1956), is incompatible with the model of word intension assumed by both Clark and Nelson. Complexive word use is the use of a word for different referents such that no set of necessary features can be found which differentiates referents from nonreferents. A frequently cited example of this is one child's use of "quah" to refer to a duck in a pond, liquids, an eagle on a coin, and several coinlike objects (Vygotsky, 1962). Thomson and Chapman (1977) analyzed pictures of animals and objects which two-year-olds named. For 17 of 20 names, the investigators were unable to derive a set of necessary and jointly sufficient features that distinguished referents from nonreferents. For example, of all the pictures one child called "Daddy," none of the following features was found in even 80% of the depicted persons: a certain hair length; glasses; facial hair; a certain hair color; a certain style of clothing; maleness; or adulthood. Although it is conceivable that some other feature governed the child's use of "Daddy," the failure of the most obvious attributes to account for its use argues against Clark's and Nelson's assumption that early word intensions are sets of necessary and jointly sufficient features.

Bloom (1973) proposed that complexive word use reflects cognitive immaturity and that its frequency should diminish once a child reaches Stage VI of object permanence. However, Bowerman (1978a) reported that in her daughters' speech, both complexive and feature-consistent word use was present from the beginning of the one-word stage. Complexive word use was most frequent a few months *after* the one-word stage began and continued well beyond the third year.

Bowerman (1978a) reported that all of the referents of any one of her children's complexively used words shared at least one feature with a central instance. For example, Eva used "moon" in reference to the real moon, a grapefruit half, shiny green leaves, lemon slices, and hangnails. All referents shared some feature(s) with the real moon. This pattern of complexive word use is, in Vygotsky's terms, associative rather than chain-like. In chain complexive usage, each referent shares a feature with the previous referent, but not necessarily with a single central instance. The "quah" example illustrates chain complexive usage. Bowerman observed no chain complexive usage in her daughter's speech. The central instance of Bowerman's daughters' complexive uses were usually both the first referent the children named and the most likely referent of their mother's use of the term. Rescorla (1980) also has reported associative, but no chain complexive usage in early speech.

The Relative Importance of Form and Function

Several reports have challenged Nelson's claim that only functional features are defining. Clark (1975) has pointed out that some of the overextensions reported in diary studies cut across functional boundaries known to children. For example, one child used the same word to refer to the bars of his crib and to a toast rack. It is unlikely that the child was identifying the toast rack as something that might have the same function as the bars of his crib. Bowerman (1978a) found very few overextensions in her daughters' speech that were based on functional similarity independent of static feature similarity. The few observed occurred rather late in lexical development. On the other hand, many overextensions based on static feature similarity alone were observed.

Laboratory experiments also have provided a fair amount of evidence against Nelson's claims. Anglin (1977) found no overextensions based solely on functional similarity, but a substantial number based solely on formal similarity in three-year-olds' acceptance of labels for depicted objects. However, since Anglin's experiment involved pictures, functional information was not directly available. This argument cannot be made against the findings of an experiment by Gentner (1978) in which children and adults were taught names for two complex apparatuses which were very different in both function and form. Contrary to the implication of Nelson's hypotheses, 82% of 2½- to 5-year-olds thought a third apparatus that looked like one apparatus (but functioned like the other) should be given the same name as the formally similar apparatus.

One could argue that Nelson's hypotheses only apply to names learned spontaneously, that is, names which tag the child's existing functional core concepts. Children in Gentner's experiment were compelled to perform in a name-based feature abstraction paradigm which, according to Nelson, is not a good analogy to the way children ordinarily learn the reference of names. Also, Nelson never claimed that functions have primacy in a name-based feature abstraction process. Rather than limiting the scope of Nelson's hypotheses in this way, a second argument can be made that there were several functions which the children discovered about each machine in addition to the designated function. Although moving the lever on the transfer machine did not produce the same result as moving the lever on the formally similar machine, the children may have inferred from the static features of the transfer machine that it shared many more functions with the formally similar machine than with the functionally similar machine. This argument has the disadvantage of being less parsimonious than the argument that children think that similar looking things have the same name, however. A third argument is that children may have encoded the two training machines' functions equivalently as moving-the-lever-produces-an-interesting-movement. The child could only base their naming on other inferable functional differences. This argument is not only unparsimonious, but also serves to highlight a weakness already identified in Nelson's account—namely, its vagueness concerning the level of abstractness of functions in the cores of concepts. Also, the designated function (whether or not a machine delivers jelly beans), should have been salient to children.

Tomikawa and Dodd (1980) reported that 3-year-olds could learn the names of blocks much more easily if blocks of the same name had identical shapes but different functions, than if blocks of the same name had identical functions but different shapes. Again, one could argue that the experimenter-defined functions were not the effective functions for the child. Also, even if the experimenter-defined functions were salient to the child, the difficulty in learning the names of the functionally identical objects may be a reflection of the lack of a reliable way of inferring the function of an object at rest. One way to test this would be to have the child both hear the things named and later have to name them while the functions of the things are being demonstrated. This would provide the child with a reliable way to identify a function without having to make an inference based on a form-function correlation. Another way to test this would be to examine whether it is easier to learn names whose extensional boundaries coincide with correlated form-function differences than with just form differences alone.

Even if some of the interpretations of the experiments of Gentner (1978) and Tomikawa and Dodd (1980) I have offered in defense of Nelson's functional core hypothesis are correct, it has become clear that Nelson's functional core hypothesis cannot be applied in a straightforward way to predictions of which objects will be included in the extensions of children's words.

Tomikawa and Dodd (1980) and Currie-Jedermann (1981) have found that preschool children are much more likely to spontaneously sort objects according to form than according to function even when the functions of objects are explicitly demonstrated to the children and the children are able to describe the functions of the objects. However, the categories adhered to in children's sorting are not necessarily those upon which names are based. There is a well-documented tendency for 3-year-olds to sort according to color (Suchman & Trabasso, 1966; Perlmutter & Ricks, 1979), but overextensions are rarely based on color (Clark, 1973a). Nevertheless, the sorting results stand as evidence against a claim of the general conceptual primacy of function.

Contexts of Naming

Bowerman (1978a) reported that Nelson's prediction that early object word use would be restricted to contexts of defining functions was not upheld in Bowerman's daughters' behavior. Many of Christy's and Eva's object words were first uttered in reference to objects which were neither moving nor being manipulated. Bretherton, Bates, McNew, Shore, Williamson, and Beeghly-Smith (1981) also reported that 13- and 20-month-olds most often used a label for an object upon first seeing it or while inspecting or showing it, but rarely while performing an action upon it.

New Models of Natural Concepts

Both Clark's and Nelson's proposals held that learning the reference of a name involves associating to the name a set of necessary and jointly sufficient features. Recently, many arguments have been made, chiefly by Labov and Rosch, that the classical model of the word intension as a set of necessary and jointly sufficient features is inadequate. Two phenomena which are difficult to reconcile with the classical model of word intension have already been discussed: (a) complexive word use and (b) children's tendency to overextend in production, but not comprehension.

Feature interdependence. Labov (1973) emphasized the fact that natural categories have vague boundaries. Labov constructed drawings of containers that varied in width, depth, and contour. He found that adults always labeled some drawings "cup" and other drawings "bowl," but that the label given to most of the drawings depended upon the functional context in which adults were asked to imagine the container, for example, as containing coffee versus soup. Labov concluded that the necessity of features and the allowable ranges of feature values depend on the other features and feature values manifest in a referent. For example, the intension of "cup" must specify a wider range of acceptable width-to-depth ratio values for containers with handles or for containers used for drinking coffee than for other containers. Thus, contrary to the stipulations of the classical model, the features (has a handle) or (for drinking coffee) are relevant for only *some* decisions concerning the application of "cup" to a referent—namely, only when the referent's width-to-depth ratio is within certain ranges. According to the classical model, all referents of a term must possess all of the features specified in the term's intension. One type of new model which could account for Labov's finding specifies *disjunctive* sets of necessary and jointly sufficient features. For example, the intensions of "cup" might consist of (container) and ([(has handle) and (width-to-depth ratio between X and Y)] or [(used for drinking) and (width-to-depth ratio between W and Z)] or [(width-to-depth ratio between U and V)]). Another type of model assigns weights to various features or dimension values and accepts a referent only if the combined weights of its features or dimension values exceeds some threshold (see Smith & Medin, 1981).

Typicality. Rosch and her colleagues (Rosch, 1973; Rosch & Mervis, 1975; Rosch et al., 1976b; Rosch, 1978; Mervis & Rosch, 1981) have argued that the vagueness of category boundaries is a reflection of the fact that members of a natural category differ in their typicality. For example, soccer is considered a more typical sport than shuffleboard. In fact, different sports can be ordered according to how good an example of a sport each is. Boundary vagueness enters this ordering where examples becomes increasingly less typical. At some point, people disagree concerning whether something is an atypical example or not an example at all. Even before this point is reached, however, examples can be ordered according to their typicality.

Neither Nelson nor Clark anticipated typicality effects in their original formulations. Several studies have documented the importance of typicality considerations to an account of lexical development. For example, Rosch (1973) found 9- to 11-year-old boys to be more likely to reject atypical instances than typical instances as referents of concrete nouns. Anglin (1977; Kay & Anglin, 1982) provided additional evidence that 2- to 5-year-olds learn to categorize typical instances before they learn to categorize atypical instances. Mervis and Pani (1980) found that for six artificial object categories which mimicked natural categories in their pattern of shared features, five-year-olds were most accurate in generalizing category names to novel instances if they had been taught just the names of the most typical instance of each category rather than the names of both typical and atypical instances or just the names of the least typical instances. These results suggest that the typicality of the referent to which a child first applies a name may influence the extent of the child's subsequent extension errors with that name.

Basic level categories. Rosch and her colleagues also have explored the structure of natural object category hierarchies. They have identified the basic level object category as one having certain optimal properties. The roots of the notion of the basic level category can be found in a paper by Brown (1958) in which he set forth several hypotheses about what people consider the "best fitting" name for something. Brown proposed that the best fitting name reflects an object's usual level of behavioral equivalence, which is the number of differences between that object and other objects that can be ignored in behavior addressed to those objects. The higher the level of behavioral equivalence, the broader the set of objects treated equivalently. According to Brown, the levels of behavioral equivalence associated with names other than the best fitting names are useful for fewer, more specialized purposes. For example, it is best to call a dime "dime" rather than "money" or "1968 dime" since in most interactions involving dimes one ignores differences among dimes, but not differences between dimes and other forms of money. Brown suggested that adults name objects for children at the perceived level of behavioral equivalence for children, which may or may not be the same as the level of behavioral equivalence for adults. For example, parents may call a dime "money" for their toddler because the parents realize it is not necessary for the child to distinguish dimes from other forms of money until he or she is older, but it is necessary that the child distinguish money from objects lacking monetary value. Finally, Brown proposed that children will find it difficult to learn a word extension that cuts across distinctions maintained in their behavior toward objects. If the child knows different names for mutually exclusive sets of objects, it will be very difficult for the child to learn the superordinate name common to those objects.

Rosch et al. (1976b) have elaborated on Brown's hypotheses by proposing that there is a basic level in most hierarchies of object categories which is the most inclusive level at which there is a cluster of attributes common to all members. This level represents an optimal tradeoff between category distinctiveness and category cohesiveness. The greater cohesiveness of lower level of basic level categories has less value cognitively than the greater distinctiveness of basic over lower level categories. For example, although two sparrows are more similar to each other than are any two birds, the similarity among birds is sufficient to easily learn to group them into the same category. However, the low distinctiveness of the sparrow category is problematic. Sparrows are easily confused with contrast categories such as wrens or buntings. Birds are not easily confused with contrast categories such as bats or butterflies. On the other hand, the greater distinctiveness of higher level over basic level categories is outweighed by the greater cohesiveness of basic level over higher level categories. For example, although invertebrates are more distinct from vertebrates than birds are distinct from bats, it is not difficult to distinguish birds from bats. However, the similarity among two invertebrates may not be sufficient to easily learn to group them into the same category.

Basic level terms are essentially the same terms Brown identified as the best fitting names for things. A basic level term conveys information which suffices for most object language activity. It is usually not necessary to convey the finer distinctions entailed by a lower level term, but it is usually necessary to convey more distinctions than a higher level term entails.

Neither Nelson's nor Clark's original accounts of the acquisition of the reference of terms gave attention to the effect of a term's level of inclusiveness. Nelson's account was vague concerning the breadth of the extension of functional core concepts and the manner in which the child decided which of several concepts with overlapping extensions to tag. In Clark's account, the only claim made concerning the acquisition of categorically related terms is that children may treat a pair of terms as if they were synonyms until a differentiating feature is attached to the lower level term.

Several observations indicate that basic level terms may play an important role in the acquisition of other terms. Rosch et al. (1976b) reported that one child's speech in the two-word period contained *only* basic level object terms. Preschoolers' picture naming (Anglin, 1977) also indicates that most of the first object terms learned are basic level terms. Given Rosch et al.'s findings of adults' great tendency to name objects with basic level names, the data on children's early vocabulary is not surprising. Rarely will members of a pair of categorically related nouns be acquired in close temporal proximity; the basic level member is usually acquired well in advance of the other member. When children finally begin to acquire other terms, this acquisition will involve coordinating these terms with the basic level terms already in the vocabulary.

The fact that children's early object names are predominantly basic level terms suggests that parents' perceived best fitting names for children and for adults are usually both basic level names. However, this does not imply that the perceived level of behavioral equivalence for the child is the same as the level of behavioral equivalence for the adult. Mervis and Mervis (1982) have shown that mothers use some basic level terms more broadly in speech to their 13-month-olds than in speech to older children and adults. For example, mothers may name a van "car" for their children rather than use the appropriate basic level name "van." Mervis and Mervis introduce the term *child basic category* to denote the extension of a basic level term addressed to or used by a young child. Child basic categories overlap but do not coincide with adult basic categories.

Brown's (1958) hypotheses suggest that the few instances in which parents introduce nonbasic level terms to their children should be those in which parents want their children to maintain finer or broader distinctions in their behavior toward objects than the children normally would maintain. Parents should use a subordinate or proper name in reference to a person or thing they want their children to treat specially. Parents should use superordinate terms when they want their children to ignore certain distinctions between objects in their behavior toward those objects. Consistent with this last prediction, both Blewitt (1983b) and Whitehurst, Kedesdy, and White (1982) found that adults are more likely to use superordinate terms in speech in children when referring to groups of objects, for example, "Put away your *toys*" or "Eat that *food*," rather than when referring to single objects.

Anglin (1977) has provided some support for Brown's hypotheses. Preschool children were more likely to use "money" appropriately before "dime" or "coin," confirming Brown's suggestion that children's broader level of behavioral equivalence with respect to money might be reflected in their initial acquisition of a higher level term than the adult basic level term. Anglin (1977) also reported that whether mothers imagined themselves to be addressing their 2-year-olds or another adult affected their choice of names for 6 of 25 depicted objects. In all cases in which most mothers chose the same term in speech to toddlers and adults, the term was a basic level term. When different terms were chosen, the more general term was used in speech to the toddler.

Rosch et al. (1976b) have argued that basic level object categories capture the object distinctions and equivalencies that toddlers are mostly likely to make. Presented with three depicted objects, 3-year-olds were able to pick the two from the same basic level category 99% of the time, but were at chance in picking two from the same superordinate category, but different basic level categories. In the first task, the odd item was not from the same superordinate category as the items to be matched. Stronger evidence would have been provided for the claim that basic object categories mark salient distinctions and equivalencies for toddlers if high level matching performance were found when the odd item was from a contrastive basic level category, for example, two shoes and one pants. In fact, Blewitt (1983a) has carried out such an experiment. Her results supported the hypothesis that basic level matching is easier than superordinate matching, but the difference was not great. Three-year-olds made 68% of basic level matches correctly versus 60% of superordinate level matches.

Mervis and Crisafi (1982) demonstrated that ten of ten 2½-year-olds could match two figures which shared three more static features with each other than with a third figure. The experimenters argued that this pattern of feature sharing was analogous to that characterizing real world objects belonging to basic level categories within the same superordinate category. There are no criteria for deciding how close a contrasting natural category the analog category of the odd object was, however.

Daehler, Lonardo, and Bukatko (1979) found that 22-, 27-, and 33-month-olds were better able to match an object to another object from the same basic level category than to make superordinate level matches. Since the distractor items in the matching task bore no obvious relation to the standard, the experiment only showed that basic level categories have a greater cohesiveness than superordinate categories for toddlers. The experiment did not demonstrate the optimality of the combined cohesiveness and distinctiveness of basic level over superordinate categories for toddlers. Also, since even the 22-month-olds' matches at the superordinate level had above chance accuracy, the experiment demonstrated that very young children have some sensitivity to the superordinate level of object categorization. In fact, habituation studies have indicated such a sensitivity in 12-month-olds (Ross, 1980).

The fact that toddlers do make considerable overextensions in their use of basic level terms and that mothers occasionally model an overextended use of a basic level term to a toddler (Mervis & Mervis, 1982) indicate that basic level object categories do not correspond exactly to the object distinctions and equivalencies the toddler is most likely to make. However, there is ample evidence that basic level object categories approximate toddlers' categories much more closely than do adult categories of other levels and that toddlers are more likely to hear basic level names for things than names from other levels.

Revisions and Extensions

Clark and Nelson have responded to the developments that followed the publication of their original proposals by discarding some of their hypotheses, revising other hypotheses, and providing additional arguments and evidence in support of other hypotheses. Several inadequacies and inconsistencies remain in both of these revised systems.

Clark's Initial Revisions

Clark (1975) revised her theory to account for asymmetric overextension and complexive word use. She reasoned that an overextension in production only is not indicative of the full featural composition of a word intension. Clark accepted Bloom's (1973) proposal that such overextensions reflect the child's attempts to communicate about objects for which the child lacks labels. The child chooses to label with the term in her vocabulary whose semantic features only partially match those of the object named. For example, although three-year-olds overextend "cup" to some glasses (Andersen, 1975), they realize a glass does not possess all of the necessary features of "cup," but decide that it possesses enough such that "cup" is the best available name for it. Since a child will not call every glass "cup," there must be some criteria of feature possession for "cup" to be used as its name. Also, a child might even use "cup" as an approximation when "glass" is in his or her vocabulary if the intension of "glass" does not fit as well as the intension of "cup," that is, if the intension of "glass" specifies an underextended range.

Clark (1975) also suggested that some overextensions in production only, rather than being knowing misapplications of a term, may be *uncertain* applications. Clark cited Labov and Labov's (1974) observation of their child's use of "cat" as evidence for this. The more features an animal shared with the family cat, the less the child hesitated in referring to the animal as a "cat." A child who overextends a name to a novel referent which exhibits only a few of the features shared by other referents of the name may be less certain of the appropriateness of the name for the novel referent. Clark and Clark (1977) also suggested that in some cases of uncertainty, the child may use a term just to find out from the feedback of an adult listener whether that use is correct. Brown (1956) maintained that this pattern of adult-child interaction, termed the *original word game*, is critical to the acquisition of the reference of all terms. However, Clark and Clark considered this pattern to characterize how the child learns only a few of the referents of a few terms.

The inclusion of certainty considerations is a laudable amendment. Since a child's word intensions must change with development, it makes sense that there should be times in which a child is uncertain of the importance of certain features and hence the acceptability of certain referents. Clark does not discuss procedures for determining when a child is using a word as an approximation or when the child is using a word with uncertainty. Overextensions which occur in both comprehension and production cannot be instances of word approximation. Perhaps latency to name or to accept a name could be used as a measure of certainty. Forced choice selection could also be used to measure gradients of certainty.

Complexive word use can be accounted for in terms of either gradients of certainty or word approximation. The central instance of an associative complexive extension (e.g., the real moon in Eva's complexive extension of "moon") is the instance the child is most certain bears the label she gives it. The central instance possesses most of the features the child considers to be important in decisions about the applicability of the label to things. The child may be uncertain of the degree of importance of each feature. The child's uses of the label for referents which share the fewest features with the central instance should be the child's least confident uses. Alternatively, some of the child's namings of referents which share the fewest features with the central instance could be instances of word approximation.

One consequence of Clark's revisions is that children's productions are viewed as too conservative a measure of the number of semantic features incorporated in word intensions. Thus, early word intensions are not as impoverished as Clark originally proposed. Also, Clark's allowance for gradients of certainty entails an allowance for the nonequivalence or varying typicality of members of an extension and for the possibility that accidental features, or at least features whose necessity the child is uncertain of, play a role in decisions about the reference of a name.

Clark also suggested that underextensions may be common in the first stages of the acquisition of a word's reference (Clark & Clark, 1977). There is some evidence for this claim. Rescorla's (1980) finding that the percentage of overextended to total words in 12- to 15-month-olds is smaller than it is in 15- to 20-month-olds (10% versus 26%), and that the majority of overextended words are not overextended until at least a month after they are first used, suggests that the initial extensions of the first 25 words produced are rather narrow. Although Clark acknowledged that initial word extensions may be narrow, she did not acknowledge that narrow extensions imply intensions which, contrary to her original hypotheses, consist of many general features or a few very specific features or both.

Clark's Most Recent Position

Clark (1983) has recently criticized her own original hypotheses. She has abandoned the claim that semantic features represent universal primitives of thought, largely because of the little progress made in the development of procedures for identifying primitives or rules for their combination. Clark has replaced semantic features with *lexical contrasts* which are representations of contrasts between things or events that are relevant to naming. Secondly, Clark has acknowledged that both the GBSH and the simple-before-complex hypotheses of feature addition are, at best, very limited in scope. Neither can predict why in most instances children posit the lexical contrasts they do. It is often difficult to decide which of two features is more general or complex than the other. Only in a few lexical domains do linguists agree on a hierarchially structured set of features for the intensions of words in the domain. Thirdly, even for words having an accepted hierarchy of features, the GBSH is not always upheld. Children determine the polarity of certain dimensional adjectives, for example, positive for "tall" and "deep," negative for "short" and "shallow" before they determine the relevance of the vertical dimension for them, for example, relevant for "tall" and "short," not relevant for "deep" and "shallow" (Brewer & Stone, 1975; Bartlett, 1976). Most linguists consider verticality to be superordinate to polarity in the lexical entries of these adjectives. Fourthly, the analysis of most words into semantic features is difficult, if not impossible (see Miller & Johnson-Laird's (1976) analysis of furniture words). This difficulty further limits the scope of the GBSH and the simple-before-complex hypothesis. Finally, the child's general features such as (animate) and (male) require development themselves. They do not represent the same contrasts as the corresponding adult general features. Clark maintains that the simple-before-complex hypothesis is useful for some lexical domains such as kin terms, dimensional adjectives, and verbs of possession, motion, and communication, but rejects GBSH completely.

Clark (1983) has proposed *lexical contrast theory* as a "fresh look at what is involved in the acquisition of meaning" (pp. 819-820). However, several of the hypotheses of this theory are not new. For example, according to the theory's *principle of contrast*, children assume any new word contrasts with some already known word(s). This hypothesis can be found in Clark's (1973a) paper. I have already outlined the process described in that paper of how a child partitions the extension shared by a new and old word by positing a contrastive feature. Also, according to the theory's *principle of conventionality*, children are motivated to find the conventional names for things they want to refer to. The first words children learn should refer to what children are most interested in. The salient perceptual properties of an object, usually its shape, will be taken by the child to constitute the intension of its name. Only later will children develop the tendency to search for a pertinent conceptual contrast upon hearing a novel word. These predictions are very similar to those offered in Nelson's (1974) paper and some can be found in Clark's earlier writings (1973b, 1975). As Bowerman (1978b) has observed, both Nelson and Clark offer versions of a "cognition first" theory in which nonlinguistic concepts, more than linguistic input patterns, determine the nature of the first words learned and the nature of the intensions of those first words.

Clark (1983) has claimed that nearly all overextensions are manifestations of the motivation to find a conventional word for what one wants to talk about. According to Clark, children act according to Slobin's (1973) maxim of "using old forms for new functions" (p. 821). Implicit in Clark's most recent position is the claim that most overextensions only occur in production, not in comprehension, and that these overextensions represent instances of using known words as approximations, rather than instances of word usage reflecting error in or uncertainty about the meanings of words. The evidence of overextension in comprehension (Kay & Anglin, 1982; Kuczaj, 1982) and of children's resistance to corrections of their overextensions (Mervis & Canada, 1981) does not support Clark's view.

There is a contradiction between the hypothesis that children seek the conventional names for things and the hypothesis that overextensions reflect communication strategies. If children desire to use the conventional names for things why should they knowingly use an incorrect word as an approximation? Why wouldn't they just ask what the conventional word is? If children are motivated to use the conventional name for things, then they should believe their overextensions are correct namings. One way to resolve this contradiction is to propose that children's motivation to communicate is at times greater than their motivation to use conventional names. This would allow some overextensions to be word approximations. That the motivation to communicate is sometimes greater than the motivation to use conventional words is implicit in Clark's (1983) statement that "lexical contrast theory makes communication primary" (p. 825) and is consistent with her observations that children often rely on general purpose terms such as "do" and "make." Although general purpose words are conventional words, the conventionality principle would seem to imply that children are motivated to find more fitting names than these, that is, the ones adults would use. Children use general purpose words because in certain situations they are more concerned to communicate a request or message than to retrieve or request the conventional name for something.

Clark (1983) observes that children occasionally invent words. This tendency is clearly incompatible with the conventionality principle—invented words are unconventional words. For Clark, invented words are manifestations of the operation of the principle of contrast. This principle apparently not only implies that children assume that any new word contrasts with some known word(s), but that any considerably novel thing is deserving of a new name. In this sense, the principle of contrast is different from the hypotheses found in Clark's earlier writings. For the child, it is not sufficient to call what looks like a dog but has horns and eats grass a "dog." This novel animal merits a novel description such as "funny dog" or "grass dog" or "cow." The principle of contrast operates both when a child decides what a new word means and when a child decides how to describe a thing or event that is considerably different from things or events previously encountered. The principle of contrast overrides the principle of conventionality, at least in some instances.

The principle of contrast appears to operate in only one direction in the early stages of word learning. It guides the child's decisions about what to call things, but it does not guide the child's comprehension of new words. This follows from Clark's view that the formation of concepts to match a pattern of a new word's use is a late development.

If the principle of contrast operates when the child is deciding how to describe things or events, the tendency to make word approximations and to use general purpose words should be limited. The principle of contrast suggests that a child should not use either general purpose words or word approximations to refer to things that are appreciably novel. The motivation to communicate may override the principle of contrast in some cases, however, allowing for the use of general purpose words or word approximations in reference to appreciably novel things.

Another implication of the principle of conventionality is that children should not overextend a word or use an invented word when they already have the correct name for the referent in their vocabulary. Barrett (1978) was the first to propose this kind of hypothesis and provided support for it with evidence from the same diary studies Clark (1973a) analyzed. This hypothesis has not been upheld in several investigations, however. Thomson and Chapman (1977) found that in 16% of the instances in which two-year-olds overextended a name to a depicted person or object, the children had used the correct name for that person or object in reference to other depicted persons or objects, for example, calling a strange adult "Daddy" although "man" was in the vocabulary. Rescorla (1980, 1981) has documented the same phenomenon in her naturalistic observations. If one counts instances of comprehension, but not production of a new word, violations of the hypothesis are numerous (Nelson, 1979b; Rescorla, 1980, 1981; Fremgen & Fay, 1980).

A Summary Evaluation of Clark's Hypotheses

Clark has abandoned her original view that early word intensions are small sets of general and mostly appropriate necessary features and that general features are added to these word intensions before more specific ones. There is much evidence against these claims. However, Clark's recent proposals are unsatisfactory in many ways. The principles she has set forth have conflicting implications as well as implications which have been disconfirmed. I have attempted to resolve some instances of conflict by proposing that the motivation to communicate occasionally overrides the motivations to use conventional names for things, to contrast novel words with known words, or to find new words for novel concepts and that the motivation to find new words for novel concepts occasionally overrides the motivation to use conventional names for things. Future research is clearly necessary to explicate the situations in which one motivation overrides the others.

The proposals of lexical contrast theory are much less specific than Clark's original proposals. A chief difference between lexical contrasts and semantic features is that much less can be said about what lexical contrasts are or about the order in which they are acquired. Lexical contrasts, unlike semantic features, are not universal cognitive primitives. They are merely cognitive distinctions mapped onto lexical differences. Lexical contrasts, unlike semantic features, are not thought to be acquired in a general-to-specific order. A simple-to-complex lexical contrast acquisition hypothesis is only applicable to a small set of words. Lexical contrast theory is vague about the structure and processing of children's word intensions. Word intensions appear to be sets of contrastive features. Only segments of these sets are evoked by different contexts. This process of evocation has not been explicated. It is not clear how this model accounts for typicality effects. The model does not incorporate feature interdependence considerations nor does it make predictions about how nonbasic level terms become integrated with basic level terms in a semantic system. A much more powerful theory than lexical contrast theory is needed to adequately explain how children learn the reference of names.

Nelson's Revisions

Nelson and her colleagues have revised some of Nelson's original hypotheses and have provided further elaborations upon the role of nonlinguistic concepts and functional information in the acquisition of the reference of concrete nouns.

One correction that has been made is to allow first names to be attached to concepts at any point in the concept-formation process, rather than constraining attachment until after formation is complete (Nelson, Rescorla, Gruendel, & Benedict, 1978). This modification represents a concession of a greater role to linguistic input. This modification was necessitated, in part, by demonstrations of the early and rapid development of word comprehension. Ironically, Nelson now grants somewhat more of a role to linguistic input than does Clark. Nelson and her colleagues still maintain, however, that the usual sequence in word acquisition is functional core formation, then static attribute abstraction, and finally name learning.

Nelson et al. (1978) claim that most early words will be applied to a narrow range of objects initially, perhaps only to a single referent or class of indistinguishable items, for example, raisins. Only later will terms be applied more generally. They contend that this period of specific application may be apparent for some terms only in comprehension. No extensive comprehension studies have been carried out to corroborate this claim. I have already mentioned Rescorla's (1980) evidence for initially narrow word extensions. Nelson et al. do not acknowledge that the existence of narrow early word extensions is incompatible with their hypothesis that names are usually learned only after children are capable of identifying objects on the basis of static attributes and testing those objects for concept membership on the basis of functional features. The latter implies that initially a term should be applied broadly since it tags a well-formed concept. The evidence for narrow early word extensions also suggests an answer to the question left open by Nelson's (1974) paper: How broad are functional core concepts. They contain a single referent or several indistinguishable referents. But if functional core concepts are so specific, how does the child ever learn general terms?

Nelson et al. (1978) have attempted to defend the functional core hypothesis against the evidence of overextensions that apparently disregard functions known to the child (Clark, 1975; Bowerman, 1978a) by pointing out the possibility that such instances may not be true namings. Rather, the child may be using a term to predicate something of a referent, for example, saying "Daddy" in reference to father's shoe meaning "Daddy's," or to make an analogy, for example, saying "ball" in reference to a water tank meaning "like a ball." Rescorla (1980) estimated that 45% of the overextensions observed in her sample were not true namings. However, Rescorla's coding scheme treated any use of a word in reference to an object not close to the word's standard referent in an adult lexical taxonomy as an analogical statement. It is difficult to determine whether a child who says "ball" in reference to a water tank is merely noting the tank's similarity to a ball or is actually calling it a ball. The child certainly realizes the difference between a water tank and an ordinary ball, but it remains an open question whether the child believes both can be called "ball." Some support for Rescorla's scheme comes from her finding that the proportion of overextensions that were not true namings declined from 66% to 29% over the period from ages 12- to 18- or 20-months-old and that the peak in predicate statement overextensions occurred in the month before the onset of two-word speech. These findings are consistent with the notion that syntactic immaturity prevents children from expressing intended relational meanings. With syntactic development, children become able to say "doll all gone" rather than merely "doll" in reference to any empty crib or to say "it's like a comb" in reference to a centipede. However, Anglin (1977) found that three-year-olds occasionally overextend a name *in comprehension* to an object that is only contextually associated with an acceptable referent of the name, for example, "horse" as a name for a saddle. Therefore, some of what Rescorla identified as predicate statement overextensions are likely true namings which reflect incorrect word intensions. Also, Bowerman (1978a) has made the valid argument that it is useless to distinguish naming from analogizing without additional evidence that a toddler can appreciate the distinction between naming and analogizing. Research on the development of metaphor suggests that this appreciation is gained late in the preschool years (Vosniadou & Ortony, 1983).

In contrast to Clark's principle of contrast, Nelson et al. (1978) proposed that the motivation behind analogical statements and naming overextensions is that of elaborating the *similarities* between objects. Clearly a theory of the many motivations governing child name selection is needed.

The allowance for predicate statements and analogical statements entails the rejection of Nelson's original hypothesis that children's first uses of object names imply the functional core and no more. Another problem for Nelson et al.'s position is that associative complex overextensions which occur beyond the one-word stage, such as Bowerman (1978a) reported, cannot be interpreted as either comments on analogy or as predicate statements since the child has the syntactic means for making such comments and predications explicit. Further research is needed to assess the extent of complexive word use in older children and to determine whether it disregards functional differences between referents.

Nelson has not altered her theory to accommodate the notions of typicality and feature interdependence. In her original account, concepts had internal structure in that features were weighted for reliability, with static features less reliable than functional features. This internal structure is not adequate for explaining the effects of typicality and feature interdependence.

Nelson has not defended her claim that words will be first used only in the context of defining relations against the evidence of Bowerman (1978a) and Bretherton et al. (1981), but she has weakened it. Nelson et al. (1978) propose that early word productions are contrained to the context of the concept forming instance in any relation or to the context of a novel instance in a defining relation. This hypothesis is disconfirmed by the observations of Bretherton et al. (1981).

Nelson et al. (1978) have outlined the following general progression of lexical development:

> "1. From ten to thirteen months: match adult words to existing child concepts in comprehension. Here, words are likely to be underextended, as the child's concepts may be based on one instance. Generalization to new instances will be based on perceptual similarity and action components.
> 2. From eleven to fifteen months: acquire a small number of words in production which are constrained to use in the context of a particular instance or in conjunction with the action-function component of the concept to which they are bounded; begin to differentiate concept domains in comprehension in line with adult usage.
> 3. From sixteen to twenty months: acquire new productive words for old concepts, form new concepts to match novel words, and begin to use words in new contexts and symbolically to categorize, to propositionalize, to analogize. Overextension appears as words are used categorically; comprehension-production discrepancies appear and then disappear as vocabulary expands to map the conceptual range." (p. 966)

One question I have about this progression is why first-word productions must be constrained to the context of a particular instance or function when those same words have been comprehended for a long time in a variety of contexts. If concept domains in comphension have already been differentiated in line with adult usage, then later productions should reflect a well-differentiated concept domain. According to Rescorla's (1980) findings, productive overextensions do occur in the 12- to 15-month period, although they are infrequent. On the other hand, Kay and Anglin (1982) did find evidence of narrower productive than receptive extensions of names children could comprehend, but had to be trained to produce. Nevertheless, research is needed to explore whether words which have been comprehended for several months before they are produced are less likely to be constrained to an instance or two in production than words not previously comprehended.

Although many arguments against Nelson's original hypotheses have been advanced, Nelson has gathered evidence which at least supports the claim that functional information is important in infant and toddler categorization. I have already mentioned Nelson's (1979a) study showing a correspondence between the number of action schemes elicited by objects and the speed with which children learned labels for the objects. Nelson (1979a) also has reported the preliminary results of two experiments involving 8- to 12-month-olds. In the first, infants exhibited greater dishabituation to a change in the way a mobile moved than to a change in the constituents of the mobile. In the second, 10-month-olds showed greater puzzlement and more sustained attention to an object that had been surreptitiously substituted for an identical object possessing different functional properties than to a substituted object that was formally, but not functionally different from the object it had replaced. However, 12-month-olds showed a significant trend in the opposite direction. Nelson does not offer an explanation of the 12-month-olds' behavior. A serious problem in both experiments, which Nelson acknowledges, is that of equating the magnitude of perceived functional and formal changes. Nevertheless, the experiments demonstrate that infants are sensitive to certain functional differences between objects.

Nelson's Extensions to Later Lexical Development

In addition to her attempts to revise and defend her original hypotheses, Nelson (1979a) has offered proposals about the course of lexical and conceptual development beyond the toddler period. These proposals concern the elaboration of the conceptual foundations laid during the infancy and toddler period. According to Nelson, functional information maintains its privileged position in the structure of concepts into the preschool period and beyond.

Nelson (1974) proposed that children are likely to comment on temporary states of objects in their first one-word utterances, for example, "broke." Nelson also proposed that such comments were only made about objects that were associated with well-formed concepts. One criticism is that it is unlikely that associated concepts could be that well formed so early in life. Nelson's (1979a) position implicitly accepts this criticism since these early comments are now taken to reflect the child's appreciation of the generality of such temporary states across all objects. Only the later use of color and size adjectives is more directly connected with object concepts having well-formed functional cores. Children's motivation for using these adjectives is to temporarily individuate instances of the same functional object concept. At an even later stage, children use modifiers to differentiate an object category such that a more permanent subcategory is established. For example, *Christmas tree* comes to be recognized as a subcategory of *tree*. This subcategory somehow enjoys a structural existence more distinct from that of the original category than do the subcategories designated by such phrases as "big tree" or "green tree." Nelson's (1976) analysis of toddlers' use of adjectives revealed a developmental decrease in the use of adjectives describing temporary states and a developmental increase in the use of other types of adjectives. However, the use of the general adjectives did not begin earlier than that of taxonomic modifiers.

It is difficult to evaluate the claim that expressions such as "Christmas tree" or "teddy bear" reflect the establishment of new conceptual types in a way that expressions containing common adjectives do not. There is no question that there are syntactic differences between these two types of expressions. "Christmas" and "teddy" are not adjectives, but noun adjuncts. They are rather unique to the nouns they modify. Their relation to the nouns they modify is opaque. For example, a green tree is a tree that is green and a big tree is a tree that is big, but a Christmas tree is not a tree that is Christmas. The relations between noun adjuncts and the nouns they modify vary and are never the same as the relation between an adjective and the noun it modifies. The relation between noun adjuncts and the nouns they modify is similar to that between components of compound words. For example, "dogsled" does not convey the nature of the relation between dog and sled (Clark, 1983). Also, the phonetic segmentation between the adjective and noun in expressions such as "green tree" appears more marked than that between the modifier and noun in expressions such as "Christmas tree."

Nelson et al.'s (1978) claim that first terms have initially narrow extensions suggests that functional core object concepts are very specific, but Nelson's (1979a) interpretation of developmental changes in modifier use suggests that functional core concepts are more general. These concepts must at least be more general than the subordinate categories that are ultimately differentiated from them. The best way of resolving this conflict would be to abandon the claim that functional cores are completely established and most identifying features are isolated before names are attached to concepts.

Both Nelson and Clark agree that contrastive object terms, which are the precursors of adult lexical fields, can be found very early in children's vocabularies. Children's first 50 productive words often consist of a disproportionate number of animal, vehicle, toy, or food terms (Nelson, 1973b; Rescorla, 1981). Children usually acquire many terms from a lexical field before acquiring the name for the field, for example, "duck," "dog," "kitty" before "animal" (Rescorla, 1981). Nelson et al. (1978) have suggested that before the name for the field is acquired, one of the lower level terms may be used as the name for the field as well as the name for a subcategory of the field. This term would be *polysemous*. This term may also be the first term within the field acquired. It should be noted that this sort of use has a precedent in the structure of some English lexical fields, for example,

Also, adults sometimes make mistakes reflecting the overgeneralization of this structure, for example,

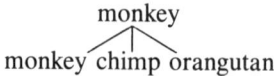

This structure could also account for some of the asymmetry observed between comprehension and production such as comprehending "kitty" and "squirrel," but calling squirrels "kitties." It is compatible with the dual naming observed by Rescorla

(1980, 1981) and Fremgen and Fay (1980). I know of no research which has explicitly tested for this kind of structure in toddlers' lexicons.

Nelson (1979a) has discussed a study by deVos and Carmazzo (1977) which traced the developmental differentiation of names for small containers. According to Nelson, the results indicated that these terms were first used rather indiscriminately, then used only in appropriate functional contexts, for example, if the container was used for drinking water, it was called "glass," then used according to certain form criteria, for example, height-to-width ratio distinguished a "cup" from a "glass," and finally used in such a way that form was integrated with function. The finding of an initial period of indiscriminate use and a later period in which form criteria determine lexical decisions is inconsistent with the hypotheses that labels initially tag functional core concepts and that functional information is always more reliable than form information. Nelson (1979) did not acknowledge these inconsistencies in her discussion of the study, but only noted that the study "demonstrates the way in which an originally holistic concept (cup=thing to drink from) may be broken down along functional lines, with the original (concept formation) sequence recapitulated for the resulting subconcepts" (p. 65).

Prawat and Wildfong (1980) found that 7- to 8-year-olds were more likely than preschoolers to vary their naming of containers that were intermediate in their resemblance to cups and bowls as a function of depicted function, for example, for holding drink versus food. The preschoolers labeled containers having the physical dimensions of a prototypical cup "cup" and of a prototypical bowl "bowl" regardless of the depicted function. Both of these results suggest that the subconcepts associated with "bowl" and "cup" were first differentiated along formal rather than functional lines, contrary to Nelson's (1979) prediction and to the reported results of the study by deVos and Caramazzo (1977)

Other proposals made by Nelson imply that subcategory differentiation *need not* always recapitulate the sequence of early concept formation. Nelson (1974) and Nelson et al. (1978) have asserted that beyond the age of two or so, name-based feature abstraction can occur. In this process, a child, after hearing a new word used on different occasions, selects an element of context that co-occurs with the word's use as an element of the word's intension. This element may be formal or functional. Thus, after the age of two or so, some object words will not be associated with functional core concepts. This is true of words for newly differentiated subconcepts as well as words for new concepts. According to this account, the child might form a functional core object concept consisting of the functional features (can contain) and (can be lifted). At an early age, the child learns "cup" as a tag for this concept. After this, the child hears "bowl" used in certain instances in which the functional criteria for "cup" are satisfied. The child attends to the contexts of usage of "cup" and "bowl" so as to differentiate their usage. Prawat and Wildfong's (1980) results suggest that the child is most likely to seize upon the contrasting physical appearances of cups and bowls as criterial. Thus, some of what Nelson has written can be reconciled to demonstrations of the importance of form in older children's lexical decisions. Nelson's functional core hypothesis does imply, however, that contrastive terms acquired *before* the age of two or so should tag different functional core concepts and that functional differences should be more important than formal differences in children's decisions about the extensions of these terms.

Functional features which form the core of an early word intension could serve to differentiate a small set of terms from all other terms, but not serve to differentiate within that set of terms. The fact that "bowl" shares core functional features with "cup" may be critical to the child's realization of the relation of "bowl" to "cup" in meaning and to the child's search for ways to differentiate the meanings of "bowl" and "cup."

Nelson (1979a) has argued that the continued importance of functional information in older children's word intensions is evident in preschoolers' explanations of what words mean and of what they know about the referents of words. Nelson (1978) asked 3- and 4-year-olds to "Tell me what X is" or to "Tell me what you know about X". When X was a basic level term such as "car" or "apple," children were most likely to list functions in response to both questions. Static attributes were listed with substantial frequency only in response to the "know about" request. According to Nelson, this pattern of response indicates that static attribute information is secondary to functional information in the structure of children's word intensions. When X was a superordinate term such as "animal" or "fruit," children were even more likely to mention functions in response to the "what is" request, but tended to list instances in response to the "know about" request. They rarely mentioned static attributes in response to either request. According to Nelson, this pattern indicates that superordinate object concepts are represented by a core of defining functions and a list of typical instances.

Adults tend to define basic object terms by giving a superordinate term and differentiating properties, for example, *an elephant is an animal that is large, grey, has a long trunk* (Anglin, 1977), but preschool children do not, even when the superordinate term is known to them (Anglin, 1977; Nelson, 1978). Nelson (1979a) has proposed that, with development, superordinate terms come to substitute for the functional component of children's object concepts in their definitions. This claim requires testing, but one problem with it is that certain functions children are likely to mention in their definitions are not entailed by superordinate terms, for example, a young child may say *a dog is something that barks, can be petted, and wags its tail*, but none of these core functions are entailed in the statement that *a dog is an animal*. Thus, the superordinate term is only a suitable substitute for general functions in the cores of children's object concepts.

Prawat and Cancelli (1977) have reported that both 5- and 8-year-olds are faster at verifying sentences attributing dynamic properties to basic level objects, for example, a dog can run, than they are at verifying sentences attributing ego-relational properties, for example, a dog can obey, or static properties, for example, a dog has a tail. If the dynamic properties in this experiment are the ones most likely to be found in the functional cores of early object concepts, this result supports the claim of the primacy of functional core features in later semantic organization. However, Nelson (1974) made no distinction between dynamic and ego-relational properties with respect to their membership in functional cores. Nelson (1979a) has reported the preliminary results of a study showing that 4-year-olds respond to, "Tell me some things that (are, can) X" faster if X is a function rather than a static attribute. In contrast to this finding and that of Prawat and Cancelli, Nelson and Kosalyn (1975) found no difference between dynamic and static properties in the speed with which grade school children or adults verified sentences attributing these properties to various animals. Further research is needed which compares preschool to grade school groups and uses better techniques to guarantee that properties tested include ones likely to be constituents of functional cores. Nelson (1974) stipulated that not all functional features, but just ones in functional cores, are important in the organization of object word meaning.

The last paradigm which has provided Nelson (1979a) with evidence for the primacy of function in later lexical organization is the word association task. Nelson (1977) concluded from a review of research that 6- to 7-year-olds' noun associations reflect their awareness of many semantic relations of nouns—superordination, subordination, coordination, and associated static and dynamic properties—but preschoolers' noun associations reflect chiefly an awareness of associated functional properties. For example, "boy" – "talk," "bread" – "eat," and "doctor" – "fix people" are typical noun associations of preschoolers. However, there have been very few studies of preschoolers' word associations. Also, Nelson does not discuss the implications of the changes in noun associations from preschool to early grade school for the role of functional information in lexical organization.

The primacy of functions in preschoolers' lexical knowledge does not extend to all tasks. Cramer (1974) found that although 5-year-olds give more functions than contrastive words in a word association task, they are more likely to falsely recognize contrastive words than functions in a memory task.

A Summary Evaluation of Nelson's Hypotheses

Several instances in which Nelson's hypotheses are either internally inconsistent or irreconcileable with external evidence have been presented. The claim of initially narrow word extensions is compatible with the claim that functional cores are formed and identifying features are abstracted usually before names are associated with concepts only if functional cores specify very narrow extensions. If such is the case, however, there is no account of how word extensions ever broaden since the nature of functional cores is not supposed to change after names become associated. If functional cores are allowed to change after names become associated, then this represents a greater role for the process of name-based feature abstraction than Nelson (1974) intended. The prediction that names are first produced only in reference to a certain object or in reference to objects in certain functional contexts has not been upheld. There is a need for empirical support for the claim that first productive uses of a term are more constrained than the term's contemporaneous comprehension. Nelson's original claim that first-word productions imply the functional core and no more is not reconcilable with her later claim that early word productions can be predicate statements or comments on analogy. Several experiments and naturalistic observations have found that children tend to generalize names on the basis of similarities in form despite differences in function. Although arguments have been made in defense of the functional core hypothesis against this evidence, these arguments have the effect of removing considerable predictive power and testability from the hypothesis. The evidence that toddlers alter their decisions about the appropriateness of a name for an object after receiving functional information about that object does not entail that function has primacy over form in word intensions. The evidence that the likelihood of a toddler learning the name for an object is positively correlated with the number of action schemes the object elicits does not entail that function has primacy over form in word intensions. Finally, Nelson has not revised her hypotheses to accommodate typicality, feature interdependence, or complex naming.

Although the case *against* the claim of the primacy of function over form in toddlers' word intensions is strong, Nelson has build a case *for* the primacy of function over form in the organization of older children's lexicons. However, the studies of children's noun definitions, noun associations, and noun-attribute verifications are few and not without discrepancies. Even if further experimentation in these paradigms supports the claim of functional primacy, it is most likely that this primacy is, contrary to Nelson's claims, a result of abandoning old representations of word meanings and adopting more complex representations. Function most likely assumes a greater importance in object word meanings as development proceeds. The results of studies by Prawat and Wildfong (1978) and Gentner (1978) indicate a developmental increase in the effect of certain functional information on noun interpretations. Howard and Howard's (1977) finding of a developmental decrease in the effect of size and of a developmental increase in the effect of predativity and domesticity on children's decisions about the relatedness of animal names is consistent with a perceptual-to-functional feature shift. Functions are more important general organizers of objects than forms. The few properties that dictionaries (Nelson, 1979a) and adults (Rosch et al. 1976b) list as common to members of superordinate categories are functional attributes. Most inanimate objects are best thought of as functional artifacts. Also, Callanan (1982) has observed that mothers are more likely to mention functional properties and included members when teaching superordinate terms to their three-year-olds than when teaching terms from other levels. Thus, one does not have to propose a functional core formed in the first two years of life to explain why children's first definitions of superordinate terms consist of functional properties and included members. Perhaps it is not until a child is four or five years old that he or she begins to realize the usefulness of functions for making general distinctions between noun domains.

Conclusions and Some Suggestions for Future Research

In reviewing any large body of research, one must be selective both in choosing the research to be reviewed and the order in which to review it. A historical approach has been taken in this paper in presenting, comparing, and evaluating general hypotheses about children's acquisition of the reference of concrete nouns.

This approach was taken in order to elucidate the observations and inferences which justified both the initial proposal of a hypothesis and its subsequent revision, extension, or abandonment. Some hypotheses, such as Nelson's hypothesis that children first use object words only in the context of defining relations, had little justification from the beginning. Others, such as Clark's GBSH, accounted for the data base from which they were induced, but were disconfirmed by subsequent research. This paper also has focused chiefly on the hypotheses specified in two evolving theories—Clark's and Nelson's. This approach was taken both because these theories have guided a good deal of research in the last 10 years and because it permitted the evaluation of hypotheses not only in terms of their consistency with observations of children's performance but also in terms of their logical consistency with other hypotheses proposed in the same theory. There are several instances of internal inconsistency in the theories of both Clark and Nelson.

Clark's decisions to abandon her original claim that word intensions are initially small sets of general semantic features is justified by several lines of evidence. Although Clark has replaced semantic feature theory with lexical contrast theory, the latter has incorporated some of the claims of the former. Lexical contrast theory requires much more elaboration and some corrections. The theory's principles of contrast and conventionality can be used to generate conflicting predictions as well as predictions which have been disconfirmed.

Although it is likely that the salience of the functions of an object is related to the likelihood of a child learning the name of the object, there is substantial evidence against Nelson's claim of the primacy of functional information in the object noun intensions of toddlers and against her claim that first uses of a noun are constrained to a particular instance or particular functional context. Nelson's claim of initially narrow word extensions is not compatible with her claim that names are associated with concepts late in the concept formation process. Finally, the most recent theories of both Nelson and Clark fail to accommodate the findings of typicality effects, feature interdependence effects, or category level effects on children's lexical performance.

Although I have focused on the weaknesses in Clark's and Nelson's accounts, I have offered little in the way of an alternative account. I have none to offer. Nor have the critics of Clark's account of developmental change in the meaning of other parts of speech (Richards, 1979; Carey, 1982) offered alternative accounts. However, like Carey, I will offer some suggestions of aspects of word meaning acquisition we need to know more about before an account can be developed. First, given that children learn the meanings of common basic level names first (Rosch et al., 1976a; Anglin, 1977), we need to know more about how children relate the intensions of new words to the intension they have constructed for the basic level name they know. Do children assume that new words contrast with the words they know, as Clark (1983) and Barrett (1978) suggest? If so, then they should have difficulty accommodating their vocabularies to new words that are not contrastive to the words they know. They should have less difficulty with a new contrastive name than with new superordinate, subordinate, synonymous, or overlapping names. Secondly, we need to know more about the ways in which the relation of a new name to known names is marked in input and whether children are sensitive to such marking. For example, Whitehurst et al. (1982) have documented that superordinate names occurring in input to the child are more likely to be used in reference to groups of objects rather than single objects, for example, "Put your *toys* away" or "Don't play with your *food*." Markman and her colleagues (Markman, Horton, & McLanahan, 1980; Callanan & Markman, 1982) have demonstrated that this kind of input pattern fosters the mistake of interpreting the new name as a collective rather than a class noun. Adams and Bullock (1983), Callanan (1982), and Blewitt (1983b) have provided other evidence of how the nature of the relation of new names to names a child knows affects the way adults introduce new names to the child. This research is suggestive of certain mistakes to which children's interpretations of new names should be prone, but investigations of such mistakes have yet to be carried out. Finally, there has been some investigation of what might be termed *metalexical ability*, that is, children's awareness of lexical relations. Investigation has focused primarily on word definition and word association (Anglin, 1977; Nelson, 1979a). We need to know how developmental changes in metalexical ability influence the course of lexical development itself. For example, to what extent can children's decisions about the reference of a name be affected by giving children a definition of the name in addition to showing examples. Horton and Markman (1980) have found that verbal specification of defining features facilitates reference decisions only after the age of four and only for superordinate, not basic level names. This provocative finding clearly merits replication and extension. Other kinds of nouns should be examined and variations in the specification of defining features should be explored.

If the lines of research proposed here are pursued and attempts are made to correct for points of weakness that have been identified in the accounts of Clark and Nelson, then development of a more accurate and more complete account of how children learn the reference of concrete nouns is a likely consequence.

References

Adams, A. K., & Bullock, D. (1983). *Anomaly and context effects in maternal labeling of category examplars*. Paper presented at the biennial meeting of the Society for Research in Child Development, Detroit.

Andersen, E. S. (1975). Cups and glasses: Learning that boundaries are vague. *Journal of Child Language, 2*, 79-104.

Anglin, J. (1977). *Word, object, and conceptual development*. New York: Norton.

Barrett, M. D. (1978). Lexical development and overextension in child language. *Journal of Child Language, 5*, 205-219.

Bartlett, E. J. (1976). Sizing things up: The acquisition of the meaning of dimensional adjectives. *Journal of Child Language, 3*, 205-219.

Benedict, H. (1978). Language comprehension in 9-15-month-old children. In R. N. Campbell & P. T. Smith (Eds.), *Recent advances in the psychology of language: Language development and mother-child interaction*. New York: Plenum Press.

Benedict, H. (1979). Early lexical development: Comprehension and production. *Journal of Child Language, 6,* 183-200.

Bierwisch, M. (1970). Semantics. In J. Lyons (Ed.), *New horizons in linguistics.* Harmondsworth, England: Penguin Books.

Blewitt, P. (1982). Word meaning acquisition in young children: A review of theory and research. In H. W. Reese (Ed.), *Advances in child development and behavior* (Vol. 17). New York: Academic Press.

Blewitt, P. (1983a). *What determines order of acquisition of object categories?* Paper presented at the biennial meeting of the Society for Research on Child Development, Detroit.

Blewitt, P. (1983b). *Dog* versus *collie:* Vocabulary in speech to young children. *Developmental Psychology, 19,* 601-609.

Bloom, L. (1973). *One word at a time—the use of single word utterances before syntax.* The Hague: Mouton.

Bowerman, M. (1978a). The acquisition of word meaning: An investigation into some current conflicts. In N. Waterson & C. E. Snow (Eds.), *The development of communication.* New York: Wiley.

Bowerman, M. (1978b). Semantic and syntactic development: A review of what, when, and how in language acquisition. In R. L. Schiefelbusch (Ed.), *Bases for language intervention.* Baltimore: University Park Press.

Bretherton, I., Bates, E., McNew, S., Shore, C., Williamson, C., & Beeghly-Smith, M. (1981). Comprehension and production of symbols in infancy: An experimental study. *Developmental Psychology, 17,* 728-736.

Brewer, W. E., & Stone, J. B. (1975). Acquisition of spatial antonym pairs. *Journal of Experimental Child Psychology, 19,* 299-307.

Brown, R. W. (1956). Language and categories. Appendix to J. S. Bruner, J. J. Goodnow, & G. A. Austin. *A study of thinking.* New York: Wiley.

Brown, R. W. (1958). How shall a thing be called? *Psychological Review, 65,* 14-21.

Callanan, M. A. (1982). *Parental input and young children's acquisition of hierarchically organized concepts.* Unpublished doctoral dissertation, Stanford University.

Callanan, M. A., & Markman, E. M. (1982). Principles of organization in young children's natural language hierarchies. *Child Development, 53,* 1093-1101.

Carey, S. (1982). Semantic development—state of the art. In L. Gleitman & E. Wanner (Eds.), *Language development—state of the art.* Hillsdale, NJ: Erlbaum.

Chambers, J. C., & Tavuchis, N. (1976). Kids and kin: Children's understanding of American kin terms. *Journal of Child Language, 3,* 62-80.

Chomsky, C. (1969). *Acquisition of syntax in children from 5 to 10.* Cambridge, MA: MIT Press.

Clark, E. V. (1971). On the acquisition of "before" and "after." *Journal of Verbal Learning and Verbal Behavior, 10,* 266-275.

Clark, E. V. (1973a). What's in a word? On the child's acquisition of semantics in his first language. In T. E. Moore (Ed.), *Cognitive development and the acquisition of language.* New York: Academic Press.

Clark, E. V. (1973b). Non-linguistic strategies and the acquisition of word meanings. *Cognition, 2,* 161-182.

Clark, E. V. (1975). Knowledge, context, and strategy in the acquisition of meaning. In D. P. Dato (Ed.), *Georgetown University round table on language and linguistics.* Washington, DC: Georgetown University Press.

Clark, E. V. (1983). Meanings and concepts. In P. H. Mussen (Ed.), *Carmichael's Manual of Child Psychology: Vol. 3. Cognitive Development.* New York: Wiley.

Clark, H., & Clark, E. V. (1977). *Psychology and language: An introduction to psycholinguistics.* New York: Harcourt Brace Jovanovich.

Cramer, P. (1974). Idiodynamic sets as determinants of children's false recognition errors. *Developmental Psychology, 10,* 86-92.

Currie-Jedermann, J. (1981). *The role of function in conceptual development.* Paper presented at the biennial meeting of the Society of Research in Child Development, Boston.

Daehler, M. W., Lonardo, R., & Bukatko, D. (1979). Matching and equivalence judgments in very young children. *Child Development, 50,* 170-179.

Dale, P. S. (1976). *Language development: Structure and function.* New York: Holt, Rinehart, & Winston.

Danziger, K. (1957). The child's understanding of kinship terms: A study in the development of relational concepts. *Journal of Genetic Psychology, 91,* 213-232.

deVos, L. F., & Caramazzo, A. (1977). *The role of form and function in the development of natural language concepts.* Paper presented at the biennial meeting of the Society for Research in Child Development, New Orleans.

Donaldson, M., & Balfour, G. (1968). Less is more: A study of language comprehension in children. *British Journal of Psychology, 59,* 461-472.

Donaldson, M., & Wales, R. J. (1970). On the acquisition of some relational terms. In J. R. Hayes (Ed.), *Cognition and the development of language.* New York: Wiley.

Eilers, R. E., Oller, K. K., & Ellington, J. (1974). The acquisition of word meaning for dimensional adjectives: The long and the short of it. *Journal of Child Language, 1,* 195-204.

Fremgen, A., & Fay, D. (1980). Overextensions in production and comprehension: A methodological clarification. *Journal of Child Language, 7,* 205-212.

Gentner, D. (1978). On relational meaning: The acquisition of verb meaning. *Child Development, 49,* 988-998.

Glucksberg, S., Hay, A., & Danks, J. H. (1976). Words in uttterance contexts: Young children do not confuse the meanings of *same* and *different. Child Development, 47,* 737-741.

Goldin-Meadow, S., Seligman, M. E. P., & Gelman, R. (1976). Language in the two-year-old. *Cognition, 4,* 189-202.

Haviland, S. E., & Clark, E. V. (1974). 'This man's father is my father's son': A study of the acquisition of English kin terms. *Journal of Child Language, 1,* 23-48.

Horton, M. S., & Markman, E. M. (1980). Developmental differences in the acquisition of basic and superordinate categories. *Child Development, 51,* 708-719.

Howard, D. V., & Howard, J. H. (1977). A multidimensional scaling analysis of the development of animal names. *Developmental Psychology, 13,* 108-113.

Huttenlocher, J. (1974). The origins of language comprehension. In R. L. Solso (Ed.), *Theories in cognitive psychology: the Loyola symposium.* Potomac, MD: Erlbaum.

Katz, N., Baker, E., & MacNamara, J. (1974). What's in a name? A study of how children learn common and proper nouns. *Child Development, 45,* 469-473.

Kay, D. A., & Anglin, J. (1982). Overextension and underextension in the child's expressive and receptive speech. *Journal of Child Language, 9,* 83-98.

Kuczaj, S. A. (1982). Children's overextensions in comprehension and production: Support for a prototype theory of object word meaning acquisition. *First Language, 3,* 93-105.

Labov, W. (1973). The boundaries of words and their meanings. In C-J. N. Bailey & R. Shuy (Eds.), *New ways of analysing variation in English.* Washington, DC: Georgetown University Press.

Labov, W., & Labov, T. (1974). *The grammar of "cat" and "mama"*. Paper presented at the annual meeting of the Linguistic Society of America, New York.

Lewis, M. M. (1951). *Infant speech: A study of the beginnings of language*. New York: Humanities Press.

Markman, E. M., Horton, M. S., & McLanahan, A. G. (1980). Classes and collections: Principles of organization in the learning of hierarchical relations. *Cognition, 8*, 227-242.

McCarthy, D. A. (1954). Language development in children. In L. Carmichael (Ed.), *Manual of child psychology* (2nd ed.).

Mervis, C. B., & Canada, K. (1981). *Child-basic categories and early lexical development*. Paper presented at the biennial meeting of the Society for Research in Child Development, Boston.

Mervis, C. B., & Crisafi, M. A. (1982). Order of acquisition of subordinate-, basic-, and superordinate-level categories. *Child Development, 53*, 258-266.

Mervis, C. B., & Mervis, C. A. (1982). Leopards are kitty-cats: Object labeling by mothers for their thirteen-month-olds. *Child Development, 53*, 267-273.

Mervis, C. B., & Pani, J. R. (1980). Acquisition of basic object categories. *Cognitive Psychology, 12*, 496-522.

Mervis, C. B., & Rosch, E. (1981). Categorization of natural objects. In M. R. Rosenzweig & L. W. Porter (Eds.), *Annual Review of Psychology* (Vol. 32). Palo Alto, CA: Annual Reviews Inc.

Miller, G. A., & Johnson-Laird, P. N. (1976). *Language and perception*. Cambridge, MA: Harvard University Press.

Nelson, K. (1973b). Some evidence for the cognitive primacy of categorization and its functional basis. *Merrill-Palmer Quarterly, 19*, 21-39.

Nelson, K. (1974). Concept, word, and sentence: Interrelations in acquisition and development. *Psychological Review, 81*, 267-285.

Nelson, K. (1976). Some attributes of adjectives used by young children. *Cognition, 4*, 13-30.

Nelson, K. (1977). The syntagmatic-paradigmatic shift revisited: A review of research and theory. *Psychological Bulletin, 84*, 93-116.

Nelson, K. (1978). Semantic development and the development of semantic memory. In K. E. Nelson (Ed.), *Children's language* (Vol. 1). New York: Gardner Press.

Nelson, K. (1979a). Explanations in the development of a functional semantic system. In W. A. Collins (Ed.), *Children's language and communication—the Minnesota symposium on child psychology*: Vol. 12. Hillsdale, NJ: Erlbaum.

Nelson, K. (1979b). Features, contrasts, and the FCH: Some comments on Barrett's lexical development hypothesis. *Journal of Child Language, 6*, 139-146.

Nelson, K., Rescorla, L., Gruendel, J., & Benedict, H. (1978). Early lexicans: What do they mean? *Child Development, 49*, 960-968.

Nelson, K. E., & Kosslyn, S. M. (1975). Semantic retrieval in children and adults. *Developmental Psychology, 11*, 807-813.

Perlmutter, M., & Ricks, M. (1979). Recall in preschool children. *Journal of Experimental Child Psychology, 27*, 423-436.

Piaget, J. (1928). *Judgment and reasoning in the child*. London: Routledge & Kegan.

Postal, P. M. (1966). Andre Martinet, 'Elements of general linguistics'. *Foundations of Language, 2*, 151-186.

Prawat, R. S., & Cancelli, A. A. (1977). Semantic retrieval in young children as a function of type of meaning. *Developmental Psychology, 13*, 354-358.

Prawat, R. S., & Wildfong, S. (1980). The influence of functional context on children's labeling responses. *Child Development, 51*, 1057-1060.

Reich, P. (1976). The early acquisition of word meaning. *Journal of Child Language*, *3*, 117-123.

Rescorla, L. A. (1980). Overextension in early language development. *Journal of Child Language*, *7*, 321-335.

Rescorla, L. A. (1981). Category development in early language. *Journal of Child Language*, *8*, 225-238.

Richards, M. M. (1979). Sorting out what's in a word from what's not: Evaluating Clark's semantic features acquisition theory. *Journal of Experimental Child Psychology*, *27*, 1-47.

Rosch, E. H. (1973). On the internal structure of perceptual and semantic categories. In T. E. Moore (Ed.), *Cognitive development and the acquisition of language*. New York: Academic Press.

Rosch, E. H., & Mervis, C. B. (1975). Family resemblances: Studies in the internal structure of categories. *Cognitive Psychology*, *7*, 573-605.

Rosch, E. H., Simpson, C., & Miller, R. S. (1976a). Structural bases of typicality effects. *Journal of Experimental Psychology: Human Perception and Performance*, *2*, 491-502.

Rosch, E. H., Mervis, C. B., Gray, W., Johnson, D., & Boyes-Braem, P. (1976b). Basic objects in natural categories. *Cognitive Psychology*, *8*, 382-439.

Rosch, E. H. (1978). Principles of categorization. In E. H. Rosch & B. Lloyd (Eds.), *Cognition and categorization*. Hillsdale, NJ: Erlbaum.

Ross, G. S. (1980). Categorization in 1- to 2-year-olds. *Developmental Psychology*, *16*, 391-396.

Slobin, D. (1973). Cognitive prerequisites for the development of grammar. In C. A. Ferguson & D. Slobin (Eds.), *Studies of child language development*. New York: Holt, Rinehart, & Winston.

Snow, C. E. (1977). Mother's speech research: From input to interaction. In C. E. Snow & C. A. Ferguson (Eds.), *Talking to children: Language input and acquisition*. Cambridge, MA: Cambridge University Press.

Suchman, R. G., & Trabasso, T. (1966). Stimulus preference and cue function in young children's concept attainment. *Journal of Experimental Child Psychology*, *3*, 188-198.

Thomson, J., & Chapman, R. W. (1977). Who is 'Daddy' revisited: The status of two-year-olds' overextended words in use and comprehension. *Journal of Child Language*, *4*, 359-375.

Tomikawa, S. A., & Dodd, D. H. (1980). Early word meanings: Perceptually or functionally based? *Child Development*, *51*, 1103-1109.

Vosniadou, S., & Ortony, A. (1983). The emergence of the literal-metaphorical-anomalous distinction in young children. *Child Development*, *54*, 154-161.

Vygotsky, L. S. (1962). *Thought and language*. (E. Haufmann, & G. Vakar, Trans.). Cambridge, MA: MIT Press.

Werner, H. (1948). *Comparative psychology of mental development*. New York: International Universities Press.

Werner, H., & Kaplan, B. (1964). *Symbol formation*. New York: Wiley.

Whitehurst, G. J., Kedesdy, J., & White, T. G. (1982). A functional analysis of meaning. In S. A. Kuczaj (Ed.), *Language development* (Vol. 1). Hillsdale, NJ: Erlbaum.

2. Early Semantic Representations and Early Word-Usage

Martyn D. Barrett

In this chapter, I would like to address the following two questions: (a) What are the principal phenomena which characterize the early development of word-usage in young children? and (b) What theoretical constructs do we need to posit in order to explain these phenomena? In an attempt to provide answers to these two questions, I will not only draw upon the findings from existing studies, but also report some further findings which are derived from observations that I have been making of the early linguistic development of my son, Adam. The chapter will be structured as follows. I will begin by describing some of the principal phenomena which characterize the early development of word-usage; in the course of this description, I will also start to introduce some of the pertinent theoretical constructs that seem to be required in order to explain these phenomena. I shall then present a summary description of the theoretical framework which is being proposed, and show how this framework can be used to explain the various patterns of developmental change which are exhibited by young children's early lexical productions. The chapter will conclude with a brief discussion of some of the outstanding issues which require further investigation for proper elucidation.

The Principal Phenomena Characterizing Early Word-Usage

The Event-Bound Nature of Early Word-Usage

It has frequently been observed in previous studies that many early words, when they are first produced, are only used by the child in very limited contexts. Bloom (1973), for example, reports that her daughter, Allison, began to produce the word *car* when she was 9 months old only while she was looking at a car moving on the street below, as she watched from the living room window. She never produced this word in any other context at this age (for example, when she was in a car, when she saw a car standing still, or when she looked at pictures of cars). Similarly, Bates, Benigni, Bretherton, Camaioni, and Volterra (1979) report that, in their study of 25 children (aged between 9 and 13 months), nearly all of the earliest words that were acquired by these children were initially produced only in the context of highly specific events. Thus, one child initially produced the word *bye* only while putting a telephone receiver down; another child initially produced the word *papa* only when he heard the sound of the door. The longitudinal study of two children by Barrett (1983) yielded further illustrations of this phenomenon. For example, one of the two children studied, Tina, initially produced the word *catch* (when she was 19 months old) only while she was throwing an object to another person; the other child, Emily, initially produced the word *there* (at 17 months) only while she was engaged in the process of placing an object in a location.

Many further examples could be selected from the available literature in order to illustrate the highly restricted nature of initial word-usage by young children. However, I would instead like to document this phenomenon in greater detail here by reporting some new instances which I have observed in my son, Adam. In Table 2-1, data pertaining to Adam's early use of four different words are presented: *chuff-chuff*, *duck*, *dog*, and *no*. The aspect of these data which will be considered here is the initial context of use of each word. Consider the word *chuff-chuff*. This word was initially produced by Adam only while he was engaged in the process of pushing a toy train along the floor. The fact that Adam never produced this word in any other situation at this initial stage suggests that although he had learned that this particular situation provided him with an appropriate context for the production of the word, he had not yet acquired the understanding that this word could be used to refer to his toy train in any situation, or indeed that he could use this word in order to refer to real trains. In other words, Adam did not yet appear to have learned that this word could function as a name for a particular object or class of objects. Instead, his behavior suggests that he had simply identified one particular event in the context of which it was appropriate for him to produce the word *chuff-chuff*.

Adam's initial use of the word *duck* (which he usually pronounced *dut*) can also be interpreted in a similar way. This word was initially produced by Adam only while he was engaged in the process of hitting one of his toy yellow ducks off the edge of the bath (which is where they were normally kept). He was never observed producing this word in any other situation at this initial stage: he never produced it while he was playing with his toy ducks in other situations, or while he was looking at or feeding real ducks. This behavior therefore tends to suggest once again that Adam had not yet learned that the word *duck* could be used to refer to either his toy ducks or real ducks. Instead, his behavior suggests that he had simply identified one particular event in the context of which it was appropriate for him to produce the word *duck*.

A third example is provided by Adam's early use of the word *dog*. His first use of this word was a direct imitation of my own use, and it occurred while he was looking

Table 2-1. Adam's Use of the Words *chuff-chuff*, *duck*, *dog*, and *no*

Word	Contexts of use[a]
chuff-chuff	Initial context of use: while pushing a toy train along the floor (1;6;2). Subsequent contexts of use: while looking at pictures of trains in books (1;6;6); after being asked, "How does a train go?" (1;6;6); on seeing real trains (1;6;20); on hearing the sound (resembling that of a train) made by an airship on television (1;6;23)[b]; on seeing railway bridges on which he had previously seen trains (1;6;25); while looking at and scratching a pattern on a rug which consisted of an elongated rectangular shape roughly resembling the shape of a whole train (1;7;22)[b]; while looking at a long jointed toy caterpillar (1;7;22)[b].
duck	Initial context of use: while hitting any one of his three toy yellow ducks off the edge of the bath (1;0;2). Subsequent contexts of use: while playing with his toy yellow ducks in any situation (1;0;15); after being asked "What's that?" in reference to his toy yellow ducks (1;0;15); on seeing a toy yellow duck (1;0;17); while looking at real ducks (1;1;6); while looking at a stylized multicolored picture of a duck (1;2;7); while approaching a river, apparently in anticipation of seeing ducks (1;2;9); while looking at realistic pictures of ducks (1;3;25); after being asked "What's that?" in reference to pictures of ducks (1;3;25); while looking at real swans (1;5;18); while looking at real geese (1;5;18); while looking at a picture of a quail (1;6;7); while looking at pictures of swans (1;7;11).
dog	Initial context of use: first imitated the word while looking at a picture of a dog on a bib, after his father had been pointing to the picture and repeatedly saying the word (1;1;10); first spontaneous use of the word after being asked "what's that?" by another person who was pointing to the picture of the dog on the bib (1;1;10). Subsequent contexts of use: while looking at and pointing to the picture of the dog on the bib (1;1;30); while looking at real dogs (1;2;2;); after being asked "what's that?" in reference to dogs (1;2;8).
no	Initial context of use: while Adam was actively refusing to comply with an action which another person was trying to impose upon him, for example, while struggling against his father who was trying to take him out of a room in which he wanted to stay, while turning his head away from some food which was being held to his mouth by his mother, while struggling against his father who was trying to put him to bed against his will (1;5;20). Subsequent contexts of use: while performing an action which he knew was forbidden, for example, while he was pulling handfuls of books off a shelf onto the floor, while he was attacking and savaging plants in plant-pots (1;8;9); to express his refusal to comply with a verbal directive, for example, after his mother said "tidy your toys", after his mother said "have some milk" (1;8;27).

[a] Adam's age at the first occurrence of each usage is given in parentheses in years, months and days.
[b] These usages were unique occurrences which were not subsequently repeated.

at a picture of a dog on the front of a bib, after I had been pointing to this picture and repeatedly saying the word. His first spontaneous use of the word occurred later on the same day, when I pointed to this same picture and asked *what's that*? He subsequently began to produce the word *dog* when anyone pointed to this picture while asking *what's that*? He did not, however, yet say *dog* in any other context (for example, when he himself was pointing to this picture on the bib, when other pictures of dogs were being pointed to, or when real dogs were being pointed to). Consequently, Adam's behavior once again suggests that he had simply identified one particular event (which was defined in terms of another person pointing to this picture on the bib and asking *what's that*?), and that he interpreted the occurrence of this particular event as providing him with the appropriate context for the production of the word *dog*.

Thus, what I would like to suggest here is that, although some early words may be used by the child in such a way that they give the appearance of functioning as the names of objects (e.g., Adam's use of the word *dog*, in particular), this may well be an overinterpretation of the actual use of those words by the child. Instead, these words can often be interpreted merely as ritualized responses to the occurrence of particular events (in which the child may be involved either as a participant or as a spectator), events which the child interprets, in a holistic manner, as providing appropriate contexts for the production of those words.

The final example contained in Table 2-1 concerns Adam's initial use of the word *no*, which differs from the three previous examples in that it is clearly not an object name. Adam initially produced this word while he was engaged in the process of actively refusing to comply with an action that another person was trying to impose on him. Although the full range of event instances in which Adam produced this word was much broader than the range of event instances in which the three previous words were produced, it can nevertheless be seen that the production of the word *no* was still always tied to the actual occurrence of a particular type of event, that is, an event in which Adam actively refused to comply with an action that was being imposed on him.

If my interpretation of these examples of early word-usage is correct (i.e., that these initial word uses should properly be interpreted as being event-bound), then we can begin to explore how this phenomenon might be explained. To this end, it is helpful to return to the first example provided by Adam's use of the word *chuff-chuff*. It will be recalled that Adam initially produced this word only while in the process of pushing his toy train along the floor. The fact that Adam produced this word on many separate occasions, but only when this particular event was occurring, shows that he was treating various separate instances of this event as being equivalent to one another (in the sense that he regarded all of these separate instances as providing him with appropriate contexts for the production of the word). This in turn suggests that Adam had acquired a mental representation of this event, by reference to which he was able to recognize the equivalence of these separate instances. This event representation is depicted in Figure 2-1(a). The three different elements (*Adam*, *pushing*, and *toy train*) are included here because the presence of all three of these

(a) $\begin{bmatrix} \text{Adam} \\ \text{pushing} \\ \text{toy train} \end{bmatrix}$

(b) $\begin{bmatrix} \text{Adam} \\ \text{hitting} \\ \text{toy yellow duck (e.g. } duck_1, duck_2, \text{ or } duck_3) \end{bmatrix}$

(c) $\begin{bmatrix} \text{another person (e.g. mummy, daddy, \ldots etc.)} \\ \text{pointing} \\ \text{to picture of dog on bib} \\ \text{and saying 'what's that'} \end{bmatrix}$

(d) $\begin{bmatrix} \text{another person (e.g. mummy, daddy, \ldots etc.)} \\ \text{imposing action on Adam (e.g. taking out of room, offering food, \ldots etc.)} \\ \text{-----------------} \\ \text{Adam} \\ \text{refusing to comply with other person's dictates (e.g. struggling, turning head} \\ \text{away, \ldots etc.)} \end{bmatrix}$

Figure 2-1. The event representations hypothesized as underlying Adam's initial uses of the words (a) *chuff-chuff*, (b) *duck*, (c) *dog*, and (d) *no*. *Note.* The information in parentheses in these figures is included here for illustrative purposes only. It remains an open question as to whether an event representation includes an explicit specification of each individual slot-filler, or whether slots are specified solely at the superordinate level and thus only implicitly specify the appropriate fillers. Square brackets are used in these figures to indicate the holistic nature of each event representation. It should be noted that the term *holistic* as it is used here does not necessarily preclude the possibility that an event representation is ultimately specified in terms of sets of more specific primitive features; rather, it is meant to imply that, however the representation is ultimately specified, any given event instance must necessarily display *all* of the specifed features in order to be recognized as an instantation of that representation.

elements was required in any given event instance in order for that instance to elicit Adam's production of the word (thus, he did not produce the word when another person pushed the train, or when he himself performed another action on the train, or when he himself pushed another object such as a toy car).

Exactly the same reasoning can be applied to the other three examples described in Table 2-1. In each case, it can be postulated that Adam had acquired a mental representation of an event, and that he was producing the appropriate word when he recognized the occurrence of the appropriate event. In the case of the word *duck*, Adam hitting any one of three different toy yellow ducks provided the context for his production of the word. Thus, the event representation underlying his use of this word can be depicted as in Figure 2-1(b), the word *duck* being produced when Adam recognized an instance in which this type of event was occurring. In the case of the word *dog*, it can be postulated that Adam had acquired the event representation depicted in Figure 2-1(c), and that he was producing the word *dog* when he recognized an event instance in which this type of event was occurring. Finally, in the case of the word *no*, Adam appeared to have acquired the event representation depicted in Figure 2-1(d), consequently producing this word when he recognized an instance in which this type of event occurred.

Two principal characteristics of these hypothesized event representations are apparent from Figure 2-1. First, it can be seen that the event representations which underlie early word-usage are rather limited in scope, the represented events sometimes involving just a single person, a single action-scheme, and a single object. They are thus much more limited in scope than the event representations which have previously been discussed in the literature (Nelson, 1982) and which contain specifications of the entire range and sequence of activities involved in very general events such as *meal-time* and *getting dressed*. Second, it appears that these very limited event representations which governed Adam's early word-usage nevertheless contained, in several cases, *slots* which could be variously filled by different people, actions, and objects. In the case of the word *duck*, for example, Adam had three different toy yellow ducks, and his hitting any one of them provided a sufficient context to elicit his production of the word. Similarly, Adam also produced the word *dog* when anybody pointed to the picture of the dog on the bib and asked *what's that?* Adam himself appeared to be the only person who could not fill this particular slot at this stage. There were also several different specific people and actions which could fill the slots in the event representation underlying his use of the word *no*. However, Adam's use of the word *chuff-chuff* does indicate that, in some cases, these slots might only be filled by one particular person, action, and object. In this case, he only produced the word while he himself was pushing just one particular toy train along the floor. Thus, the evidence from Adam suggests that, depending upon the event representation, the constituent slots may be filled to varying extents by alternative possible fillers.

Finally, the way in which these event representations might initially be acquired by the child can be considered. To this end, it is relevant to note that, in the case of Adam's use of the words *chuff-chuff*, *duck*, and *no*, the represented events were events in which Adam had frequently and regularly participated prior to his acquisition of these words. It therefore seems plausible to suppose that, during this period prior to his use of these words, he was gradually acquiring a knowledge of these routine events in which he was regularly participating, and building up a knowledge of the various ways in which these particular types of event could be instantiated. And in the fourth case, that of the word *dog*, it will be recalled that Adam only began to use this word after an episode in which I had been repeatedly pointing to the picture on the bib and modelling the word for him. Thus, the data from Adam is consistent with the hypothesis that an event representation is acquired through the child repeatedly experiencing instances of a particular type of event (Nelson, 1982, 1983).

The Modification of Event-Bound Word-Usage

I shall now turn to a second phenomenon which characterizes the development of early word-usage. The available data suggest that, in some cases, once the child has acquired the initial event-bound use of a word, the child's use of that word may subsequently change, even though it remains event-bound. Often, this change appears to consist of the generalization of the use of the word to a broader range of event instances. For example, I have previously reported in Barrett (1983) that, about one month after Tina had acquired her initial use of the word *catch* (to accompany her actions of throwing an object), she began to produce this word not only while she herself was throwing an object, but also when she saw another person throwing an object. However, she still did not use the word in any other context. Thus, the word was still tied to the occurrence of a particular event. However, this event now seemed to be specified at a more general level in the sense that *any* person, not just Tina herself, could now perform the action entailed in that event. Consequently, we can hypothesize that Tina had acquired the event representation depicted in Figure 2-2(a) to govern her initial use of this word. Similarly, the event representation which appeared to be governing her generalized use of this word can be depicted as in Figure 2-2(b). By comparing Figures 2-2(a) and 2-2(b), it can be seen that the generalization of the use of this word was due to the broadening of the range of the people who could fill one particular slot in the initial event representation, the word thus coming to be produced in a wider range of event instances.

The same phenomenon was also exhibited by Adam. For example, Table 2-1 shows that, about 3 weeks after Adam had acquired his initial use of the word *dog*, he began to produce this word not only while another person was pointing to the picture of the dog on the bib, but also while he himself was pointing to this picture. Thus, the word was still tied to the occurrence of a particular event; however, once again, this event was now specified at a slightly more general level in that any person, including Adam himself, could now perform one of the actions which was entailed in that event (i.e., pointing). Furthermore, the event instances which now elicited the production of the word did not always involve the production of the question *what's that?* (i.e., those instances in which Adam himself pointed to the picture on the bib). Consequently, we can explain these developments by postulating that the event representation which had governed Adam's initial use of this word (see Figure 2-1(c)) had been modified and now had the form depicted in Figure 2-2(c), the word thus coming to be used when this more general type of event was instantiated.[1]

Another example which illustrates the generalization of event-bound word-usage is provided by Adam's use of the word *no* (see Table 2-1). It will be recalled that when Adam first acquired this word, he only used it when he was actively refusing to com-

---

[1] Alternatively, it could have been the case that the element "saying *what's that*" had not been deleted from the initial event representation, but had instead become a conditional element (conditional upon a person other than Adam doing the pointing). If this element had been deleted, then we would predict that Adam should sometimes have produced the word *dog* in situations in which another person merely pointed to the picture (without asking *what's that?*); if it had become conditional, then Adam should never have produced the word *dog* in these situations. Unfortunately, I did not think of performing this critical test at the appropriate time, and in all of the recorded instances in which another person spontaneously pointed to the picture, that person did always ask *what's that?*

(a) $\begin{bmatrix} \text{Tina} \\ \text{throwing} \\ \text{object} \end{bmatrix}$

(b) $\begin{bmatrix} \text{any person (e.g. Tina, mummy, daddy, \ldots etc.)} \\ \text{throwing} \\ \text{object} \end{bmatrix}$

(c) $\begin{bmatrix} \text{any person (e.g. Adam, mummy, daddy, \ldots etc.)} \\ \text{pointing} \\ \text{to picture of dog on bib} \end{bmatrix}$

(d) $\begin{bmatrix} \text{Adam} \\ \text{refusing to comply with other person's dictates} \end{bmatrix}$

Figure 2-2. The event representations hypothesized as underlying (a) Tina's initial use of *catch*, (b) Tina's generalized use of *catch*, (c) Adam's generalized use of *dog*, and (d) Adam's generalized use of *no*.

ply with an action which another person was trying to impose on him. However, about 3 months later, Adam also began to produce this word while he was engaged in the process of performing an action which he knew was forbidden by another person (for example, while he was pulling handfuls of books off a shelf onto the floor, and while he was attacking and savaging plants in plant-pots). This development can be explained by hypothesizing that the event representation underlying Adam's initial use of the word *no* (see Figure 2-1(d)) had been modified, such that it now had the form depicted in Figure 2-2(d). Thus, in the case of the word *no*, it appeared that one of the components of the initial event representation had been deleted, the behavior represented in this component no longer being a necessary element of the event instances eliciting his use of this word.[2]

[2] It can be noted here that the data do permit an alternative explanation: it could have been the case that Adam acquired a second and distinct event representation (of the form [Adam / performing forbidden action]) to govern his new use of this word, which then functioned alongside the initial representation. This explanation would therefore suggest that the word *no* became polysemous at 1;8;9. Furthermore, the same argument could also be applied to the other two examples discussed above (*catch* and *dog*), with the new, generalized, uses of each word also being due to the acquisition of a second event representation (rather than to the modification of the initial representation). Although this alternative explanation cannot be ruled out, such an explanation would, however, fail to explain why there were such marked similarities between the initial use of each word and the generalized use of each word, an aspect of the data which is explained if it is proposed that it was the modification of the initial event representation which had led to the broader use of the word. Nevertheless, it does have to be conceded that there are certain cases in which event-bound words appear to be polysemous: for an example of such a word (*there*, which was used in two quite distinct contexts by Emily early in her development), see Barrett (1983).

Thus, all three of these examples (*catch*, *dog*, and *no*) show that the use of an event-bound word may sometimes change due to a change in the child's underlying event representation. For several further examples of words which displayed this phenomenon (produced by both Tina and Emily), and which can be accounted for in an identical manner, see Barrett (1983). Before leaving our discussion of this phenomenon, however, it should be noted that not all event-bound words exhibit changes of this sort. For example, neither Adam's use of *chuff-chuff* nor his use of *duck* developed in this way after their initial contexts of use had been established. Nevertheless, there are many words which do exhibit these changes. And consequently, one of the advantages of using the theoretical construct of an event representation is that it enables us to model the changes which seem to be occurring in the child's internal representations as that child's use of words changes during this intermediate stage of development.

The Decontextualization of Early Word-Usage

The third phenomenon to which I would now like to turn is the decontextualization of early word-usage. This phenomenon has been documented in many previous studies (see, for example, Dore, Franklin, Miller, and Ramer, 1976; Lock, 1980; Barrett, 1983), with perhaps the most explicit documentation being provided by Bates et al. (1979). Bates et al. report that, at the outset of their study, nearly all of the words which they observed being produced by their 9-month-old subjects were used only in extremely limited contexts while the children were performing particular actions (i.e., these words were nearly always event-bound at this stage). However, by the time of the final observation session, when the children were 12- to 13-months old, the same words were being used in a much wider range of situations, often in the absence of any particular action by the child. It should perhaps be made clear that the term *decontextualization* as it is used to denote this type of change in early word-usage is intended to imply that the use of a word is dissociated from the occurrence of just one particular type of event. This notion will perhaps become clearer if we explore some specific examples.

The first example we can consider is Adam's use of the word *duck* (see Table 2-1). About 2 weeks after Adam had begun to produce this word while hitting a toy yellow duck off the edge of the bath, he also began to produce this word in a variety of new situations. He began to produce it while he was playing with these toy ducks in any situation (for example, while he was sitting on the floor in the lounge manipulating the ducks, while he was playing with the ducks in the bath at bath-time, etc.); when he was asked *what's that?* in reference to these toy ducks; and (2 days later) when he noticed one of the toy ducks lying on the floor in the lounge. It is thus apparent that Adam had now begun to use this word in a much more flexible manner, no longer using it solely in the context of just one particular event.

How can this transition from event-bound word-usage to decontextualized word-usage be explained? We have seen that Adam's initial use of the word appeared to be governed by an event representation, with the word being produced when he recognized the instantiation of this representation. By contrast, his new uses of this word indicate that Adam had fundamentally reorganized his knowledge of the situations which could provide appropriate contexts for his production of this word, with the word now being produced when he was attending to one of his toy yellow ducks, irrespective of the behavioral context in which that duck was located. This development is therefore explicable if we postulate that, at this stage, Adam had decided that it was the presence of one of his toy yellow ducks which actually motivated the appropriate use of the word, rather than the instantiation of the event representation as a whole. Consequently, we can hypothesize that, at this stage, Adam disembedded the specification of these toy yellow ducks from the event representation which governed his initial use of the word, with this specification subsequently functioning as an internal representation of the type of object which could be appropriately labelled with the word. Thus, Adam began to use the word *duck* in order to refer to his toy yellow ducks in any situation, and not just while he was engaged in the process of hitting them off the edge of the bath.

A second example of decontextualization is provided by Adam's use of the word *no*. It can be seen from Table 2-1 that, about 3 weeks after Adam had generalized his event-bound use of this word, he also began to use this word in purely conversational contexts to express his refusal to comply with verbal directives (such as *tidy your toys*, *have some milk*, etc.). Thus, Adam's use of this word was no longer tied exclusively to the overt enactment of an event, this word now sometimes being used in the absence of any overt action by Adam. However, in spite of this change which occurred in Adam's use of this word, there was nevertheless a basic continuity between his event-bound and his decontextualized uses of *no*: all of the situations in which Adam produced this word were characterized by Adam refusing to comply (whether at a behavioral or at a conversational level) with the dictates of another person. This continuity therefore suggests that Adam had reorganized his assumptions about the use of this word, and decided that this word could be used to designate his refusal to comply in the absence of the overt performance of any action (this particular designatum having been derived from the information which was contained in the event representation that had previously been governing his event-bound use of this word).

Several further examples of words (produced by both Tina and Emily) which exhibited decontextualization, and which can be accounted for in an identical manner, are presented in Barrett (1983). Here we may simply note that these data seem to suggest that decontextualization marks a major shift in the format of the child's internal representations, with event representations being superseded at this stage by specifications of the types of object or action-scheme which are designated by particular words. If this is the case, then decontextualization can be viewed as marking a fundamental transition in the child's early linguistic behavior, away from the use of words only in the context of specific enacted events, to the use of words as names which designate objects and actions. This point is not new, having been made previously by several authors, in particular by Dore (1978) and McShane (1979, McShane & Whittaker, 1982), both of whom have also argued that children acquire the understanding that words can be used as names only after those children have already been producing words in a nonreferential manner for a while. However, the fact that decontextualization occurs at different times for different words (for example, *duck* was decontextualized when Adam was age 1;0;15, while *no* was only decontextualized when he was age 1;8;27) indicates that this understanding, once it has been acquired, is not applied simultaneously to all the words in the child's vocabulary. Instead, it indicates that the child only gradually ascertains which particular words in his or her vocabulary are able to function as names, successively identifying and disembedding the relevant constituent element from each individual event representation in turn at the stage of decontextualization.

The Extension of Decontextualized Object Names to Novel Referents

From the previous discussion of Adam's use of the word *duck*, it is apparent that immediately after this word had been decontextualized, it was radically underextended, being used by Adam to refer to only a small subset of the full range of objects which are properly labelled with this word in the adult language. However, it can be seen from Table 2-1 that Adam gradually began to extend his use of this word to refer to certain other objects: real ducks, pictures of ducks, swans, geese, and a picture of a quail. Thus, the extension of this word was gradually broadened to include novel referents that had not previously been labelled with this word, some of these labels being overextensions.

Both underextension and overextension have been investigated in considerable detail in previous studies. For example, it has been found that between 12% and 29% of object names may be underextended by children during early lexical development, the precise figure depending upon the method of vocabulary assessment which is used (Anglin, 1977). And similarly, estimates of the proportion of object names which are overextended during early lexical development have usually been found to fall within the range from 7% to 33% (Anglin, 1977; Gruendel, 1977; Barrett, 1978; Rescorla, 1980; K. E. Nelson, 1982). Patterns of overextended word use, in particular, have been subjected to detailed scrutiny in many of these studies, and one of the principal points to emerge has been the finding that the objects which the child eventually labels with a given word do not necessarily have any features in common with each other; however, each one of the objects which is labelled with a word does usually have at least one feature in common with the object which originally functioned as the initial referent of that word (Bowerman, 1978; Barrett, 1982; K. E. Nelson, 1982). To give a specific example, one child, Hildegard, used the word *ball* to refer to (amongst other objects) balls, an observatory dome, and crumpled pieces of paper which she used in the game of catch (see Leopold, 1939, 1949). While the observatory dome and the crumpled paper do not have any features in common with one another, both objects have at least one feature in common with a ball, which was the initial referent for this word. Thus, Hildegard appeared to overextend the word *ball* to label an observatory dome because it shared the single perceived feature of sphericality with a ball, and she appeared to overextend *ball* to label crumpled pieces of paper because she used these pieces of paper in the same way that she used a ball in the game of catch. However, while both perceptually and functionally based overextensions have been found to occur, it does seem to be the case that the majority of object name overextensions are perceptually based, and that only a minority are functionally based (Clark, 1975; Barrett, 1978; Bowerman, 1978; Rescorla, 1980).

In the light of this evidence, it has been argued by Bowerman (1978; see also Barrett, 1982) that the meaning of an object name is acquired through the operation of the following processes. It appears that the child first constructs, on the basis of his or her experience with referential exemplars, a mental representation of a prototypical referential exemplar for the word (thus, this prototypical exemplar might simply consist of a representation of the initial referent in connection with which the child first experiences the word). This prototypical referent then functions for the child as a specification of the type of object which can be labelled with the word. At this point in development, the meaning of the word simply consists of this representation, and the word is only used at this stage to refer to objcts which closely resemble the prototype (i.e., the word might be underextended at this stage).[3] Subsequently, the child identifies and abstracts some of the principal perceptual or functional features which characterize the prototypical referent. The meaning of the word thus now consists of both the representation of the prototype and a specification of some of its principal features, the word being used to label any object which shares one or more of these features with the prototype (i.e., the word would now be extended to label novel referents, and would possibly become overextended in the process).[4]

To return to Adam's use of the word *duck*, then, it can be seen that his decontextualized use of this word can be explained by postulating that he used the specification of the type of object which could be labelled with this word (i.e., the specification which he had disembedded from the event representation at the stage of decontextualization) to construct a representation of a prototypical referent for this word. Thus, immediately after decontextualization, this word was only used by Adam to refer to objects which closely resemble this prototype (i.e., his toy yellow ducks). Subsequently, however, Adam began to identify and abstract some of the principal features which characterized the prototype, and he consequently began to extend this word to label novel referents on the basis that they shared one or more of these features with the prototype (i.e., to label real ducks, swans, geese, etc.).[5]

---

[3]As in the case of event representations (see Figure 2-1, footnote), it could be argued that prototypes are holistic in nature (see Greenberg & Kuczaj, 1982). Once again, we may note that a prototype must ultimately be specified in terms of a set of primitive features in order to permit the matching of category exemplars to the prototype to occur (on a feature-by-feature basis); the term *holistic* simply implies that, in order for an object to be matched with the prototype, that object must necessarily display *all* of the specified features of the prototype (that is, these features are obligatory rather than optional).

[4]If it is maintained that the prototype is holistic in nature (see footnote 3), then this second process can be interpreted in terms of the primitive features of the prototype becoming optional rather than obligatory, with new instances of the category being identified on the basis that they share one or more of these optional features with the prototypical exemplar.

[5]It should be clear from the above account that a theoretical distinction is being drawn here between the event representation which governs the initial event-bound use of a word, and the prototype which governs the decontextualized use of a word. Although the event representation could, in a sense, itself be construed as functioning as a prototype (i.e., the child's representation of the initial context of event-

Adam's uses of the words *chuff-chuff* and *dog* also developed in a similar way, except that in these two cases the words were decontextualized and extended to label novel referents simultaneously (see Table 2-1). Thus, *chuff-chuff* was decontextualized when Adam was age 1;6;6, when he began to extend his use of this word in order to refer to pictures of trains. The nonreferential use of *chuff-chuff* in response to the question *how does a train go?*, which also began at 1;6;6, possibly comprised a separate, ritualized use of the word. Similarly, *dog* was decontextualized at 1;2;2, when Adam began to extend its use in order to refer to real dogs. This suggests that when the representations of the prototypical referents of these two words (i.e., representations of the toy train and of the picture of the dog, respectively) were disembedded from their event representations at the stage of decontextualization, these prototypes were immediately analyzed into their constituent features, these features then guiding the application of these words to novel referents. In the case of *chuff-chuff* (but not *dog*), overextensions subsequently occurred. Two of the overextended applications of *chuff-chuff* (to label the pattern on the rug and to label the toy caterpillar) can be explained by reference to the features which these overextended referents shared with the prototypical referent of the word. The other two overextended applications (to label the airship sound and to label railway bridges) instead appeared to be based upon associations through contiguity, with the word being used to refer to things which had previously been experienced in the presence of genuine referential exemplars and which therefore probably served to remind Adam of trains by association (see Anglin, 1977, 1983, and Barrett, 1978, 1982, for further examples and discussions of associative overextensions).

The Acquisition of Decontextualized Object Names in the Absence of an Initial Period of Event-Bound Word-Usage

Up to this point in the discussion, I have only considered the acquisition of word meaning in relationship to words which, when first acquired, were used in an event-

---

bound use could be construed as being the source of the features which determine the child's later uses of the word), this interpretation is not made here for the following reasons. Firstly, this move would obscure the importance of decontextualization as marking a major transition in early lexical development (from event-bound word-usage to naming) and would not explain why this transition occurs. However, by maintaining the distinction between event representations and prototypes, this transition can be explained in terms of the child disembedding prototypical information from event representations, this disembedded information then being used to guide the child's subsequent use of the word as a decontextualized name. Secondly, the identification of event representations with prototypes would result in the conflation of two distinct phenomena, namely the modification of event-bound word-usage, and the extension of decontextualized object names to label novel referents (both of which would be explained in terms of the extension of the word's use to new situations on the basis of the features which are shared by those new situations and the initial situations of use). However, by drawing a distinction between an event representation and a prototype, the distinction between these two phenomena is respected at the theoretical level, these phenomena being explained by reference to different underlying processes. Thus, the position being advocated here is that prototypes are distinct from event representations, these being two different forms of internal representation that are acquired by the child.

bound manner by the child. However, it is clear from previous studies (Clark, 1973; Bowerman, 1978; Barrett, 1982) that many object names are acquired by the child without an initial period of event-bound usage. That is, many object names are used from the outset in a decontextualized manner by the child. In view of the large number of examples of this phenomenon which are already available in the literature, I will present just a single new example here.

In Table 2-2, Adam's uses of the word *tick-tock* are described. His first use of this word occurred when he was looking at a picture of a clock in a book. However, later on the same day, he also produced this word when he was playing with a clock and when he was pulling at my wristwatch. These various uses of *tick-tock* therefore suggest that Adam's use of this word was decontextualized from the outset, and was not initially governed by an event representation. It seems that Adam's production of this word was instead governed from the outset by a representation of a prototypical referent which he had acquired, the word being used immediately to refer to objects which shared one or more features with this prototypical referent. In addition to these referential uses of the word, Adam also began, on the same day, to produce *tick-tock* in response to questions of the form *how does a (the) clock (watch) go?*, which possibly comprised a separate, ritualized, use of the word.

Adam began to overextend *tick-tock* about one month later, when he used this word whenever he was looking at a picture of wallpaper which was patterned with circles bearing radiating spikes. He later also overextended the word to label circular blue road signs, and, on one occasion, to label a barometer which had a circular dial with a hand pointing to the figures. These overextensions are all explicable by reference to one or more features which these referents shared with the prototypical referent of the word; that is, by reference to the information contained in Adam's semantic representation for this word.

Examples such as this demonstrate that not all words go thorugh a period of event-bound usage when they are first acquired, and that the production of some words may be governed from the outset by representations of prototypical referents.[6] Nevertheless, the studies by Dore et al. (1976) and Bates et al. (1979) suggest

---

[6]It can be noted here that there are three possibilities as to how the child acquires these prototypical referents which underlie the use of words which are decontextualized from the outset. Firstly, they could be acquired at the same time as the productive use of the word is acquired, by means of the child observing the type of referential exemplar in connection with which other people typically produce the word. Secondly, it could be the case that, prior to the child producing the word, the child engages in the process of constructing a receptive meaning for that word (a process which could be tapped by the use of comprehension tests), the word only beginning to be produced by the child at the stage at which the prototypical referent finally becomes disembedded from an event representation. And thirdly, it could be the case that these prototypical referents are acquired prior to the child's production of these words, not as the core of receptive meanings for words, but as the core of prototypically-organized non-linguistic cognitive categories (i.e., categories which could be examined by the use of non-linguistic techniques such as habituation), categories onto which these words are subsequently mapped when they are eventually acquired. Until studies are conducted to explore these three possibilities (such studies would need to examine cognitive data, lexical comprehension data, and lexical production data in relationship to each other), it would be premature to prejudge this issue by opting for any one of these possibilities over any of the others.

Early Semantic Representations and Early Word-Usage 53

Table 2-2. Adam's Use of the Word *tick-tock*

Word	Contexts of use
tick-tock	Initial context of use: while looking at a picture of a clock in a book (1;6;2). Subsequent contexts of use: while looking at or playing with any clock or watch (1;6;2); in response to the question "How does a/the clock/watch go?" (1;6;2); while looking at a picture of wallpaper patterned with circles bearing radiating spikes (1;7;1); while looking at and pointing to a circular blue road sign (1;9;1); while looking at and pointing to a barometer which displayed a circular dial with a hand pointing to the figures (1;9;1).[a]

[a] This usage was a unique occurrence which was not subsequently repeated.

that this is a pattern which usually only begins to emerge after lexical development has already commenced with the use of event-bound words. That is, the earliest phase of lexical development seems to be typically characterized by the initial use of words only in the context of enacted events, this initial phase being succeeded, within a few months, by a second phase in which: (a) new words are acquired that are decontextualized from the outset; (b) new event-bound words continue to be acquired; and (c) existing event-bound words are gradually decontextualized.

The Rescission of Object Name Overextensions

It has been seen that after the decontextualized use of an object name has been acquired, such a word may sometimes be overextended by the child to label objects which are not normally labelled with that word in the adult language. However, as the child's lexical development proceeds, these overextensions are gradually rescinded by the child. It has been found in previous studies that the rescission of overextensions often occurs in conjunction with the acquisition of new object names which then take over the labelling of the overextended domain (Barrett, 1978, 1982; Rescorla, 1981). To give a specific example, Leopold (1949) reports that Hildegard initially acquired the word *cookie* to refer not only to cookies but also to crackers and cakes. She later acquired the word *cracker* to refer to crackers, and at this moment in time, the overextension of *cookie* was partially rescinded, this word now being used only to refer to cookies and cakes. Finally, she acquired the word *cake* to refer to cakes, which resulted in the further restriction of the extension of *cookie* to include cookies alone.

Exactly the same phenomenon was also observed in Adam. For example, it will be recalled that, after Adam had begun to use the word *duck* as a decontextualized name, he used this word not only to refer to ducks (from 1;1;6 onwards), but also to refer to swans (from 1;5;18), to geese (from 1;5;18), and to a picture of a quail (from 1;6;7). However, at 1;7;16, Adam acquired the word *swan*, which he used from this point on as a decontextualized name for swans. After this point in time, Adam was never observed using *duck* to refer to swans again. At 1;8;23, he also acquired the word *geese*, which he began to use from this time on to refer either to a single goose or to a group of geese. He subsequently never used the word *duck* to refer to geese again. As far as the picture of the quail is concerned, Adam did not acquire the word *quail* during the period in which I was documenting his vocabulary development, and he continued to use the word *duck* to label this picture.

These two examples from Hildegard and Adam suggest that these words (*cookie*, *cracker*, and *cake*, and *duck*, *swan*, and *geese*) had been organized into semantic fields by each child (the meanings of the words within each semantic field being interdependent). The examples also suggest that, as a new word is added to a given semantic field, the meanings of the words which are already included within that field are adjusted by the child, these meanings being differentiated from the meaning of the new word in such a way that all of the words within the field come to acquire mutually exclusive extensions.

Consequently, these developments can be explained in the following way. Initially, the child assigns the overextended word, together with its semantic representation (which, it will be recalled, consists at this stage of both a representation of a prototypical referent and a specification of some of the principal features which characterize this referent), to a particular semantic field. Thus, the child groups this word with certain other words as they are acquired (possibly on the basis that the prototypical referents of these words have various salient features in common with each other). The child then identifies the features which differentiate the prototypical referents of these words from one another, and adds these contrastive features to the semantic representations of the words. Thus, to consider the example from Adam, it would seem that he grouped the words *swan* and *duck* together in the same semantic field, identified those features which served to distinguish the prototypical referent of *duck* from the prototypical referent of *swan*, and added these features to the semantic representations of these words. He consequently came to use these new contrastive features to delimit the boundary between the extensions of the two words, the meanings of which became mutually exclusive, with the overextension of *duck* being partially rescinded. The same process seemed to be at work in Adam's acquisition of the word *geese* and the further restriction of the extension of *duck* which occurred in conjunction with this acquisition.

To summarize, it can be hypothesized that the meaning of an object name eventually contains four types of information: (a) a representation of the prototypical referent of the word; (b) a specification of some of the principal perceptual and/or functional features which characterize the prototype; (c) a specification of the semantic field to which the word has been assigned; and (d) a specification of the contrastive features which differentiate the prototype of the word from the prototypes of the other words which have been assigned to the same semantic field.[7] Thus,

---

[7]It should be noted here that if the child acquires the wrong contrastive feature for a pair of words (i.e., wrong from the point of view of the adult language), then one of these words might be overextended while the other word is underextended, the extensions of the two words nevertheless still being mutually exclusive. For example, Lewis (1951) reports that, after one child had acquired the words [hɔʃ] (horse) and [gɔgi] (doggie), he used [hɔʃ] to refer to horses and large dogs, and [gɔgi] to refer to small dogs and toy dogs. In this example, it appears that the child had mistakenly used size as a contrastive feature to

on the basis of this hypothesis, the rescission of an overextension would be attributed to the addition of further information (i.e., the contrastive features) to the semantic representation of the overextended word. For a more detailed exposition of this hypothesis, and of the evidence which it can be used to explain, see Barrett (1978, 1982).

However, it is clear from the available data that not all overextensions are rescinded in conjunction with the acquisition of new words which subsequently take over the labelling of the overextended domains. For example, Adam sometimes rescinded overextensions *before* he had acquired more appropriate names for the overextended referents; he also sometimes produced overextensions *after* he had acquired more appropriate names for those referents.

The former pattern, for example, was exhibited by Adam's overextensions of *tick-tock* to refer to the circular road signs and to the barometer (see Table 2-2). These two overextensions were both rescinded before he had acquired more appropriate names for these objects. He only used *tick-tock* to refer to the barometer on one occasion, and this use was not immediately followed by the acquisition of another name for this object. His use of *tick-tock* to refer to the road signs was more persistent, being produced on many separate occasions from 1;9;1 onwards; however, it spontaneously disappeared about one month later, from which time onwards Adam no longer referred to these objects, not having acquired an alternative name for them.

There are at least two different ways in which the occurrence of these rescissions could be explained. One such explanation would be to propose that the opportunities for these overextensions to occur were no longer available to Adam. This explanation would seem to be quite plausible in the case of the barometer: this object was located on a rather cluttered shelf, and on the one occasion when he produced this overextension, I was holding him up so that he could see the various objects on this shelf. Thus, it is quite likely that he simply did not notice the barometer again after this episode, and that he therefore had no further opportunity to label it, consequently appearing to have rescinded this overextension.[8]

A second explanation would be to propose that an overextension can occur, not because the child regards the overextended referent as a legitimate example of the category designated by the overextended word, but because the child is confronted by a situation in which he or she wants to draw attention to this object for which, however, an appropriate name has not yet been acquired. Consequently, in order to

---

differentiate between the extensions of the two words, one of which therefore became overextended, the other of which became underextended. This type of overextension and underextension is therefore to be distinguished from the types of overextension and underextension previously discussed, which are explicable by reference to different underlying processes. For a more detailed discussion of these issues, see Barrett (1982).

[8]This possibility indicates a weakness in the use of diary records. Although these records can provide a very rich source of naturalistic data on children's early word-usage, the data which are collected are not based upon a systematic control of extensional opportunities, and may therefore contain irresolvable ambiguities at the level of interpretation. For a lucid discussion of the various weaknesses associated with diary studies, see Anglin (1983).

draw attention to this object, the child might deliberately overextend that word which has been acquired whose prototype has the most features in common with this object, in order to fulfill the immediate communicative requirements of the situation. That is, some overextensions might not be categorical in nature, but strategic solutions to communicative problems (see Bloom, 1973; Clark, 1978; and Barrett, 1982, for further discussions of this notion).[9] And if this is the case, then the rescission of this type of overextension might be attributable to a change in the child's communicative strategies (whereby the child simply stops trying to draw attention to the object by overextending a word which he or she knows to be inappropriate). This second proposal could therefore explain why Adam stopped using *tick-tock* as a label for the road signs, even though he had not yet acquired a more appropriate name for these objects.

In addition to these examples of overextensions being rescinded in the absence of the acquisition of new words, Adam also sometimes produced overextensions after he had already acquired more appropriate names for the overextended referents. For example, he continued to use *chuff-chuff* upon seeing railway bridges (see Table 2-1) well after he had acquired the word *bridge*. Other examples occurred both when Adam occasionally misnamed pictures of animals in books, even though he had previously produced the correct names for these animals, and when he occasionally engaged in what appeared to be the wilful misnaming of objects. Several different explanations seem to be required in order to account for these various examples.

In the case of the use of *chuff-chuff* to refer to railway bridges, it has already been seen that this overextension was probably associative rather than categorical in nature. Consequently, its continued production after the acquisition of the more appropriate word *bridge* can be explained in terms of the continuing influence of the association which had been established between bridges and trains, the sight of bridges still reminding Adam of trains. Other examples to which this explanation probably also applies occurred when Adam saw or was playing with an object, and named the person to whom that object belonged (even though he had already acquired the correct name of that object). These examples (termed *predicate statement overextensions* by Rescorla, 1980) can also be explained in terms of an established association between the object and the person who is named.

As far as the misnamed pictures of animals are concerned, though, these seemed to be primarily due to processing errors by Adam. In these instances, if the appropriateness of his incorrect label was challenged, he typically took another look at the picture and then responded with the correct name of the animal. These overextensions could have been caused either by errors in the perceptual identification of the referents (e.g., mistaking a donkey for a horse, through not paying sufficient attention to the picture) or by lexical retrieval errors (e.g., retrieving the word *horse* rather than the word *donkey*, even though the creature had been correctly perceived as a donkey).

---

[9]This possibility could be empirically tested by seeing whether or not the child also overextends the word to the overextended referent in comprehension as well, the absence of overextension in comprehension indicating a noncategorical overextension, as opposed to a categorical overextension where the child would overextend the word both in production and in comprehension.

Finally, Adam very occasionally engaged in what appeared to be wilful misnaming. This usually entailed the paradigmatic substitution of another name from the same semantic field in place of the correct name. These instances could be distinguished from the processing error overextensions, as they were typically characterized by laughing and/or smiling and a steadfast refusal by Adam to produce the correct name of the referent (which he had previously shown that he knew) despite persistent requests to do so.[10]

In conclusion, then, it appears that the rescission of an overextension can occur for a variety of different reasons. In the case of a categorical overextension, the rescission often seems to result from the acquisition of another word which is assigned to the same semantic field as the overextended word, and to the subsequent differentiation of the extensions of those words from one another. In other cases, however, the apparent rescission might simply be due to the lack of appropriate opportunities for reproducing the overextension. Third, in the case of non-categorical overextensions, the rescission might be due to a change in the communicative strategies which are being employed by the child. And finally, some overextensions might continue to be produced after the acquisition of more appropriate names, either when there are established associations between objects, when perceptual recognition and/or lexical retrieval errors occur, or when the child engages in wilful misnaming.

The Acquisition of Decontextualized Action Words in the Absence of an Initial Period of Event-Bound Word-Usage, and the Extension of Action Words to Novel Actions

Whereas object names have received considerable attention in previous studies of early lexical development, action words have received far less attention. As a result, there is far less available evidence on action words which can be tapped in trying to understand the processes which are responsible for the development of the meanings of these words.[11] Unfortunately, the evidence from Adam is also not particularly revealing about these processes, as he acquired relatively few action words during the time in which I was documenting his vocabulary development. When he had 50 words in his productive vocabulary at the age of 1;6;20, only 3 of these words were unambiguously not either object names or words which were to develop into object

---

[10]Perceptual recognition errors, lexical retrieval errors, and wilful misnaming might, of course, also be responsible for some of the overextensions which occur prior to the acquisition of more appropriate names for the overextended referents. However, when the more appropriate name has not yet been acquired (and the child therefore cannot be expected to correct the overextension in response to adult feedback), it is more difficult in practice to identify those overextensions which might be due to these factors.

[11]The absence of properly detailed longitudinal data on the ontogenesis of individual action words is a particularly acute problem here, with the paper by Bowerman (1978) being a notable exception. In addition, Gopnik (1981, 1982) has provided a useful documentation of some of the more salient phenomena characterizing early action word usage (in particular, event-bound usage and decontextualization); however, she does not report her data in a form which enables the ontogenesis of individual words in individual children to be traced.

names. Furthermore, he tended to use the few action words which he had acquired rather infrequently.

However, the small amount of evidence I did collect from Adam suggests that, once the child's lexical development is under way, the child may begin to acquire some action words which do not go through an initial period of event-bound usage, these words instead being decontextualized from the outset. For example, when Adam was aged 1;11;12, he began to use the word *cut* both as a comment while he was watching another person cutting food and as a request for another person to cut his food for him. Thus, *cut* appeared to be used from the outset to designate a particular action. This word was also underextended at this stage, being used to refer to only a subset of the actions which are designated by this word in the adult language.

In addition, it appears that once the child has acquired the decontextualized use of an action word to refer to a particular action, that word may then be extended by the child to label novel actions. Perhaps the clearest examples which illustrate this phenomenon are those reported by Bowerman (1978). For example, her daughter, Christy, initially used the word *open* to refer to the action of opening drawers, doors, boxes, etc., but subsequently came to use this word to also refer to actions such as unscrewing a plastic stake from a block and turning on a light. Bowerman argues that these new uses of the word are similar to object name overextensions, in that they can be accounted for by construing the initial action which is designated by the word as a prototype which is then analyzed by the child into its constituent features. Thus, the prototype in the above example appeared to be analyzed by the child into two features: (a) separation of parts which are in contact; and (b) causing something to be revealed or become accessible. The word was then extended by the child to refer to novel actions on the basis that they had one or more features in common with the prototypical action.

Consequently, the available data would seem to suggest that the meanings of action words develop by means of the same processes which are responsible for the development of the meanings of object names. However, there is little substantial data in the literature on the rescission of action word overextensions, and rather than argue solely on the basis of an analogy with object name overextensions, it would seem preferable to reserve any conclusions which could be drawn about the rescission of action word overextensions until further evidence becomes available.

The Development of Semantic Representations: A Summary of the Proposed Model

Having surveyed the principal phenomena which characterize early word-usage, we can now summarize the theoretical framework that has been proposed to account for these phenomena. It has been argued that, at the outset of lexical development, the child links words to mental representations of events. These representations contain specifications of the people, actions, and objects which are involved in the represented events, and may contain slots representing the roles that can be variously filled by different people, actions, or objects in those events. Each event representation is most probably acquired as a result of the child repeatedly experiencing various instances of a particular type of event. Thus, the highly ritualized routines in which young children frequently participate (in caretaking activities, in free play with objects, and in interactive social play, for example) may well provide a very rich source from which the young child identifies categories of recurrent events, and builds up a knowledge of the various alternative ways in which each individual category of event can be instantiated. These event representations subsequently function, in effect, as recognitory schemata, in the sense that they enable the child to recognize specific event instances as being instances of a particular category of event. At this initial stage of lexical development, then, a word may be produced when the child recognizes the instantiation of a particular event representation. That is, the child's production of a word may occur when he or she recognizes the occurrence of a particular type of event, the child apparently regarding the occurrence of this event, in a holistic manner, as providing an appropriate context for the production of the word. Thus, at this initial stage, the child begins to produce words in an event-bound manner.[12]

Having acquired the initial event-bound use of a word, the underlying event representation may be subsequently modified by the child, either through the broadening of the range of the entities which can fill one of the slots in the representation, or through the deletion of entire elements from the representation. The effect of these modifications is the generalization of the child's use of the word to a broader range of event instances.

Eventually, however, the child may identify the presence of just one particular element in the eliciting event instances as being the critical element which actually justifies the appropriate use of the word (rather than the instantiation of the event representation as a whole). The child may consequently disembed the specification of this element from the event representation, and use it as a specification of the type of object or action which can be designated with the word. Consequently, the word now becomes decontextualized, being used by the child to designate objects or actions in a variety of different contexts, contexts which do not necessarily entail the overt enactment of any particular event.

This specification of the type of object or action which can be labelled with the word (i.e., the specification which has been disembedded from the event representation) is then used by the child to construct a representation of a prototypical object or action which is designated by the word. In certain cases, the word may then be used only to refer to objects or actions which closely resemble this prototype (thus

---

[12]The present theoretical framework therefore helps to explain why *formats* (that is, standardized interaction patterns between adults and children which contain clearly demarcated roles; see Bruner, 1983) might be particularly important in the initial stages of lexical development. Such formats would provide the child with ideal situations in which to acquire event representations (owing to both their clarity and their regularity), representations which could then be used by the child to guide the initial event-bound use of words.

possibly being underextended at this stage), and the child may only subsequently go on to identify the features which characterize the prototype. In other cases, however, the child may immediately identify these features. In either case, the net result of this latter process is the extension of the word to label novel objects or actions which share one or more of these features with the prototype (the word possibly becoming overextended in the process).

Once lexical development is under way, the child may begin to acquire further object names and action words which are decontextualized from the outset. In these instances, the child appears to map these words directly onto representations of prototypical objects and actions (i.e., these words are not initially governed in their use by event representations). The prototypes of these new words may then also be analyzed into their constituent features by the child, these words similarly being extended to label novel objects or actions on the basis that these objects or actions share one or more of these features with the prototype.

Finally, I have suggested that each object name is assigned to a particular semantic field, possibly on the basis of the most salient features which are displayed by the prototypical referent. The child then compares the prototypical referent of that word with the prototypical referents of the other object names which have already been assigned to the same semantic field, and identifies those features which differentiate these prototypes from one another, adding these contrastive features to the semantic representations of the various words. Thus, the object names within a semantic field come to acquire mutually exclusive extensions. In addition, if an object name which had previously been assigned to the semantic field had hitherto been overextended, this overextension may now be rescinded by the child, with the new object name taking over the labelling of the overextended domain.

This model is summarized in Figure 2-3 which describes: (a) the processes which are hypothesized as underlying the development of semantic representations; (b) the criteria which govern the use of a word at each particular stage of development; and (c) the observable phenomena which are associated with each stage of development. The arrows in Figure 2-3 indicate the possible sequences in which the various processes can, in principle, occur. This model can account for at least eight different patterns of development which may be exhibited in early word-usage. These eight patterns are described in Table 2-3. The letters in Table 2-3 refer to the stages of development described in Figure 2-3.

Pattern 1 consists simply of the acquisition of an event-bound word which does not subsequently undergo any further development. Adam did not in fact produce any word which exhibited this particular pattern of development, but I have previously reported data concerning Tina's use of two different words which did display this pattern: the word [hIjɑ:], which Tina only produced in situations in which she was giving an object to another person; and the word [kju:], which she only produced in situations in which she was taking an object from another person (Barrett, 1981). Neither of these two words exhibited any further development. Instead, they remained event-bound throughout Tina's early linguistic development, appearing to function throughout this time as pure *performatives* (that is, they were only produced in

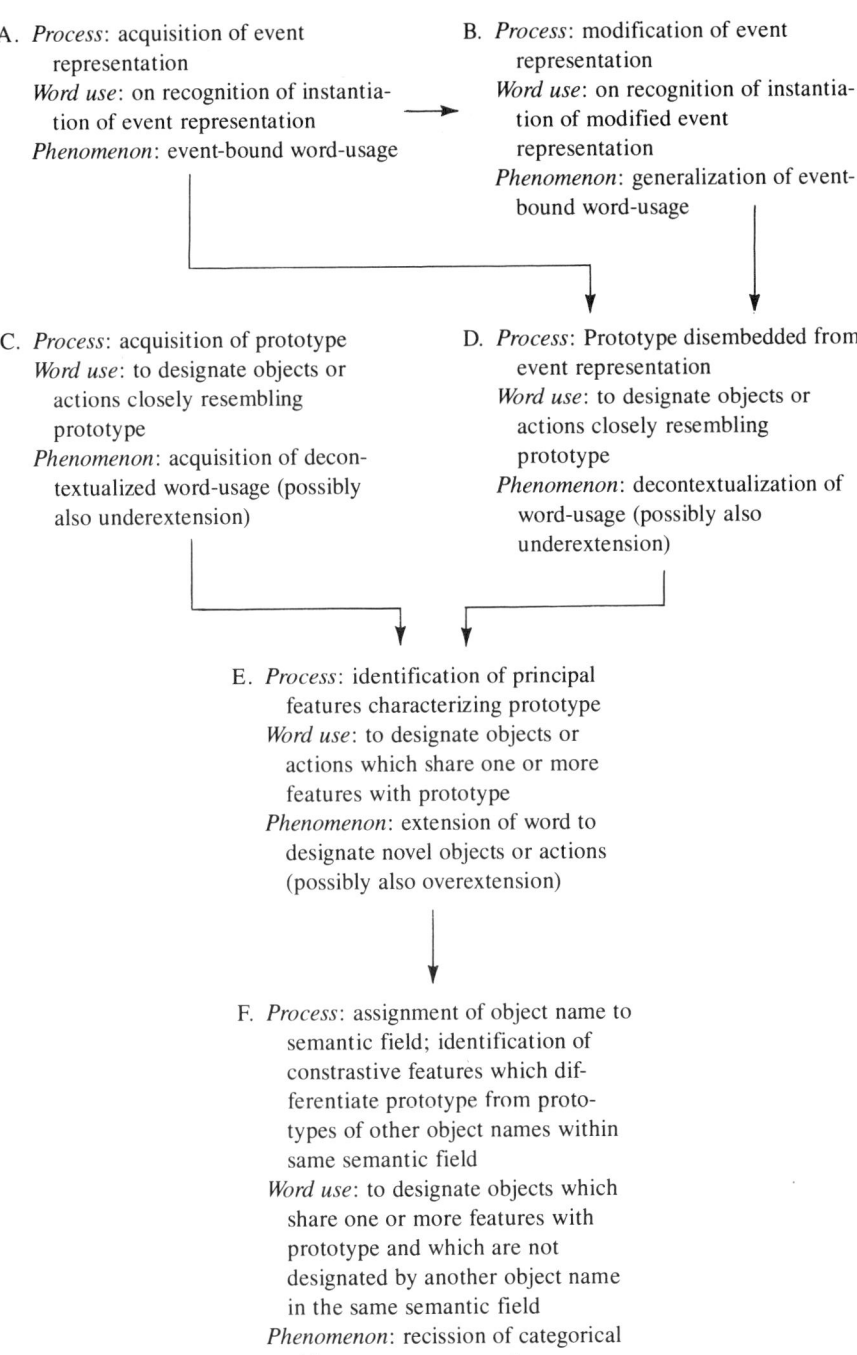

Figure 2-3. A summary of the proposed model.

Table 2-3. Patterns of Development Exhibited in Early Word-Usage

Pattern of word development[a,b]	Word category at end of development	Example[c]
1. A	performative	[hIjaː]
2. A+B	performative	bye-bye
3. A+D(+E)	action word	run
4. A+B+D(+E)	action word	no
5. C(+E)	action word	cut
6. A+D+E+F	object name	duck
7. A+B(+D)+E(+F)	object name	dog
8. C+E+F	object name	tick-tock

[a] See Figure 2-3 for descriptions of the developmental stages encoded by each letter.
[b] Stages are placed in parentheses if the example given did not exhibit the phenomena associated with these stages. The inclusion of these stages here is theoretically rather than empirically motivated.
[c] See text for descriptions of these examples.

a context of ongoing actions, and did not appear to have any meaning or use outside the context of those actions).

However, not all performatives are used in this unmodified manner throughout early lexical development. Some performatives exhibit changes in their use. For example, Adam initially used the word *bye-bye* at 1;5;26 when he waved to a person or object from which he was in the process of moving away. However, from 1;6;6 onwards, he also began to use this word when he was waving to a person or object which was in the process of moving away from him. Thus, his initial event-bound use of this word was subsequently modified, a development which can be accounted for by hypothesizing a change in the event representation underlying his use of this word. However, in spite of this change, the word still continued to function as a performative, a pattern of development which is represented in Table 2-3 as Pattern 2.

Pattern 3 represents the course of development followed by certain action words, which are initially used in an event-bound manner but which subsequently come to be used in a decontextualized manner to refer to particular actions. For example, Adam acquired the word *run* at the age of 1;11;12, which he initially used only while he was actually running. At 1;11;24, however, he also began to use this word as a request for me to run with him, and, after having run, as a comment on the activity which he had just performed. Thus, he now appeared to be using the word to refer to the action of running, no longer using it solely while performing the action. Alternatively, some action words may come to be used in a decontextualized manner only after the initial event representation has been modified in one way or another (Pattern 4). As we have seen, Adam's use of the word *no* exhibited this pattern of development; further examples which were produced by Tina and Emily are reported in Barrett (1983). Pattern 5 represents a third developmental pattern which may be displayed by some action words. These words do not go through an initial period of event-bound usage but are instead decontextualized from the outset. Adam's use of the word *cut*, described earlier, provides an example of this pattern of development.

Pattern 6 represents the course of development exhibited by certain object names. These words are initially used in an event-bound manner. They are subsequently decontextualized, and then extended to label novel referents, possibly becoming overextended in the process. If a categorical overextension occurs, then this overextension is eventually rescinded as the child acquires new words to take over the labelling of the overextended domain. As we have seen, Adam's use of the word *duck* followed this pattern of development. Alternatively, the event representation which governs the initial use of an object name may sometimes be modified prior to the decontextualization of the word (Pattern 7). For example, Adam's initial event-bound use of the word *dog* appeared to be modified in this way prior to decontextualization. And finally, Pattern 8 represents the developmental course followed by certain other object names which do not go through an initial period of event-bound usage, being decontextualized from the outset. The word *tick-tock* is an example of a word displaying this pattern of development, a comparatively mature pattern which tends to emerge only after the child's lexical development has already commenced with the acquisition of event-bound words.[13]

These eight patterns, however, do not necessarily exhaust all the possible patterns of development which might occur on the basis of the present model. The model does not preclude the possibility that several of the constituent processes might occur in very rapid succession for particular words. If this does happen, then the child would acquire a relatively mature use of these words within a very short period of time, without one or more of the intermediate developmental phenomena (e.g., event-bound usage, underextension, overextension) being displayed by these words. Adam did sometimes acquire quite mature uses of certain words within a very short period of time (for example, the word *ball*, which he first produced when he was aged 1;6;11 and which he began to use immediately in a decontextualized manner to refer to any ball, without ever appearing to either underextend or overextend the word as far as I could ascertain). The very rapid acquisition of these words can therefore be explained in terms of the underlying processes occurring in quick succession to one another.

In addition, it is possible that although some of the earlier developmental phenomena (e.g., event-bound usage and underextension) may not be displayed in the child's production of a particular word, these early phenomena may nevertheless still be displayed in the child's comprehension of that word before he has begun to produce it (the late appearance of the word in production perhaps stemming from phonological/articulatory production difficulties). There is evidence from previous studies which tends to suggest that this may indeed occur. For example, Reich (1976) has reported the following developmental sequence which characterized his son's early comprehension of the word *shoes* prior to his production of this word. Initially, whenever the child heard the question *where's the shoes?*, he would crawl to his mother's closet and play with his mother's shoes which were situated on the floor

---

[13]In Table 2-3, stage F for the word *tick-tock* appears without parentheses because the "overextension" of this word to refer to watches was rescinded when Adam was aged 1;10;21, when he acquired the word *watch* for referring to watches.

of the closet. Furthermore, if some of his mother's shoes were placed outside the closet, the child simply disregarded these shoes, and went around them in order to get at the shoes which were in the closet. He also disregarded his father's shoes which were situated in an adjacent closet. This suggests that the word *shoes* was being responded to in an event-bound manner, the question *where's the shoes?* simply triggering the enactment of an event (consisting of the child crawling off to play with the shoes which were in his mother's closet). Subsequently, however, this event was broadened such that the child, when he heard this question, sometimes crawled to his father's closet to play with the shoes that were located there as well. This development can be explained by reference to a modification in the underlying event representation. Reich does not report the data in a form which enables us to ascertain the precise point at which this word became decontextualized. However, he does suggest that by the time that this word was eventually produced by the child several months later, it may well have been overextended to label not just shoes (in any context) but also boots, ice-skates, etc. This example therefore suggests that the semantic representation of the word developed in a manner which is compatible with the model depicted in Figure 2-3, but with the earlier developmental phenomena being displayed only in comprehension.

Consequently, this model can account for the occurrence of many different developmental patterns which may be exhibited in early word-usage. However, this model also implies that there will be certain constraints on these patterns, not in terms of the phenomena which will necessarily be displayed in the development of any given word, but in terms of the *sequence* in which the phenomena should occur if these phenomena are displayed in the development of a word. Thus, this model, although it permits a wide variety of different developmental pathways, nevertheless posits certain constraints upon the possible sequences of phenomena which may be observed whenever we attempt to trace the development of particular words.

Conclusions

In this chapter, I have described some of the principal phenomena which characterize the early development of word-usage, phenomena which range from the early acquisition of event-bound word-usage through to the rescission of object name overextensions. I have also tried to articulate a model of the development of early semantic representations which can account for these various phenomena.

Although this model is able to account for a wide variety of different developmental patterns of early word-usage, it should not, however, be interpreted as providing a comprehensive account of early lexical development. For example, this model does not account for the acquisition of the meanings of proper names (such as *mummy*, *daddy*, *Adam*, etc.) which children often begin to produce during their second year. Nor does it account for the acquisition of the meanings of personal pronouns (such as *I* and *you*) which children also begin to produce in this period.

In addition, I have not attempted to discuss the role that linguistic input might play in the early acquisition of word meaning. For example, it could be the case that event-bound word-usage results from the prelinguistic child regularly hearing particular words being produced by others primarily in the context of very limited events and subsequently imitating this over-restrictive modelled use of these words. On the other hand, it could be the case that although the prelinguistic child hears each particular word being modelled in connection with a wide variety of different events, he or she is unable to cope with the variance which is inherent in such a broad usage. Consequently, the child might strategically oversimplify the linguistic and perceptual input by focusing upon only a small subset of these word-event complexes. Further studies, in which the linguistic input is systematically examined in relationship to the routines and events which occur in the environment of the child, and in relationship to the child's own initial use of words, are required in order to resolve this issue. Similarly, the role of linguistic input in later processes, such as the modification of event-bound word-usage and decontextualization, also remains to be assessed. It could be the case that these processes occur spontaneously. On the other hand, it could be the case that the linguistic input provides crucial guidance to children, by illustrating to them that their initial word-usage is indeed over-restricted and that these words can be used in a very much broader manner. Thus, the role of linguistic input in both the early acquisition and the later development of word meaning is a topic which still requires detailed investigation.

Finally, I have not attempted to deal in this chapter with the relationship which exists between the child's lexical-semantic representations and the child's non-linguistic cognitive representations. The evidence which I have discussed has been taken entirely from observations of children's linguistic behavior, and as such it can only inform us about how the child's linguistic development proceeds, not about how such development relates to the child's cognitive system. However, if we are to obtain a full understanding of early lexical development, it is clearly necessary to elucidate the nature of the relationship which pertains between the child's lexical and cognitive systems. For example, it could be the case that words map directly onto the child's cognitive representations, the child's use of words thus being a direct index of cognition itself. Alternatively, it could be the case that lexical-semantic knowledge comprises a second representational system which is distinct from the child's nonlinguistic cognitive representations. Or, it could be the case that initial event-bound word-usage is due to the child initially mapping words directly onto cognitive representations of events, but that decontextualization is due to the child then setting up a second representational system containing representations of specifically lexical-semantic prototypes to govern decontextualized word-usage, prototypes which are derived by disembedding information from the cognitively-based event representations. This is clearly a complex issue on which it would be premature to draw any firm conclusions. But although a comprehensive account of early lexical development has not been provided here, it is nevertheless hoped that the model presented in this chapter will serve as a useful theoretical background against which some of these issues may be profitably addressed by future research.

Acknowledgments. Part of this chapter was presented as a paper at the British Psychological Society Developmental Section Annual Conference, Oxford 1983, under the title *Scripts, Prototypes, and the Early Acquisition of Word Meaning.* I would like to express my gratitude to Stan Kuczaj, John McShane, Chris Sinha and John Morton for extensive comments which they provided on the material contained in this chapter, and to my wife, Annette, who both participated in and endured the process of recording Adam's early linguistic productions.

References

Anglin, J. M. (1977). *Word, object, and conceptual development.* New York: Norton.

Anglin, J. M. (1983). Extensional aspects of the preschool child's word concepts. In T. B. Seiler & W. Wannenmacher (Eds.), *Concept development and the development of word meaning.* Berlin: Springer-Verlag.

Barrett, M. D. (1978). Lexical development and overextension in child language. *Journal of Child Language, 5,* 205-219.

Barrett, M. D. (1981). The communicative functions of early child language. *Linguistics, 19,* 273-305.

Barrett, M. D. (1982). Distinguishing between prototypes: The early acquisition of the meaning of object names. In S. A. Kuczaj (Ed.), *Language development, volume 1: Syntax and semantics.* Hillsdale, NJ: Erlbaum.

Barrett, M. D. (1983). The early acquisition and development of the meanings of action-related words. In T. B. Seiler & W. Wannenmacher (Eds.), *Concept development and the development of word meaning.* Berlin: Springer-Verlag.

Bates, E., Benigni, L., Bretherton, I., Camaioni, L., & Volterra, V. (1979). *The emergence of symbols: cognition and communication in infancy.* New York: Academic Press.

Bloom, L. (1973). *One word at a time.* The Hague: Mouton.

Bowerman, M. (1978). The acquisition of word meanings: An investigation into some current conflicts. In N. Waterson & C. Snow (Eds.), *The development of communication.* Chichester: Wiley.

Bruner, J. (1983). *Child's talk: Learning to use language.* Oxford: Oxford University Press.

Clark, E. V. (1973). What's in a word? On the child's acquisition of semantics in his first language. In T. E. Moore (Ed.), *Cognitive development and the acquisition of language.* New York: Academic Press.

Clark, E. V. (1975). Knowledge, context and strategy in the acquisition of meaning. In D. P. Dato (Ed.), *Devlopmental psycholinguistics: Theory and Applications. Georgetown University roundtable on languages and linguistics 1975.* Washington, DC: Georgetown University Press.

Clark, E. V. (1978). Strategies for communicating. *Child Development, 49,* 953-959.

Dore, J. (1978). Conditions for the acquisition of speech acts. In I. Markova (Ed.), *The social context of language.* Chichester: Wiley.

Dore, J., Franklin, M. B., Miller, R. T., & Ramer, A. L. H. (1976). Transitional phenomena in early language acquisition. *Journal of Child Language, 3,* 13-28.

Gopnik, A. (1981). Development of non-nominal expressions in 1-2 year olds: Why the first words aren't about things. In P. S. Dale & D. Ingram (Eds.), *Child language: An international perspective.* Baltimore: University Park Press.

Gopnik, A. (1982). Words and plans: Early language and the development of intelligent action. *Journal of Child Language*, *9*, 303-318.

Greenberg, J., & Kuczaj, S. A. (1982). Towards a theory of substantive word-meaning acquisition. In S. A. Kuczaj (Ed.), *Language development: vol. 1. Syntax and semantics*. Hillsdale, NJ: Erlbaum.

Gruendel, J. M. (1977). Referential extension in early language development. *Child Development*, *48*, 1567-1576.

Leopold, W. F. (1939). *Speech development of a bilingual child: A linguist's record: Vol. 1. Vocabulary growth in the first two years*. Evanston, IL: Northwestern University Press.

Leopold, W. F. (1949). *Speech development of a bilingual child: A linguist's record: Vol. 3. Grammar and general problems in the first two years*. Evanston, IL: Northwestern University Press.

Lewis, M. M. (1951). *Infant speech: A study of the beginnings of language*. London: RKP.

Lock, A. (1980). *The guided reinvention of language*. London: Academic Press.

McShane, J. (1979). The development of naming. *Linguistics*, *17*, 879-905.

McShane, J., & Whittaker, S. (1982). *The role of symbolic thought in language development*. Paper presented at the Conference on the Acquisition of Symbolic Skills, Keele.

Nelson, K. (1982). The syntagmatics and paradigmatics of conceptual development. In S. A. Kuczaj (Ed.), *Language development, volume 2: Language, thought and culture*. Hillsdale, NJ: Erlbaum.

Nelson, K. (1983). The conceptual basis for language. In T. B. Seiler & W. Wannenmacher (Eds.), *Concept development and the development of word meaning*. Berlin: Springer-Verlag.

Nelson, K. E. (1982). Experimental gambits in the service of language acquisition theory: From the Fiffin Project to Operation Input Swap. In S. A. Kuczaj (Ed.), *Language development: vol. 1. Syntax and semantics*. Hillsdale, NJ: Erlbaum.

Reich, P. A. (1976). The early acquisition of word meaning. *Journal of Child Language*, *3*, 117-123.

Rescorla, L. A. (1980). Overextension in early language development. *Journal of Child Language*, *7*, 321-335.

Rescorla, L. A. (1981). Category development in early language. *Journal of Child Language*, *8*, 225-238.

3. Constraints on the Representation of Word Meaning: Evidence From Autistic and Mentally Retarded Children

Helen Tager-Flusberg

There is a girl in England called Nadia whose exceptional drawing ability has captured the attention of psychologists from around the world. Her unusual talents, which allowed her to draw like a skilled adolescent when she was only 4 years old, are all the more striking since she is an autistic child. Her graphic skills blossomed when she was a preschooler, even though at that time she could hardly communicate, she had poor gross motor skills, and her intellectual level was in the retarded range. This remarkable child has interested numerous researchers (Gardner, 1983; Selfe, 1977), in part because it is often the exceptional ability or unique disorder which can inform us most about the nature of human cognition.

Nadia was born in 1967 to emigré parents from eastern Europe. Her development during the first years followed the classic path of many autistic children. As an infant she was uninterested in people, happy to lie alone in her crib for hours. She did not nestle comfortably against her mother or seek her mother's help when distressed. After acquiring several words before she was 1 year old, her language development gradually slowed down until, by 18 months, she stopped speaking. Even by the time she was 6, she only spoke about ten words, mostly echoing the speech of others. During the second year, she showed a general decline in development with delayed motor milestones reflecting her retardation. She was extremely compulsive and rigid in her behavior, resistant to changes in her environment, and still quite detached from people. Later, like many other autistic children, she did become interested in people and showed some peculiar obsessive attachments, yet she retained a distinct lack of social empathy, which is a hallmark of the autistic syndrome.

But unlike other autistic (or normal) children, Nadia began displaying a most remarkable artistic talent at around 3½ years of age. She only drew with her left hand, only using a ballpoint pen, on scraps of paper or anything else available. She drew very few subjects: mostly animals, particularly horses and humans. Her drawings were influenced by pictures she had seen, but they were not copied, nor were they faithful reproductions. Her drawings were indeed wonderful. They were executed rapidly and with great skill, and they demonstrated fluidity and movement. Nadia seemed to gain a good deal of enjoyment from the activity of drawing, although once the pictures were complete, usually in less than a minute, she showed little interest in the final product.

Where did this talent come from? Nadia possessed this single isolated skill, an island of intelligence, like other so-called *idiots savant*. Selfe (1977), who studied Nadia most intensively, suggests that one reason why she drew so well at such an early age was precisely because she lacked other conventional cognitive and linguistic abilities. Selfe believes that Nadia's inability to formulate verbal or semantic concepts allowed her perceptual skills to dominate her drawing. Unlike other children, she did not draw what she knew, only what she saw. Selfe based her conclusions about Nadia's conceptual limitations on her inability to recognize the relationship between members of the same class of objects, her inability to form categories and generalize her knowledge, and her very limited language skills.

Are Nadia's conceptual difficulties peculiar to her or do they represent a cognitive deficit common among children with autism? It is generally acknowledged that cognitive and linguistic difficulties are among the cardinal signs of the autistic syndrome (Rutter, 1978; Schopler, 1978), and during the past 20 years researchers have been investigating what the precise nature of these deficits, specific to autism, might be. While there is little agreement, it has been proposed that autistic children are deficient in semantic-conceptual development. Both Fay and Schuler (1980) and Menyuk (1978) suggest that autistic children do not form even basic semantic categories and do not develop organized semantic and underlying conceptual systems. This hypothesized conceptual deficit provides a plausible interpretation for many aspects of behavior associated with the disorder. For example, many autistic children, like Nadia, are resistant to changes in their routine or environment. Changes and novelty are not easily integrated into existing representations of the world when those representations are not based in a flexible organized conceptual structure. It has also been noted that even autistic children who do learn language are very slow in acquiring words or signs and they do not usually generalize words to novel referents or contexts (Bonvillian, Nelson & Rhyne, 1981; Harris, 1975).

There is, however, little direct evidence supporting this interpretation of the cognitive deficits specific to all children with autism. The most relevant research, conducted by Hermelin and O'Connor (1967, 1970), showed that autistic children, unlike retarded and normal children, fail to use meaning to facilitate recall. Their experiments, however, did not distinguish between the autistic child's representation of meaning from their ability to use meaning in a cognitive task. Is it possible, as Menyuk and Fay and Schuler implicitly suggest, that autistic children fail to represent semantic concepts, or represent them differently from normal children? When they are shown different examples from the same general class of objects, such as chairs, do they fail to categorize and form a unified concept of *chair*? When they learn a word for a specific example, such as a kitchen chair, do they fail to generalize to other examples which share perceptual or functional features with the original object? The answers to these questions are important not only for understanding the nature of autism, but also for general theories of semantic representation and word meaning, as the questions offer the possibility that there may be alternative formats for representing concepts and that the process of developing concepts and word meaning may not be universal.

This chapter will offer some evidence from work that I have done with autistic and retarded children which argues against this radical interpretation of the nature of the cognitive deficit in autism. Instead, the data that I have gathered show that the representation of meaning and lexical development are strikingly similar across widely different groups of children, suggesting that these capacities are highly constrained aspects of human cognitive development.

One of the primary sources of evidence for the nature of the development of semantic representation comes from children's early word use (Bowerman, 1978; Clark, 1974; Seiler & Wannenmacher, 1983). We have learned a good deal about how normal children's concepts develop, what their first words refer to, and how their meanings for words gradually come to match the meanings of adults. My work has explored how autistic and retarded children, whose language development is severely delayed, organize their conceptual knowledge, represent the meanings of words, and how they name both familiar and unfamiliar objects. This chapter will focus on how autistic, retarded, and normal children name objects from different kinds of categories, and will present data both from correct naming and error patterns of overextensions and underextensions, looking for similarities and differences among the groups of children in this study, and drawing parallels between this study and other related research.

The Study

The subjects who participated in this study included 14 autistic, 14 retarded, and 14 normal children. The autistic children were diagnosed using the criteria described by Rutter (1978). Their essential characteristics and developmental histories were much like those described for Nadia: they began displaying different behaviors at a very early age, well before they were 2 years old; they were very impaired in social attachments and social relationships in general; their language development had been significantly delayed; and they each had some idiosyncratic obsessive or compulsive characteristics. As a group, the children were older than Nadia was when she began her drawings. They were, on average, 10½ years old; they had near-normal nonverbal IQs (as assessed on the Raven's Colored Progressive Matrices, a test of visual-spatial ability), but were fairly retarded on verbal measures. Using the Peabody Picture Vocabulary Test, the autistic group had an average verbal mental age of about 5 years. They all spoke and comprehended some language, though other language measures were not taken. As a group, the autistic children represent a select, higher functioning segment of the population as a whole, though, as Rutter (1983) points out, these are the children to study in order to identify cognitive deficits specific to the autistic syndrome.

The retarded children were chosen to match the autistic group on chronological age and verbal mental age. Their nonverbal IQs were significantly lower than those of the autistic children. The normal children matched the other groups only on verbal mental age.

The study involved asking the children to name two series of pictures consisting of line drawings of objects. The pictures had been used to test the children's understanding of several words using two different methods. After their comprehension had been assessed, the children were asked to name all the pictures. Here, we will only discuss the naming data in detail as the comprehension studies are presented elsewhere (see Tager-Flusberg, in press). The pictures were selected to provide several examples from a number of basic level and superordinate level categories. The examples were chosen to vary along the dimension of prototypicality, as defined by Rosch in her seminal work (cf. Rosch, 1975). Adult judges were asked to rate pictures from a number of categories along a scale from 1 (very central or excellent example of the category label) to 7 (very peripheral or poor example). The categories and pictures were selected for this study from the pool rated in this way. Table 3-1 shows the complete list of examples and the prototypicality rating for each picture. Half the categories had six examples; the other half had four examples. The comprehension experiments had also included foil pictures which the children named too, but these data will be omitted here.

Each child was presented with the pictures in random order and were encouraged to identify the picture for the experimenter. None of the subjects had difficulty with the task.

Results

Children's responses were initially coded into two categories: correct and incorrect. Correct responses included any name that was suitable in reference to a particular picture. There was frequently more than one possible correct response. For example, in reference to the drawing of an eagle, some children called it an *eagle*, some a *bird*, and a few called it *birdie*. For the purpose of data analysis, the examples for each category were divided into central and peripheral, based on the adult ratings of prototypicality. Table 3-2 shows the distribution of correct and incorrect responses over the various examples, collapsing across the four basic level categories and four superordinate level categories.

What is most striking about these data is the similarity of response patterns across the groups of subjects. Looking first at the basic level categories (*bird*, *boat*, *fish*, and *house*), we see that all three groups of subjects made significantly more errors on the peripheral examples. That is, children had more trouble naming the penguin, or barge, or igloo than naming the cardinal, sailboat, or colonial house. For basic level categories, prototypicality plays a significant role in naming performance.

Table 3-1. Stimuli Used in the Naming Study (Prototypicality ratings in parentheses)

Category	Central category members		Peripheral category members	
Basic level				
Boat	sailboat	(1.4)	submarine	(3.6)
	tugboat	(2.0)	barge	(5.8)
	canoe	(2.7)	raft	(5.9)
Bird	cardinal	(1.3)	rooster	(4.3)
	eagle	(2.3)	penguin	(5.2)
	owl	(3.4)	ostrich	(5.3)
Fish	bluefish	(1.5)	skate	(5.2)
	shark	(3.3)	seahorse	(5.4)
House	colonial	(1.2)	houseboat	(5.3)
	igloo	(3.9)	tent	(5.4)
Superordinate level				
Food	chicken	(1.3)	ice cream	(3.4)
	apple	(1.8)	ketchup	(5.4)
	bread	(2.2)	lollipop	(6.1)
Tool	hammer	(1.5)	scissors	(3.9)
	wrench	(1.6)	pencil	(4.7)
	ladder	(3.7)	nail	(4.9)
Kitchen utensil	pot	(1.7)	toaster	(2.9)
	rolling pin	(2.6)	broom	(6.1)
Musical instrument	guitar	(1.3)	harp	(1.9)
	trumpet	(1.6)	bell	(4.6)

This, however, was not true for the examples from the superordinate level categories. In fact, children in all three groups did slightly better in naming the peripheral examples, but the difference between the central and peripheral examples is not significant. This contrasts with the findings from the comprehension study in which performance was worse on the peripheral members than on the central members for both the basic level and superordinate level words (see Tager-Flusberg, in press).

Why doesn't prototypicality play a role in the naming data for superordinate categories? The answer is fairly straightforward. Take, for example, the category *tool*. A central member of that category may be *hammer* or *wrench*. Peripheral members include *pencil* and *scissors*. While *pencil* is peripheral for the category *tool*, the drawing of the pencil was nevertheless a good example of the basic level category *pencil*. *Pencil*, too, may be a central member of another superordinate level category, *writing implement*. The same is true for many of the peripheral examples of the other superordinate level categories. The pictures of all the examples for the superordinate categories were highly prototypical for their respective basic level

Table 3-2. Percentage of Correct and Incorrect Naming Responses

	Autistic		Mentally retarded		Normal	
	Central	Peripheral	Central	Peripheral	Central	Peripheral
Basic level						
Correct	88	72	89	63	89	63
Incorrect	12	28	11	37	11	37
Superordinate level						
Correct	81	90	74	81	77	81
Incorrect	19	10	26	19	23	19

categories and thus were fairly easy to name. This suggests that prototypical basic level examples are the most easily named by all the children and, indeed, the data support this conclusion.

What kinds of names did the children give to the different pictures? One way to investigate this is to classify the correct responses, such as "eagle" and "bird," as subordinate or basic level names. The picture could also have been correctly named "animal," a superordinate level name for the same object. Children's correct responses to all the pictures were classified in this way, according to the hierarchical level of the name used for each picture. These data are shown in Table 3-3.

The data for the superordinate level categories again show no differences for central and peripheral examples. Almost all the names given to these pictures were basic names. The few correct superordinate responses, such as "tool" or "food" may well have been influenced by the comprehension task conducted prior to the naming study in which children were provided with the superordinate level word and asked if the picture was an example of that word. In this later naming study, if a child could not find the basic word for a picture, such as for "wrench," he or she

Table 3-3. Breakdown of Correct Names: Percentage of Subordinate, Basic and Superordinate Level Names

	Autistic		Mentally retarded		Normal	
	Central	Peripheral	Central	Peripheral	Central	Peripheral
Basic level categories						
Subordinate	27	51	17	39	22	39
Basic	73	48	83	60	78	61
Superordinate	0	1	0	1	0	0
Superordinate level categories						
Subordinate	1	0	1	0	5	3
Basic	96	96	92	94	94	94
Superordinate	3	4	7	6	1	4

may have remembered being asked earlier if it was a "tool," and used this word again to name the same picture.

The response pattern to the examples from the basic level categories is more complex. For these pictures, children used more varied names and the differences between central and peripheral examples again showed up. Only an isolated one or two superordinate names were used for these stimuli, which is not surprising since the children never heard their superordinate labels used in the comprehension task. Compared to the superordinate categories, the proportion of basic names is lower because of the dramatic increase in the number of subordinate, more specific names being used. In all three groups of subjects, children were more likely to use a subordinate name on peripheral examples than on central examples. For example, children usually called the cardinal a "bird" whereas the penguin was given its specific name, "penguin." The autistic children showed a slightly higher tendency to use subordinate names for these pictures. Otherwise, the similarity across the groups clearly held up. Once again, then, we find the children differentiating between central and peripheral examples, supporting the view that prototypicality, at least in basic level categories, significantly influences the children's word use. Furthermore, these data overall show the primacy of the basic level of naming that was first noted by Brown (1958). These issues will be discussed later, when we address theories of semantic representation.

The next analysis shows a breakdown of the kinds of errors made by each group of children. An exhaustive coding of errors across all subjects yielded 14 error categories—but most of them contained only one or two examples. For instance, one rare error was to give some picture a proper name, such as "Big bird" for a picture of an ostrich or "Mr. Tool" for a wrench. Other rare errors included associations ("eskimo" for igloo), naming a part of the whole ("cap" for bottle of catsup), gesturing, neologisms, phonological errors ("art" for arch), and giving a completely unrelated response ("flower" for skate). There were, in addition, occasional interference errors from previously presented pictures. There were also four major error categories which accounted for the majority of errors: *semantic*—when the child responded with a semantically related, but incorrect name ("duck" for rooster, "screwdriver" for wrench); *perceptual*—when the child mistook the item for something quite other than what was intended because of perceptual similarity "crayons" for raft); *functional description*—when the child described with one or several words the function of the object ("cutter" for scissors, "you row it" for canoe); and *no response*—when the child said nothing, even after prompting by the experimenter. Table 3-4 shows the distribution of errors among these response categories, grouping all the rare response types under *other*.

There are a number of interesting features in these error patterns. First, it is clear that the majority of errors fall in the semantic category. For all the groups, more than half of the errors on the central examples from both basic and superordinate level categories are semantic. More than any other data, these semantic errors are evidence for the *meaningful* organization of the lexicons in all the children. These naming errors are much like those found among groups of adults for whom there is abundant evidence that their lexicons are semantically organized. Perceptual errors

Table 3-4. Breakdown of Error Responses: Percentage of Semantic, Perceptual, Functional Descriptive, and Other Error Responses

	Autistic		Mentally retarded		Normal	
	Central	Peripheral	Central	Peripheral	Central	Peripheral
Basic level						
Semantic error	56	43	79	60	60	32
Perceptual error	11	37	0	16	13	36
Functional/ description	0	2	14	4	27	15
Other	0	5	7	18	0	15
No response	33	13	0	2	0	2
Superordinate level						
Semantic error	52	33	65	47	53	33
Perceptual error	5	8	6	0	4	8
Functional/ description	5	17	3	11	18	38
Other	22	17	16	26	18	17
No response	17	25	10	16	7	4

account for more errors among the basic level categories, particularly on peripheral examples, than among superordinate level categories. Again, this probably reflects the fact that in the latter categories all the pictures were prototypical for their basic level and, hence, less confusable with examples from other categories (cf. Rosch, Mervis, Gray, Johnson, & Boyes-Braem, 1976). The remaining errors are distributed among the response categories differently for the normal, retarded, and autistic groups. Normal children tended to use functional descriptions. Nearly 25% of their errors fall in this category, compared to only 6% of such errors by the autistic group, and 8% by the retarded group. In contrast, the autistic children were most likely to give no response if they could not name the picture. The retarded children showed more interference errors and provided associations more frequently than either of the other groups. These differences among the groups—the only significant ones to emerge in this study—reflect different *strategies* used by the children when faced with a picture for which they had no name. These errors are the only ones not linked to semantic or lexical representation, but rather are means of handling incomplete representations. Normal children, who were younger than the other groups, described what they saw, or tried to show that they knew the function of the object; autistic children preferred to keep quiet; and the retarded children were more easily distracted (as shown by their interference errors) or gave single word associations to the pictures.

The final pieces of data to be mentioned here address the relationship between comprehension and production. Each of the pictures named in this study had been tested in a comprehension task using either a basic level name (for the basic level categories) or a superordinate level name (for the corresponding superordinate level categories). Comprehension errors in connection with these pictures would all be classified as underextensions, that is, not recognizing the example as a member of the category named by the experimenter. We can compare each child's comprehension and naming performance on each picture to check consistency between these measures. Consistent performance would include correct comprehension and production as well as incorrect comprehension and production. Inconsistent performance would include correct comprehension but incorrect production and incorrect comprehension but correct production. All four possible performance patterns were obtained by children in all the groups, as can be seen in Table 3-5.

Table 3-5 also shows that comprehension does not clearly precede production. Thus, we do not find children in any group with a dominant inconsistent pattern of correct comprehension but incorrect production. In fact, the opposite pattern (correct naming but incorrect comprehension) is more dominant, especially on peripheral examples which children tend to underextend in comprehension (cf. Anglin, 1977; Kuczaj, 1982). The large proportion of correct naming for peripheral

Table 3-5. Relation Between Comprehension and Production: Percentage of Responses in Different Patterns

Comprehension/ production	Autistic		Mentally retarded		Normal	
	Central	Peripheral	Central	Peripheral	Central	Peripheral
Basic level						
Correct-correct	89	59	85	48	82	44
Incorrect-incorrect	3	12	1	24	4	24
Correct-incorrect	5	14	7	9	4	13
Incorrect-correct	3	15	7	18	10	19
Superordinate level						
Correct-correct	79	66	73	50	69	50
Incorrect-incorrect	2	0	1	6	4	13
Correct-incorrect	7	6	9	13	9	10
Incorrect-correct	12	28	17	32	18	27

examples of superordinate categories shows up once more in the data presented in Table 3-5. To understand the various inconsistent response patterns found in this analysis, we need to go back to some of the results presented earlier. Children's correct comprehension but incorrect productions reflect the semantic naming errors described in the previous paragraph. Thus a child might have correctly recognized an eagle as a *bird* in the comprehension task but then called it a *dove* in the naming task. These errors are related to the child's difficulty with subordinate names in production whereas the comprehension performance shows mastery of the basic level name. Correct naming coupled with a lack of comprehension reflects different taxonomic disparities in the child's developing lexicon. For basic level categories, for example, children know the name for a penguin, but may not yet have learned that it is a bird (since it is peripheral and shares few features with other birds). At the superordinate level, children name correctly at the basic level, but have not yet fully developed more abstract, higher order categories and so, for example, may know what a lollipop is called, but do not realize it belongs to the same superordinate food category as bread or chicken. These errors and disparities between comprehension and production demonstrate the similar developing hierarchical structure in the autistic, retarded, and normal children's lexicons. For all children, the basic level name is learned first, especially for central members of a category.

Discussion

The most consistent finding is the similarity in performance across the three subject groups. The fact that children in all groups correctly named about the same proportion of pictures (see Table 3-2) is not particularly surprising or revealing since the groups were initially matched on the Peabody Picture Vocabulary Test, a standardized and reliable measure of vocabulary level. But we are interested more in what the *patterns* of responses, both correct and incorrect, summarized in Tables 3-2, 3-3, 3-4, and 3-5 reveal about how the different groups of children represent the semantic knowledge tapped in this study, both conceptually and lexically. The obvious similarities among the children in the kinds of correct names used, in the error patterns, and in the relation between comprehension and production, suggest that the same factors are important for all the children—autistic, retarded or normal.

Two main factors influenced the patterns of data. First, for the basic level categories, performance was related to the prototypicality of the examples. Thus, children made more errors on peripheral items, named them differently (with a subordinate rather than basic level name), and were less likely to recognize them for what they were (as shown by the increase in perceptual errors). Prototypicality played a less significant role in the naming of examples from superordinate level categories, as explained earlier in the chapter, but the comprehension data shows that all the groups were sensitive to this factor at all taxonomic levels (Tager-Flusberg, in press). Thus, prototypes play an important role in the way the concepts underlying the words that were tapped are represented and in the development of word meaning, not only in adults (Rosch, 1975; Rosch et al., 1976) and not only in normal children (Mulford, 1979), but in *all* children who develop some conceptual knowledge. The second factor which influenced the children's naming performance was the primacy of the basic level in lexical development and related conceptual representation. Most of the names used by chidlren, especially on the superordinate level items, were basic level names. Thus, these data support other findings in the normal literature on the developmental primacy of this level in children's early lexicons (Anglin, 1977; Brown, 1958). The central role of prototypes in semantic representation, and the psychological significance of the basic level were found to be similar in all groups of children, as well as in adults (cf. Medin & Smith, 1984).

Even the naming errors made by the children are revealing about the organization of their lexicons. Specifically, the children did not typically make random or unsystematic errors. Instead, the majority of errors were semantic, that is, using an incorrect name from a conceptually and categorically related item. This was true of the autistic children as well as the normal and mentally retarded, demonstrating the semantic organization of their conceptual and lexical knowledge.

The findings from this study refute the hypothesis proposed by Menyuk (1978) and Fay and Schuler (1980) that children with autism are specifically deficient in developing concepts, in relating categorically similar objects or words, and in the development of meaning. These autistic children who participated in the study, and had developed some language, acquired a conceptual system and processed semantic information just like other groups of children. For reasons that we do not understand, autistic children are severely delayed in their language development relative to their nonverbal mental age. This was true of the autistic children in this study, who were more advanced than the normal or retarded children in nonverbal intelligence, yet their naming performance was comparable to their verbal mental age matched peers. Overall, autistic children are delayed in semantic development (as well as other aspects of language, see Tager-Flusberg, 1981), but they show no specific deficit or deviance in the way they represent meaning once they have begun to acquire such knowledge.

The similar systems of semantic representation and the process of developing word meanings in the widely different groups of children in this study supports the view that they are highly constrained. We find that children of diverse ages, with quite different developmental histories, organic impairments, sensory deficits, patterns of cognitive abilities, and social awareness, are developing representational systems for concepts and words that are organized in the same way, using the same formats. This provides probably the best evidence for universal, possibly innate, constraints on this aspect of human cognition. These constraints are what make the development of concepts and word meanings possible in all children, no matter what other deficits they might have.

What of Nadia? Lorna Selfe believed that Nadia had no conceptual knowledge, no access to meaning, and therefore drew exactly as she saw things. We have no way of knowing whether this was true, but I suspect that since Nadia did begin to make progress in language, she must have developed some basic conceptual knowledge, like the autistic children in this study. Even her drawings of semantically related subjects (animals) suggests that already by age four there was the ability to categorize things. Otherwise, her world would have been too chaotic to bear. Nevertheless, her remarkable and unique drawing talent remains a mystery.

Acknowledgements. Preparation of this chapter and the research described in it were supported by a grant from the National Institute of Mental Health (5 R01 MH 37074). I am grateful to the teachers and students at the following schools in Massachusetts for their help and participation in the study: The League School, Newton; St. Colletta's Day School, Braintree; The Osgood School, Cohasset; South Shore Collaborative, Hingham; and the University of Massachusetts Child Care Center, Boston. I am also indebted to Helene Chaika for her help in preparing stimuli, data collection and coding; and to Kathleen Quill, Wendy Barrett and Gail Rex Andrick for their assistance with the research.

References

Anglin, J. (1977). *Word, object and conceptual development*. New York: Norton & Co.
Bonvillian, J. D., Nelson, K. E., & Rhyne, J. (1981). Sign language and autism. *Journal of Autism and Developmental Disorders, 11,* 125-137.
Bowerman, M. (1978). The acquisition of word meaning: An investigation into some current conflicts. In N. Waterson & C. Snow (Eds.), *The development of communication*. New York: Wiley.
Brown, R. (1958). *Words and things*. New York: Free Press.
Clark, E. V. (1974). Some aspects for the conceptual basis for first language acquisition. In R. L. Schiefelbusch & L. L. Lloyd (Eds.), *Language perspectives: Acquisition, retardation and intervention*. Baltimore: University Park Press.
Fay, W. H., & Schuler, A. L. (1980). *Emerging language in autistic children*. Baltimore: University Park Press.
Gardner, H. (1983). *Frames of mind*. New York: Basic Books.
Harris, S. (1975). Teaching language to nonverbal children—with emphasis on problems of generalization. *Psychological Bulletin, 82,* 565-580.
Hermelin, B., & O'Connor, N. (1967). Remembering of words by psychotic and subnormal children. *British Journal of Psychology, 58,* 213-218.
Hermelin, B., & O'Connor, N. (1970). *Psychological experiments with autistic children*. Oxford: Pergamon Press.
Kuczaj, S. A. (1982). Young children's overextensions of object words in comprehension and/or production: Support for a prototype theory of early object word meaning. *First Language, 3,* 93-105.
Medin, D. L., & Smith, E. E. (1984). Concepts and concept formation. *Annual Review of Psychology, 35,* 113-138.
Menyuk, P. (1978). Language: What's wrong and why. In M. Rutter & E. Schopler (Eds.), *Autism: A reappraisal of concepts and treatment* (pp. 105-116). New York: Plenum Press.
Mulford, R. (1979). Prototypicality and the development of categorization. *Papers and Reports on Child Language Development, 16,* 13-25, Stanford University, California.

Rosch, E. (1975). Cognitive representations of semantic categories. *Journal of Experimental Psychology: General, 104*, 192-233.

Rosch, E., Mervis, C. B., Gray, W. D., Johnson, D. M., & Boyes-Braem, P. (1976). Basic objects in natural categories. *Cognitive Psychology, 8*, 382-439.

Rutter, M. (1978). Diagnosis and definition. In M. Rutter & E. Schopler (Eds.), *Autism: A reappraisal of concepts and treatment* (pp. 1-25). New York: Plenum Press.

Rutter, M. (1983). Cognitive deficits in the pathogenesis of autism. *Journal of Child Psychology and Psychiatry, 24*, 513-531.

Schopler, E. (1978). National Society for Autistic Children definition of the syndrome of autism. *Journal of Autism and Childhood Schizophrenia, 8*, 162-167.

Selfe, L. (1977). *Nadia: A case of extraordinary drawing ability in an autistic child*. New York: Academic Press.

Seiler, T. B., & Wannenmacher, W. (1983). *Concept development and the development of word meaning*. New York: Springer-Verlag.

Tager-Flusberg, H. B. (1981). On the nature of linguistic functioning in early infantile autism. *Journal of Autism and Developmental Disorders, 11*, 45-56.

Tager-Flusberg, H. B. (in press). The conceptual basis for referential word meaning in children with autism. *Child Development*.

4. Semantic and Conceptual Knowledge Underlying the Child's Words

Jeremy M. Anglin

In this chapter I would like to comment upon two general kinds of studies in terms of their relevance for inferences that can be drawn concerning the meanings and concepts underlying the words of young children. The studies I will discuss have investigated the referential, semantic, and conceptual aspects of some of the words learned by English speaking children between the ages of 1 and 6 years. The two general kinds of studies I will be concerned with are: (1) extensional investigations of the tendency of children to generalize words referentially in both (a) naturalistic studies (e.g., diary studies) of spontaneous speech production, and (b) more controlled quasi-experimental studies of this tendency in tests of speech production and comprehension; and, (2) interview studies in which preschool children are asked to define words and to tell what they know about the meanings and concepts encoded by them. With respect to the first kind of study, in this chapter I will be concerned with object names such as *dog*, *animal*, *car*, *money*, *flower*, *basket*, and so on. With respect to the second kind of study I will comment upon investigations of verbs such as *jump*, *walk*, *play*, and *talk* as well as of studies of nouns.

I would like to make two general points at the outset. The first is of a theoretical nature, and concerns a debate regarding whether conceptual and semantic development precede or follow initial word learning. Two extreme positions on this issue are: (1) the child's initial learning of a word is essentially an invitation for him or her to form a concept and conceptual and semantic development follow and are aided by word learning; versus (2) the child's learning of a word basically involves concept matching, and concept formation and semantic development precede word learning. My own opinion is that there must be some partial truth to both these views. Initial word learning must, at least often in the early stages of language development, build upon the child's preceding conceptual development. However, most of my work on conceptual and semantic development suggests that there are important changes in the semantic and conceptual structure underlying many words *after* they have been initially acquired as well.

The second general point is a methodological one. No single method of studying semantic and conceptual development, including those being discussed here, can provide all or even most of the answers to questions concerning the semantic and conceptual structure underlying the child's words. Each of the methods to be discussed is useful in some respects and each provides some clues as to the nature of semantic and conceptual development. Moreover, each method is considerably more useful in this respect than simply keeping a list of the words learned by a given child as he or she grows up. Nonetheless, each of these methods is associated with certain problems and limitations concerning the inferences they permit vis à vis semantic and conceptual development. Put otherwise, I am concerned with characterizing the nature of semantic and conceptual knowledge in children (and also in adults) but this knowledge is not directly observable. The methods to be discussed (as well as other relevant methods) provide windows to aspects of this knowledge but only to some aspects. Moreover, the windows themselves may be somewhat colored or clouded for various reasons. Because of this, a variety of methods, including the ones to be discussed as well as others, will be necessary to come up with a reasonably complete account of the acquisition of word meanings and word concepts.

For my purposes here I will define a *word concept* as the knowledge possessed by an individual about a category of objects or events, each such category being denoted by a word in the language of that individual. This knowledge includes both the knowledge an individual has of the category's *extension* or denotative scope—what things or events are instances of the category—and the knowledge he or she has of its *meaning* or *intension*—those properties that are true of and important for defining the category. Thus, according to these definitions, a *word meaning* is a subset of the knowledge included in a *word concept*. A *word meaning* refers to the essential properties which define the word for a particular individual whereas a *word concept* is more encyclopedic encompassing these essential properties but also other kinds of knowledge an individual possesses about the word including knowledge of how to identify referents of it. For elaboration of these working definitions see Anglin (1977, 1983). The only additional point I will make here about my definitions of these terms is that I have defined them from the point of view of an individual child's or adult's understanding and knowledge. Thus for my purposes the *meaning* or the *concept* underlying a word refers to the semantic or conceptual knowledge respectively, possessed by an individual about that word. These terms have not always been defined by others in this way (see for example Macnamara's [1982] definition of *concept* or Putnam's [1975] definition of *meaning*).

Extensional Studies

The first type of extensional or referential study to be discussed has often been used in the investigation of the semantic and conceptual development underlying the child's first words. In these studies researchers have kept diaries or chronological records of children's spontaneous speech production, recording over a certain period of time what the child says and in what context. Such diaries have been kept by numerous investigators of language acquisition (e.g., Bloom, 1973; Chamberlain & Chamberlain, 1904; Leopold, 1939, 1949; Lewis, 1959; Moore, 1896; Piaget, 1962). One use to which the resulting observations have been put has been the examination of children's natural tendency to extend and overextend their early words to refer to various things (or events, etc.) in their environment. Such observations have been analyzed to formulate hypotheses and even theories of what words might mean to children given these generalization patterns (e.g., Barrett, 1978, & this volume Chapter 2; Brown, 1958; Bloom, 1973; Bowerman, 1977; Clark, 1973; Nelson, Rescorla, Gruendel, & Benedict, 1978; Rescorla, 1980). I myself kept such a diary of my first daughter, Emmy's, language development which, among other things, allowed me to reflect on the limitations as well as the virtues of this approach. With respect to my topic here I will only mention that in keeping this diary I observed that Emmy would often use the words she spoke between 1 and 2 years to refer to things that I had used or would use them for as well. However, Emmy, who learned various words and especially object names early and rapidly and who produced such words relatively frequently, sometimes used them in ways that suggested that the range of objects to which she was willing to apply them was not always the same as the range of objects to which I would be inclined to apply what I thought were the corresponding words in my vocabulary. In particular there appeared to be cases in which some of Emmy's words were *overextended* (applied more generally), *underextended* (applied less generally), and, for some words, both overextended and underextended (applied to some things I would use the word for, but not to all such things, and, at the same time applied to some things I would not be inclined to use the word for) suggesting a pattern of *overlap* of reference between the extension of her word and my corresponding word.

Overextensions have often been noted in the child's early speech production (e.g., Clark, 1973; however, see also Clark & Clark, 1977; Clark, 1979). In Emmy's case, although a number of factors and combinations of factors may have been at work in enticing her to overextend her first words, or at least use them apparently to refer to things that I would not, the most frequent bases for such word generalization seemed to be *perceptual similarity* and *functional similarity*. An example of an early word which Emmy seemed to extend on the basis of perceptual similarity was her word for *dog* which she pronounced [gagi] to refer not just to real dogs and pictures of dogs but also to pictures in her books of lambs, cats, wolves, cows, etc. (cf. Clark, 1973). An example of an early word that Emmy generalized apparently on the basis of functional similarity was her word for *hat* which she first pronounced [æt] but soon correctly as [hæt]. She used this word in reference to her sun hat at first but soon thereafter to numerous objects which she put on her head including a plastic bowl, a bag, an empty diaper box, a washcloth, a juice can, her blanket, and even her sneaker (Anglin, 1983; see also Gruendel, 1977; Nelson, Rescorla, Gruendel, & Benedict, 1978).

Although most striking, overextensions (or more general applications of words) were not the only way in which Emmy's word use was different from my own. There were also apparent cases of underextension. For example, Emmy at first used her word for *bottle* which she pronounced [bʌbʌ] only for her plastic drinking bottles and not for various other kinds of bottles (e.g., coke bottles) when I asked what they were. Furthermore, there were also some apparent cases of overlap of reference as described above in which Emmy both overextended and underextended a given word relative to adult standards. For example, Emmy at first could name both real umbrellas and pictures of umbrellas [bɛlə] provided they were open. She also used the word [bɛlə] on a number of occasions to refer to a large green leaf in one of her picture books which a monkey was holding over its head when it was raining. She also used this word to refer to kites, both real kites and pictures of kites. However, she did not recognize closed umbrellas as [bɛlə] in real life or in picture books. If I would ask her what a closed umbrella was she would most often say [seya?] or [waseya?] which was her way at that time of asking me "What's that?". Also once or twice when I asked her what a closed umbrella in one of her picture books was she responded [kændi keyn]. Thus, Emmy used her word for *umbrella* to refer to some things adults would use it for, but some things they would not, and at the same time, she did not use it for some things adults would.

Overall, apparent cases of overextension were more numerous in Emmy's spontaneous naming behavior recorded in my diary than underextensions which in turn were more numerous than cases of overlap of reference, although all three types of relations were observed. This is the impression obtained from diaries of others in which overextensions have been reported most frequently, underextensions less, and cases of overlap only infrequently. One might be inclined to conclude from this that most often the denotative scope of the child's words is greater than that of the corresponding adult words, which in turn might be interpreted as implying that most often the meanings of the child's words are more general than those of adults, a conclusion which has often been reached on the basis of these kinds of diaries (e.g., Clark, 1973; however, see also Clark, 1979; Clark & Clark, 1977).

However, there are several problems with using the spontaneous naming behavior of children recorded in such diaries as the sole basis for coming to conclusions about the extension of the child's words, let alone about their meaning or intension, four of which I will mention here (for further elaboration see Anglin, 1983). First, because of the way the data in diaries of children's spontaneous speech production are collected, recorded, and interpreted, such diaries are systematically biased to suggest overextension rather than underextension and overlap of reference (e.g., Anglin, 1977; 1979). This is so because the words used by a child actually recorded in a diary will either be used appropriately or inappropriately from the point of view of adult standards. Whenever they are used appropriately they will be viewed as having been applied correctly; whenever inappropriately they will be viewed as having been applied incorrectly and as overextended. Thus the words used by a child will rarely be viewed as underextended; underextension can only be inferred indirectly when words are not used when they should have been *and* when there is independent evidence that these words are in the child's productive vocabulary. Thus underextensions, and also cases of overlap which involve underextension as well as overextension, are not as clearly suggested by diaries as are overextensions. Second, a number of recent studies have indicated asymmetries in children's tendency to overextend words in speech production as compared to speech comprehension. These results raise questions about inferences that can be drawn concerning the semantic and conceptual structure underlying the child's words when only speech production is studied (e.g., Gruendel, 1977; Fremgen & Fay, 1980; Huttenlocher, 1974; Rescorla, 1980; Thomson & Chapman, 1977; however see also Kay & Anglin, 1982; Kuczaj, 1982). Third, diaries of spontaneous speech are good for giving a rough overview of language development in specific children but they are usually not systematic, controlled or intensive enough to allow a confident assessment of the denotative breadth of a child's individual words. More systematic assessment of the extension of a given child's words, involving the testing of a reasonably large range of referents and nonreferents of the words (from the adult point of view), is necessary to come to correct inferences regarding extensional aspects of the child's words such as whether the relation between the extension of a given word for a given child and that of adults is one of overextension, underextension, overlap of reference, or whatever. Fourth, in the second year of their life and beyond many children *often* engage in pretense and symbolic play in naturalistic settings which is often accompanied by nonliteral pretend talk (e.g., Bates, 1976; Piaget, 1962; Winner, 1979). Such pretend talk is fascinating and of relevance to semantic development in its own right but the ever-present possibility that the child may be just pretending when he or she seems to use a word differently than we might does complicate the task of specifying the extension of the child's words on the basis of naturalistically occurring spontaneous speech alone. (A number of cases of Emmy's seemingly applying her words more generally than I might and particularly some of the ones apparently involving functional similarity, may well have been cases of pretend talk, although, especially in the early stages of Emmy's language development (12-19 mos.) as in the example of her word for *hat* described above, it was often difficult to know for sure whether she was pretending or not.)

To an extent these four problems can be overcome through the use of more systematic, controlled, and intensive laboratory tests in which a child is asked for fairly large numbers of both referents and nonreferents which he or she thinks are referents of a given word in both production (by asking "What's this?" for each stimulus) and in comprehension (by asking "Is this a _____?" or some variant of this question for each stimulus). Increasingly my own quasi-experimental studies of the extension of the child's words tended to approximate these conditions (e.g., Anglin, 1977) and one relatively recent investigation conducted with Deborah Kay (Kay & Anglin, 1982) had most of the relevant features included in its design.

In this study after pretesting and training (see Kay & Anglin, 1982 for details), 2-year-old children were assessed for their extension of one of five words (*basket*, *candle*, *wheel*, *pin*, and *card*) with respect to several referents and nonreferents, and in both *production* (by asking "What's this?" for each stimulus) and *comprehension* (by asking "Is this a *basket*?" etc. for each stimulus). When we counted overextensions and underextensions only when they were made by a given child in both production *and* comprehension, we found that although each of the three patterns (discussed above) of overextension, underextension, and overlap of reference occurred, the pattern of overlap of reference was actually the most common, the pattern of underextension second most common, and the pattern of overextension the least common, which is the exact reverse of the relative ordering of these three patterns as suggested by diaries (see above). This indicates, at the very least, that the relative frequencies of the referential patterns I have been discussing that are observed depends upon the particular method used to assess the extension of the child's words.

When one combines results from diaries with those from more controlled tests of the extension of the child's words in comprehension and production I believe it becomes possible to come to some correct conclusions regarding the extension of the child's words. Moreover, on the basis of these combined results it is also possible to formulate *hypotheses* concerning their meaning or intension for young children, three examples of which I will summarize here based on extensional studies such as those described above. First, if I am right that overextension, underextension, and overlap of reference are all relations which can and do occur, then one hypothesis which would appear to have support is that there is probably no single simple way of characterizing the relation between the child's word meanings and those of adults in terms of generality. Cases of overextension are at least compatible with the view that the child's word meanings are more general (defined by fewer and/or more general properties) than those of adults. Similarly, cases of underextension are at least compatible with the view that the child's word meanings are more specific (defined by more and/or more specific properties) than those of adults. However, cases of overlap are compatible with neither view; rather they imply that the child's meanings are somewhat different from those of adults but not simply too general or too specific.

A second hypothesis of a more affirmative nature suggested by some of the research briefly discussed above is that the meanings of the child's words (at least their object names) include properties of a perceptual and/or functional nature as indicated, for example, by the fact that overextensions so often seem to be based on perceptual and/or functional similarity. That is often the meanings of the child's names for things typically specify how referents of the word look (as well as how they sound, feel, taste, etc.) and how referents of the word function or are used.

A third hypothesis suggested by some of the studies alluded to above and related research is that the child's understanding of the meanings of object words may often be based upon his or her representation of prototypical referents (presumably including both perceptual and functional aspects of these prototypical referents) of the words (see Rosch, 1973; 1978). For example, in the study by Kay and Anglin children were far more likely to include within the categories referents rated previously by adults as prototypical or "central" instances of those categories in the tests of both comprehension and production, than they were for instances rated as atypical or peripheral. Various other kinds of evidence have also suggested that early meanings may be based upon the child's representation of prototypical referents (e.g., Anglin, 1977, 1979; Barrett, 1982; Bowerman, 1977; Kuczaj, 1981, 1983; Mulford, 1977; Rosch, 1973; 1978; see also Barrett, this volume Chapter 2), although there is considerable debate and uncertainty concerning the exact nature of this representation.

Thus, controlled tests of the extension of children's words combined with information gained from diaries of naturalistically occurring speech can lead to at least some general tentative hypotheses about the nature of their meanings for children. However, all extensional or referential methods including controlled tests such as that of Kay and Anglin (1982) have limitations with respect to inferences that can be drawn from them with respect to the *meanings* and *knowledge* underlying children's words, three of which I will briefly mention here. First, one of the deepest problems as philosophers such as Nelson Goodman (1972) have pointed out is that if one establishes for a large but finite number of things those which are included versus those which are not in the extension of a given word for a given person, there is always an indefinitely large number of rules or properties which could have been the basis for classifying those things in that particular way. Thus, the intension or meaning of a word for a particular individual will always be underdetermined by extensional tests. A second limitation relates to a distinction between the core of a concept or the essential meaning of a word versus the identification procedure which enables classification or naming (e.g., Anglin, 1977; Miller & Johnson-Laird, 1976; Nelson, 1974; Smith & Medin, 1981), a distinction which is similar in a number of respects to that made earlier by Bruner, Goodnow, and Austin (1956) in their book, *A Study of Thinking*, between concept formation and concept attainment. It can be argued that extensional methods which are basically categorization, classification, or concept attainment methods are more revealing of the identification procedure than they are of the conceptual core or essential meaning of a word since such studies merely consist of having subjects *identify* things as either belonging or not belonging to a given concept or to the denotative scope of a given word (e.g., Anglin, 1982). The third and last limitation of extensional methods that I will mention concerns the domains of words to which such methods can be applied. Such methods can be used in the study of object names, as in my previous research and that of many others, and in the study of other domains of words (e.g., proper nouns, color terms, verbs of motion, etc.) for which it is possible to show the child referents and nonreferents of the word in question and to examine the child's tendency to include such stimuli within the denotative scope of the word in production and/or comprehension. However, it is harder to apply such methods to other interesting domains of words (e.g., relational terms such as *brother*, abstract nouns such as *idea*, verbs denoting mental processes such as *think*, functors such as *but*, etc.) because it is harder to show children in a clear and unambiguous fashion referents and contrastive nonreferents of such words.

Interview Studies

Given these and related problems with extensional methods, my students and I have turned to others, one of which I would like to comment upon here. This method—"the interview method"—is one in which, in our research, young children from about 3 years up to about 6 years as well as adults are interviewed and asked questions with respect to their knowledge of the meanings and concepts underlying certain words. In these studies this is accomplished by asking standard definition questions such as "What is a _____ ?" or "What does _____ mean?" for nouns or "What does to _____ mean?" or "What is _____ing?" for verbs. These questions are supplemented by a variety of other follow-up questions to probe the child's (and adult's) knowledge of the words further. Thus this approach is a kind of combination of the definitional procedure used by Feifel and Lorge (1950) and others and the clinical interview method used by Piaget (1929) and others. It is a method which can be used with children as young as 3 years in some cases at least, and it can be used to study a number of domains of words for which the extensional methods considered above are not appropriate. Moreover, the other problems associated with extensional methods discussed above do not really apply to the interview method, although as will become clear, this procedure does have its own problems and limitations. Still, my students and I have learned a number of interesting things using this method and have always found what the children say in the interview studies we have conducted fascinating.

I have reported the results from four of the first studies we have conducted using this method elsewhere (Anglin, 1977; 1978; 1985), and will just summarize a few of our findings here by comparing briefly the kinds of knowledge expressed by children and by adults for some fairly simple object names (e.g., *dog, car, flower, apple*, etc.) versus some fairly simple verbs (e.g., *eat, walk, play, talk*, etc.). In our interviews concerning concrete nouns or "basic level" names (e.g., Rosch, 1978; see also Anglin, 1977; Brown, 1958) preschool children proved to be most adept in describing their knowledge of four kinds of properties: (1) the appearances of referents of the words (e.g., "*round*" or "*red*" for *apple*), (2) their uses (e.g., "*you eat an apple*"), (3) their actions (e.g., "*it barks*" for *dog*), and (4) their locations (e.g., "*in the garage*" for *car*). Thus, they could often describe what referents of the word look like, how they are used, what they do, and where they are found (see also Norlin, 1980). Adults for these same words could also provide these kinds of information but would in addition frequently mention others such as superordinates of the word (e.g., "an apple is a *fruit* . . ."), and often more than one (e.g., "a dog is a *pet* . . . an *animal* . . . a *mammal* . . ."), the relations of referents of the word to other things (e.g., "A dog *has a brain which is bigger than a fish's but smaller than a human's*."), the constituents of referents of the word (e.g., "An apple *has a core and seeds inside it*."), the origins of referents of the word (e.g., "Some flowers *come from seeds*.") as well as some metaphorical extensions or derivative senses of the word (e.g., "*used in a derogatory sense to refer to someone held in low esteem*" for *dog*). Thus adults could often describe superordinate categories to which referents of the word belong, their relations to other things in the world, what they are made of, and where they come from, as well as metaphorical extensions and derivative senses of the words in addition to the four basic kinds of properties preschoolers could often describe.

In contrast, for relatively simple verbs preschool children in a number of studies have been found to be most adept at describing the *participants* in the activities or processes denoted by the verbs (e.g., "*People* walk.", "*Adults* kiss.", "*I* jump." etc.), the *objects* of the activities (e.g., "I eat *popcorn*.", "Mommy kisses *Daddy*.", "You bounce *balls*." etc.), the *locations* of the activities (e.g., "I eat *at the dinner table*.", "You play *in the park*.", "You float *on water*."), the situational contexts in which the activities take place (e.g., "You help someone *when they are hurt*.", "You kiss someone *good night*.", "You shake *when you are cold*."), and the instruments with which the activities are performed (e.g., "You eat *with a fork*.", "I talk *with my voice*.", "I kick *with my foot*."). Thus children in these studies have tended to provide information which answers the questions: "Who or what does it?"; "To what or whom is it done?"; "Where is it done?"; "When is it done?"; and "With what is it done?" (see also Nelson, 1978). Although they could occasionally produce information answering the question "How is it done?" they did not describe *processes* nearly as frequently as adults for whom description of processes was often the most frequent kind of response (e.g., "Eating involves *biting, chewing, and swallowing*.", "You float *by paddling your arms and kicking your feet gently*.", "You jump *by applying force through your legs and feet to impel you off the ground*."). Adults, who could express the kinds of information mentioned by children, could also provide information concerning the functions or purposes of the activities whereas children almost never did (e.g., "You eat *in order to nourish your body*.", "You talk *to communicate*."). Adults also often provided superordinates for the verbs (though not so frequently as for nouns) whereas children rarely did (e.g., "Thinking is a *mental process* . . .", "liking is a *feeling* . . .", "Jumping is *a physical activity* . . ."). Adults also provided more often than children other types of information such as metaphorical extensions and derivative senses of the words (e.g., "You can grow *emotionally*.", "*being on top of the world, a happy feeling*" for *float*, "*A cheque can bounce*." for *bounce*). Thus, when discussing the activities or processes denoted by the verbs we have studied, preschool children are fairly adept at stating who or what does it, to whom or what it is done, where it is done, when it is done, and with what it is done. However, although they occasionally mention how it is done, they do so far less often than adults for whom description of processes was often the most frequent kind of response. And children rarely mention why it is done, what kind of activity or process it is, or other statements including metaphorical extensions and derivative senses of the verbs which adults fairly often do. [It is interesting that much of what the children say about verbs can be captured by Fillmore's (1968) case categories whereas this is less true of what adults say.]

Although there are a few similarities in terms of the general kinds of information provided by children and adults for basic level nouns versus relatively simple verbs (e.g., mention of locational information by children in both cases; mention of superordinates and metaphorical extensions or derivative senses by adults but not by children in both cases) the differences are more numerous and striking. This has led me to the feeling that it is difficult to overestimate the importance of the semantic differences between different domains of words (see also Miller & Johnson-Laird, 1976), certainly between nouns and verbs (see Gentner, 1978, 1981, 1982). For example, many of the properties mentioned by children for verbs are simply different from those mentioned for nouns (e.g., instruments, participants or objects for verbs but not for nouns). This is true for adults also. One of the differences, I think, is worthy of special mention. Numerous previous studies of children's definitions and descriptions of words (e.g., Al-Issa, 1969; Feifel & Lorge, 1950; Nelson, 1978; Norlin, 1980; Watson, in press; Wolman & Barker, 1965) including some of my own studies (Anglin, 1977, 1978) have consistently reported that children often define words in terms of use or function. However, all of these studies focused primarily, and in many cases exclusively, on concrete nouns. In the studies of verbs alluded to above, however, although we found that adults often mentioned use or function in describing the verbs, preschool children rarely did for any of them. Thus the tendency in preschool children to define words in terms of use or function seems to apply especially to concrete nouns, but not to verbs.

Even in the cases of some of the apparent similarities in the information provided by adults and children for nouns versus verbs, there were differences. For example, metaphorical extensions and derivative senses were mentioned more frequently by adults for verbs than for nouns (cf. Gentner, 1981, 1982). With respect to the production of superordinates preschool children, while not adept at producing them in either case, did occasionally mention them for concrete nouns but virtually never did for relatively simple verbs. Adults who usually mentioned superordinates for nouns and often a number of them (e.g., *"pet"*, *"mammal"*, *"animal"*, *"living thing"* for *dog*) only occasionally mentioned more than one superordinate per verb and sometimes none at all. Adults also mentioned subordinates infrequently for the verbs whereas they usually mentioned many for the nouns (at least for basic level nouns and superordinates) suggesting that verbs do not have the hierarchical depth that many nouns do.

Thus, simple nouns appear to differ semantically from relatively simple verbs in adults as well as in children as Gentner (1978, 1981, 1982) has suggested. Also as Gentner has argued, it is my impression that preschool children often have a better appreciation of the meanings of simple nouns than they do of relatively simple verbs, at least as indicated by their definitions and descriptions.

In spite of these and other differences between nouns and verbs, there are some very general and quite related similarities in the ontogenetic trends we have found in all of our studies of children's and adults' definitions and descriptions of words, four of which I shall mention briefly here (see Anglin, 1985 for elaboration). First, younger children appear to base their responses upon their recollection of personal experiences to a greater degree than older children and adults. Second, younger children tend to mention more perceptually observable or concrete properties of the words. Increasingly with age, they mention in addition more subtle, more relational, and more abstract kinds of properties. Third, younger preschool children infrequently assign the words to a superordinate class. Increasingly with age and especially by adulthood they do so more frequently. Fourth, increasingly with age children, in their descriptions of words, approximate definitions, by which I mean they tend to supply the kinds of properties which are included in dictionary definitions of the words and which tend to specify all and only the referents of the words. One can postulate a continuum of word descriptions in terms of the extent to which they approximate definitions from not known, to responses based on personal experience, to characteristic properties, to some defining properties, to all or most defining properties. As children grow older their responses tend to move up this kind of scale as well (see Litowitz, 1977; see also Feifel & Lorge, 1950; Keil & Batterman, 1984).

I do believe interview studies such as these are of relevance to semantic and conceptual development in children, and I will indicate why I think so below, but I would like to describe first three of the limitations of this method which are important to bear in mind. First, this procedure is not suitable for use with children who are younger than about 3 years, even though there is no doubt that many children begin to learn about words and their meanings earlier than this, often beginning around their first birthday. Other methods will be necessary to study the semantic and conceptual development underlying the child's words during the earliest periods of language development. Second, because of the use of probe and follow up questions used in these interviews, there is always the possibility of suggesting to the child information about the words which he or she would not have been able to come up with on his or her own. Actually in the studies discussed above I believe this was rarely a problem since a deliberate attempt was made to use general probes which did not supply specific relevant information. Nonetheless, it should be mentioned that care should be taken in this kind of study to avoid leading questions lest one overestimate what the child knows. Third, there is the opposite and far more serious possibility of underestimating what the child knows on the basis of interview data. The interview task assesses what knowledge children can (or are willing to) articulate or express verbally about the words they attempt to describe. It is quite possible, indeed probable, that because of the metalinguistic nature of the task and/or constraints in children's powers of verbal expression, they may not always reveal all they know implicitly or tacitly about the words they are discussing. In at least two very important instances there is evidence that this is indeed the case. First, although in the studies of verbs mentioned above young children did not often describe how to perform the actions denoted by the verbs, they could more often show how to act out the verbs, actually or in pretense, when asked to do so by means of requests such as "Show me how to jump.", "Show we how to talk.", "Show me how to eat." and so on. Thus, it seems at some tacit level they appreciated the processes involved in the actions denoted by the verbs to a greater degree than they revealed in their verbal descriptions (see Anglin, 1985). Second, although our studies and those of others of the child's definitions and descriptions of concrete nouns have found that preschool children infrequently mention superordinates (such as *"animal"* for *dog*, *"plant"* for *flower*, or *"toy"* for *doll*) there is evidence from other studies using other methods (especially comprehension methods) which suggests that many preschoolers of 3 years and older do appreciate that dogs are called *"animals"*, that flowers are *"plants"*, and that dolls are *"toys"* etc. (see Anglin, 1977; Macnamara, 1982; Watson, in press).

Thus, in drawing inferences about the meanings of words for children and of the concepts they encode on the basis of interview data, I now feel that one can be fairly safe in attributing what the child expresses about words to his or her understanding of them (and this is often quite a lot), provided this knowledge was not suggested by leading questions. Thus, for example, on the basis of the interview studies summarized above even 3-year-old children can often be given credit for some understanding of the appearances, functions, actions, and typical locations of the referents of the kinds of nouns I have discussed. And they can often be given credit for some knowledge of the participants and objects, at times, of the instruments, and typical situational contexts and locations and, occasionally, of the processes associated with the kinds of verbs I have discussed. Therefore, such studies are relevant to our understanding of the semantic and conceptual knowledge underlying the child's words. But the interview method may well not tell us everything the child understandings implicitly or tacitly about his or her word meanings and word concepts, such as superordinates for nouns in *some* cases and processes for verbs in *some* cases, as indicated above.

Conclusion

I have argued that both extensional studies and interview studies are of some relevance for our understanding of the semantic and conceptual knowledge underlying the child's words, at least for the types of nouns and verbs that I have been discussing. For each kind of study I have tried to indicate at least some of the reasons why I think so in this chapter. However, as I have also suggested each of these methods, and ultimately I would argue all empirical methods, provide only indirect assessments of the nature of the semantic and conceptual knowledge underlying the child's words. Moreover, each of these methods is associated with certain limitations as far as assessing this knowledge is concerned.

I have emphasized these methodological issues not so much to be critical about my own work and related work of others but rather in the hope of coming to some valid conclusions about semantic and conceptual development. With respect to studies based on the methods I have been discussing, I believe that after one has taken into account their limitations and biases, there remains a residue of information which really is relevant to our understanding of the child's meanings and concepts as I hope I have indicated. Moreover, I would argue that, although each of these methods and presumably all empirical methods are associated with certain limitations and biases, the limitations and biases are not the same for different methods. This leads me to suggest that ultimately developmental psychologists and psycholinguists should use not one but a variety of different but complementary methods, if their goal is to come up with a relatively complete characterization of the child's word meanings and word concepts.

Undoubtedly various methods, in addition to those considered in this chapter, that have been and will be used by researchers in this field are and will be relevant to characterizing the knowledge underlying children's words. In this regard, I suspect that various kinds of comprehension tests and also careful examination of the child's use of words in naturalistic discourse and/or more controlled settings may prove to be especially illuminating.

Acknowledgments. Parts of this chapter were presented in a talk entitled "The child's word concepts and word meanings" which was my contribution to a symposium entitled *Concepts, Words, and Meanings: Interrelationships between Semantic and Conceptual Development* held at the *Society for Research in Child Development* in Toronto, Canada, April, 1985. An earlier version of it was also presented in a talk entitled "Recent research in semantic development" given in June, 1984, at the *Fifth International Summer Institute for Semiotic and Structural Studies* sponsored by the Toronto Semiotic Circle in a symposium entitled *Phylogeny and Ontogeny of Communication Systems*. A summary of the proceedings of the latter conference is to be published by the *Toronto Semiotic Circle*. I would like to thank the students who helped with the studies referred to here and in particular Marc Fiedler, Sophia Cohen, Deborah Kay, Lois Campbell, Joanne Gallivan, and Janet McPharlin. While writing this paper I have been supported in my research on language development by a grant from the Natural Sciences and Engineering Research Council of Canada, support for which I am most grateful.

References

Al-Issa, I. (1969). The development of word definitions in children. *Journal of Genetic Psychology, 114*, 25-28.

Anglin, J. M. (1977). *Word, object, and conceptual development*. New York: Norton.

Anglin, J. M. (1978). From reference to meaning. *Child Development, 49*, 969-976.

Anglin, J. M. (1979). The child's first terms of reference. In N. R. Smith & M. B. Franklin (Eds.), *Symbolic functioning in childhood*. Hillsdale, NJ: Erlbaum.

Anglin, J. M. (1982). Modeling conceptual structure. Review of E. Smith and D. Medin, *Categories and concepts. Canadian Journal of Psychology, 9*, 554-558.

Anglin, J. M. (1983). Extensional aspects of the preschool child's word concepts. In T. Seiler & W. Wannenmacher (Eds.), *Concept development and the development of word meaning*. New York: Springer-Verlag.

Anglin, J. M. (1985). The child's expressible knowledge of word concepts: What preschoolers can say about the meaning of some nouns and verbs. In K. E. Nelson (Ed.), *Children's language: Volume 5*. Hillsdale, NJ: Erlbaum.

Barrett, M. D. (1978). Lexical development and overextension in child language. *Journal of Child Language, 5*, 205-219.

Barrett, M. D. (1982). Distinguishing between prototypes: The early acquisition of the meaning of object names. In S. A. Kuczaj (Ed.), *Language development, volume 1: Syntax and semantics*. Hillsdale, NJ: Erlbaum.

Barrett, M. D. (in press). Early semantic representations and early word usage. In S. A. Kuczaj & M. D. Barrett (Eds.), *The development of word meaning*. New York: Springer-Verlag.

Bates, E. (1976). *Language and context*. New York: Academic Press.

Bloom, L. M. (1973). *One word at a time*. The Hague: Mouton.

Bowerman, M. (1977). The acquisition of word meaning: An investigation of some current conflicts. In N. Waterson & C. Snow (Eds.), *Proceedings of the third international child language symposium*. New York: Wiley.

Brown, R. (1958). How shall a thing be called? *Psychological Review, 65*, 14-21.
Bruner, J. S., Goodnow, J., & Austin, G. (1956). *A study of thinking.* New York: Wiley.
Chamberlain, A. F., & Chamberlain, J. C. (1904). Studies of a child I. *Pedagogical Seminary, 11*, 264-291.
Clark, E. V. (1973). What's in a word? On the child's acquisition of semantics in his first language. In T. E. Moore (Ed.), *Cognitive development and the acquisition of language.* New York: Academic Press.
Clark, E. V. (1979). Building a vocabulary: Words for objects, actions, and relations. In P. Fletcher & M. Garman (Eds.), *Studies in language acquisition.* Cambridge: Cambridge University Press.
Clark, H. H., & Clark, E. V. (1977). *Psychology and language.* New York: Harcourt Brace Jovanovich.
Feifel, H., & Lorge, I. (1950). Qualitative differences in the vocabulary responses of children. *Journal of Educational Psychology, 41*, 1-18.
Fillmore, C. (1968). The case for case. In E. Bach & T. Harms (Eds.), *Universals in linguistic theory.* New York: Holt, Rinehart, and Winston.
Fremgen, A., & Fay, D. (1980). Overextensions in production and comprehension: A methodological clarification. *Journal of Child Language, 7*, 205-211.
Gentner, D. (1978). On relational meaning: The acquisition of verb meaning. *Child Development, 49*, 988-998.
Gentner, D. (1981). Some interesting differences between verbs and nouns. *Cognition and Brain Theory, 4*(2), 161-178.
Gentner, D. (1982). Why nouns are learned before verbs: Linguistic relativity versus natural partitioning. In S. Kuczaj (Ed.), *Language development: Language, cognition and culture.* Hillsdale, NJ: Erlbaum.
Goodman, N. (1972). On likeness of meaning. In N. Goodman (Ed.), *Problems and projects.* New York: Bobbs-Merrill.
Gruendel, J. M. (1977). Referential extension in early child language. *Child Development, 42*, 1567-1576.
Huttenlocher, J. (1974). The origins of language comprehension. In R. L. Solso (Ed.), *Theories in cognitive psychology.* Hillsdale, NJ: Erlbaum.
Kay, D., & Anglin, J. M. (1982). Overextension and underextension in the child's expressive and receptive speech. *Journal of Child Language, 9*, 83-98.
Keil, F. C., & Batterman, N. (1984). A characteristic to defining shift in the development of word meaning. *Journal of Verbal Learning and Verbal Behavior, 23*, 221-236.
Kuczaj, S. A. (1982). Young children's overextensions of object words in comprehension and/or production: Support for a prototype theory of early object word meaning. *First Language, 3*, 93-105.
Kuczaj, S. A. (1983). On the acquisition of the notion of types of flying objects: Support for prototype-based theories of word meaning development. In D. Rogers & J. A. Sloboda (Eds.), *The acquisition of symbolic skills.* New York: Plenum Publishing Corporation.
Leopold, W. F. (1939). *Speech development of a bilingual child: A linguist's record, Vol. 1. Vocabulary growth in the first two years.* Evanston, IL: Northwestern University Press.
Leopold, W. F. (1949). *Speech development of a bilingual child, vol. 3. Grammar and general problems in the first two years.* Evanston, IL: Northwestern University Press.
Lewis, M. M. (1959). *How children learn to speak.* New York: Basic Books.
Litowitz, R. (1977). Learning to make definitions. *Journal of Child Language, 4*, 289-304.
Macnamara, J. (1982). *Names for things: A study of human learning.* Cambridge, MA: The M.I.T. Press.

Miller, G. A., & Johnson-Laird, P. N. (1976). *Language and perception*. Cambridge, MA: Harvard University Press.

Moore, K. C. (1896). The mental development of the child. *Psychological Review Monograph Supplements*, *1*(3).

Mulford, R. (1977). Prototypicality and the development of categorization. Paper presented at the Boston University Child Language Conference.

Nelson, K. (1974). Concept, word and sentence: Interrelations in acquisition and development. *Psychological Review*, *81*, 267-285.

Nelson, K. (1978). Semantic development and the development of semantic memory. In K. E. Nelson (Ed.), *Children's language* (Vol. 1). New York: Gardner Press.

Nelson, K., Rescorla, L., Gruendel, J., & Benedict, H. (1978). Early lexicons: What do they mean? *Child Development*, *49*, 960-968.

Norlin, P. F. (1980). The development of relational arcs in the lexical semantic memory structures of young children. *Journal of Child Language*, *8*, 385-402.

Piaget, J. (1929). *The child's conception of the world*. London: Routledge and Kegan Paul.

Piaget, J. (1962). *Play, dreams, and imitation in childhood*. New York: Norton.

Putnam, H. (1975). The meaning of "meaning". In K. Gunderson (Ed.), *Language, mind, and knowledge, vol. 7. Minnesota studies in the philosophy of science*. Minneapolis, MN: University of Minnesota Press.

Rescorla, L. (1980). Overextension in early language development. *Journal of Child Language*, *7*, 321-335.

Rosch, E. (1973). On the internal structure of perceptual and semantic categories. In T. Moore (Ed.), *Cognition and the acquisition of language*. New York: Academic Press.

Rosch, E. (1978). Principles of categorization. In E. Rosch & B. Lloyd (Eds.), *Cognition and categorization*. Hillsdale, NJ: Erlbaum.

Smith, E. E., & Medin, D. (1981). *Categories and concepts*. Cambridge, MA: Harvard University Press.

Thomson, J. R., & Chapman, R. S. (1977). Who is 'Daddy' revisited: The status of two-year-olds' overextended words in use and comprehension. *Journal of Child Language*, *4*, 359-375.

Watson, R. (in press). Toward a theory of definition. *Journal of Child Language*.

Winner, E. (1979). New names for old things: The emergence of metaphoric language. *Journal of Child Language*, *6*, 469-491.

Wolman, R. N., & Barker, E. N. (1965). A developmental study of word definitions. *Journal of Genetic Psychology*, *107*, 159-166.

5. Thoughts on the Intensional Basis of Early Object Word Extension: Evidence From Comprehension and Production

Stan A. Kuczaj, II

Children begin to build what will eventually become an extensive and well-integrated lexicon by learning to comment on salient aspects of their environment. Although a few of children's first words may refer to actions or states (e.g., *up*, *off*) or serve a social function (e.g., *hi*, *night-night*), the vast majority of the words that children first learn to use refer to important and/or interesting objects, such as people, animals, vehicles, toys, body parts, clothes, and household items (Anderson, 1978; Benedict, 1978, 1979; Clark, 1983; Nelson, 1973; Nice, 1915; Rescorla, 1980). Not surprisingly, then, many investigators have attempted to determine the manner in which young children learn object words (see Clark, 1983, for a discussion of this literature). Although there are many important aspects of this phenomenon (e.g., why do young children focus on objects in their environment rather than actions or states? What sorts of objects are young children most likely to learn to name?), this chapter will focus on only one aspect of object word meaning: the relation of children's extension patterns in production and comprehension, and the implications of these extension patterns for our understanding of the nature of object word meaning in young children's lexicons.

Object Word Meaning

The meaning of object words consists of two related components: extension and intension. *Extension* has to do with the referents of an object word and may be represented by listing the exemplars. Thus, the extension of *dog* is all of the dogs in existence but nothing that is not a dog. *Intension* has to do with the criteria for determining what is and is not an exemplar. Thus, intension determines extension. It is difficult, however, to study intension in any direct manner, and so researchers have typically examined children's extensional decisions in order to infer the intensional bases of these decisions (Clark, 1973; Nelson, 1974). The assumption underlying such investigations is that by studying children's *use* (extension) of words, one may somehow ascertain the nature of the meaning (intension) children attached to words.

Children's Extension Errors

Perhaps the best example of this approach to the study of early lexical development is that which focuses on the errors that young children make when using object words. Although children may err by using words in some inconsistent fashion, errors that occur consistently (at least for a particular word for a particular child) are theoretically more interesting, for consistency of use (correct or incorrect) is necessary if one hopes to ascertain the intensional bases of extensional decisions.

There seem to be three types of consistent extension errors that occur in the speech of young children (Clark, 1983): (1) overextension errors, (2) underextension errors, and (3) overlap errors. Overextension errors occur when a child uses a word to refer to an overly broad array of objects. For example, *dog* might be used to refer to sheep, cats, and goats as well as to dogs. If one assumes that extension reflects intension, then it would seem that children who overextend terms have attached too broad a meaning to the overextended terms.

Underextension errors occur when a child uses a word to refer to only a limited set of the appropriate exemplars. For example, *dog* might be used to refer to only a particular dog or to a particular type of dog. Assuming that extension reflects intension, children's underextension errors result from children attaching too narrow a meaning to the underextended terms.

Overlap errors are those in which a child's use of a word overlaps partially with two or more adult words. For example, *dog* might be used to refer to only large dogs and calves, but not to smaller dogs or to cows, and so would overlap partially with the adult meanings of *dog* and *cow*. Overlap errors involve a combination of overextension and underextension, and so would seem to reflect meanings which are both too broad and too narrow by adult standards.

Overextension, underextension, and overlap errors are interesting not only because they demonstrate that children do not always know the correct extension of a term when they are able to produce the term, but also because such errors suggest that the intension (meaning) of such terms is qualitatively different than that of adults, the qualitative difference between child and adult meanings having to do with breadth of extension. Children's extension errors seem to reflect the entire range of possible errors in intensional decisions: overly broad intensions, overly narrow intensions, or a combination of the two.

The Comprehension/Production Issue

In the above discussion of children's extension errors, I assumed that such errors reflect the intension that children have attached to the terms for which the errors occur. In other words, the reference errors that children make in their use of object words may reflect the meaning that the children have attached to the object words. The assumption, then, is that use (reference) reflects meaning. If reference and meaning are sufficiently linked to yield accurate hypotheses about meaning from reference data, then one might expect errors in production to also be reflected in comprehension, and vice versa. After all, if meaning determines use, then it should not make much difference if the use is in the production mode or the comprehension mode. However, many investigators have noted that children seem more likely to understand a word than to produce it (Benedict, 1978; Goldin-Meadow, Seligman, & Gleman, 1976; Grégoire, 1937; Huttenlocher, 1974; Leopold, 1949; Lewis, 1951; Rescorla, 1976). Thus, there seems to be an asymmetry between production and comprehension that is at odds with the notion that intension determines extension, at least insofar as the use of object words by young children is concerned.

Regarding overextension, underextension, and overlap errors, one might expect that if, in fact, children's extension errors mirror the actual meanings that children have attached to the misextended terms, children who misextend terms in production should also do so in comprehension, and vice versa. However, such has not always proved to be the case. Young children's overextensions in production are not always reflected in comprehension. In a pioneering study, Thomson and Chapman (1977) provided children who had overextended words in production with a forced-choice comprehension situation in which they were asked to indicate which of a pair of objects was an exemplar of an overextended term. Each pair of objects consisted of an appropriate exemplar and an object to which the child had overextended the term in production. In this situation, children either overextended the term in both comprehension and production (40% of the cases) or overextended the term only in production (60% of the cases). Fremgen and Fay (1980) conducted a similar study in which the results were even more straightforward: none of the children tested overextended words in comprehension that they had overextended in production.

The lack of correspondence between children's use of a term in production and in comprehension has been thought to reflect task difficulty (Fremgen & Fay, 1980; Huttenlocher, 1974; Thomson & Chapman, 1977) and/or deliberate misuse by the child of the overextended word (Bloom, 1973; Clark, 1978; Fremgen & Fay, 1980; Hudson & Nelson, 1984; Nelson, Rescorla, & Gruendel, 1978). Nelson et al. proposed that what have been termed overextensions may in fact be merely assertions of similarity between two objects (judgments of analogy rather than equivalence), a view anticipated by Bloom (1973), as illustrated in the following statement concerning overextension errors:

> It is almost as if the child were reasoning, 'I know about dogs, that thing is not a dog, I don't know what to call it, but it is like a dog.' (p. 79).

Similarly, Clark (1978) argued that young and relatively inarticulate children are applying words from their limited lexicons that best fit the context. In this view, at least some of the children's overextensions are partial rather than complete, such inappropriate uses appearing because children apply the *overextended* words when there is a certain degree of overlap between what they have perceived as the appropriate conditions of application and the properties of the objects to which they wish to direct the listener's attention. In other words, Clark assumed that some overextensions result because of a communication strategy employed by young children rather than as a result of an erroneous attachment by the child of an overly broad meaning to the terms in question. Clark suggested that at least some overextended terms do in fact reflect the too general meanings children have attached to them (Clark, 1983), but she has abandoned her earlier assertion (Clark, 1973) that all overextensions in some sense reflect the meanings the child has attached to the overextended terms.

The asymmetry between production and comprehension is not always such that comprehension is more accurate than production. Children may produce words that they do not accurately comprehend (Leonard, Newhoff, & Fey, 1980; Leonard & Schwartz, 1981; Nelson & Bonvillian, 1978; Rice, in press; see Leonard, 1983, for a discussion of the methodological difficulties inherent in studies that indicate production before comprehension). Rice (in press) suggested that production before comprehension occurs when the word is easier to recall than is the concept. Thus, children are able to produce the word, but are not able to recall the meaning of the word.

Asymmetries in comprehension and production, then, seem to reflect different types of difficulties in relating words and meanings. When production occurs in the absence of comprehension, children have failed to recall the word's meaning (or what they knew of it) even though they are able to produce the word. Such results are similar to young children's counting skills, in which they are able to produce a string of numbers, but evidence no understanding of what the numbers mean (Gelman & Gallistel, 1978). When comprehension seems to either procede or be more accurate than production, children have either failed to acquire words that can express what they know, or are unable to recall the word that they know even though they can recall the meaning.

Clearly, both production and comprehension must be considered in accounts of lexical development. In production, children have in mind the concept to which they intend to refer, and must choose from the words they know in order to try to succeed at their referential attempt. In comprehension, children attempt to recognize the words that they hear, and then determine the concept to which they refer. According to Clark (1983),

> Production is not simply the inverse of comprehension: the two processes are quite distinct. Production requires an active search for available words and expressions combined with an evaluation of whether they are appropriate to label the concepts to be conveyed and to call up these concepts in the addressee. Comprehension requires recognition of a word as known, followed by a search for the conceptual category usually picked out by that term to arrive at the speaker's intended meaning (p. 911).

Keenan and MacWhinney (1984) have offered an account of the relation of production and comprehension that emphasizes the similarities and differences between two modes of lexical processing. Their account assumes that there are three developmental processes involved in comprehension and production: (1) the acquisition of the concept to which the form refers, (2) the acquisition of the form itself, and (3) the acquisition of the mapping relations between the form and concept. Production and comprehension are similar in that the concept to which the form refers is similar in both modes. The form is also similar in production and comprehension, although the processes involved in producing a form are different than those involved in recognizing a form. The main difference between comprehension and production is in the mapping relation between form and function (as Rice, in press, has also noted). Comprehension involves a mapping from form to concept, whereas production involves a mapping from concept to form.

Given all this, it is not surprising that there are asymmetries in production and comprehension in the early phases of lexical-meaning acquisition. Lexical-meaning acquisition involves both comprehension and production, but mastery in one does not guarantee mastery in the other. Under certain circumstances, children may have better mastery in production than in comprehension. Under other circumstances, children may be better able to comprehend an item than to produce it.

Summary

Historically, a fair amount of theorizing has focused on the discovery that young children frequently overextend the meaning of early object words. For example, the term *doggy* might be used to refer to a variety of animals, only some of which are dogs. Overextensions were initially thought to reflect an overly broad intensional system on the part of the young child, the basic notion being that the overextensions directly reflected the meaning children had granted the overextended object terms (Clark, 1973; Nelson, 1974). The fact that overextension errors in production were not always reflected in comprehension (Huttenlocher, 1974; Thomson & Chapman, 1977) cast some doubt on the assumption that overextension errors have any direct relation to intension, suggesting that such errors instead reflected the children's limited vocabularies and/or communicative strategies (Bloom, 1973; Clark, 1978; Nelson, Rescorla, & Gruendel, 1978). This possibility resulted in a shift in emphasis in regard to children's early overextension errors. Rather than attempting to describe the intensional bases for these errors, researchers instead began to ascertain the relation between such errors in production and in comprehension. These efforts suggested that there are indeed asymmetries in overextension errors in production and in comprehension, highlighting possible processing differences between production and comprehension.

The Notion of Prototypes and Its Implications for the Comprehension/Production Issue

It is not necessarily the case, however, that there is no relation between production and comprehension in young children's lexicons. Young children can produce and comprehend many words equally well. Moreover, overextension errors in production are at least occasionally reflected in comprehension. Thomson and Chapman (1977) did find some overextensions in comprehension as well as in production despite the general finding of more overextensions in production than in comprehension. Other investigators have also reported overextensions in both comprehension and production (Anglin, 1977; Chapman, Leonard, Rowan, & Weiss, 1983; Kay & Anglin, 1982; Mervis & Canada, 1983). Moreover, children's failure to overextend words in comprehension that they do overextend in production may reflect an overly broad meaning *of a particular type* that at least some comprehension tasks would fail to accurately diagnose. The phrase *overly broad meaning of a particular type* will be expanded upon below in the discussion of a prototype approach to object word meaning (based on Rosch's work on category formation and structure, see Rosch & Lloyd, 1978). Basically, this approach assumes that the meaning a child grants an object word is based on a small number of prototypic exemplars (best examples) and that overextension errors result from the child erroneously relating the referents to which the word is overextended to the prototype(s) the child has for the overextended term. Although there is considerable disagreement about the exact nature of a concept's prototypes and the role such prototypes play in concept intension and extension (Anglin, 1977; Bowerman, 1975; Greenberg & Kuczaj, 1982; Mulford, 1977), the concern here is with the degree to which a prototype-based theory of object word meaning acquisition can account for the relative lack of overextensions in comprehension situations.

It is possible that in the comprehension of a word the child *begins* by looking for a prototypic exemplar but will choose less prototypic exemplars, including those to which the word is overextended, if given the opportunity. Thus, if the meanings children attach to object words that they overextend in production consist of prototype-based representations of appropriate referents (appropriate to the child, that is) and overly broad intensional bases for extension, children might fail to overextend terms in comprehension that they do overextend in production because the representations of an object word's prototypic referents might dominate initial comprehension decisions (decisions involving recognition skills) more so than initial production decisions (decisions involving recall skills).

In one attempt to assess this possibility, Kuczaj (1982) assessed six children's comprehension of words that they were overextending in production. The comprehension task differed from that of other investigators (e.g., Thomson & Chapman, 1977; Fremgen & Fay, 1980) in that children were provided with an array of objects from which to choose the target exemplar(s). For each target word, the child was shown a group of six objects (two appropriate exemplars, two objects to which the term had been overextended in production, and two obvious nonexemplars), and asked to give or show the investigator a *target word*. Following each response, the child was again asked to give the investigator a *target word*. This procedure was repeated until the child declined to give the investigator any of the remaining objects. This procedure provided information concerning the number of objects a child would give the investigator for a particular term and information concerning the order in which the child chose the objects. The nonexemplars were used to insure that children were not giving objects simply to give objects.

In the comprehension task, children were more likely to choose correct exemplars as referents of the target words than to choose the objects to which they had overextended the terms in production. Children were also more likely to choose the objects to which the terms had been overextended in production than to choose the obvious nonexemplars. The data were also interesting in regard to the relations between children's choices and the order in which these choices were made. Appropriate objects were most likely to be chosen on children's first and second choices while overextended objects were most likely to be chosen on children's third and fourth choices. The total number of objects chosen on the fifth and sixth choices was three and zero respectively, suggesting that the children were not simply choosing all of the objects in each referent array but were instead in most cases choosing those objects that they considered to be exemplars of the target terms.

These data suggest that the terms children overextend in production may also be overextended in comprehension if the comprehension task provides sufficient opportunity for overextension errors. Children may not appear to overextend terms in comprehension because they tend to choose objects that are prototypic insofar as the concepts underlying their use of the terms is concerned. Although the prototypes of particular concepts may vary from child to child and from child to adult (Carey, 1978), the prototypes are most likely to be appropriate exemplars (assuming that such exemplars are most frequent in the context in which the child hears the terms, this increasing the likelihood that some appropriate exemplars will be viewed as prototypic by the child). The result is that children will view at least some appropriate exemplars as prototypic or more prototypic than exemplars to which they overextend particular terms and so initially choose such appropriate exemplars rather than the overextended exemplars. The important point is that such a pattern does *not* mean that children will invariably fail to overextend terms in comprehension. Instead this reflects the more prototypic status of the appropriate exemplars, the less prototypic exemplars (including at least some to which the term is overextended) being chosen after the more prototypic exemplars *if* children are given the opportunity to make subsequent choices.

The following study supports and refines these findings and speculations. This sample of 20 children who overextended certain terms and underextended other terms in production consisted of ten males and ten females ranging in age from 1;11 to 2;7, with a mean age of 2;4.

Initially, a set of six words was individually constructed for each child, based on parental reports and pilot testing. Three of these words were overextended by the child in production. Three other words were underextended in production. Based on this, a production task was constructed in which the child was asked to name 72 objects (six appropriate exemplars for each term, 3 objects to which each term was thought to be overextended for the overextended terms or to which each term could possibly be overextended in the case of underextended terms, and 18 objects that bore no relation to any of the target terms). As will be shown, children did in fact overextend some terms and underextend others in the production task. Such a pattern is not surprising, for children most definitely overextend and underextend words in production (Anglin, 1977; Clark, 1983). How, though, were these errors reflected in children's comprehension?

The comprehension task involved the simultaneous presentation of twelve objects for each of the words assessed in production. Six objects were appropriate exemplars, three objects were either objects to which the word had been overextended in production (for overextended terms) or objects to which the term might be overextended (for underextended terms), and three objects were obvious nonexemplars. Upon being presented with the array of objects for a target term, the child was asked to give the investigator a *target term*, asked to do so again after the object the child had offered was noted and put away, and so on until the child ceased to give an object when asked to do so. This procedure was repeated for each target term for each child.

Results

In both the comprehension task and the production task, children's responses were scored as appropriate, underextended, overextended, or inappropriate. Appropriate responses were those in which the child chose or labeled an object with the appropriate word. There were six appropriate objects for each term, and so children's scores for each term could range from zero to six appropriate responses. Underextension responses were those in which a child failed to choose or label an exemplar with the appropriate term. Given the six appropriate objects for each term, children's underextension scores for each term could range from zero to six. However, the sum of the appropriate responses and the underextended responses could be no more (and no less) than six for any of the target terms, given that the two response types were assessed with the same six objects. Overextension responses were those in which a child chose or labeled one of the designated *overextendable* objects with a word. There were three objects to which each term might be overextended in both tasks. Moreover, there were a variety of other objects available for labeling in the production task and for choosing in the comprehension task. These objects were occasionally inappropriately labeled (in the production task) or chosen (in the comprehension task), but such errors were sufficiently rare (and never consistent across tasks) to preclude further consideration. In the following, the consideration of overextension errors reflects children's use of the objects that were legitimate contenders for overextension errors.

Certain results are summarized in Tables 5-1 and 5-2. Table 5-1 shows the average number of appropriate exemplars labeled in the production task and chosen in the comprehension task for each of the six target terms (three overextended terms and three underextended terms per child). Table 5-2 shows the average number of objects to which a term was overextended in the production task and in the comprehension task.

To assess the statistical significance of the differences shown in Tables 5-1 and 5-2, the responses given by each child were grouped according to word-type (overextended and underextended), response-type (the number of times an appropriate exemplar was chosen or labeled; the number of times a word was overextended), and task (production vs. comprehension). Initial analyses failed to yield significant sex differences, and so gender was not considered in later analyses.

Children were more likely to correctly label appropriate exemplars with overextended words than with underextended words in the production task; $t(19)=22.74$,

Table 5-1. Mean Number of Appropriate Exemplars Chosen in the Comprehension Task or Labeled in the Production Task per Target Term in the First Testing Session

Type of term	Comprehension	Production
Overextended	4.7	5.4
Underextended	2.2	1.6

$p < .001$. Similarly, appropriate exemplars were more likely to be correctly chosen for overextended words than for underextended words in the comprehension task; $t(19) = 12.29$, $p < .001$. In both the comprehension and production tasks, then, children were more likely to correctly use appropriate objects in connection with overextended words than with underextended words.

Nonetheless, there were differences between the comprehension and production tasks in regard to the use of appropriate exemplars. Moreover, these differences interacted with word-type. For overextended words, children were more likely to label appropriate exemplars in production than to choose them in comprehension; $t(19) = 3.59$, $p < .01$. However, children were more likely to choose appropriate exemplars in comprehension than to label them in production insofar as underextended terms were concerned; $t(19) = 3.9$, $p < .001$.

To no one's surprise, I am certain, children were more likely to label the overextendable objects in the production task and to choose them in the comprehension task when using an overextended term than when using an underextended term; $t(19) = 26.29$, $p < .001$ for the production task; $t(19) = 15.83$, $p < .001$ for the comprehension task. Overextension errors were more likely to occur in production than in comprehension for overextended words; $t(19) = 2.69$, $p < .05$. However, underextended words were more likely to be overextended in comprehension than in production; $t(19) = 6.48$, $p < .001$.

The data considered above demonstrate that we were successful in selecting children who overextended and underextended words. Words that were thought (by the parents and investigators) to be overextended were in fact overextended, while words that were thought to be underextended were extended in this manner, particularly insofar as production was concerned. Given that children were selected in regard to their use of words in production, this is not surprising. Although the data summarized in Tables 5-1 and 5-2 are useful in determining our accuracy in selecting children who exhibited the extensional patterns of interest, they are useless in regard to the issue of whether asymmetry or symmetry is the rule insofar as extension in production and comprehension is concerned. The data discussed to this point have

Table 5-2. Mean Number of Objects to Which a Term Was Overextended in Comprehension and Production in the First Testing Session

Type of term	Comprehension	Production
Overextended	2.6	2.8
Underextended	.7	.1

been group data, but data about the relation of a word's extension in production to its extension in comprehension is necessary in order to address the issue of symmetry (or its lack) across the two communication modes.

First, a word about the scoring decisions is in order. A word was viewed as overextended but not underextended if all six of the appropriate exemplars were labeled or chosen, and at least one of the overextendable objects was incorrectly labeled or chosen. A word was viewed as underextended but not overextended if it was used in connection with only some of the appropriate objects and none of the overextendable objects. A word was categorized as both overextended and underextended (an overlap error) if the child used the word in connection with some but not all of the appropriate exemplars, and also used the word in connection with at least one of the overextendable objects. By categorizing each word as either overextended, underextended, or an overlap error in production and doing the same in comprehension, it became possible to determine whether each of the 120 words studied involved symmetry or asymmetry in regard to their extension in comprehension and in production.

Using the above criteria, there were 61 instances of symmetry and 59 instances of asymmetry, hardly sufficient evidence to resolve the issue. Nonetheless, a finer-grained look at the extension patterns is a bit more illuminating. The most common type of symmetry was that in which an overlap pattern occurred for a given word in both comprehension and production. This occurred for 30 words, 25 of which were originally designated as overextended words (obviously, the remaining 5 words were initially designated as underextended words). Of the 31 remaining instances of symmetry, 18 involved words that were underextended in both comprehension and production, and 13 involved words that were overextended in both comprehension and production. Thus, in regard to symmetry of word extension in comprehension and production, overlap errors were most frequent, followed by underextension errors which, in turn, were more frequent than overextension errors.

There were two main types of asymmetry that occurred. The most common type of asymmetry involved words that were underextended in production, but for which overlap errors occurred in comprehension. This pattern was observed for 35 words. The other main type of asymmetry, which occurred for 21 words, consisted of overextension errors in production but overlap errors in comprehension. The remaining three instances of asymmetry involved three words for which overlap errors occurred in production, two of these words being underextended in comprehension, the remaining word being overextended in comprehension.

The significance of these patterns depends, in part, on the extent to which they are consistent for individual children. Perhaps all children employ each of the above patterns, depending on the word being acquired and its phase of acquisition. If so, the relation between extension in comprehension and extension in production depends on the word being acquired (and its relation to other words in the child's lexicon) and how much (and what sort of) meaning the child has attached to it. Or, children might exhibit the same symmetrical (or asymmetrical) pattern consistently, but differ from one another because they employ different strategies in their acquisition of word meaning. For example, some children might overextend in production but not in comprehension, others might consistently overextend in both, and so on. The following analyses, although far from sufficiently rich to resolve the issue of general developmental patterns versus individual differences, suggest the general direction in which such a resolution might go.

Each child was categorized as having exhibited each of the observed extensional relations for no words, 1 word, 2 words, or 3 words. (There were no instances in which a child used one of the patterns with more than three words.) The 13 words that were overextended in production and comprehension (symmetry) were used by five children. Moreover, four of the children accounted for 12 of these words (three words each). The 18 words that were underextended in production and comprehension (symmetry) were used by nine children. Three children accounted for 3 words each, three other children for two words each, and three other children for 1 word each. Curiously, eight of these nine children and four of the five children who exhibited symmetrical overextension patterns did not overlap with one another. The one child who exhibited symmetrical patterns for both an overextended term and an underextended term did so for one overextended term and one underextended term. It seems that children who exhibit symmetrical overextension patterns are most likely to do so for all or most of the words that they overextend, and that they are also unlikely to exhibit symmetrical underextension patterns. Children who exhibit symmetrical underextension patterns are unlikely to do so for overextended terms, but may exhibit symmetrical extension patterns for only some, most, or all of the words that they are underextending. These patterns suggest that individual differences exist in regard to symmetrical extension patterns. Some children are more likely to produce them for overextended terms, while other children are more likely to do so for underextended terms. Apparently, rarely the twain shall meet (my apologies to Kipling).

The remaining 30 words for which symmetrical extension patterns were observed were those for which overlap errors occurred in both production and comprehension. The 5 of these words that were primarily underextended were used by five different children (one word each), while the 25 words that were primarily overextended were used by eleven children. Six children accounted for 18 of these words (3 words each), two children for 2 words each, and three children for 1 word each. Although children were much more likely to exhibit symmetrical overlap errors for overextended terms than for underextended terms (in regard to the primary extension pattern), it is unclear whether children who do so for overextended words are unlikely to do so for underextended words. Although seven children who exhibited this pattern for overextended terms did not do so for any underextended term, four children exhibited the pattern for both overextended terms and one underextended term (a different underextended term for each of the four children).

The asymmetrical patterns that were observed were rather evenly spread across the sample of 20 children, particularly for those words that were underextended in production, but for which overlap errors occurred in comprehension. Of the 35 words that fell into this category, five children accounted for 3 words each, eight children for 2 words each, and four children for 1 word each. Only three children did not use a word that fell into this category, suggesting that this pattern may be a prevalent one in the acquisition of object word meaning.

The 21 words that were overextended in production but overextended and underextended (overlap errors) in comprehension were accounted for by 10 children. Four children accounted for 3 words each, three children for 2 words each, and three children for 1 word each. (The other three instances of asymmetry, discussed earlier, were produced by three different children.) Although children were more likely to produce asymmetrical patterns for words that were underextended in production than for words that were overextended in production, it did not seem to be the case that one type of asymmetrical pattern consistently precluded the other for individual children.

Only one child produced symmetrical extension patterns for all six target words (three underextended words and three overlap errors). The remaining 19 children produced both symmetrical and asymmetrical patterns.

These findings suggest that each of the extension patterns may be used by children, depending on the phase of acquisition of the words being acquired, with one possible exception. Children who produce symmetrical overextensions do not produce symmetrical underextensions, and vice versa. These speculations are somewhat lacking in that they are based on data obtained from children at one point in time. Thus, they do not provide much information about developmental patterns for extensional symmetries and asymmetries. In order to provide a better data base from which to ascertain such developmental patterns, 18 of the 20 children were retested with the original production and comprehension tasks 6 to 7 weeks after they had been given the first set of tasks (the remaining 2 children were unavailable for retesting).

Results of the Second Testing Session

Of the 108 words assessed in the retesting (6 words each for 18 children), there were 84 instances of symmetrical extension patterns across production and comprehension, but only 24 asymmetrical extension patterns. This difference is statistically significant; $t(17) = 8.72$, $p < .001$. The initial testing and the retesting differed in terms of the relative frequency of symmetrical and asymmetrical extension patterns. In the initial testing, there was virtually no difference, whereas in the retesting there was a decided difference in favor of symmetrical extension patterns. Moreover, of the 53 words with symmetrical patterns used by these 18 children in the first testing session, 39 were symmetrical in retesting. On the other hand, 45 of the 55 words with asymmetrical patterns in the initial testing had symmetrical extension patterns in the later testing. These data suggest two patterns: (1) symmetrical patterns are more stable than asymmetrical patterns, and (2) words are more likely to change from asymmetrical patterns to symmetrical patterns than vice versa. Before beginning to specify more about the nature of these changes, I shall summarize the frequency of each of the extensional patterns observed in retesting.

The 84 symmetrical patterns consisted of 24 correct extensions, 18 underextensions, 14 overextensions, and 28 overlap errors. The 24 asymmetrical patterns consisted of 9 words that were underextended in production, but for which overlap errors were observed in comprehension; 3 words that were underextended in comprehension, but for which overlap errors were observed in production; and 12 words that were extended correctly in either production or comprehension. Seven of these 12 words were extended correctly in comprehension, but both overextended and underextended in production. The remaining 5 words were extended correctly in production, 3 of which were overextended in comprehension and 2 of which were both overextended and underextended in comprehension.

How were these extension patterns related to those observed in the first testing session? Symmetrical overextensions in the first testing session either remained the same (five instances) or became symmetrical correct extensions (eight instances). Symmetrical underextensions either remained the same (nine instances), became one of a number of asymmetrical patterns (seven instances of underextension in either production or comprehension, with overlap errors in the opposite communication mode), or became symmetrical overlap extension patterns (only in one instance).

The picture for the remaining extension patterns is less clear. Of the 23 words for which symmetric overlap patterns were observed in the first testing session, only 2 remained symmetric overlap errors in the second testing session. The remaining 21 words fell into one of the following patterns: symmetric underextension (1 instance), symmetric overextension (3 instances), correct extension in comprehension but overextension in production (4 instances), correct extension in production but overextension in comprehension (3 instances), or symmetric correct extensions (10 instances).

There were 21 words for which overextension in production and overlap errors in comprehension were observed in the first testing session. None of these words reflected this extension pattern in the second testing session, suggesting that this is a developmentally unstable pattern. Sixteen of these words reflected symmetric extension patterns in the second testing session (five instances of correct extension, five instances of overlap errors, and six instances of overextensions). The five asymmetrical patterns observed in the second testing session consisted of correct extension in production but overextension in comprehension (three instances), or correct extension in pproduction but overlap errors in comprehension (two instances).

There were 31 words in the first testing session for which underextension in production and overlap errors in comprehension were observed. Three of these words exhibited this same pattern in the second testing session. Two others were underextended in comprehension, but both overextended and underextended in production. The remaining 26 words exhibited one of two symmetrical patterns in the second testing session: underextension (seven instances), or overlap errors (nineteen instances).

Finally, the three instances of infrequent extension patterns observed in the first testing session each changed in the second testing session. The two instances in which words were underextended in comprehension but both overextended and underextended in production changed to symmetric underextension (one instance) or symmetric overlap (one instance). The single instance in which an overlap error was observed in production but for which overextension was found in comprehension became a symmetrical correct extension.

These patterns are illustrated in Figure 5-1, which shows that certain extension patterns in the first testing session were more stable than others. Symmetric underextensions and symmetric overextensions were the most stable patterns, followed by the asymmetric pattern in which underextensions were observed in production but overlap patterns occurred in comprehension which were more frequent than symmetric overlap patterns. The asymmetric pattern in which overextensions occurred in production and overlap errors in comprehension proved to be the least stable between the two testing sessions.

Similarly, words that exhibited certain extension patterns in the first testing session were more likely than others to become symmetric correct extensions in the second testing session. Symmetric overextensions were most likely to become correct extensions, followed by symmetric overlaps, which were more likely to become correct extensions than words that were overextended in production but overextended and underextended in comprehension. No word that was underextended in production in the first testing session was correctly extended in the second testing session.

The above discussion has centered on the relation of a word's extension in the first testing session to its extension in the second testing session. This is important information, but tells us little about the manner in which the performance of a child in the first testing session was related to his or her performance in the second testing session. Rather than describing the many and varied types of extensional

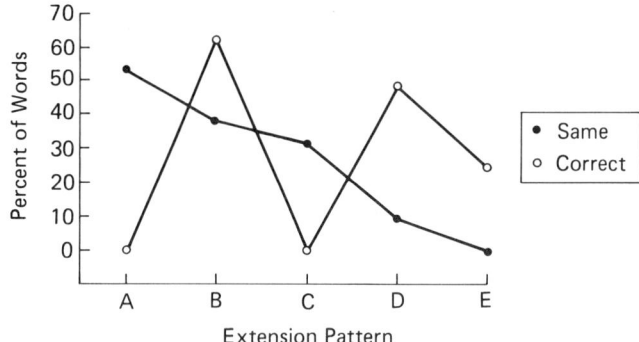

Figure 5-1. Percentage of words from each of five extension patterns in the first testing session that either remained the same or changed to correct extension in the second testing session. Extension pattern (in first testing session): A = symmetric underextension; B = symmetric overextension; C = underextension in production, overlap errors in comprehension; D = symmetric overlap errors; E = overextension in production, overlap errors in comprehension.

patterns used by the children in the two testing sessions. I shall focus on a few general patterns.

I shall first consider those children who used symmetric extension patterns for either all of the overextended words or all of the underextended words. Recall that children who exhibited such a pattern did so for either overextensions or underextensions, never both. This pattern was also observed in the second testing session. The four children who produced symmetric overextensions but asymmetric underextensions in the first testing session failed to produce symmetric underextensions in the second testing session. Similarly, the three childlen who produced symmetric underextensions but asymmetric overextensions in the first testing session failed to produce symmetric overextensions in the second testing session. This supports the notion that children who consistently produce symmetric overextensions or underextensions may be using different strategies in their attempts to determine the meaning of words. Children who produce symmetric overextensions but not symmetric underextensions may be using a strategy wherein they apply what they know too broadly. Thus, they consistently overextend some words, but produce overlap errors (overextension and underextension) for those words for which there are many peripheral exemplars or for which the children have not correctly ascertained the generality (or generalities) that underlie the word's extension. On the other hand, children who symmetrically underextend words but who produce overlap errors for overextended words may be using an overly stringent strategy. Thus, they underextend some terms but both overextend and underextend others. These children may represent the ends of a dimension. At one end, children extend the meanings of words they are acquiring as far as possible. At the other end, children limit the extension of novel words to what they know.

The children who consistently produced symmetric overextensions in the first testing session were most likely to produce symmetric correct extensions in the second testing session. In fact, 11 of the 23 words that were correctly extended in production and comprehension in the second testing session were produced by these four children. In contrast, only 1 of these 23 words was produced by a child who had consistently produced symmetric underextensions in the first testing session (and this was not a word that had been underextended but instead one for which overlap errors had been observed in the first testing sessions).

Finally, 10 of the 18 children in the second testing session produced both symmetric and asymmetric extensions; 4 produced only asymmetric extensions; and 4 produced only symmetric extensions. The latter 4 children consisted of 3 children who had consistently produced symmetric overextensions in the first testing session and 1 child who had consistently produced symmetric underextensions in the first testing session. Moreover, the other child who had produced symmetric overextensions and 1 of the other 2 children who had produced symmetric underextensions in the first testing session each produced five symmetric extensions (out of a possible total of six) in the second testing session. (The other child who had consistently produced symmetric underextensions in the first testing session produced but two symmetric extensions—both overlap errors—in the second testing session). Apparently, children may differ in regard to the likelihood of producing symmetric extensions in the early phases of lexical acquisition. Although the frequency of symmetric extensions increases with development (as evidenced by the differences in the first and second testing sessions), some children seem more likely than others to employ symmetric extensions in early lexical development.

Conclusions and Speculations

At the beginning of this chapter, I emphasized the importance of determining the relation of extension in comprehension to that in production as a first step in the understanding of the nature of object word meaning in young children's lexicons. The results of the two investigations reported in this chapter, combined with those of previous investigations, suggest that it is an oversimplification to argue for either symmetrical or asymmetrical extension patterns. Both types of patterns exist, usually in the same children. What are the implications of this conclusion for our understanding of object word meaning development?

Children are clearly confused about the correct extension of some words. The result of their confusion is overextension, underextension, and overlap errors. The available data suggest that children may employ a more conservative intensional decision in production than in comprehension for underextended terms, the evidence being the greater frequency of underextension errors in production than in comprehension. In an investigation somewhat analogous to the present one, Kay and Anglin (1982) found that underextension errors were more likely to occur in production than in comprehension. However, Kay and Anglin found that overextension errors occurred more frequently in comprehension than in production, this being the opposite of the pattern observed in the above study. Given the differences in the direction of the asymmetry between comprehension and production for overextended words in the finding of Kay and Anglin (1982) and those found in the present investigation, it is not clear if children consistently employ differently weighted intensional decisions in comprehension and production for overextended terms. Kay and Anglin's findings suggest that children are more conservative in production than in comprehension in regard to overextended terms, while the findings of the present investigation suggest that if there is a difference, it is in the opposite direction. Perhaps the intensional decisions that children employ in production and in comprehension are influenced by the phase of acquisition of the words so that children who were learning many words (as are most children) might employ different types of intensional decisions depending on how close they were to ascertaining the correct meaning of a word. This may be particularly true for overextended words, for both the present investigation and that of Kay and Anglin found that underextension errors were more likely to occur in production than in comprehension. Underextension errors, then, may be more stable across children than are overextension errors insofar as asymmetries between comprehension and production are concerned.

This possibility is tempered by the individual differences observed in the present study. Children who exhibited symmetrical overextension patterns did not produce symmetrical underextension patterns, while children who produced symmetrical underextension patters did not exhibit symmetrical overextension patterns. As mentioned earlier, these differences may be due to stylistic differences among the children. Children who consistently overextend terms seem to applying what they know as broadly as they can. These children also seem to learn the correct extension of words more quickly, quite possibly due to being corrected when they err by labeling incorrect objects. Corrections (such as, "No, that's not a dog. It's a sheep.") must help children to learn the correct extension of terms. On the other hand, children who consistently underextend terms seem to restrict their use of terms to exemplars to which they are more certain the term applies. Such children appear to take longer to figure out the correct extension of terms, perhaps because they have less feedback to guide their way. Parents rarely notice, let alone correct, underextensions.

Despite these individual differences, there are several general patterns that emerged from the data. First, underextension errors seem more likely to occur early in the genesis of a word's meaning than do overextension errors. Underextension errors were less likely to change between the two testing sessions than were other types of extension errors. When they did change, they changed to overlap or overextension errors, not to correct extensions. On the other hand, overextension and overlap errors did change to correct extensions, but never to underextension errors.

In Kuczaj (1982), I suggested that asymmetries between comprehension and production extensional decisions would be more likely to occur in the early phases of lexical acquisition, due to children's limited vocabulary and to the initial instability of word meaning. A different view has been offered by Clark (1983), who suggested that symmetry would be the rule rather than the exception in the early phases of lexical acquisition, but that asymmetry would occur in later phases as children acquire a better understanding of the intensional basis of the object words they know (and so become more accurate in comprehension) but continue to overextend in production due to limited vocabulary. Clark's view implies that children's early uses of a term may have intensional significance, but later uses may not, whereas the hypothesis suggested by Kuczaj (1982) has the opposite implications: Children's early uses of a term may not have intensional significance, but later uses do. The data from the present study suggest that asymmetrical patterns are more likely to occur in the early phases of object word meaning acquisition, and that symmetrical extension patterns are more likely in the later phases of acquisition. Moreover, symmetrical patterns were developmentally more stable than were asymmetrical extension patterns. The extensions of the words studied were more likely to change from asymmetrical patterns to symmetrical patterns than vice versa. It appears, then, that asymmetrical patterns are more likely to occur in the early phases of the acquisition of a word's meaning than in later phases.

An Unembarrassed Return to the Notion of Prototype-Based Word Meaning

Near the beginning of this chapter, I suggested that children's early object-word meaning might be prototype-based. This hypothesis, like most of those concerned with the nature of early object word meaning, has little difficulty accounting for symmetrical extension patterns. A child who correctly extends a term such as *car* in both comprehension and production is assumed to use the same intensional bases for the extension of car, regardless of whether the word is being produced or comprehended by the child. The common intensional bases could be a set of critical features, a prototype or set of prototypes, or even some sort of generalized script. Similarly, a child who overextends *car* in both comprehension and production is assumed to be using the same intensional information in comprehension and production. Common intensional information would also be assumed for the child who consistently underextended *car* in comprehension and production. Of course, the intension would be different for correct extension than for underextension or overextension. These differences are readily explained by most accounts of early object word meaning, but only if extension is symmetrical in comprehension and production. Thus, the findings of the study reported above are consistent with the notion of prototyped-based object word meaning, but are also readily explained by other theories.

Nonetheless, there is some support for a prototype-based approach. The order in which children chose the exemplars in the comprehension task is similar to that found in an earlier investigation (Kuczaj, 1982). In general, children first chose appropriate exemplars, and then chose overextendable exemplars (if they chose any such exemplars). This pattern fits well with the notion of prototype-based object word meaning if one assumes that appropriate exemplars are more prototypic than overextended exemplars (Kuczaj, 1982). Moreover, comparing the order of objects chosen in the first testing session with that observed in the second testing session supports the notion that children first choose prototypic objects when confronted with a multiple-choice task. In both testing sessions, appropriate exemplars were more likely to be chosen before overextended exemplars. Moreover, objects that were chosen for underextended words in the first testing session were usually chosen first in the second testing session, even in those instances in which the word was no longer underextended. This pattern suggests that children may consider the objects to which they initially apply underextended terms to be prototypic exemplars.

The asymmetrical patterns may also be explained in terms of prototype-based word meaning. First, it is important to note that asymmetries were usually a matter of degree rather than of kind. In other words, children never showed one extension pattern in production and a completely different one in comprehension. There were differences in the exemplars chosen in the two communicative modes, but there was still considerable overlap. This is reflected in the fact that of the asymmetrical extension patterns, none involved overextension in one mode and underextension in another. Instead, children would overextend or underextend in one mode, and exhibit overlap errors (overextension and underextension) in the other. In all cases of asymmetry, children seemed to experience difficulty with peripheral examples, sometimes using them in conjunction with a term and sometimes failing to do so. Perhaps the mapping relation between a form and its intension is best for prototypic exemplars and worst for peripheral exemplars, regardless of whether production or comprehension is involved. It is less clear that the mapping relation is easier in production than in comprehension, or vice versa (see Keenan & MacWhinney, 1984, for a discussion of such mapping relations).

The basic argument, then, is that children's extensional decisions in production and comprehension may be based on intensions that utilize prototyped-based concepts, regardless of whether symmetrical or asymmetrical extension patterns are observed (Kuczaj, 1982; Kay & Anglin, 1982; Mervis & Canada, 1983). The possibility is further supported by the results obtained in the investigation reported in this chapter. How, though, may we best characterize the prototype structure of children's early object word intensions? Although the notion of prototypes has been used in theories of lexical meaning acquisition (Anglin, 1977; Mulford, 1977), there has been little agreement about the nature of the prototype-based concept structure and formation process thought to underlie the acquisiton of object word meaning (Greenberg & Kuczaj, 1982). As Rosch (1978) has noted, adherence to the notion of prototypes as important in concept structure and formation does not entail acceptance of any particular view of prototype-based concepts and their acquisition. Greenberg and Kuczaj (1982) offered a prototype-based account of object word meaning acquisition in which it was assumed that children store holistic information about individual experiences with concept exemplars (or supposed exemplars) and that children are capable of making holistic comparisons in order to decide if a novel object is or is not an instance of a particular concept. Other prototype-based theories have suggested that prototypes may be viewed as special sets of criterial features (Rips, Shoben, & Smith, 1973; Clark & Clark, 1977), or that prototypes are abstract idealized forms (Mulford, 1977). Although the data reported above may be accounted for in terms of any of these theoretical approaches, the criterial feature approach to concept formation and structure encounters twin difficulties. First, it is difficult to justify theoretically the notion of criterial or defining features (Greenberg & Kuczaj, 1982; Miller, 1979). Second, the empirical evidence fails to support the notion that criterial features play a role in children's acquisition of object word meaning, particularly in the early phases of acquisition (Greenberg & Kuczaj, 1982; Richards, 1979; Thomson & Chapman, 1977).

The notion of abstract prototypes is not as readily dismissed as is the notion of criterial features. However, Greenberg and Kuczaj (1982) viewed the possibility that young children formulate abstract prototypes of object concepts to be less than the possibility that children store and use holistic information about individual experiences with concept exemplars, an assumption supported by the work of Brooks (1978). If children do in fact store and use holistic information about concept exemplars, then the results of the myriad array of studies concerning the relation of comprehension and production extensional decisions may be explained in the following manner. Children have experience with concept exemplars and come to store and organize holistic information about these exemplars, some of which come to have prototypic status. Thus, in the comprehension task, the children initially choose objects which are prototypic or close to prototypic, only subsequently choosing less prototypic instances.

In addition to assuming that children create prototype-based intensions based on their early experiences with exemplars, this view of early object word meaning development also assumes that children's early use of object words is primarily based on extension (the one or two exemplars which the child believes the word labels) and only gradually comes to have a true intensional basis. In other words, the young child initially assumes that a word applies to a very limited set of objects (perhaps only one object), and so has little inkling of what the word *means*. Instead, the child knows a bit about a small set of objects to which the word refers. Although one might argue that even this limited extension has an intensional basis, the intensional basis is more similar to that for a proper name than that for an object term such as *dog* or *car*. With experience, the child learns to relate the word to additional exemplars, the comparisons of these exemplars to those already associated with the word causing the child to broaden her intensional basis for the word's extension. With development, the intension of the word becomes independent of any single exemplar (even if the exemplar is the prototype). Thus, intension comes to determine extension, whereas extension may have determined intension in the child's early use of words.

In closing, I would like to acknowledge that it is also possible to account for the present findings by appealing to prototype family resemblance structure, such structure consisting of bundles of noncriterial features (Rosch & Mervis, 1975; Bowerman, 1976; Mervis & Canada, 1983). The same basic arguments can be made, the difference between the two accounts resting on differing concepts of prototype concept structure and formation (holistic vs. featural). Although additional data are needed in order to better determine the nature of prototype-based concepts in object word meaning development, it seems reasonable to assume that some sort of prototype-based intension influences much of object word meaning development and that a common intension may be used in comprehension and production, regardless of whether the object word is overextended, underextended, both overextended and underextended, or appropriately extended. Symmetry in extension between comprehension and production seems to be the rule in early object word meaning development. Asymmetry seems to be the exception. Moreover, when asymmetrical patterns are observed, they usually involve the use or nonuse of peripheral exemplars rather than completely different extensional patterns in the two communication modes. Extension in comprehension and in production is more similar than it is different, such similarity suggesting a common intensional basis between the two communication modes.

Acknowledgments. I am grateful to Kathy Alred, Bob Borys, Meg Mullen, and Danny Wilcox for their assistance in locating and testing children, as well as for analyzing the data. Special thanks to Martyn Barrett for his comments on an earlier draft of this chapter.

References

Anderson, E. (1978). Lexical universals of body-part terminology. In J. H. Greenberg (Ed.), *Universals of human language: Vol. 3. Word structure*. Stanford, CA: Stanford University Press.

Anglin, J. M. (1977). *Word, object, and conceptual development*. New York: Norton.

Benedict, H. (1978). Language comprehension in 9-15 month-old children. In R. N. Campbell & P. T. Smith (Eds.), *Recent advances in the psychology of language: Language development and mother-child interaction*. New York: Plenum.

Benedict, H. (1979). Early lexical development: Comprehension and production. *Journal of Child Language, 6*, 183-200.

Bloom, L. M. (1973). *One word at a time: The use of single word utterances before syntax*. The Hague: Mouton.

Bowerman, M. (1975). The acquisition of word meaning: An investigation of some current conflicts. Paper presented at the Third International Child Language Symposium, London.

Brooks, L. (1978). Nonanalytic concept formation and memory for instances. In E. Rosch & B. Lloyd (Eds.), *Cognition and categorization*. Hillsdale, NJ: Erlbaum Associates.

Carey, S. (1978). The child as word learner. In M. Halle, J. Bresnan, & G. A. Miller (Eds.), *Linguistic theory and psychological reality*. Cambridge, MA: MIT Press.

Chapman, K., Leonard, L. B., Rowan, L. E., & Weiss, A. L. (1983). Inappropriate word extensions in the speech of young language-disordered children. *Journal of Speech and Hearing Disorders, 48*, 55-62.

Clark, E. V. (1973). What's in a word? On the child's acquisition of language in his first language. In T. E. Moore (Ed.), *Cognitive development and the acquisition of language*. New York: Academic Press.

Clark, E. V. (1978). Strategies for communicating. *Child Development, 49*, 953-959.

Clark, E. V. (1983). Meanings and concepts. In P. H. Mussen (Ed.), *Handbook of Child Psychology, 4th ed., Vol. III*. New York: John Wiley & Sons.

Clark, H., & Clark, E. (1977). *Psychology and language*. New York: Harcourt, Brace, Jovanovich.

Fremgen, A., & Fay, D. (1980). Overextensions in production and comprehension: A methodological clarification. *Journal of Child Language, 7*, 205-211.

Gelman, R., & Gallistel, C. R. (1978). *The child's understanding of number*. Cambridge, MA: Harvard University Press.

Goldin-Meadow, S., Seligman, M. E. P., & Gelman, R. (1976). Language in the two-year-old. *Cognition, 4*, 189-202.

Grégoire, A. (1937). L'apprentissage du language, vol. 1, les deux premières années. Liège and Paris: Librairie Droz.

Greenberg, J., & Kuczaj, S. A. II. (1982). Towards a theory of substantive word-meaning acquisition. In S. A. Kuczaj II (Ed.), *Language development: Syntax and semantics: vol. 1*. Hillsdale, NJ: Erlbaum.

Hudson, J., & Nelson, K. (1984). Play with language: Overextensions as analogies. *Journal of Child Language, 11*, 337-346.

Huttenlocher, J. (1974). The origins of language comprehension. In R. L. Solso (Ed.), *Theories in cognitive psychology*. New York: Wiley.

Kay, D. A., & Anglin, J. M. (1982). Overextension and underextension in the child's expressive and receptive speech. *Journal of Child Language, 9*, 83-98.

Keenan, J. M., & MacWhinney, B. (1984). Understanding the relationship between comprehension and production. In H. W. Dechert & M. Raupach (Eds.), *Psycholinguistic models of language production*. New York: Ablex.

Kuczaj, S. A. II (1982). Young children's overextension of object words in comprehension and production: Support for a prototype theory of early object word meaning. *First Language, 3*, 93-105.

Leonard, L. B. (1983). *Production before comprehension: Some methodological issues*. Paper presented at the biennial meeting of the Society for Research in Child Development, Detroit.

Leonard, L. B., Newhoff, M., & Fry, M. E. (1980). Some instances of word usage in the absence of comprehension. *Journal of Child Language, 7*, 189-196.

Leonard, L. B., & Schwartz, R. (1981). *Factors influencing lexical acquisition in children with specific language disability*. Paper presented at the biennial meeting of the Society for Research in Child Development, Boston.

Leopold, W. F. (1949). *Speech development of a bilingual child: A linguist's record: Vol. 3*. Evanston, IL: Northwestern University Press.

Lewis, M. M. (1951). *Infant speech: A study of the beginnings of language*. London: Kegan Paul.

Mervis, C. B., & Canada, K. (1983). On the existence of competence errors in early comprehension: A reply to Fremgen & Fay and Chapman & Thompson. *Journal of Child Language, 10*, 431-440.

Miller, G. (1978). Comments on the acquisition of word meaning. *Child Development, 49*, 999-1004.

Mulford, R. (1977). *Prototypicality and the development of categorization*. Paper presented at the Boston University Child Language Conference, Boston.

Nelson, K. (1973). Structure and strategy in learning to talk. *Monographs of the Society for Research in Child Development, 38* (Serial No. 149).

Nelson, K. (1974). Concept, word, and sentence: Interrelations in acquisition and development. *Psychological Review, 81*, 267-285.

Nelson, K., Rescorla, L., Gruendel, J. M., & Benedict, H. (1978). Early lexicons: What do they mean? *Child Development, 49*, 960-968.

Nelson, K. E., & Bonvillian, J. (1973). Concepts and words in the 18-month-old: Acquiring concept names under controlled conditions. *Cognition, 2*, 435-450.

Nice, M. M. (1915). The development of a child's vocabulary in relation to environment. *Pedagogical Seminary, 22*, 35-64.

Rescorla, L. (1980). Overextensions in early language development. *Journal of Child Language, 7*, 321-335.

Rescorla, L. (1976). *Concept formation in word learning*. Unpublished doctoral dissertation. Yale University, New Haven, CN.

Rice, M. (in press). A cognition account of differences between children's comprehension and production of language. *Western Journal of Speech Communication*.

Richards, M. (1979). Sorting out what's in a word from what's not: Evaluating Clark's semantic features acquisition theory. *Journal of Experimental Child Psychology, 27*, 1-47.

Rosch, E., & Lloyd, B. (1978). *Cognition and categorization*. Hillsdale, NJ: Erlbaum.

Rosch, E., & Mervis, C. (1975). Family resemblances: Studies in the internal structures of categories. *Cognitive Psychology, 7*, 573-605.

Thompson, J. R., & Chapman, R. S. (1977). Who is "daddy"? The status of two-year-old's overextended words in use and comprehension. *Journal of Child Language, 4*, 359-375.

6. Lexical Acquisition Strategies in the Preschool Child

Julie Dockrell and Robin Campbell

> That's not a *cow*, that's a *patas*.
> (Rachel, 4;3)

Rachel was a subject in one of the studies we shall be reporting in this chapter. This sentence was taken from a natural play session in the nursery Rachel was attending. She was informing another playmate (who had not taken part in our study) that calling the novel toy animal a *cow*[1] was incorrect—an overextension, in other words. What information had allowed Rachel to make this inference? What inference had Rachel made? Was *patas* (a nonsense word in our study) a label for all unknown toy animals or all unknown toys? Or had she progressed further in mapping out the meaning of this new lexical item? If Rachel had identified a range of items for which she regarded this new lexical item as appropriate, what hypotheses had she developed in the process? Were these hypotheses similar to those used by her peers who participated in the same study?

These questions comprise the focal concerns of this chapter. Specifically, we are concerned with the ways in which children manage to map out the meanings of novel lexical items. Preschool children bring substantial information to the word-learning task both in terms of knowledge about their language and knowledge about the world. Our aim is to suggest ways in which these types of knowledge interact with the input the child receives. Children's vocabulary growth at this age is substantial (Carey, 1978a). Our plan is to outline some aspects of what the child brings to the word-learning task and the potential sources of information available to children that may help them to solve such problems. We will then proceed to report a number of studies which monitor the child's development of word meanings over time.

---

[1]We have used the following typographical conventions to assist the reader. Single quotations are used to indicate that a word's meaning is being considered; italics are used to refer to the word qua lexical item and for emphasis; and upper case letters are used to indicate denotations.

What's in a Word?

Any attempt to study word meaning requires a framework through which we can evaluate the status of the child's lexical entries. Children's early word meanings are frequently not like those of adults, and have sometimes been viewed as incomplete (Clark, 1973). But in what way are they incomplete? Let us consider two possible cases of partial or incomplete meaning. Child A correctly identifies the range of vessels commonly described as cups, but fails to understand that cups are a type of drinking vessel.[2] Child B takes the term *cup* to include bottles, mugs, bowls and *cups* (that is, overextends the term), but clearly produces evidence that cups, like glasses, and so forth, are drinking vessels. The term *glasses* applies to the appropriate set of items for Child B. Both children's meanings are incomplete and do not match the adult criteria for the meaning of 'cup'. However, to classify both children as having incomplete lexical entries fails to acknowledge that Child A and Child B have acquired quite different kinds of information about these terms. In fact, in many comprehension tasks Child A, but not Child B, would appear to have grasped the meaning of 'cup'. We shall propose a framework which will aid in discussing these quite different kinds of errors and provide a working definition of what is entailed by acquiring the meaning of a word.

The issue of what is acquired in the acquisition of word meaning is by no means straightforward. Bierwisch (1981) argues "that two aspects of meaning are to be distinguished that are organized according to independent though interacting principles: *Semantic structure* determined by the rules of language and thus pertaining to the realm of tacit linguistic knowledge: *Conceptual structure*, based on rules in terms of which mental representations of the world are built up" (p. 341). For Bierwisch, then, a specification of lexical entries includes phonological, syntactic, semantic, conceptual, and perceptual information (if the latter is involved) with the key connections being those between phonetic, syntactic, and semantic information for each lexeme. We are concerned here primarily with the semantic information which determines the meaning of a word across various situations. But it should be clear that in certain cases it will be quite difficult to distinguish the semantic and conceptual structures which may be involved. The framework we offer is simpler than that proposed by Bierwisch. It does, however, cover major distinctions which have rarely been explicitly stated; our framework is intended to provide a working model for evaluating the child's lexical entries.

Following Lyons (1977), we make a three-fold distinction between sense, reference, and denotation. We use the term *reference* to describe the relationship which exists between an object and a particular expression on a particular occasion of utterance. Reference, therefore, should not be regarded as a property of words, *per se*. It is an arbitrary relationship. An object can be referred to in any number of ways and it is "the person who refers who invests the expression with reference by the act

---

[2]It would be empirically possible to devise a means of tapping a child's knowledge about drinking vessesl and to see whether cups were included in this set, e.g. we might investigate the way in which the child acted with drinking vessels.

of referring" (Lyons, 1977, p. 177). *Denotation*, on the other hand, describes the relationship that exists between a linguistic term and a set of objects, properties, and so forth, external to the language system. For example, the denotation of the term *red* is a particular property and its denotata are all red objects (Lyons, 1977). Equally, the term *cup* denotes a particular set of objects, that is, cups. Child A in our earlier example would be credited with knowing the set of objects denoted by the term *cup*. Knowing the denotation of a term (that is, the range of objects or instances to which a term can be appropriately applied), entails that denotation will determine reference in referring expressions. The opposite is not the case. A child may know how to make successful reference using the word *brother* (in utterances where she refers to her brother) without knowing anything about the denotation of the term (except that it may be used to refer to her brother).

We should like to elucidate two issues related to denotation which will bear on later discussions. Firstly, it is not necessarily the case that the denotation of a word is clearly defined. The denotational boundaries may be fuzzy; there may, for example, be no rigid criteria to determine the denotata of *cup*. This point has been argued quite convincingly from a theoretical stance (Labov, 1973; Lehrer, 1970; Lennenberg, 1967) and from empirical evidence (Rosch et al., 1976). Thus, while knowing the denotation of a lexeme entails identifying the range of application of the lexeme there may be instances whose status is indeterminate with respect to a particular lexeme.

Secondly an object, attribute, and so forth, may be the denotatum of more than one lexeme. A cow is a denotatum of both the term *cow* and the term *animal*. There is, thus, a one to many mapping from entities in the world to lexemes. It is therefore not the case that once one relationship is established between a lexeme and a denotatum that other relationships are precluded. As we shall discuss later, this notion causes difficulties for the young word learner.

The final element of this tripartite distinction is sense. While both denotation and reference involve entities external to the language system, sense has to do with relations entirely within the language system. That is, sense has to do with the ways in which various words are connected or distinguished within the language itself—with meaning relations (e.g., *white* and *red* are incompatible terms). The sense relationship is said to hold between the words or expressions of a language independently of the relationship, if any, which holds between those words or expressions and their referents or denotata (Lyons, 1977). The nature of the sense relations will depend on the central meaning postulates within a semantic field (Miller & Johnson-Laird, 1976) be they perceptual (e.g., for color), functional (e.g., for drinking vessels), or relational (e.g., for in/on). The relations which hold a semantic field such as 'animals' together are likely to be quite different from those that hold a semantic field like 'motion' together.

Neither sense nor denotation are regarded as logically or psychologically basic by Lyons (1977). However, it seems clear that while sense may not determine denotation, it surely limits denotation. Knowing the meaning of x and the sense relationship between x and y imposes limits on the denotation of y. If we know that (1) x and y denote drinking vessels, and that (2) x is incompatible with y—whatever is x is not *y* and vice versa, and that (3) *x* denotes *glasses* then we know that (4) *y* denotes some drinking vessels which are *not glasses*. Note the similarity between these conditions and the type of responses given by Child B discussed above. What we are arguing then, is that knowing the semantic domain of a term (that is, the words to which the term is closely bound by sense relationships), helps set up the boundary conditions for application of that term. However, knowing the denotation of a term does not necessarily help us to discover its sense unless we have some *a priori* knowledge of the object denoted (for example, a cup is a drinking vessel). To say that a child or adult has the full meaning of a term would require evidence for knowledge of both sense and denotation. Further, this allows us to classify erroneous or partial meanings. Child A has clearly circumscribed denotational criteria but has not grasped the sense of the term; Child B has few criteria for restricting denotation but has acquired an understanding of the key sense relations (that is, cups are drinking vessels which are not glasses).

Briefly, what are the implications of these distinctions for studies of the child's lexicon? Reference is an arbitrary relationships Being able to decipher the referent of a referring expression on one particular occasion can be due to anything from a clever guess to knowledge of the expression's meaning. Clearly, it must be possible to work from successful reference to a knowledge of denotation and sense. It is equally clear, however, that knowledge of reference alone cannot be sufficient. Information about the sense and denotation of children's words is also necessary. The latter is far more accessible to experimental study and has dominated the research literature. Sense is much harder to assess empirically and frequently requires insightful guesses on the part of the experimenter or observer.

Sense, reference, and denotation provide us with rough guidelines for an operational definition of what is entailed in knowing the meaning of a word. This is, of course, a more rigid formulation than a vague entity called "full adult meaning," as it forces quite specific guidelines for crediting a child or adult with knowledge of a word's meaning and allows an analysis of the criteria which form the basis of a particular meaning. Moreover, it allows a degree of latitude in assessing semantic development for it is possible from this perspective for different words to be learned in different ways by the same child or for the same word to be learned in different ways by different children.

Data Bases and Strategies

What does the preschool child bring to the word learning task? We will distinguish between two different types of information which the child may use: *data bases* and *strategies*. Data bases denote different structured sets of knowledge to which the child has access. Further, we can subdivide data bases into: (1) nonlinguistic knowledge about the way the world is organized and the way it functions; and (2) linguistic knowledge which is relevant to the language system and the lexicon. Knowing that something is a drinking vessel is part of a nonlinguistic data base; knowing that *s* marks the plural is part of the language data base (Berko, 1958).

Strategies, on the other hand, indicate that there are certain regularities in the child's decisions in particular situations. There is no requirement that the child be aware of these strategies (or data bases). Strategies may be related to either linguistic or nonlinguistic information. A child's consistent choice of the array the experimenter alters in a conservation task would be an example of a nonlinguistic strategy. Focussing on the order of terms in an utterance to determine the actor would be an example of linguistic strategy (Slobin & Bever, 1982). Strategies and data bases will interact. Knowing a particular regularity about the world may influence the strategy that is executed. For example, if we know that *hats* go on *heads* and are told "Zurk hat", then one strategy might be to put the hat on our head. If we cannot draw on a data base that tells one that hats go on heads, a different strategy would need to be invoked. Strategies are, in effect, responses to demands to act. There is no guarantee that one will learn from using a strategy. However, performing particular strategies may well lead to learning and, therefore, to a change in the data bases available. What these mechanisms of change might be have yet to be elaborated but feedback—implicit or explicit—may well play a role.

Some Strategies

Odd Name—Odd Element? We shall consider here a number of strategies and data bases which may influence children's acquisition of novel lexical items. Carey 1978a,b) identifies a linguistic strategy which can be generalized as follows: An odd name refers to an odd, unnamed attribute, object, or event. The precise element which is isolated by the referring act will depend on the context of utterance and the child's existing vocabulary. Such a strategy would serve to delimit the range of hypotheses a child needs to entertain when he or she encounters a new word. Initially, the child need only focus on the unnamed element. Comprehension data collected (Dockrell, 1981) in a task where children had to identify a referent from a picture when an unknown word was used, showed that children had significantly greater problems identifying the target object if they already had a name for it—if it was "captured" by a known lexical item. In other words, use of the novel term to refer to the known object was preempted by a known term. There are a number of implications of such a strategy. For example, once a child has learned a name for an object, that object would then be "captured" and other names should not be overextended to include this instance. Clark (1983) provides evidence in support of this contention. Further, children should find it difficult to establish reference when different words refer to the same object, for example, *dog* and *animal*, or when the same word refers to different objects, since both instances are contrary to the initial strategy. The following naturalistic example will serve to illustrate some of these points.[3]

Brian (2;6) was playing with his railway when his mother refers to "the lines". Brian misinterprets *lines* as *lions*:

---

[3]We are grateful to John McShane for allowing us to use this example.

B: Not lion?
M: They're railway lines.
B: No, not railway lion.
M: No, not a lion, a lion is an animal—a line.
B: Where's the lion? Where's the lion? And it's a railway, not a lion, a railway.

It is irrelevant that Brian has failed to spot the subtleties of phonology, for this might well have been a homophone. Brian knew what lions were and he had a name for the object—*railways*. He appears to be working on the assumption that an object cannot have two names (Kuczaj, 1982a, develops a similar argument). Further evidence for this line of reasoning comes from Curtis (1974) who has shown that learning to master subordinate/superordinate and synonymy relations cause difficulties for the early word learner. A child who followed a preemption strategy would encounter exactly these types of problems. Evidence from Macnamara (1982) indicates that such problems cannot simply be attributed to a failure to understand hierarchical relations: "There is abundant evidence that many 2½-year-olds are reluctant to apply a superordinate term to an individual object" (p. 80) even though they appear to have formed adult-like relations among certain hierarchically related ideas.

One way a child might circumvent the problems which occur when a novel-name is used for a captured object is to mark it in some way (provided the demands of the situation clearly indicate that the same object is being referred to). McShane (1980) remarks that when some of the children in his study were told they were using an animal name incorrectly and when supplied with the correct name, the children incorporated the correct name into their vocabulary as an attribute word (or possibly as a hyponym). "Thus Brian, told that what he called ducks were turkeys, called the toys *turkey ducks* . . ." (p. 112). As if preemption was at work, Brian appears to have avoided the possibility that an object can have two names by allowing *turkey* to modify *duck* in some way. Of course, we have no idea what hypotheses Brian entertains at this point with respect to the meaning of *turkey*.

Carey's odd name—odd referent strategy will only work if the child realizes a lexical gap exists. Problems arise if reference is preempted, either because of lexical capture or because the word used has a different meaning for the child. Strategies, by their very nature, are situation bound. It is not necessary that because a child has grasped hyponymy or synonymy in one particular instance that the child should totally disregard an odd name—odd element strategy. It may be necessary, initially at least, to learn such instances item by item or set by set. However, such a strategy alone cannot account for the full development of word meaning. For, in no way, can such a strategy explain how the child deciphers whether an object, action, or attribute is being referred to, nor can such a strategy explain how the child identifies denotational criteria or sense relations, or what criteria determine the existence of a lexical gap.

What's Around at the Time? Another strategy which children might employ is to link novel words with the specific nonlinguistic context in which the word first occurred. Barrett (1983) provides evidence that early action-related words occurred only in conjunction with specific actions, "The words gave the appearance of being highly ritualistic and almost redundant accompaniments to their corresponding action-schemes" (p. 199). Nygren (1972) demonstrates that context is similarly important for the preschool child. She asked 3- to 11-year-olds questions containing instrumental verbs, many of which had a semantically unusual combination of elements, for example, "Can you saw cheese with a knife?" Her results indicated that the kindergarten children in contrast to older children had the largest percentage of responses that indicated that the usual verb/instrument pair had to be kept intact (that is, initial understanding of a verb often involves pairing the action with a particular object or situation). Such a strategy would result in the initial word meaning closely reflecting the child's encounters with the word and the world. Carey's (1978b) study of spatial adjectives supports the presence of just this type of procedure. She argues that the child's representation of the meaning of these words contains specific information about typical objects to which the word applies. However, as McShane and Dockrell (1983) point out, despite the obvious appeal of such a notion, "it is virtually impossible to know in what contexts a child will have acquired a word and therefore it will be impossible to predict patterns of results in advance of a comprehension test . . . [unless] specific predictions can be derived about the relation between particular 'adjectives' and 'entities' " (p. 65). Moreover, it may well be the case that context is more important for certain word classes than for others.

There are other strategies which the child may use as default mechanisms when failing to understand a new term. Some of these procedures will be more informative than others. Phonetic associations, although used by children (Dockrell, 1981), are a particularly unsatisfactory procedure. Monitoring a speaker's gaze might prove more fruitful in eliminating options. We shall close our discussion of strategies by emphasizing two points. Firstly, we have primarily been concerned with strategies for comprehension. Production is not simply the opposite of comprehension (Campbell et al., 1982; Kuczaj, 1982b; McShane & Dockrell, 1983). There may well be a different set of strategies put into operation for production, for example, using general purpose words where a lexical gap exists or extending words whose denotational boundaries are vague. Gentner (1978) suggests that using the words you know is a good working strategy.

Secondly, strategies *cannot* explain by themselves the process of learning new words. Although they may help children to isolate the initial element referred to, they *do not* explain either the development of denotation or sense. We must turn to the child's data bases for further help.

Some Data Bases

We have described the sets of knowledge which the child can access as data bases. As Clark (1983) states, "by the age of two or so, it is clear that young children have already acquired a large fund of knowledge about objects in the world around them". The existence of these data bases is inferred from children's performance on experimental tasks and from behavior in the world. We are concerned here principally with data bases which will influence the word learning task.

The Way the World Is. Children appear to understand from early on that there are certain orders of events (Leslie, 1984) and arrangements of objects which are expected (Freeman et al., 1980). Gelman et al. (1980) present data from older children (3 and 4 years of age) showing that they can use information about events to predict what the transformed state of a sequence might be, given the initial state and the instrument; deduce the initial state, given the instrument and final state; and describe actions which might link the initial state with the final state. Such data would serve to restrict the possible meanings a child would entertain about a novel term presented in such a context. Further evidence about such data bases comes from children's awareness of the appropriateness of object configurations. Grieve et al. (1977) and Hoogenraad et al. (1978) studied children's understanding of instructions containing *in*, *on*, and *under*. Whereas younger children's responses were largely determined by the natural canonical relations of the objects used in the test, older children's responses were largely determined by the linguistic instructions. So, for example, young children put cups on saucers regardless of the instructions given. Such experiments support the view that early meanings are incomplete (Donaldson & Balfour, 1968; Palermo, 1973, 1974). While it is undoubtedly the case that these early theories were wrong about the child's partial representations of these terms (Richards, 1978), the contextual constraints provided by situations in the real world may assist the child to build up meanings for a word. It is likely that the child's early experience of such terms will be in canonical situations which, in turn, may guide the child's hypotheses about the possible meanings of a word. How the child proceeds from performance in canonical situations to acontextual meaning must still be explained.

Categorization—What Helps? Categorical information could serve as data bases in two distinct ways. Firstly, the level at which children naturally form categories may influence the level at which they initially form lexical categories, which in turn may influence their inferences about the intended referent (Rosch & Mervis, 1975). Secondly, the categories the child has previously established may provide information in that a child who hears a new word may search for already existing nonlinguistic categories to map onto the new term (see Kuczaj, 1982a, for a clear discussion of this issue).

When Can Children Form Categories? The ability to categorize and thereby form concepts is a prerequisite to acquiring a lexicon. Even if it were the case that words stood for single unchanging instances, one would need to be able to distinguish instances from noninstances. Otherwise, each occurrence of an instance would need to be treated independently, making communication impossible. As it is, words denote particular classes of objects, actions, or attributes. Our task here is two-fold. Firstly, we shall examine the evidence concerning children's abilities to categorize and to see to what extent, if any, this knowledge may influence the child's lexical acquisition process. Secondly, we shall briefly comment on the nature of the categories that are formed and to see how this might influence the word learning process.

At least two methods exist to assess the child's early categorical knowledge—sorting tasks and habituation studies. As we shall see, the data acquired from both sorts of tasks is both equivocal and methodologically questionable. There is considerable need for further work in assessing the young child's early categorical abilities.

Early studies of children's categorical abilities relied heavily on sorting tasks (Inhelder & Piaget, 1964; Vygotsky, 1962). The results of these studies suggested that children's classification behavior was deficient in comparison with adults and older children. Rather than forming categorical groups as an adult would, the children were more likely to create graphic collections or "associative complexes." More recent sorting studies have suggested that children can in fact perform rudimentary classification by kinds if not by attributes. Ricciuti (1965) found some rudimentary grouping behavior even at the earliest age (12 months) with objects grouped into kinds. On the whole, however, many of the younger subjects either did not sort objects into groups or formed groups that were incomplete. In contrast, Nelson (1973) found that children between 1;7 and 1;10 could sort toys into separate groups, for example, different types of toys. The evidence is far from conclusive. Part of the problem appears to rest with the methodology of the tasks themselves. Younger children may well be more influenced by the process of sorting than the objects themselves (Markman, Cox, & Machida, 1981).

In contrast to the sorting studies, habituation studies seem more promising in terms of results achieved (Cohen & Strauss, 1979). For example, Ross (1980) assessed categorization abilities in one- to two-year-olds. Children were presented with a series of habituation trials followed by a choice between a new member of the familiarized category or a member of a novel category. The results suggest that children of this age recognize conventional categories such as men, animal, food, and furniture. Moreover, Ross's results make it clear that: "Conclusions about children's categorization skills are dependent on the methodology employed, the response required and the categories presented" (1980, p. 395). The evidence is tentative, but on the whole there is a clear indication that children have a predisposition to form natural kind categories early on.

As we stated earlier, categorization is a prerequisite to acquiring a working lexicon. Whether these categories are of any use in the development of word meanings is a moot point. (Nevertheless, see Kuczaj, 1982a for an interesting translation of this information into strategies children can use.) It is evident that word meanings tap only part of our conceptual domain, and that languages differ in the conceptual domains which are represented lexically (cf. Clark, 1983). Hence, direct mappings will not always be possible and, in fact, may not occur.

Recently, in a study designed to assess children's constraints on word meaning, Markman and Hutchinson (1984) found evidence that children limit the hypotheses they entertain about the meaning of novel terms. Specifically, children constrain the meaning of new nouns to refer to specific categorical relations as opposed to thematic relations. This result was significantly different from a condition where no new noun was used and thematic associations predominated. These results were obtained with three- and four-year-olds. As yet, we have to determine the extent to which younger children might use categorical information. It seems safe to assume that the manner in which children use conceptual knowledge to derive the sense of a new term depends on the child's conceptual knowledge regarding a particular domain. If, for example, a child's conceptual knowledge regarding a particular domain is differentiated, for example, in the case of animals (Nelson, 1973; Ross, 1980), and if the child is aware that the object being referred to is an animal, then considerably more information is given to the child than "*x* is a polysaccharide," for example. Harris (1975) has demonstrated that if an unknown word is introduced as a member of a familiar class (that is predicated as a familiar entity), for example, a *mib* is a bird, five-year-old children will ascribe the same properties to its referents that they would ascribe to the entity.

The Nature of Concepts. A further question remains. To what extent do the types of categories children form influence the types of meanings which they entertain? Recent work on adult categories (Rosch & Mervis, 1975; Rosch et al., 1976; Rosch, 1978) suggests that there are three guiding principles of concept formation:

1. Natural categories are formed on the basis of family resemblances, not a single defining attribute.
2. There are key or prototypical exemplars of each category.
3. Attributes come in correlated groups which reflect the structure of the real world, that is, natural kinds.

While there are indications that children's early concepts may be prototypical in nature (Mervis & Pani, 1980) and that early word representations are prototypical (Bowerman, 1978), little has been said about the notion of correlated attributes and the implications for word learning. Since attributes in the real world appear to come in correlated bundles and children use these data to categorize the children may also be able to use this data as a basis for hypotheses about initial acts of reference (and possibly for the subsequent development of denotation).

This argument in no way suggests that cognitive categories determine linguistic categories but rather, rests on the notion that the environment sensitizes the child to particular types of groupings early on and that this information may be used in making inferences about initial referents. So, for example, a child may be more likely to assume that a novel term refers to an unlexicalized type of object (e.g., *animal*) rather than an unlexicalized attribute (e.g., *it has spots*). Such an inference will be determined by other data to which the child has access, for example, level of specificity for which reference is usually made for the child (Brown, 1965) and the context in which the term occurs (Cruse, 1977). This analysis leads to a number of direct predictions. When all data bases predict the same level of specificity, initial mappings should be facilitated. If, on the other hand, the data bases are in conflict, a more extended mapping process with greater errors might be predicted, for example, in the case of noncanonical uses of relational terms.

Other data bases exist which the preschooler may access for assistance. The range and size of the child's lexicon may serve as data in two ways, firstly in conjunction with a preemption strategy (as discussed earlier) and secondly, in terms of the data the child has accumulated about the relationship between words (sense). Since we have argued that sense relations may restrict denotation, a crucial developmental question concerns the manner in which a child becomes aware of relationships within and between semantic fields? Bowerman (1974) has argued that for causative verbs the child's knowledge of the relationships that these verbs contract with other verbs in the lexicon is acquired *after* the child has been using the term in a denotationally correct manner. In contrast, evidence from children's knowledge of color terms suggest that they know something about the sense of the word before they are sure of the denotation of the term. Children realize that x is a color before they have mapped out which color x actually denotes. The possibility therefore exists that if a new word is a member of a semantic field for which the child has a number of features which are already established as lexical organizers (as long as the child realizes the new term belongs to this semantic domain), then that word may be acquired more easily.

We have attempted to indicate the ways in which data bases may influence the development of a lexicon. Considerable scope exists for identifying these data bases and specifying their role in the word acquisition process. These knowledge sets cannot be ignored when we look at the preschoolers word-learning ability if we hope to specify the processes involved.

The Input

The linguistic context in which the child first meets a novel lexical item is a source of hypotheses about the term's denotation and sense. To what extent do children use this information? We will outline some of the information that is potentially available to the young child and present evidence concerned with the manner in which children use such information.

Several studies have focussed on the ways in which adult speech to children differs from speech to adults (Snow & Ferguson, 1977; Vorster, 1975). On the whole, little attention has been paid to how speech content may influence lexical development. Ninio and Bruner (1978) found that the mother invariably drew attention to the referent before naming it. Ninio (1980) found that ostensive definitions were used almost exclusively to name objects.[4] However, Ninio also noted that when mothers named parts of objects, they avoided misunderstanding of the level of reference either by naming the part immediately after naming the whole, or by including a reference to the whole in the definition of the part. These data, although informative, do not tell us much about the nature of maternal labeling of objects.

Objects can be referred to by a variety of different terms (Brown, 1958). Brown (1965) maintained that in speech to children adults anticipate the appropriate level of reference—the 'maximum level of utility' (that is, the level at which objects share

---

[4]Ostensive definition is a process of providing the meaning of a word be it by pointing to or using some other means to focus the child's attention on a particular referent. Ostensive definition, of itself, is never sufficient for learning the meaning of a word since the child must know in advance the significance of the pointing gesture and be able to identify the object or attribute correctly.

common appropriate behaviors). Evidence in support of this prediction comes from White (1982). He found that mothers rarely used a superordinate term to refer to pairs of atypical instances of a category (that is, objects which are not behaviorally equivalent), but did so to refer to pairs of typical instances.

Maternal input to children can be used as a guide in identifying the referent—an essential prerequisite to semantic development. Rogers (1975, 1978, 1979) has gone one step further. From his analysis of protocols dealing with animals (1978, 1979) and household utensils (1979), Rogers has been able to identify two main aspects of maternal speech which are potentially helpful to children in learning the meanings of words: "elaborative linkages" and "semantic extensions." Elaborative linkages are cases where the mother supplies a comment which would add to the child's knowledge about a word or about a world in which the word can be used. Rogers distinguishes four main classes of elaborative linkages:

1. Substitutions which are either instances of synonymy, hypernymy, or hyponymy.
2. Contrastive linkages which indicate that the two words belong to the same semantic field but are not synonyms, for example, "It's short—not very long."
3. Statements of equivalence which are similar to substitutions but are more definitional in nature, for example, "A dog is an animal."
4. Inclusion, for example, "An x is a kind of y."
(It is not clear in Rogers' writing how one distinguishes between inclusion and hyponymy.)

Semantic extensions, on the other hand, are cases where the mother supplies the child with further *relevant* information without employing another nominal from the same domain. The criteria for 'relevancy' is problematic, as Rogers acknowledges. He has, moreover, been able to identify just two categories of semantic extensions: functional and "other." Bridges (1979) reports a similar set of behaviors where the mother referred to the target object in terms of the children's background knowledge of the objects' functions or associations.

We think it is plausible to argue that elaborative linkages are involved in specifying the sense of the term, that is, specifying the semantic domain to which the term does or does not belong. However, one can also envisage them used to correct denotation. For example, "No, that's a lion and this one's a tiger." Semantic extensions, on the other hand, are better thought of as relating to general knowledge. An example of a functional extension will serve to illustrate this point.

Object: Icing syringe.
Mother: It's an icing machine, to ice cakes with. An icing machine for Christmas and birthday cakes. You fill it up with icing and press that down and it squirts icing out (Rogers, 1979, p. 19).

The majority of the information presented in this excerpt is merely contingent and not necessary. The issues in determining essential properties versus contingent ones are controversial and we do not wish to enter the debate at this point. But many cases are perfectly clear. Surely, interchanges such as

Mother: What's that?
Child: Pussy.
Mother: Yes, pussy like Nana's.

are not germane to the meaning of *pussy*. Semantic extension is possibly a misnomer.

The implications of Rogers' work are intriguing. He has provided us with strong evidence that mothers provide their children with linguistic information which could be used in working out the meanings of words, especially in the case of elaborative linkages. However, it is unclear whether children can and do use this information. Rogers (1979) reported a pilot study directed specifically to the question of whether children make use of contrastive information. While his results suggest that children do, the experiment is fraught with difficulties: The sample in each group is small (3); the materials are complex; and the sample size causes problems for the statistical analysis. There is considerable room for clarification and modification before we can determine to what extent children can or do use the information present in elaborative linkages.

K. E. Nelson (1982) reviewed a number of studies which examine the degree to which the child's initial vocabulary can be directly influenced by the semantic and conversational input of adults. He argued, "that children can learn to comprehend and produce some new labels for specific referents on the basis of brief, controlled exposure to referents and names" (p. 186). Unfortunately, the majority of studies Nelson reviews depend solely on naming, so it is impossible to determine the influence of different types of lexical input. It is certainly significant that children learn from these exposures even if some of the exposures are somewhat contrived. In the "rabbit gambit" (pp. 174-175), the child heard the live exemplar named "about 24 times"! It is surely unusual to label an object 24 times in a short period of time and certainly unrepresentative of the natural word-learning task.

Despite this lack of ecological validity, it is difficult to ascertain in many of the studies reported by Nelson what the child has, in fact, learned. There is no assessment of the sense of the new terms and denotational options are often sharply circumscribed. Learning to label a series of varying two-dimensional geometric shapes by a single lexeme may investigate denotational boundaries but hardly studies sense relations. In fact, in these studies it is questionable what sense relations, if any, might be established. The studies focus on denotation but there are three problems here. Firstly, it is not clear in some cases that anything more than correct reference is established, for example, in the rabbit gambit. Secondly, pictures of strange shapes are somewhat lacking in ecological validity. We think it is significant that in Nelson's own data (another labeling task) "thin background-free toys" elicited more naming at every level. Children are much more likely to have had experience of labeling toys. Thirdly, it is very difficult from most of these studies to discern what alternative hypotheses, apart from the intended one, the children might entertain. This is unfortunate since short-lived incorrect hypotheses might well be missed. It is these short-lived hypotheses which may provide us with a significant insight into the word-learning process (Carey, 1982).

We will report Carey's work in some detail since the method she uses is the basis for our own studies. Carey's (1978a) novel experimental approach combines both longitudinal and cross-sectional methods in examining the acquisition of unfamiliar terms by preschool children. She studied the course of development of a single color term in the lexicon of 14 3- to 4-year-olds. Carey chose the term *chromium* and intended it denote the color OLIVE GREEN. The children first encountered the term in a situation which, Carey maintained, allowed the child the possibility of gaining the full meaning of the novel lexical item. Carey does not define "full meaning"; so we shall resort to our own definition of "full meaning" which entails knowing the sense and denotation of a term.

In the introducing event, children were asked to, "Bring me the chromium tray, not the blue one." There were only two trays available, one blue, one olive green. Clearly, successful performance in this introducing situation did not require the child to pay specific attention to the new word *per se*. Carey then plotted the development of the new color term over a period of 6 months, both in a natural playgroup situation and in a number of production and comprehension tasks. Prior to the introducing event, the children were presented with a color identification task and their preferred term for olive green was established. The children tended to label olive green either as *green* or *brown*. Throughout the 6-month testing period it became clear that two distinct forms of response to this experience emerged: one group of children interpreted *chromium* as a synonym of *green*; the other group of children seemed to realize that olive was an odd color that required an odd name, but they did not necessarily produce this name. Carey describes these two types of responses as "fast mappings". In a fast mapping, the child picks up some but not all of the relevant information about the new word. By the end of the 6 months, only one child had established full mapping of the term. It is impossible, however, to see whether full mapping had been established from the limited nature of the assessment as there was no investigation of the sense of the new term. Aware of this, Carey repeated the experiment employing a number of design modifications (1978b). These alterations included a hyponym task assessing whether the children had learned that *chromium* named a color regardless of whether they had learned that *chromium* designated a particular hue. Children were asked if *purple* was a color, if *cold* was a color, and so forth. Included in these question frames was *chromium* and a nonsense word, *tearval*. To be credited with a correct response, children had to respond that all the named colors and *chromium* were a color and that *tearval* and the noncolor terms were not colors. The task was not very informative; the majority of children replied to all questions in either the negative or to all in the affirmative, although there were a few children (6/20) who gave the correct response sequence. In the replication, two of the children established full mapping, six children could clearly be credited with some information about the novel term, eight children demonstrated no learning whatsoever, and two children were difficult to score. Carey concludes:

> At one level, these results are demonstrational: they show that half of the children picked up something about the new word "chromium" or the naming of olive from a single experience with the word. They managed to display that knowledge at an assessment one week later, in a context totally different from the one in which the introducing event had occurred.

That almost half of the children learned nothing indicates that these presentation and assessment conditions might be close to the limit of a three-year old's ability to achieve a fast mapping for a new colour word. Nonetheless, the first demonstrational results confirm the existence of a fast mapping, at least under these conditions. (1978b, p. 28)

Carey's study potentially presents the children with more information than a single ostensive definition. Her introducing event sets up a contrast between *chromium* and a common color term. She has in effect presented the child with a lexical contrast.

Lexical contrast, by its very nature, allows the child both to set up a semantic field and to limit the denotation of the term involved. When two terms are contrasted lexically this serves as an indication that the two terms are similar but that they differ in some manner that is not explicitly defined, for example, "this is a boy, not a girl." The informative nature of the contrast depends on the terms involved and their semantic fields. Provided with a lexical contrast, such as the example, in a situation where reference is clear, the child not only knows that the two lexemes are related but the child is also able to limit the range of denotata to which the term can be applied, human juveniles that are not female.

Barrett (1978) has proposed a theory of semantic development in which learning the relevant contrasts between objects is crucial. Barrett's theory emphasizes an important aspect in the acquisition of word meanings—the differentiation process through contrasts.

To make use of lexical contrast the child must (a) have some idea of which semantic field is involved, and (b) be able to differentiate the field. Rogers (1979) has pointed out that mothers use two different forms of lexical contrast in their speech to young children: contrast *within* fields and contrast *between* fields. The existence of contrast between fields is problematic for the notion that it is an important source of delimiting information to the child. Contrast between fields does not delimit the child's denotation nor help to structure the semantic field in the same way that contrast within fields does. Rogers makes a similar point:

> Clearly, contrastive linkages cannot serve as an infallible indicator of relations between terms in a domain, because of the occurrence of between-category [field] contrasts. However, these are usually well marked as corrections, and show some intonational differences from within-category [field] contrasts. (p. 13)

Experimental Evidence

Carey (1982) argues that the way forward in building a theory of semantic development is to:

1. Examine the role of the linguistic context in which a child first meets a word and assess the child's use of this information.
2. Isolate, if possible, any short-lived hypotheses that the child might entertain.
3. Consider whether differences exist between the types of words children learn.

4. Examine whether constraints on human concepts rule out meanings that children might entertain.
5. Assess whether any differences in children's concepts and, hence, meanings constrain a theory of semantic development.

Some of the evidence we have presented so far bears on these issues. The experiments we are about to report are relevant to statements 1, 2, and 3.

Rather than supplying clearcut answers, the *chromium* study raises a number of questions. Are children's mapping strategies always as idiosyncratic as Carey's data suggest? Is the lexical domain to which the word belongs important? Does Carey's procedure really test the limits of the child's abilities? Our experiments are designed to answer some of these questions.

A Novel Animal Term

This experiment was designed to test the acquisition of a new animal term in the vocabularies of three- and four-year-old children. We chose an animal term for two reasons. Firstly, we suspected that part of the reason that Carey found so few children reaching full mapping of the color term was because of the complex nature of the color vocabulary. Several studies (Miller & Johnson-Laird, 1976, pp. 350-355) have suggested that the color vocabulary is rather complex. The correct use of color terms by children generally develops rather late. Further, Campbell et al. (1982) presented data on developing color vocabularies where the agreement between the range of application of a word in production and comprehension is extremely poor. The extent to which such asymmetries generalize to other semantic domains is a moot point. The difficulty with color terms appears to be a semantic one since children are able to sort objects into their respective color piles. It has been shown that children as young as 15 days have been able to discriminate between colors (Chase, 1937). It may be that because colors lie on a perceptual continuum, children have difficulty isolating the appropriate denotational range. By choosing an animal term, we are presenting the children with a distinct perceptual entity. In addition, children appear to have fairly well-differentiated knowledge about animals. That is, there are data bases which the children may use if the inference "X is an animal" is established. How does a child go about learning a new word which fits into a firmly established conceptual framework?

The present experiment is designed to give children a series of quasi-natural contexts to develop the meaning of a word and has the following goals:

1. to explore the child's ability to acquire a new animal term;
2. to explore the child's ability to produce and comprehend this term in natural conditions with peers;
3. to investigate whether the child does associate the new word with a particular type of animal;
4. if the child associates the new word with a particular type of animal, how does the new term relate to her general concept of animal. For example, does she ascribe it with animate characteristics?

Sixteen children took part in the study which ran for fourteen weeks. Five experimental stages were involved.

Stage 1, Week 1. A base line was established. We wanted to ascertain that the children could name the farm animals (pig, sheep and cow) and that the children had no correct or consistent lexical entry for the animal to be chosen as unknown (tapir).

Stage 2, Week 2. Children were introduced to the novel animal under the pretext of putting animals away. The child was provided with the necessary syntactic and lexical information to form a full mapping, as defined by the experimental task, of the unknown referent. For example, "Pass me the patas, not the pig, the sheep, or the cow but the patas." *Patas* was the nonsense name given to the new animal. Children were then asked for each of the other farm animals in turn.

Stage 3, Week 3. This was a comprehension task embedded in the form of a game. The experimenter played the buyer of animals from the child (who had a farm with pigs, sheep, cows, and tapirs). There was a further test designed to assess the child's ability to attribute animate characteristics to the new term.

There were six question frames (three animate, three inanimate). Eight individual lexical items were inserted in the six question frames: three inanimate objects, *ball*, *car* and *plate*; three farm animals, *cow*, *sheep* and *pig*; *patas*, and a control, meaningless word, *withy*. Any child who asked what a *withy* was, was told that *withy* was a long piece of straw. To assess the effect of the introducing event, a group of children from a different nursery who had not experienced the introducing event carried out the same task.

Stage 4, Week 5. A play situation was arranged twice a week for the children in the nursery. On each occasion, the nursery nurse brought the farm and the animals into the play group and placed them on a table. Playing with the farm and animals was completely voluntary. These sessions were continued for a period of 6 weeks. During this period, the experimenter had no contact with the children or the nursery. Video recordings were made of all these sessions through a one-way mirror.

Stage 5, Week 13. Children were individually tested in a series of production and comprehension tasks including telling the experimenter the names of all the animals they knew, naming known and unknown animals from pictures and responding to the same questions that were asked at Stage 3.

The results were dramatic. The perceptual and lexical contrasts in the experiment allowed all the children to form an initial referential relationship between a sharply circumscribed set of objects. This was done almost immediately. By Stage 3, 13 of the 16 children correctly chose the tapir as the referent for *patas* on the first trial and continued to do so thereafter. Only 1 child, the youngest (2;11), had considerable difficulties with the task saying she "couldn't find the patas." The other 2 children who were classed as initial failures were categorized as such because they asked for reassurance that they had chosen the correct object. On the second trial, every child chose the tapir when asked to "pass the patas". Further, in Stage 5 the children did not overextend the new term to other unknown animals. This suggests that the denotation of the term had been limited. However, not only did the children recognize that *patas* denoted a physical object satisfying some set of perceptual criteria, but they also realized that *patas* designated an animal. That is, the new term had been incorporated into a particular semantic domain. Data to support this contention comes from the children's responses to the questions in Stages 3 and 5. Children treated the term *patas* as they did other animal names and *patas* was unambiguously differentiated from the meaningless control word and the inanimate object names. (There was no observed disassociation between comprehension and production. The new term was used and apparently understood both in the structured testing situation, in the free play in the nursery, with peers, and with other adults.)

We have strong grounds to suggest that the children knew the sense of the term and were in the process of delineating denotation. It seems that for all the children, full mapping of this new term was well on the way to completion. Superficially, this data might appear contradictory to Carey's results where only one child established "full mapping" after a 6-month period. We do not believe this to be the case. There are two major differences between Carey's study and the present one. Firstly, color vocabulary may well be more complex. Secondly, the conceptual framework onto which the novel color term is to be mapped may be less well-established. The actual physical characteristics of the animal in our study were qualitatively different and salient as opposed to the (gradable) differences in color. It is interesting to note that many of the play group interactions that focused on the *tapir* elicited comments about the object's salient perceptual features, for example, its long nose or clear black and white markings. No such comments were noted about the other animals. Being able to identify distinctive features of an object is a clear advantage in isolating one particular referent from a group of possible referents. There are no defining attributes of a particular color and even adults may have problems identifying a particular color. Another peculiarity of the color lexicon is the ease with which color terms denoting perceptually similar groups of colors can be interchanged. While one might label an object as *blue*, another adult might label it as *green*, and a third might label it *turquoise*. It would be a bizarre situation, indeed, were the same object to be labelled as *cat*, *dog*, and *rat* by different adults.

As we have mentioned, 3- and 4-year-old children have fairly firm, if often erroneous, criteria for animal concepts. Suppose a child already knows what an animal is. When the child is exposed to a new term which he or she takes to denote a type of animal, the child need only add this new animal term to his or her previously established lexical/conceptual framework. Bartlett (1978), in a discussion on the acquisition of color words, makes a similar point:

> We must emphasize once again that lexical development depends on both the store of phonological units available for the child to use as words *and the conceptual system available* for mapping meaning onto these units. (pp. 104-105)

New words which are members of semantic classes that have not been firmly defined or that are themselves ill-defined are open not only to the ambiguity of the referential situation, but also the ambiguity or possibly complete lack of conceptual organization of the appropriate reference domain. If the child does not realize that certain verbs are *relational*, the child is unlikely to succeed in deriving their meaning regardless of the situation in which the verb is encountered. It may be that in such situations the context of the word's presentation is given undue weight (Donaldson & McGarrigle, 1974). In such cases, the ontogeny of word meanings is a long, drawn-out procedure with many possibilities for errors.

These factors are only important if the child sees the new word as referring to an animal. We think it is clear that in this situation the child does, although it is perfectly justifiable to argue that there may be no alternative. What governs the level of analysis the child chooses to use? Here, the initial choice of tapir is governed by the alternatives given to the child and the structure which controls the comprehension task. There is a farm on which there are three animals for which the child has already firmly established lexical entries and the child has previously received information as to the nature of the game (i.e., that animals are to be passed between the experimenter and the child). So, once explicitly and once implicitly, the child has been told what the key items are—animals. In many ways, the level of analysis is determined by this information, and the child appears to be sensitive to these cues. Anglin (1977) has shown that children first learn words at intermediate levels of generality, usually at the level at which the objects are functionally equal (in this particular case, animal). We doubt that the task would have been as easy if the new word referred to the specific color patterning of the animal and had been contrasted with the patterning of the other animals.

The present experiment has shown that lexical *and* strong perceptual contrast in one particular semantic domain allows the child to be extremely adept at picking up certain aspects of a word's meaning. If more unknown animals had been present, as in the study by Braun-Lamesch (1973), or if the contrast had been purely linguistic (e.g., "I like cabbage, not aubergines"), or if the new word had been preempted, the results might have been very different.

Before moving on to the next study, we would like to report an unexpected result from the control group, who experienced no introducing event. Children in this group showed no significant difference in choosing the tapir as a patas in the comprehension trials from those children who did experience the introducing event. Thus, the introducing event, *per se*, had no significant effect on the children's performance in the comprehension session. However, a ceiling effect was probably operative here for both the control and experimental groups. The children were extremely efficient at figuring out that the unknown word referred to an unfamiliar object and therefore, to the tapir. Accordingly, even the control group (with no prior information about 'patas') performed at a high level immediately—an unanticipated result. This result was replicated with a different semantic domain, that of fruit terms, and the conclusions remain the same. This is an extremely useful strategy for the early word learner.

A Novel Shape or Pattern or Color Term?

By the end of the 2 months, thirteen of the sixteen children produced the term *patas* appropriately and all but one child presented evidence of comprehension.

What we appear to have is a group of children who have nearly all completed the full mapping process in a period of 2 months. The children proved so adept in making the appropriate inference that it was not possible to identify any partial meanings or idsiosyncratic responses along the way. As we shall show, this is not always the case.

Both Carey's study (1978a,b) and the patas study have attempted to look for a gap in a particular semantic domain. In both, the child was presented with sufficient information to determine the referent intended by the experimenter, and the child's performance was then assessed in a series of well-defined task contexts. These are not effective ways of evaluating the relative importance of the information provided linguistically and nonlinguistically. Apart from the denotation intended by the experimenter, what alternatives did the children have? The opportunities for children to make wrong guesses in these studies is sharply circumscribed. Carey's testing procedure practically forces the inference that *chromium* denotes a range of colors including olive green, while our procedure forces the inference that *patas* denotes a range of animals including tapirs. These studies show that 3-year-old children can make these inferences.

By contrast, it seems evident that there must frequently be cases where there is doubt about which attribute, value, or range of values is being referred to—either because of the ambiguity inherent in a particular referential situation and/or because of the child's limited vocabulary. As we have noted, mothers of young children evidence some awareness of their children's problems (Bridges, 1979; Rogers, 1978) and, in fact, sometimes the mothers structure the information which accompanies the encounter with the new term so as to restrict the range of possible denotations. The following experiment was designed to trace the acquisition of a single term where the range of possible denotations spanned three distinct attributes: shape, color, and pattern.

Building blocks were used as the experimental stimuli. The test simulus was an hexagonal block with an unusual pattern on it (silver grey stripes on a tangerine background). Would the children take the new term to denote (a) hexagons, (b) a range of shapes including hexagons, (c) striped things, or (d) a range of patterns including striped or the constituent colors? The children were given different introducing events in order to determine whether it was possible to affect their guesses by means of different lexical contrasts. The main question then is, given a range of possible denotations, how does variation in the input affect acquisition?

There are several possible problems with the present study which we would like to comment upon before describing it. Firstly, it might be argued that, for some reason, one of the attributes might have some kind of potency or saliency for the child and therefore, there might be a tendency to assume that the potent or salient attribute was what was meant by the unknown term, with no account taken of the particular lexical contrast drawn. The general consensus from the literature is that nursery school children tend to prefer color, there being a shift to form preference around the age of 4½ to age 6 (Suchman & Trabasso, 1966). Preferences do appear to depend on the type and complexity of the stimulus. A prediction from this conclusion might be that children should find it easier to learn an unknown color term, but there is no guidance about the relative salience of pattern. Moreover, such findings tell us little about the salience of *particular* colors and shapes. However, if the introducing event has any effect, these perceptual criteria might be overruled.

The second possible criticism concerns the use of pattern as a stimulus. Contrasting pattern with known color is clearly unusual. However, there is good reason for this choice. It was found in a pilot study that when children encounter colors for which they have no name, they commonly overextend known color terms to include this new instance. This did not occur with unknown shapes or patterns and since we were looking for a gap in the lexicon, we chose pattern for the main experiment. We have, however, included a supplementary control study where an unknown color is contrasted with known colors. This study will be reported after the results of the main study have been presented.

Plan of the Experiment

Sixteen children, mean age 4;0 (range 3;0– 4;11) were tested. Fourteen children completed the study, six children in the shape contrast group and eight in the pattern contrast group.

Stage 1, Week 1. Prior to any exposure to the new word, a baseline level of performance was obtained. A selection of blocks of various colors, shapes, and patterns and a number of filler items were presented to the children in an attempt to assess their production vocabulary for shape, color and pattern.

Stage 2, Week 2. The introducing event occurred one week later. Children left the play group with the experimenter under the pretext of hearing a story. Three objects were present on the table in the testing room and these were to be removed before the story could commence. The three objects were a red cube, a green sphere, and a striped hexagonal prism. They are henceforth referred to as a square block, or a round block, or a hexagonal block. Children were asked to pass the blocks one by one to the experimenter as she requested them. For half the children (the pattern group), the following request was used:

Pass me the *gombe* block, not the red one or the green one, but the *gombe* one.

For the other children (the shape group) the following request was used:

Pass me the *gombe* block, not the round one or the square one, but the *gombe* one.

Henceforth, we will refer to the children receiving the second instruction as the "shape group". After the *gombe* block had been given to the experimenter, the other two blocks were requested.

Stage 3, Week 3. One week later, the children's comprehension of the term *Gombe* was examined. The comprehension test was embedded in a game. The game involved the child building some edifice of choice with a puppet. The order in which the puppet requested the blocks was predetermined. The blocks present in this session included three *gombe* blocks, two green squares, one red square, two red circles, and one green circle. For children in the shape group, blocks were requested by means of shape adjectives or *gombe*, for example, *a gombe, a square*. For children in the pattern group, blocks were requested by means of color adjectives of *gombe*, for example, *a red one, a Gombe one*. In this session there were no opportunities for the children to extend *gombe* beyond its known range unless they took the term to refer to a known shape or color for which they had a familiar term—a highly unlikely outcome.

Stage 4, Week 4. One week after the completion of Stage 3, children's comprehension of *gombe* was assessed again in the same game situation. However, on this occasion, the two attributes present in the *gombe* block were separated, that is, there were striped square and round blocks and plain-colored hexagonal blocks. On completion of the game, the blocks were removed from view and the children were asked to answer some questions for the experimenter. Inappropriate and appropriate uses of color and shape terms were included in the question frames, for example, "Can you paint a car red?", "Can you paint a car square?" Included in these sentence frames were the term *gombe* and a meaningless control word. The final questions were a hyponym task concerning color and shape (cf. Carey, 1978b).

Stage 5, Week 5-11. This stage was effectively a 6-week break during which the child was not exposed to the term *gombe*. The possibility of spontaneous production could not be precluded. Twice weekly the nursery nurse brought the blocks into the play group and children were free to play with them if they wished. These sessions were videorecorded through a one-way mirror.

Stage 6, Week 13. This was the final stage in the assessment procedure. The follow-up session involved both a production and a comprehension session carried out in the form of the game. Afterwards, the explicit knowledge of the children's understanding of the term was investigated. The format of this final assessment varied between children and was very much influenced by the child's comments. Both the production and the comprehension tasks presented opportunities for the child to extend the use of the term to other shapes, other colors, and other combinations of colors for the pattern.

The results were analyzed by looking at the overall performance of the shape and pattern groups and by looking at the development of the meaning of the term for each child.

In the final comprehension session *all* of the children in the shape group took the term *gombe* to denote hexagonally-shaped objects. In the pattern group, two children took *gombe* to denote tangerine and grey striped objects. Only one child showed no learning at all. The other children produced interpretations of various intermediate types. There were two complete reversals where pattern children took *gombe* to denote hexagonal shapes. The mapping strategies for these children are presented in Figure 6-1.

Production was more difficult to elicit. Of course, it was not possible to ask the children to name a particular attribute, since that would have introduced a heavy

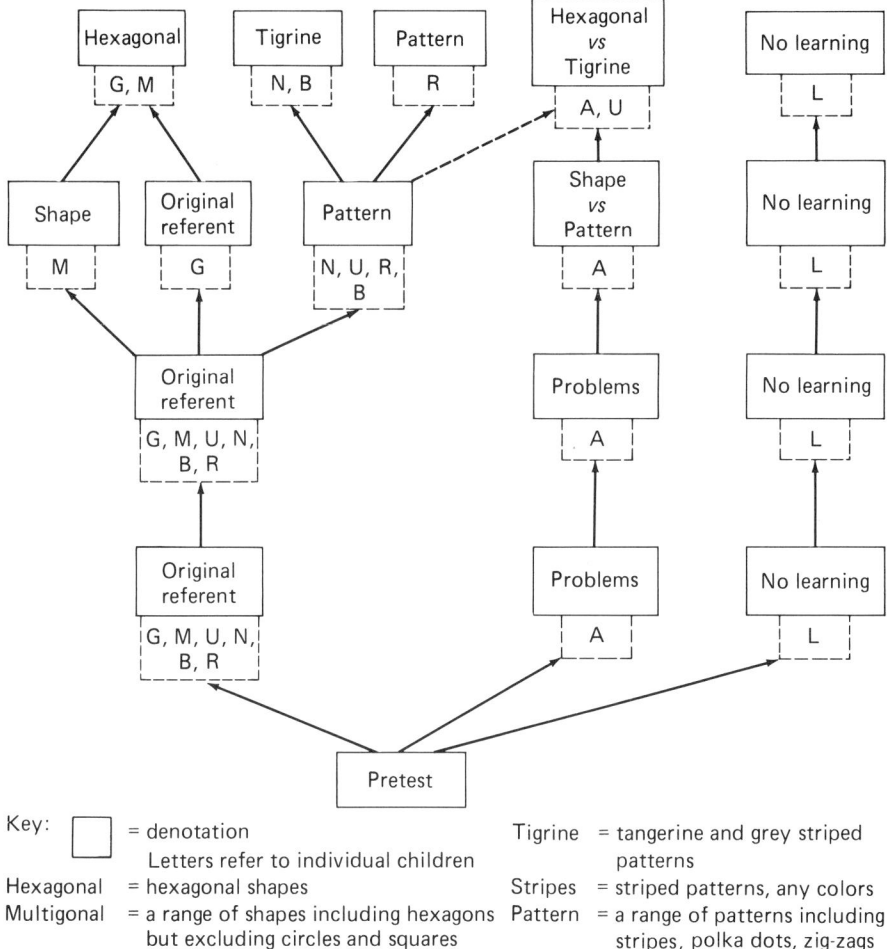

Figure 6-1. Pattern group mapping strategies (comprehension data).

bias. Five children did spontaneously produce the term when requesting a block. However, production did not always reflect the results obtained in the comprehension task. For example, the child for whom *gombe* appeared to denote hexagonal shape in the comprehension task, referred to a block of a different shape but the original pattern as a *gombe* block in the production session (see also Kuczaj, 1982b; Thompson & Chapman, 1977).

Overall, the results would appear to indicate that children are capable of using implicit contrastive information to determine exactly which attribute is being indicated in a potentially ambiguous situation. However, many idiosyncratic hypotheses or 'fast mappings' occur.

Given the idiosyncratic mappings of the pattern contrast group, we decided to test whether these strategies arose because the lexical contrast invited a search for a new color which could not be found. Accordingly, a lexical contrast between *gombe* and known color terms was employed as an introducing event (as formerly), but the referent (gombe block) differed from the other objects in shape and color only. That is, all blocks were self-colored, without patterning of any sort. The color chosen for the referent was selected to minimize the possibility of preemption by other known color terms.

Seven children (2;8–4;0) took part in the study. Apart from the change from pattern to color, the procedure was identical to the original study. The results are presented in Figure 6-2. Strikingly, only one child (N) took the new term to denote the new color (silver fern). Five children took *gombe* to denote HEXAGONAL and another child (J) took *gombe* to denote only the original stimulus. The simplest

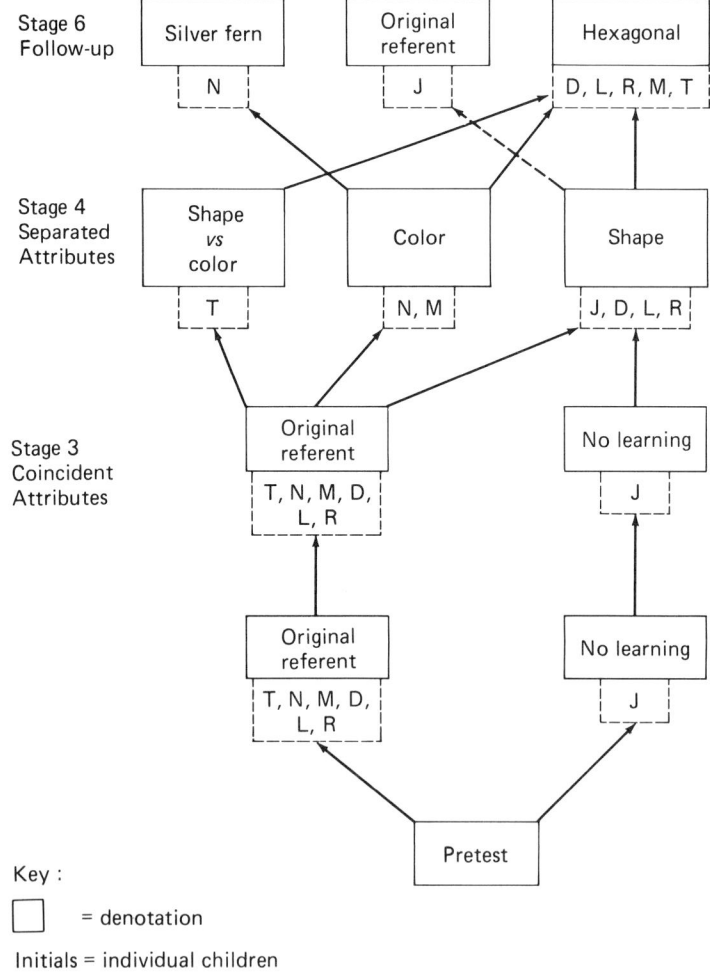

Figure 6-2. Color control group mapping strategies (comprehension data).

interpretation of these results is that color terms are more easily extended than shape terms. This leaves a gap in the shape vocabulary but not in the color vocabulary and therefore, children take *gombe* to note SHAPE in this situation. Apart from the fact that children do learn new color terms, albeit with difficulty (Bartlett, 1978; Campbell et al., 1982; Carey, 1978a; Rice, 1980), and that they do learn synonyms and superordinates and subordinates, such an explanations fails to take into account two factors present in the control experiment: children's denotation changed from Stage 4 to 6 and occasional asymmetries between production and comprehension.

Two of the children who responded as if *gombe* denoted HEXAGON in Stage 6 had responded quite differently in Stage 4. The only child (M) to admit she had no term for 'silver fern', took *gombe* to denote SILVER FERN in Stage 4 —a mapping we might predict—and changed her criteria in Stage 6 and responded as if *gombe* denoted HEXAGONAL. One possible explanation is that some semantic reorganization took place between Stages 4 and 6—possibly in her color lexicon.

(T)'s performance in Stage 4 could best be described as an either/or both property strategy. By Stage 6, (T) had restricted the denotation to hexagonal. Although his Stage 4 strategy allowed for flexibility in the mapping process, it is unclear what made him focus on shape, let alone a particular shape at that?

In contrast, (J) performed in Stage 4 as if *gombe* denoted HEXAGONAL. By Stage 6 she had restricted the denotation to the original stimulus. The reasons for such a restriction are somewhat obscure. Her willingness to label all colors with other color terms may account for elimination of color as criterion, but why restrict *gombe* to shape and color? There seems no obstacle for her mapping *gombe* onto shape or even unnamed shapes. Alternatively, why can't *gombe* be just another one of these randomly assigned color terms?

Interestingly, there is evidence of semantic reorganization in the one child, (N), who took *gombe* to denote SILVER FERN. The evidence comes from (N)'s father who reported that at home (N) was labeling BLUE as *gombe*. It would appear that although the initial lexical contrast had made it clear to (N) that color was being denoted, he had not restricted the range of denotata to SILVER FERN alone.

The second point we would like to mention is the one case of striking asymmetry between comprehension and production. *Gombe* denotes HEXAGON for (D) both in Stage 4 and Stage 6 (see Figure 6-2). Much to our surprise, when asked the color of a particular block at the end of the testing in Stage 6, he replied "gombe". The color was Silver Fern. One possibility is that (D) had come to realize that he had no appropriate name for 'Silver fern' and therefore used the only name that has been associated with that color—odd color, odd name. This hypothesis is weak: since (D) performs as if *gombe* denotes HEXAGONAL, it is not an odd name.

At the end of 10 weeks, only one child had failed to learn something about *gombe*. All the other children had formed some representation of the term. It is not possible to say how many, if any, had acquired a 'full mapping' for we have no conception of what new contexts might alter these responses or what refinement will occur unprecedented. (Note the changes which occur between Stage 4 and Stage 6 when the child does not hear or produce the term.) In any case, 'full mapping' is a relative term. In this situation, it can only mean the experimenters intended denotation and sense. Normally, the child's interpretation of lexical items is contrasted with an agreed consensus. The question is *not* which children reach the experimenter's criterion for 'full mapping', but rather what these individual and group strategies tell us about the child as a word learner.

Figure 6-3 outlines the experimental variables we have considered. What sorts of conclusions can be drawn about the child as a word learner? Firstly, it is necessary to qualify our notions concerning preemption. The existence of a lexical gap when a child first meets a new word, assuming that the child can pick out the intended denotatum, allows a quick and direct mapping to take place. Certainly, preemption places added strain on the process, but it does not preclude the acquisition of the new lexical item as having the same or a similar denotation to the previously known lexemes. Of course, this result should have been expected since children *do* learn synonyms. Preemption may only be a significant variable at particular stages in particular circumstances. Interestingly, young bilingual children will sometimes only label objects by words in one language, denying the appropriateness of the word in their other language (Fantini, 1979, cited in Clark, 1980). Further evidence of a word having only one denotation comes from work on homophones by Campbell and Bowe (1978). They showed that children interpreted homophones in the most

	Unfamiliar word / Variable	Patas (Noun)	Gombe (Adjective) Shape group	Gombe (Adjective) Pattern group	Gombe (Adjective) Color control
Experimental variable	Lexical contrast	Present	Present	Unclear whether contrast appropriate	Present
Experimental variable	Supporting perceptual contrast	Present	Absent	Absent	Absent
Within child variable	Semantic framework	Present	Present	Possibly lacking	Possibly lacking
Within child variable	Gap in lexicon	Present	Present	Present	Unclear whether gap exists
Outcome	Mapping sense & denotation	Strong sense & denotation present	Sense & denotation present	Sense unclear, denotation variable	Sense unclear, denotation reversed

Figure 6-3. Factors contributing to the development of sense and denotation in minilongitudinal studies.

familiar way even when the context indicated otherwise, for example, *hare* as a strand of hair rather than an animal. Exactly how a strategy like preemption works needs to be elaborated, since it must be discarded for synonyms and hypernyms to be acquired.

Secondly, the data bases which the children have about an object or an attribute influences the word learning process, although the presence of a semantic framework into which the new word can enter appears to be more important for representation of the sense of a term than representation of its denotation. The semantic frame is set up by the initial contrast. A semantic framework shows that the children know that relations exist between words, and therefore the existence of this framework potentially allows the new term to enter into these word-word relationships. As such, the existence of a semantic frame may, in fact, be a necessary prerequisite for the development of sense relationships. So, for example, in the case of the pattern contrast group, although various denotational boundaries are constructed, the term does not enter into any coherent semantic framework for the group as a whole as evidenced from their responses to the questions. This may well be because the initial contrast is ambiguous. This is not the point, however. The point is that various denotations develop, but there is not evidence of any sense relations. In a similar vein, in the *patas* case, where a semantic framework exists, we are sure of the sense of the term for the children and can only infer the denotation of the term from the choices the children make from a limited selection of animals. It is therefore possible for sense and denotational mappings to exist independently. The sense of the term restricts denotation, and equally, knowledge of denotation may allow a sense representation to develop. When both of these representations are complete, the child may be said to have achieved full mapping of a term.

Thirdly, there is convincing evidence that input can affect the children's ensuing mappings. Lexical contrast can play a decisive role in the child's ensuing representation of a new lexical item (shape group), but this contrast is less effective when the term is preempted (color control), or when the contrast is not accurate (pattern group) and an alternative denotation is available. Children's solutions, when preemption and lexical contrast conflict, may depend on a number of factors including their ability to accept synonymity, the relative importance placed on linguistic information, the degree of ambiguity within the frame of reference, the salience of the attribute, and other similar variables. Lexical contrast need not be supported by an analogous perceptual contrast, though the presence of an appropriate perceptual contrast does seem to accelerate the ensuing mapping process.

Carey (1978a, 1978b) identified two phases in the acquisition process—a fast mapping and a more extended slow mapping. The present studies support Carey's description of the slow mapping period—a long period of semantic and lexical reorganization. Her description, however, of the fast mapping process requires some qualification. To Carey (1978), the fast mapping is only a "Small fraction of the total information that will constitute full learning of a word" (p. 18). The first point is a simple qualification of Carey's initial conclusion. In some cases, the fast mappings may provide the children with sufficient information to gain a considerably more detailed understanding of the term than Carey found with *chromium* (cf. *patas* study). The second qualification is more important. Implicit in Carey's definition is the fact that information acquired in the fast mapping process is relevant to the meaning of the new word. Certainly this is the case in her own study, but when the child has more options, as to the attribute being referred to, there is a greater potential for errors, and children make them. Therefore, fast mappings need not necessarily provide the children with information which is relevant to the meaning of the new word, but rather on some occasions the fast mappings may lengthen the word-learning process because the child has made an initially incorrect guess. Fast mappings are structured by the linguistic and nonlinguistic context in which the child encounters the word and by the nature of the episode. The more unstructured the alternatives available to the child, the more likely the child is to make an error. It would seem then that the information provided by children's caretakers, which restricts the possible meaning of the new term, are extremely valuable guidelines for the child.

Conclusion

This chapter has been concerned with the ways in which children map out the meanings of novel lexical items. We have argued that the acquisition process is a function of the type of words being acquired as well as the type of linguistic and nonlinguistic knowledge which the child brings to the task. It is clear that no single strategy (or simple set of strategies) will account for acquisition of novel lexical items, either within or between children. Rather, we must clarify the variables which determine the use of particular strategies. The child's data bases, the time and type of exposure, and the word class must be clearly delineated for a coherent picture to emerge. Where we believe our approach differs from others, is that we have attempted to draw a link between a theoretical conception of work meaning in terms of sense, reference, and denotation, and realizing these separate entities experimentally. Our reason for introducing the sense, reference, and denotation distinction was to clarify the notion of word meaning and to thereby provide a framework for assessing the child's semantic competence. Perhaps the best way to assess the success of introducing such a distinction is to see whether it was in fact empirically possible to identify the different processes and, if so, how does this conceptualizing advance our understanding of the word-learning process?

It has been possible to distinguish experimentally between reference and denotation. Children were extremely adept at guessing that an unknown word referred to an unknown animal as evidenced by our control group. Successful reference was established and children in the experimental group progressed from knowledge of reference to knowledge of denotation. However, in the *gombe* study, reference was also achieved for the majority of children but this was not an indicator of any consistent understanding of the terms denotation. It was only by assessing the child's comprehension over time that we were able to distinguish between arbitrary guesses about the intended referent and a child's attempt to develop denotational criteria.

Our attempt to assess the development of sense has been less successful. We would argue that this is a reflection of our limited methodology. We attempted to assess the development of sense relations by examining whether children treated the novel term in a similar manner to other "related terms", that is, did children treat *patas* as an animal term and *gombe* as a shape or color term. The evidence is irrefutable that *patas* was treated as an animate term and distinguished from inanimate terms. Children also tended to include *patas* in their lists of animals. The situation with *gombe* is by no means as clear. Although the shape group did treat *gombe* as a shape term and clearly differentiated it from a meaningless control, the pattern and color groups did not. When the children in this study were presented with an explicit hypernyn question, for example, Is gombe a color?, the results were random. Interestingly, their responses to known color and shape terms were also inconsistent.

Our failure to map the children's sense relations is partially due to the fact that children have great difficulty stating what they know about a particular lexical item. In fact, it is not unjustifiable to say that they are often not aware of this knowledge— it is tacit. Not only are children not aware of what they know about a word's meaning, but frequently the child's tacit understanding of the term, as viewed in spontaneous production and comprehension, does not necessarily reflect what they say about the term. So, for example, Child B in the pattern group (specific pattern strategy) behaves as if *gombe* denotes TIGRINE, clearly distinguishes between shape and color terms, but cannot explicitly distinguish between shape, pattern, or color with reference to 'gombe'. On the other hand, Child A never responds as if *gombe* denotes COLOR, does respond as if *gombe* can denote SHAPE, yet on occasion denies it is a shape and says it is a color. There appears to be a disjunction between the children's two representations of the term. Campbell (1979), making a distinction between what he calls phenic and cryptic representations notes, "What is evident to the subject is phenic, what is hidden, cryptic" (p. 420). This distinction may well be helpful in understanding the present apparent disjunction. If we view the child's production and comprehension of the term as processes employing cryptic representation which occur without the child making inferences about its meaning, asking the child to make a conscious rational decision about its meaning may well involve a phenic representations which is not yet available for use. Campbell (1979) further states:

> There is an inner domain [phenic] of the organism, the contents of which are constantly changing and available to awareness and whose dynamic is rational; there is an outer domain [cryptic], the contents of which change only slowly, are not available to awareness, and whose dynamic is causal. (p. 420)

The fact that children's representations of the new lexical items change slowly over time when no information is encountered is another indication that we may in fact be dealing with a cryptic process when we are examining the acquisition of new words. It is not surprising, therefore, that if we attempt to examine something which is initially only cryptically represented by means that tap phenic representations, we will find explaining the acquisition of word meanings a difficult if not impossible task.

Despite our methodological difficulties, we have been able to map out some differences between the different elements in the word-learning process. The theoretical distinction can be realized empirically.

What if we had failed to draw the distinction between sense, reference, and denotation? Firstly, if we had failed to draw the distinction the concepts of full meaning and partial meaning could only be subjectively assessed. Carey's (1978a) discussion of what full meaning entails is made in comparison to some adult norm rather than to any objective criterion. There is no possibility of a full meaning which is not equivalent to an adult meaning. Similarly, her concept of partial meaning refers to some amount of information which is not equal to full meaning (adult meaning). In contrast, we can state what we mean by full meaning (sense, reference, and denotation) and, by corollary, what components of meaning are present in a partial representation of a term—either sense, reference, or denotation. Talking only in terms of partial meanings, we might have been tempted to say that in the *patas* study children have grasped the full meaning of the term, whereas it is more accurate to say that the children know the sense of the term but the precise denotation remains to be empirically established. Using the full meaning or partial meaning approach with respect to the *gombe* study, either we would wish to say that most children know the meaning of the new term since they chose the correct objects when asked for the *gombe* block or we would say that nearly all children have only a partial meaning since they did not treat the new term in the same manner as they treated other shape or color terms in the questions. 'Meaning' is not imply 'full' or 'partial,' rather, it is either 'full' or one of various types of partial meaning, and it is the analysis of partial meanings in the *gombe* study which are most informative.

Secondly, we might easily have focused only on one aspect of meaning. We criticized earlier the studies summarized by K. E. Nelson (1982) for precisely this reason. While assessing the development of sense is fraught with methodological difficulties, it is an intrinsic element in the development of word meaning and its existence must at least be acknowledged (see also Kuczaj, 1982a). Equally, it is necessary to distinguish some arbitrary guess at a referent and the mapping of a denotational range whether or not the latter is correct with respect to some adult standard.

In conclusion, we suggest that the sense, reference, and denotation distinction clarifies our conception of the word-learning process, adds precision with respect to the variables involved in the mapping process, and allows us to define meaning in such a way as to be able to make predictions about the processes involved in acquiring the meaning of an unfamiliar word.

One problem which must now be investigated is the manner in which the various aspects of word-meaning are related. We would suggest that it is *not* the case that once two elements of meaning are known, the third can be deduced. Rather, knowing either sense, reference, denotation, or some combination of the three, helps in discovering the missing element(s). Consider Carey's *chromium* task. Determining the reference of *chromium* means inferring that the tray intended is not the blue one, determining the sense of *chromium* means realizing that the trays differ saliently only in color, and knowing the denotation of *chromium* means knowing the denotation of other similar color terms, for example, brown, green, and so forth. Knowing that *chromium* is "not the blue one" and "a color" does not necessarily force the inference that *chromium* denotes OLIVE GREEN. Similarly, knowing that a *patas* is "not a pig, a cow or a sheep" does not necessarily mean that it is an animal, though there is a good chance that such an inference will be made. Knowing one or other component of meaning restricts the range of possibilities, but does not determine the correct one.

Sense and denotation are two separate aspects in the word-learning process. This is true for both child and adult alike. Sense and denotation involve two different semantic processes: establishing a relationship between words and establishing the relationship between word and world. By articulating this distinction we believe it will be possible to get a clearer characterization of the child as a word learner.

Acknowledgments. We are grateful to John McShane for his critical comments on the original manuscript, and to Pat Christopher for typing. The research was supported by an S.S.R.C. postgraduate grant to Julie Dockrell.

References

Anglin, J. M. (1977). *Word, object and conceptual development*. New York: Norton.
Barrett, M. (1978). Lexical development and overextension in child language. *Journal of Child Language*, 5, 205-219.
Barrett, M. D. (1983). The early acquisition and development of the meanings of action-related words. In T. B. Seiler & W. Wannenmacher (Eds.), *Concept development and the development of word meaning*. Berlin: Springer-Verlag.
Bartlett, E. (1978). The acquisition of the meaning of colour terms: A study of lexical development. In *Recent advances in the psychology of language*. New York: Plenum Press.
Berko, J. (1958). The child's learning of English morphology. *Word*, 14, 150-177.
Bierwisch, M. (1981). Basic issues in the development of word meaning. In W. Deutsch (Ed.), *The child's construction of language*. London: Academic Press.
Bowerman, M. (1974). Learning the structure of causative verbs: A study in the relationship of cognitive, semantic and syntactic development. *Papers and Reports on Child Language Development*, 8, 142-178.
Bowerman, M. (1978). The acquisition of word meaning: An investigation of some current conflict. In N. Waterson & C. Snow (Eds.), *The development of communication*. New York: Wiley.
Braun-Lamesch, M. M. (1973). La decouverte de significations a l'aide du contexte. *Bulletin de Psychologie*, 304 XXVI, 5-9.
Bridges, A. (1979). Directing two-year-olds' attention: Some clues to understanding. *Journal of Child Language*, 6, 211-226.
Brown, R. (1958). How shall a thing be called? *Psychological Review*, 65, 14-21.
Brown, R. (1965). *Social psychology*. New York: Free Press.

Campbell, R. N. (1979). Cognitive development and child language. In P. Fletcher & M. Garman (Eds.), *Language acquisition*. Cambridge: Cambridge University Press.

Campbell, R. N., & Bowe, T. (1978). Functional asymmetry in early child language. In G. Drachman (Ed.), *Salzburger Bestrage fur linguistic 4*. Salzburg: Wolfgang Neugebauer.

Campbell, R., Bowe, T., & Dockrell, J. (1982). The relationship between comprehension and production and its ontogenesis. In F. Lowenthal (Ed.), *Language and language acquisition*. New York: Plenum Press.

Carey, S. (1978a). The child as a word learner. In M. Halle, J. Bresnan, & G. Miller (Eds.), *Linguistic theory and psychological reality*. MIT Press.

Carey, S. (1978b). Acquiring a single new word. *Papers and reports on child language, 15*, 17-29.

Carey, S. (1982). Semantic development: The state of the art. In E. Wanner & L. Gleitman (Eds.), *Language acquisition: The state of the art*. Cambridge: Cambridge University Press.

Chase, W. P. (1936). Color vision in infants. *Journal Experimental Psychology, 20*, 203-222.

Clark, E. (1983). Meaning and concepts. In P. H. Mussen (Ed.), *Carmichael's manual of child psychology: Vol. 3, Cognitive Development*. New York: John Wiley.

Clark, E. (1980). Convention and innovation in acquiring the lexicon. *Papers and Reports on Child Language Development, 19*, 1-20.

Clark, E. V. (1973). What's in a word? On the child's acquisition of semantics in his first language. In T. E. Moore (Ed.), *Cognitive development and the acquisition of language*. New York: Academic Press.

Cohen, I. B., & Strauss, M. S. (1979). Concept acquisition in the human infant. *Child Development, 50*, 419-424.

Cruse, D. A. (1977). The pragmatics of lexical specificity. *Journal of Linguistics, 13*, 153-164.

Curtis, K. (1974). *A study in semantic development*. Unpublished bachelor's dissertation, University of St. Andrews, St. Andrews, Scotland.

Dockrell, J. (1981). *The child's acquisition of unfamiliar words: An experimental study*. Unpublished doctoral dissertation, University of Stirling, Stirling, Scotland.

Donaldson, M., & Balfour, G. (1968). Less is more: A study of language comprehension in children. *British Journal of Psychology, 59*, 461-471.

Donaldson, M., & McGarrigle, J. (1974). Some clues as to the nature of semantic development. *Journal of Child Language, 1*, 185-194.

Freeman, N., Lloyd, S., & Sinha, C. (1980). Infant search tasks reveal early concepts of containment and canonical usage of objects. *Cognition, 8*, 243-262.

Gelman, R., Bullock, M., & Meck, E. (1980). Preschoolers' understanding of simple object transformations. *Child Development, 51*, 691-699.

Gentner, D. (1978). On relational meaning: The acquisition of verb meaning. *Child Development, 49*, 988-998.

Grieve, R., Hoogenraad, R., & Murray, D. (1977). On the young child's use of lexis and syntax in understanding locative instructions. *Cognition, 5*, 235-250.

Harris, P. (1975). Inferences and semantic development. *Journal of Child Language, 2*, 143-152.

Hoogenraad, R., Grieve, R., Baldwin, P., & Campbell, R. N. (1978). Comprehension as an interactive process. In R. N. Campbell & P. T. Smith (Eds.), *Recent advances in the psychology of language*. New York: Plenum.

Inhelder, B., & Piaget, J. (1964). *The early growth of logic in the child*. New York: Humanities Press.

Kuczaj, S. (1982a). Acquisition of word meaning in the context of the development of the semantic system. In C. Brainerd & M. Pressky (Eds.), *Verbal processes in children.* New York: Springer-Verlag.

Kuczaj, S. (1982b). Young children's overextensions of object words in comprehension and/or production: Support for a prototype theory of early object word meaning. *First Language, 3*(1973), 93-105.

Labov, W. (1973). The boundaries of words and their meanings. In E. N. Bailey & R. W. Shuy (Eds.), *New ways of analyzing variation in English.* Washington, DC: Georgetown University Press.

Lehrer, A. (1970). Indeterminacy in semantic description. *Glossa, 4,* 87-110.

Lennenberg, E. (1967). *Foundations of language development* (Vol. 1). New York: Academic Press.

Leslie, A. (1984). Spatiotemporal continuity and the perception of causality in infants. *Perception, 13*(3), 287-306.

Lyons, J. (1977). *Semantics 1.* London & New York: Cambridge University Press.

Macnamara, J. (1982). *Names for things: A study of human learning.* Cambridge, MA: MIT Press.

Markman, E. M., Cox, B., & Machida, S. (1981). The standard sorting task as a measure of conceptual organization. *Developmental Psychology, 17,* 115-117.

Markman, E., & Hutchinson, J. (1984). Children's sensitivity to constraints on word meaning: Taxonomic versus thematic relations. *Cognitive Psychology, 16,* 1-27.

McShane, J. (1980). *Learning to talk.* Cambridge, MA: Cambridge University Press.

McShane, J., & Dockrell, J. (1983). Lexical and syntactic development. In B. Butterworth (Ed.), *Speech production* (Vol. 2), London: Academic Press.

Mervis, C. B., & Pani, J. R. (1980). Acquisition of object categories. *Cognitive Psychology, 12,* 496-522.

Miller, G., & Johnson-Laird, P. (1976). *Language and perception.* MA: Harvard University Press.

Nelson, K. (1973). Some evidence for the cognitive primacy and its functional basis. *Merrill-Palmer Quarterly of Behavior and Development, 19,* 21-39.

Nelson, K. E. (1982). Experimental gambits in the service of language acquisition theory: From the fiffin project to operation input swap. In S. Kuczaj (Ed.), *Language development: Vol. 2, language and cognition.* Hillsdale, NJ: Erlbaum.

Ninio, A. (1980). Ostensive definition in vocabulary teaching. *Journal of Child Language, 7,* 565-573.

Ninio, A., & Bruner, J. (1978). The achievement and antecedents of labelling. *Journal of Child Language, 5,* 1-15.

Nygren, C. (1972). Children's acquisition of instrumental verbs. Unpublished doctoral dissertation, University of Chicago, Chicago, IL.

Palermo, D. (1973). More about less: A study of language comprehension. *Journal of Verbal Learning & Verbal Behaviour, 12,* 211-221.

Palermo, D. (1974). Still more about the comprehension of "less." *Developmental Psychology, 10,* 827-829.

Riccuiti, N. (1965). Object grouping and selective ordering behavior in infants 12-24 months old. *Merrill-Palmer Quarterly, 11,* 129-143.

Rice, M. (1980). *Cognition to language. Categories—word meanings and training.* Baltimore: University Park Press.

Richards, M. (1978). The acquisition of English antonyonic terms: Recent evidence and its implications for a semantic feature acquisition theory. *Journal of Experimental Child Psychology, 29,* 1-47.

Rogers, D. (1975). Maternal usage of size words: A case study. Unpublished master's thesis, University of Keele, Keele, England.

Rogers, D. (1978). Information in the speech of mothers to young children about the meaning of nouns. Animal nouns. Unpublished manuscript, University of Keele, Keele, England.

Rogers, D. (1979). Transmission of knowledge of word meanings from parent to child. Report SSRC Research Grant, Keele, England.

Rosch, E. (1976). Classification of real-world objects: Origins and replications in cognition. In S. Ehrlich & E. Tubring (Eds.), *Bulletin de Psychologie* [Special issue].

Rosch, E. (1978). Principles of categorization. In E. Rosch & B. B. Lloyd (Eds.), *Cognition and categorization*. Hillsdale, NJ: Erlbaum.

Rosch, E., & Mervis, C. B. (1975). Family resemblances: Studies in the internal structure of categories. *Cognitive Psychology, 8*, 573-605.

Rosch, E., Mervis, C., Gray, W., Johnson, D., & Boyes-Braem, P. (1976). Basic objects in natural categories. *Cognitive Psychology, 8*, 382-439.

Ross, G. (1980). Concept categorization in 1 to 2 year olds. *Developmental Psychology, 16*, 391-396.

Slobin, D., & Bever, T. (1982). Children's use of canonical sequence schema: A cross-linguistic study of word order and inflections. *Cognition, 12*, 229-263.

Snow, C. E., & Ferguson, C. A. (Eds.). (1977). *Talking to children*. Cambridge, MA: Cambridge University Press.

Suchman, R., & Trabasso, T. (1966). Color and form preference in young children. *Journal of Experimental Child Psychology, 3*, 177-187.

Thompson, J. R., & Chapman, R. S. (1977). Who is Daddy revisited: the status of two-year olds' overextended words in use and comprehension. *Journal of Child Language, 4*, 359-375.

Vorster, J. (1975). Mommy linguist: The case for motherese. *Lingua, 37*, 281-312.

Vygotsky, L. S. (1962). *Thought and language*. Cambridge, MA: MIT Press.

White, T. G. (1982). Naming practices, typicality and underextension in child language. *Journal of Experimental Child Psychology, 33*, 324-346.

7. Apprenticeship in Word Use: Social Convergence Processes in Learning Categorically Related Nouns

Alison K. Adams and Daniel Bullock

Research and theory aimed at understanding the development of word meaning has generated a wealth of information about early semantic development. To date, most of this work has focused on the task of describing changes in the child's internal representations of lexical items and, to a lesser degree, on what has been called the *process of acquisition*. An important point about this vast body of prior research is its dependence on the implicit supposition that the *acquisition process* is a process localized within children. This supposition has persisted largely undisturbed because of widespread failure to fully appreciate the social embeddedness of cognitive development, in general, and of word learning, in particular. This chapter offers a markedly different perspective on the problems of semantic development—one built on foundations laid by Vygotsky and Wittgenstein, though drawing materials from the Piagetian, social learning, and learning-theoretic traditions as well.

In accord with Vygotsky (and his contemporary proponents), we will argue that word meaning is dynamically constituted via the inherently social process of symbolization. Because parents, or other collaborators, are pivotal figures in symbolization, the acquisition process cannot be wholly localized within the child. Strictly speaking, acquisition is a *socially distributed process*. As a reminder of this bedrock fact, we will avoid the term acquisition process altogether. Instead, we will employ the more descriptive and suggestive term *social convergence process*. Though *convergence* has been used in a relevant sense by mathematical learning theorists (e.g., Estes & Suppes, 1974; Grossberg, 1982; Hamburger & Wexler, 1975), the richest treatment of semantic convergence as a *socially* mediated process can be found in the work of Wittgenstein and his modern proponents (e.g., Bloor, 1983, Bruner,

1975; Bullock, 1983, in press; Danford, 1978; Hintikka, 1973; Millikan, 1984).

With regard to Wittgenstein, we will argue that mastery of a word's meaning is best understood as mastery of its normative conditions of application. This means that word learning may be conceptualized in terms of the child's convergence toward adult patterns of usage. Wittgenstein (1953) took great pains to show that such convergence is a more complicated affair than is usually supposed. In particular, full convergence cannot occur unless the child undertakes an apprenticeship in the culture, because word usages are bound up with specific modules of cultural practice, modules Wittgenstein called *language-games*. One such game will provide an experimental anchor point for our discussion.

The child's apprenticeship in culture, while clearly dependent on interactions with social agents, cannot be fully understood without studying the child's ongoing inventive efforts. Thus, our treatment of lexical development will also sound a Piagetian theme. However, in the context of lexical development, it will not do to proceed as if the child's inventive efforts are autonomous—as Piagetians sometimes imply. We will argue that a better focus for analysis is what has been called *guided reinvention* (Lock, 1980; Fischer & Bullock, 1984). After thus subsuming lexical development under the general rubric of guided reinvention, we end by arguing that models of semantic development will mature most quickly if they attempt to show in concrete detail how human-class social interactions constrain semantic development by guiding it along paths that would have been impossible without the envelope of experience provided by human culture.

In order to elaborate this social convergence perspective, we will first outline each tradition's major contributions to theories of lexical development. The stage will then be set for a look at recent research that relates parental naming practices to children's mastery of categorically related object labels. Finally, we will use data from a new study of mother-child object labeling to advance our understanding of the processes of social regulation and active negotiation that culminate in agreements regarding usage of such terms.

The Vygotsky-Wittgenstein Legacy

We shall begin with Vygotsky (1962/1934, 1978/1934), whose works have begun to affect both contemporary Western theories of cognitive development and performance (e.g., Brown, Bransford, Ferrara, & Campione, 1983; Fischer, 1980), and emerging theories of the social bases of human cognitive development (e.g., Bruner, 1975; Bullock, 1983, 1984; Fischer & Bullock, 1984; Kaye, 1982; Laboratory of Comparative Human Cognition, 1983; Rogoff & Wertsch, 1984; Wertsch, 1979). Vygotsky argued that higher mental functions—in particular those cognitive capacities unique to humans—first take form within social interactions, on what Vygotsky called the *inter-psychological* (*between minds*) plane of activity. For advanced, uniquely human forms of mental activity, such as symbol formation and symbolic thought, the theater of development is initially interpersonal (Kaye, 1982). Once constituted in the joint activity of the parent-child dyad (or other social unit), however, socially derived symbols, as well as myriad skills defined in terms of symbol manipulation, are gradually internalized by the child. When the child has achieved independent control over the activities involved, the social origins of what came to life as a shared mental function are masked. This masking marks completion of what Vygotsky called the transition from the interpsychological to the *intra-psychological* (*within one mind*) plane of human activity. Theorists are constantly at risk of underestimating the role played by social processes in mental devlopment because this transition *masks* the social origin of symbols and of skills defined over symbols. However, the conventionality of the symbol of skill, that is, the extent to which it has arbitrary components, is learnable, and yet is shared by other members of the social group, attests to its public beginnings. Vygotsky's theory, therefore, speaks to the social processes by which culture (where *culture* is understood to include symbolic forms of thought) is first created and subsequently transmitted between successive generations.

Vygotsky's keen appreciation of the problems caused by the masking of social origins led him to insist that researchers study the process as well as the products of development (Vygotsky, 1978/1934). It also led him to his famous critique of the interpretations of *egocentric speech* offered by Piaget (1955) in *The language and thought of the child*. For Piaget, the egocentric speech of preschoolers was originally *a*social activity that needed to be further socialized. For Vygotsky, it was activity which, though originally socially constituted, was already in the process of having its social origins masked. Note that Vygotsky and Piaget agreed regarding the fundamentally constructive nature of development. The difference between the two theorists lay in what they believed to be the engine of this constructive activity. For Piaget, its engine is almost exclusively the spontaneous activity of the child, who patiently constructs each skill or symbol on his or her own, essentially reinventing the wheel in each successive generation. For Vygotsky, the engine of constructive activity is socially distributed, with components supplied by both the child and the social agents surrounding the child (Bullock, 1983; 1984; Kaye, 1982; Wertsch, 1979). Both parent and child are active participants in the child's cognitive development. Through a process of *guided reinvention* (Lock, 1980; Fischer & Bullock, 1984), the child's mental development proceeds in a culturally appropriate and powerfully adapted manner.

We recommend the term guided reinvention because it simultaneously acknowledges parental guidance and the child's inventive efforts. From this perspective, the child may be viewed as a novice performer who, in effect, is apprenticed to an expert performer, the parent. Children move from a modest skill level in some domain to full adult competence (i.e., they converge) through the support, guidance, and educational scaffolding provided by parents. Such social aids to the process of converging toward an adult form and level of performance take many forms, some very subtle. One of the most ubiquitous parental strategies is to break complex tasks into components that are separately within the grasp of the apprenticed child. This parental strategy of task simplification is dynamic and finely tuned. As the child's skill level in a particular domain increases, parents spontaneously shift task requirements upward to a level that is more congruent with the child's emerging capacities (see Cross, 1977; Kaye & Charney, 1980; Moerk, 1983; Wertsch, McNamee, McLane, & Budwig, 1980; and Wood, 1980; for empirical treatments of this phenomenon in both linguistic and nonlinguistic domains).

The child's contributions to learning the apprenticed activity are also various and dynamic. A fundamental aspect of the apprenticeship/guided reinvention situation (see Fischer & Bullock, 1984) is that acts of guidance are embedded in the flow of purposeful efforts to master some task. For example, even the process of *imitating* modeled linguistic devices and incorporating them into one's own repertoire—a process that some researchers mistakenly continue to treat as if it were a dispensable component of semantic development (but see Snow, 1983)—actually involves complex, goal-corrected activity on the part of the child. Imitation in such cases is best understood as a temporally *extended* process in which the child, in order to further other, more primary goals, adopts the goal of replicating some aspect of the model's activity and then spontaneously varies/reorganizes his or her own behavior in an attempt to achieve that goal (see Guillaume, 1971/1926; Bullock, 1981; 1983). Just as cultural transmission must be understood as guided reinvention, and not as passive inheritance, so the child's imitations, when new for the child, must be understood as guided reinventions, not as passive mimickings.

The Vygotskyan tradition, then, provides us with a rich heritage for elaborating our understanding of the development of all higher mental functions, including symbolic activity. The framework encourages us to look simultaneously at the contributions of both parent and child to the remarkable personal and cultural achievement manifested in the individual child's cognitive structures. The temporally extended process of convergence toward adult forms and levels of performance provides a natural arena for examining the real-time cognitive and social processes that enable transitions from the interpsychological to the intrapsychological plane for each new generation of speakers. Such processes of transition or convergence, moreover, appear to be best examined in the task-oriented collaborative interactions that constitute a critical subset of parent-child interactions—a suggestion corroborated by recent empirical work (e.g., Bullock, 1979; Bullock & Zare, 1980; Kay & Charney, 1980; Ninio, 1983; Ninio & Bruner, 1978; Ratner & Bruner, 1978; Saxe, Gearhart, & Guberman, 1984; Wertsch et al., 1980; Wood, 1980).

Although such an empirical focus on structured interactions shares many features with the recent focus on routinized event structures in the literature on semantic memory development (e.g., Mandler, 1983; Nelson, 1983; Nelson & Gruendel, 1981), we believe that this literature, focused as was Piaget on describing the internal representations produced during development, has neglected the social interactive process of word meaning development as such. The perspective we offer, while not incompatible with the work on memory development, has a markedly different emphasis.

This difference of emphasis can be explained by focusing on Wittgenstein's notion of language-games. In an insight that became the basis for Rosch's ground-breaking work on prototype formation (Rosch, 1978; Rosch, Mervis, Gray, Johnson, & Boyes-Braem, 1976), Wittgenstein (1953) noted that many terms, like *game*, are actually *family resemblance* terms. Such terms refer to categories whose exemplars fall in the same category not because they all share a set of necessary and sufficient features, but because each shares some features with some other exemplars, and because all exemplars resemble each other more than they resemble members of competing (alternative) categories. Though this insight has been widely appreciated by psychologists, a closely related insight has been largely neglected. For Wittgenstein, *language* itself is such a family resemblance category. Language consists of a variety of coordinable linguistic devices (e.g., imperatives, indicatives, interrogatives; object terms, relation terms, function words, property words, quantifiers) which have no more in common than, say, the variegated tools in a carpenter's tool kit. Moreover, like tools, each linguistic device serves a standard function within some organized human mode of activity that could not exist in the *same* form without the participation of linguistic devices.

Though initially odd-sounding, language-games is quite an apt term for the various language-informed activity modes elaborated through cultural evolution. When the *games* component of language-games is stressed, we are reminded that there is great diversity across exemplars of language (e.g., naming, counting, greeting) just as there is diversity within the class of games (e.g., games of skill, games of chance, card games, ball games, etc.). We are also reminded that linguistic devices are of vital importance in the performance of certain *activities*; they are not merely representational devices (Austin, 1962; Searle, 1969). Finally, we are reminded that linguistic phenomena, like the events that may be observed on a game field, are simultaneously constrained by physical law, biological functionality, and social convention. When the *language* component of language-games is stressed, we are reminded that whatever activity mode we are discussing (e.g., the mode of a defense lawyer in a court of law) owes a significant part of its form to the participation of linguistic structures. Thus, language-game is shorthand for *an organized, culturally transmitted mode of activity, performance of which depends on, and provides the rationale for, some particular linguistic device.*

There is something quite special about this definition of language-game. The particular mode of activity (e.g., quantificational activity involving the terms *all*, *some*, and *none*; or rhetorical activity involving terms like *equality for all* and *enemy of the people*) both depends on, and provides the rationale for, the linguistic device. Neither the mature form of the mode of activity, as such, nor the linguistic device, as such, is prior to the other. In practice, they must emerge together. This point has far-reaching consequences for the theory of semantic development. It implies, as Wittgenstein was quick to note, that without the mode of activity, the linguistic device lacks meaning. If so, then semantic development is fundamentally a matter of mastering modes of activity that depend on the organized deployment of linguistic devices. Learning a word, for example, is a matter of learning a module of cultural practice. From this, Wittgenstein derived the famous dictum that *meaning is use*, that is, the meaning of a linguistic device is determined by its normative role in environmentally adapted human action.

A linguistic device can play its proper role only if its use is carefully restricted. Thus, it is quite appropriate that many studies of semantic convergence have focused on the topics of underextension/overextension—that is, on the child's gradual identification of normative conditions of use, especially boundary conditions for use of common nouns. Indeed, the study we will report below is itself addressed to this problem. However, we want to note that the semantic convergence problems faced by the child are both fine-grained and coarse-grained, and the *extension of common nouns* problem is a relatively fine-grained one.

Consider, by comparison, the problem of discovering the role played by words like *three* or *six*. Such words find their proper home within modes of activity much different than words like *dog* or *cat*. Thus, if the young child misconstrues *six* as a common noun, he or she is making a much *larger* error than if he or she misconstrues *dog* as a term that refers to both cats and dogs. Whereas the dog/cat error may create the impression that the problem is merely one of unconventional category boundaries or misidentification of distinctive features, misuse of *six* as a common noun reveals that the child completely misunderstands the language-game at hand. This point is critical, because it is primarily by attending to examples of children's coarse-grained semantic convergence problems that one begins to appreciate the inseparability of semantic development from the mastery of a *variegated* set of modules of cultural practice.

Thus, for both Wittgenstein and Vygotsky, the process of word learning is best viewed as one of converging on those patterns of word use found in particular modules of the culture. The child's understanding of a word is active. The child *knows* the correct meaning of a word when he or she uses it in the same manner as adult members of the language community. Childhood language-games provide an indispensable setting for beginning to learn adult patterns of word usage.

Some Clarifications and Implications

The idea that word meanings are constructed in social contexts and that their use is governed in accordance with social norms, in no way undermines the importance of sensitivity to objective features of the environment. We agree with Rosch et al. (1976), with Schlesinger (1982), and Millikan (1984) that the physical environment provides important co-occurrence patterns and transformational regularities that symbolic representations are created to map. This environmental texture constrains the long-term evolution of representational systems, but to think that it drives rapid conceptual development in the child without the helping hand of consistent language usage by adults is a major, if common, error. This error is most easily detected whenever the linguistic/conceptual mapping of reality seems quite arbitrary and differs from one language community to the next (see Bowerman, 1982; Schlesinger, 1982). However, it is also a mistake to see the development of many nonarbitrary (e.g., biologically validated) concepts as autonomous from linguistic guidance, as we will illustrate. One desideratum is that the child often learns distinctions without ever being exposed to those original functional considerations that made the distinctions relevant, and that would be prerequisites for truly autonomous reinvention of the concept. In effect, children often are not exposed to the original language-games in which functional considerations ensure that usage will be nonarbitrary. In such instances, partial convergence with expert usage serves as an interim substitute for the full convergence that awaits exposure to primary functional considerations.

Consider briefly the case of anomalous category exemplars, such as *bats*, *penguins*, and *Newfoundlands* (a kind of dog that resembles a bear). As we document below, children are told that bats are mammals, penguins are birds, and Newfoundlands are dogs. In addition, they are *taught* features that can help them avoid assimilating these exemplars to more or equally compelling categories (bats to *bird*, penguins to *sea mammal*, Newfoundlands to *bear*), or features that provide evidence of family membership (e.g., Newfoundlands bark, just like other dogs). But it may be years before children are introduced to the language-game of tracing evolutionary lineages—and it is only then that the distinctions drawn earlier become grounded by primary functional considerations (the scientific need to accurately map the ramifying evolutionary tree). In such cases, the child's early convergence with adult concept/usage must be understood on the model of guided reinvention rather than as autonomous reinvention because data critical for the latter will not be at hand until years after the initial convergence in usage. (cf. Bates & MacWhinney, 1982 on *syntactic vestiges*.)

These considerations begin to show the complexity required of any theory of semantic development in the child. The semantic system of any language evolves in accord with the variegated needs of human activities to accurately map and manipulate aspects of reality (including, of course, social reality). In some cases, children are introduced to these activities *and* their linguistic mappings early in life. In other cases, the linguistic fruits of the activities are transmitted to children prior to their learning the activities for which the linguistic distinctions are vital. In the former case, the child masters perceptual conditions of use as well as the functional core (i.e., the mode of activity; see also Nelson, 1979). In the latter case, perceptual conditions of use may be mastered in advance of mastery of the mode of activity within which the naturalness of drawing boundaries *just so* is apparent.

The possibility of this dissociation clarifies Piaget's longstanding concern with the contrast—in our view actually a continuum—between *real development* and *mere learning*. In the present context, mere learning would refer in the extreme to learning perceptual conditions of use for a term without also learning anything of the mode of activity in which the term originally emerged to play its current normative role. The possibility of this dissociation led Piaget to conclude that the development of thought is autonomous from, and always prior to, development of language. But the conclusion is not warranted by the mere fact of dissociated use of *terms*. A defense of Piaget's conclusion would also require showing that the modes of thinking at issue could emerge and persist with the same conceptual content in the absence of any use of linguistic devices. In effect, a Piagetian would have to show that the *language* is eliminable from every *language-game* without loss of conceptual content. On the strength of our expectation that such a demonstration will not be (in many cases, logically *could* not be) forthcoming, we conclude that Piaget, like other conceptualists (see Kaufman, 1980) and rationalists (see Millikan, 1984) before and since, systematically underestimated the linguistic, and therefore the social component of *real development*.

However, to reject one of the conclusions Piaget drew from the phenomenon of *dissociation* is to reject neither his belief in the phenomenon's importance, nor various others of his conclusions. Another way of summarizing the phenomenon is to note that when children first come to use a term, they may not use it with the same import, in the same sense, as adults. It was Piaget's genius to show, over and over again, how observers tend to err in interpreting children's thinking by making too facile comparisons of child usage with adult usage. Piaget and Wittgenstein would agree that in order to establish sameness of meaning of two symbol tokens, one used by a child, the other by an adult, it is necessary to look beyond sameness in perceptual conditions of use and ask how the symbol functions in modes of activity. Sameness of meaning amounts to sameness of language-game and nothing less.

For example, we would argue that the young word learner does not, at first, understand the logical relations between terms from different levels in a Roschian-style taxonomy—despite his or her ability to use those terms correctly (i.e., with the right extensions) in most discourse contexts (see also Markman, 1984). We believe that, for young children, such alternate ways of naming an object are lexical competitors whose selection is governed by a set of communicative constraints. The child makes adaptive choices between such competing terms as *animal*, *dog*, or *Dalmatian* (or some other subordinate level name), without any cognizance of class-subclass relations. For example, *animal* might be used as a default word when a more specific name is not known. Alternatively, in its plural form it might serve as a collection term (e.g., Markman, 1981) when the goal of the utterance is to quickly refer to a nonhomogeneous group of animals. In addition, the communicative environment constrains word choice. Different language-game settings promote the use of terms that differ in generality of reference (see, e.g., Lucariello, 1983). As we will illustrate, settings that present single exemplars from a variety of basic level categories promote basic level or generic naming. Similarly, those settings in which a number of exemplars from a single basic category appear together encourage more specific, subordinate level naming. In short, different language-game contexts demand that different levels of contrast be drawn between exemplars for effective communication.

Because children learn word meaning in structured interaction frameworks, social-communicative constraints play a formative role in the development of their semantic systems, and the resultant differentiated usage in such contexts invites the impression that they use words with adult senses. However, the child's ability to correctly use words from different levels, in what to the adult appears as a class-inclusion hierarchy, in no way presupposes knowledge of class inclusion relations by the child. A child who has learned the rules which govern word choice in a variety of different collaborative goal-directed activities is able to act as a full participant in a large number of language-games. What the child has learned is not class inclusion, but the different ranges of application (i.e., perceptual and communicative conditions of use) of the different words. Only later will these differentiated patterns of word use serve as a data base from which the child—now learning a meta-linguistic language-game—reconstructs a full understanding of set/subset relations.

The Framework Applied to Maternal Labeling Research

Such considerations provide a framework for evaluating what has been accomplished by recent research on social-interactional determinants of language development. Because the study reported below focused on the use of terms that function as object labels, we will restrict our review to research on the determinants and consequences for lexical development of maternal labeling practices.

An early formulation of issues within this tradition of research occurred in Roger Brown's classic paper, "How Shall a Thing be Called?" (Brown, 1958). Brown noted that any thing may be referred to in many different ways, and posed the problem of specifying what determines choice of one label rather than another. In particular, he sought to explain the high frequency of the most commonly used name and the lower frequencies of alternative names. Given a *collie*, why are people most likely to refer via *dog*, next most likely to refer via *collie*, and much less likely to refer via *mammal*.

Brown (1958) concludes that the most common name for things "categorizes them as they need to be categorized for the community's nonlinguistic purposes. The most common name is at the level of usual utility." Thus, on Brown's formulation, *mammal* is rare because the purposes that require apprehending a collie as a member of the category *mammal* are rare; similarly *dog* is common because the purposes that require apprehending a collie as a member of the category *dog* are common (Brown, 1958). Note that Brown's conclusion is quite consonant with Wittgenstein's language-game principle—linguistic usage varies with purpose—with one notable exception. As we stressed in our critique of Piaget's language-thought position, the language-game principle implies that few of what Brown calls the community's nonlinguistic purposes, or their associated categories, are truly nonlinguistic (if use of *nonlinguistic* is restricted to structures that would take the same form in the absence of linguistic influences) (see Bullock, 1983; Fischer & Bullock, 1984; Schlesinger, 1982).

An immediate implication of Brown's utility hypothesis is that shifts in usage may correspond to shifts in, or elaborations of, purpose. Thus, to cite Brown's own example, a parent might refer to all coins via *money* when the parent's purpose is merely to mark off, and induce her child to mark off, a category of items that are neither to be played with nor discarded. Later, as the child begins to elaborate the sort of purposes current in the domain of economic exchange, a much more differentiated referring strategy (using *dime*, *quarter*, etc.) will be needed to map positions within the space of the economic exchange language-game.

We will return to the issue of usage shifts shortly. First, though, it is germane to note another feature of Brown's treatment—the idea that parental usage may play a critical role in the child's induction of categories. Brown agreed with linguistic determinists like Whorf and Sapir that perceptual factors by themselves "do not force any single scheme of categorization," and that means names applied by elders "must be the child's principal clue to the locally functioning scheme" (Brown, 1958). Thus, Brown's thesis was that verbal reference as experienced by the child (a) shifted as a function of the purpose-context of the referent, and (b) played a critical role in the induction of new semantic categories.[1]

Given the consonance of Brown's conclusions with Wittgenstein's language-game model, it is quite ironic that Brown's sketch for a *community utility* account of semantic development has been (temporarily) overshadowed in the literature by yet another of Wittgenstein's legacies, namely *prototype theory* (Barrett, 1982; Greenberg & Kuczaj, 1982; Posner & Keele, 1968; 1970; Rosch et al., 1976; Mervis, 1984). Though a full characterization of prototype theory is beyond the scope of this chapter, a few words are in order. Wittgenstein argued that "our language is not everywhere bounded by rules" (Wittgenstein, 1953) and that the ages-long attempt by philosophers to specify necessary and sufficient conditions for category membership cannot succeed. Moreover, such specification is unnecessary because categorization can be based on the relative degree of overlap between features of a given exemplar (the item to be categorized) and the features associated with the various competing categories into which the exemplar might be assimilated.

Though Wittgenstein was careful to stress that *what* features are important in category formation typically depends on the current purposes of the categorizer, recent treatments of prototype theory have tended to ignore the purpose-relativity of features.[2] Instead, most recent treatments have focused on the statistical properties of prototype learning as it occurs once a pool of features has already been made available. (However, see Mervis, 1984, for a treatment of purpose-relativity in early category evolution.) Thus, Posner and Keele (1968; 1970) demonstrated that an arbitrary dot-pattern (a prototype) could be learned as the central tendency of a serially presented set of consistently named random distortions of itself. Similarly,

---

[1] Brown is not very clear in his 1958 paper as to whether he intends language to serve a role as *inducer* or merely as selector. His 1976 paper refers to the 1958 Brown as a linguistic determinist, so we have portrayed his position as arguing that language does more than merely help the child select among preexisting category schemes.

[2] Even low-level perceptual features that everyone agrees are hardwired (or at least very highly canalized) may be presumed to be purpose-relative. As Gibson has noted, we have been tuned over evolutionary time to resonate to features that are critical for achieving our goals.

Rosch et al. (1976) have emphasized that a prototype learning mechanism that is sensitive to featural co-occurrence statistics will autonomously (i.e., without help from the language community) induce categories that correspond to the major natural kinds present in the child's perceptual world. The level of categorization favored by such co-occurrence statistics is now widely referred to as the "basic object level".

Because Brown's *level of usual utility* terms turn out to be about the same as Rosch's *basic object level* terms—both are the most common names—it might be thought that Brown's social/functional account is in competition with, or might be replaced by, Rosch's and Posner's asocial/formal account. Indeed, Brown himself appears to have abandoned discussions of utility in favor of the Roschian paradigm in subsequent papers on reference (Brown, 1976; 1978). However, several considerations argue against opposing the two approaches. First, a *form follows function* principle is a powerful determinant of the structures of natural and artificial kinds alike. Second, as noted by Wittgenstein, functional concerns may determine (during both evolution and ontogeny) what features are attended during prototype formation and later categorization of novel exemplars. Here functional and formal-statistical effects operate at different stages to determine category formation and utilization. Third, in Rosch's own work, she has often discussed object *uses* as features that exist on the same footing as perceptual characteristics for the purposes of prototype formation. Thus, *community utility* enters in disguised form at the center of even the featural-statistical theory.

The abstract possibility of such a marriage of formal and social-functional considerations has slowly begun to be concretely realized through recent research on the development of parent-child reference patterns. Note that three classes of expectations regarding such reference patterns emerge from the preceding discussion. Wittgenstein and Brown predict that such patterns can be shifted by changes in language-game context. Rosch and Posner predict that such patterns will also be controlled by statistical factors operative in the learning context. And if Vygotsky is correct, such patterns can be shifted by changes in the interpersonal context, most notably changes in the child's competence. The remaining sections show that all these expectations gain some support from recent empirical studies.

Factors Affecting Parent-Child Reference Patterns

Rosch and associates (1976) have shown that the skill of sorting objects into basic level categories (but not superordinate categories) is well established by the preschool years, and that terms referring to basic level objects are the first to enter the child's vocabulary. This finding was replicated by Anglin (1977), who also documented the potential relevance of maternal input to this pattern by verifying Brown's suggestion that the basic level is the level at which parents most often label objects for their young children. Subsequent studies (e.g., Blewitt 1983; Ninio, 1980) add further support for these findings. Thus, it is now widely accepted that parents typically label objects at the basic level and that these generic terms usually are the earliest to appear in the child's productive and receptive vocabulary.

However, substantiating this basic starting point leaves unanswered questions about how children correct errors of application due to mislocated category boundaries (e.g., false inclusions of nonmembers, or false exclusions of anomalous exemplars like *bats*), as well as how they proceed from a generic level of reference (e.g., *bird*) to more specific (subordinate) levels of reference (e.g., *robin*) and to more general (superordinate) levels of reference (e.g., *animal*).

Most researchers sensitive to the boundary problem have studied the child's progress toward restricting the use of over-extended terms. In the earliest stages of semantic development, children often extend words across (adult) basic level category boundaries (e.g., applying *dog* to many different kinds of *animals*), but children differ markedly in their tendency to overextend terms (see Rescorla, 1981) and this phase passes quickly when other terms enter the lexicon to compete with such vastly overextended terms (Barrett, 1982). Thus, presuming that such patterns of word use can serve as accurate indices of category knowledge, it appears that the differentiation observed in this early phase proceeds from often idiosyncratic general categories to conventional basic level categories like *dog*, *cat*, *horse*, and so forth. The further differentiation of basic level categories into their subordinate types (terrier, Persian, etc.) is largely unexplored. However, Blewitt (1983) has reported evidence that adults anchor subordinate terms to basic level terms when asked to speak as they would with a child interlocutor.

Because of the ubiquity of maternal labeling at the basic level, and because of new evidence reported below, we believe that even basic level differentiation often occurs as quickly as it does only because of social guidance. Nevertheless, as previously noted, underlying biological and environmental regularities may make basic level prototype formation less sensitive to social regulation than other lower (more specific) or higher (more general) levels of categorization. (For work on the role of social/linguistic guidance in the formation of superordinate categories, see Callanan, 1983; Horton & Markman, 1980; Markman, 1984; Markman & Hutchinson, 1984; and White, 1982.)

Perhaps the strongest claims and most comprehensive theory regarding the socialization of early categories and word extensions was recently offered by Mervis (1984). She studied how children partition their overextended child-basic categories into more conventional basic object categories. Her work (Mervis, 1983; Mervis & Canada, 1983; Mervis & Mervis, 1982) is noteworthy because of the central role accorded maternal labeling practices in reshaping children's category boundaries. As one of Rosch's early collaborators, Mervis continues to treat lexical development from a prototype theory perspective. She argues that the child's early samples of experience lead to the construction of child-basic categories, organized according to the same principles of hierarchy and featural contrast (Rosch & Mervis, 1975; Rosch et al., 1976; Rosch, 1978) as adult categories. Since, in the Rosch-Posner model, early category formation is especially sensitive to statistical idiosyncrasies in any individual's experience, Mervis's use of this model gives her the wherewithal to account for individual differences in both conceptual centers and boundaries (see also Greenberg & Kuczaj, 1982). Child-basic categories, apparently establishable on the basis of only one instace (Zimmerman, 1979), form the starting point for a process of category evolution. In agreement with Anglin (1977), Mervis notes that this starting point may differ from the adult norm in a number of ways, although she has focused on overinclusive categories. This, in turn, leads her to focus on differentiation as a major process of category evolution.

Mervis treats such differentiation as a social-convergence process and offers data supporting three major *maternal* strategies that might work to regulate the child's lexical boundaries. These include: (a) corrective relabeling with demonstration of critical attributes or functions; (b) corrective relabeling with verbal description of critical attributes or functions; and (c) corrective relabeling by itself. (Similar processes could also serve to broaden the range of initially narrow categories.) In Mervis's observational study of mothers interacting with their 13-month-olds and various toys, all three strategies occurred, with the first being most prevalent. Though our (picture-book centered) study precluded use of the first strategy, it produced evidence for high frequency use of the latter two strategies with 14-, 26-, and 38-month-olds.

In addition to focusing attention on particular parental strategies, Mervis gathered evidence regarding the transactional nature of category development. In particular, she showed that mothers' methods of instruction were correlated with their children's competence to communicate about how they divide semantic space. With children equated for when they first comprehended a particular word, mothers of normal toddlers initially follow their child's lead when the child gives evidence of having a nonstandard category boundary, whereas mothers of Down syndrome (DS) toddlers (who give much less verbal feedback at this age), continue to respect adult categorical norms in their labeling practices. Later, when DS children do begin to speak, their mothers also were more willing to follow their lead regarding category membership.

Such results raise the general issue of who leads whom when shifts occur in parent-child language-games. In agreement with Kaye (1982) and most other students of "motherese" (e.g., Bullock, 1983; 1984; Cross, 1977; Moerk, 1976; 1983; Sachs, 1983; Snow, 1977; 1983), as well as students of shifting maturity demands in other domains, we believe that both parties lead at times, but that there is a marked asymmetry in favor of leadership by the parent—albeit elaborative rather than redirective leadership. Though many parents initially go along with their child's usage, they remain concerned with the culturally normative usage pattern, and eventually make the effort, when needed, to help the child learn that normative pattern. As noted above, Mervis has mapped out three forms such efforts may take when this *pattern completion process* (Bullock, 1984) is focused on departures from normative categorization.

In our view, Mervis has begun to spell out the major components of a more veridical description of lexical development. Her framework points toward treating as fundamental both the intrinsic cognitive capacities of the child and the envelope of guidance provided by the child's co-participants in language-games. By emphasizing the interaction of a general category learning capacity with the particularities of early experience, she shows individual differences in early category structure to be inevitable. This implies that conventionalization of initially nonnormative categories will be an equally inevitable component of each child's further development.

However, many factors affecting reference patterns remain unexplored in her treatment and some of her specific claims regarding shifts in reference patterns will likely need correction. One issue especially relevant to the study reported in the next section is Mervis's treatment of atypical or anomalous exemplars. Mervis's data supports the claim that such exemplars should be the first to differentiate out of the child-basic categories and coalesce into their own (basic level) categories:

> ... when the child begins to break down an initial child-basic category, the first new category(ies) to emerge should be the one(s) represented by the most atypical member(s) of the original child-basic category. For example, when breaking down an initial child-basic *kitty* category, the child should form a *tiger* category before forming a *panther* category, because tigers are less similar to domesticated cats than panthers are (1984, p. 348).

This claim raises some subtle issues concerning the status of atypical category members, and parental reference to them, at various points in development. An alternative expectation is that peripheral members first enter the conceptual system as exemplars of their own, separate, basic level categories, precisely because they share few features with prototypical exemplars, and because parents implicitly acknowledge this in their naming practices (see below). Such categories would only later be integrated with categories that were initially based on the more prototypical exemplars. This integration would then produce a broader, more adult-like, family-resemblance category. In fact, just such an expectation was stated by Rosch and Mervis in an earlier paper (Rosch et al., 1976).

A possible resolution of the conflicting expectations involves supposing that the two claims are both apt, but with respect to different stages of category evolution. Mervis's recent prediction applies to the era when first words are being learned, whereas the earlier prediction applies to later processes of integration and coordination across basic level categories (cf. Nelson & Nelson, 1978). We think this resolution has merit and may explain some of the discrepancies between Mervis's results and our own. Certainly, our sample included older children who had moved beyond the initial child-basic stage described by Mervis. However, such an explanation cannot adequately account for the disparity between her results and ours at 14 months of age. As shown below, when we presented mother-child dyads with colored drawings of a range of exemplars from different animal categories, we found that peripheral category members were most commonly labeled with their specific subordinate-level names and not with a child-basic name. For example, in virtually all contexts, leopards were called "leopard" (not "cat") and penguins were called "penguin" (not "bird"), even at 14 months. (Naming practices in regard to more typical, yet distinguishable, exemplars were more complex, as we will illustrate below.) We did not observe the shift from a child-basic name (like "kitty") to an adult name (like "leopard") described by Mervis for peripheral category members.

Instead, most atypical category members were labeled with their conventional adult names from the start by both mothers and children.

We believe that the reasons for this discrepancy relate to subtle differences in the language-games introduced by the different tasks employed in the two research efforts. Whereas Mervis used animal models in a free-play setting, our use of a picture book task may have created a more adult-like educational setting in which parents modeled and demanded more conventional patterns of word use (see also MacWhinney, 1984). In other words, the three-dimensional and more toy-like quality of her stimuli may have created a different set of affordances than those introduced by our picture book format—a set which made parents more likely to follow their children's lead.[3] Note, however, that Mervis (personal communication) reports that the use of photographs of her stimuli replicates her original results. It is also possible that the fact that Mervis's subjects were contrasting animate with inanimate categories may have encouraged a more general level of labeling than occurred in our study, where subjects drew contrasts between animate categories (see also below). These differences in labeling patterns support our claim that subtle shifts in language-games promote different patterns of word choice geared to the functional demands of the communicative setting.

Our own results, then, come closer to confirming the original prediction made by Rosch and Mervis. Of course, any child-basic category may include, among its many diverse exemplars, a subgrouping that adult members of the culture would be able to identify as comprising all and only the typical and atypical members of a single normative category. However, this does not mean that the processes involved in differentiating the child-basic category are properly characterized as processes of separating the atypical *from* (only) the typical exemplars in the category. Instead, the child is separating many new categories from an amorphous lexical category not generally coincident with any adult grouping. Those objects that will later, through social convergence processes, come to be regarded as atypical members of a single expanded category, at first separately enter the child's differentiating conceptual network as independent basic categories. That is, *lion*, *bird*, *cat*, and *penguin* will be treated as separate categories having an approximately equal degree of unrelatedness within a field of animate types.

This phase of many nonhierarchically integrated basic objects may be one in which some of the atypical members of an adult category are lumped together in a composite cluster, based on some salient common features, for example, a *big cats*

---

[3]Incidentally, whereas the leopards in Mervis's research had mild-mannered noises (i.e., *meow*) attributed to them, ours consistently were credited with more ferocious vocalizations (e.g., *ROAR! GRRR!*)—adding further support to our claim that our task created a more adult-like setting. We were struck by mothers' ubiquitous use of animal noises for the younger children in our study. We suspect that the use of such affectively salient intonation patterns, especially in routines in which the child can be an active participant (e.g., Mother: "What does a lion say?" Child: "ROAR!") may help the child learn to discriminate between basic animal types. (See Fernald & Mazzie, 1983, for related empirical work on the uses of affect in marking new information in speech to children.) Because of their affective power, such noises may well be more perceptually salient to young children than the kinds of physical features usually discussed in theories of lexical development.

category or a *water fowl* category. For example, in our study, a number of children conflated the use of the names of the large cats, calling them all tigers or all lions. Interestingly, such errors were immediately corrected by mothers, who also pointed out the distinguishing features that separate one class from another. Eventually, such maternal strategies are applied to the conventional basic level categories themselves in order to help the child expand the scope of these categories to encompass atypical exemplars.

However, as Rosch has noted (Rosch et al., 1976), such anomalous exemplars are never fully assimilated into the basic category. Thus, they stand in marked contrast to the more typical exemplars that serve as the actual empirical base for the construction of the prototype. Indeed, typical exemplars are so close to the category's core that distinguishing between them too early might distort the process of prototype formation. We will show that typical exemplars are not assigned specific subordinate level names until the child has a well-established set of prototypes. Our data indicate that mothers usually do not introduce specific names for more typical category members until after the child has achieved productive mastery of both basic level names and specific names for atypical exemplars. This pattern adds credibility to our claim that the latter are in fact treated by mothers as separate basic level categories in the early stages of lexical development.

In accord with our earlier discussion, we presume that atypical exemplars maintain their semiindependent status because they usually function in very different language-game settings than the one in which their resemblances to typical exemplars are relevant. *Bird* simply does not capture the perceptually and functionally outstanding features of penguins. Thus, for most purposes, to refer to a penguin as *bird* would be misleading because *bird* will conjure a prototypical image in the mind of the hearer. Anyone who has unwittingly led a child to have false expectations by a careless choice of terms will know that such communicative slipups have unhappy consequences. With development, of course, children are introduced to further language-game settings and to the referential practices that have their homes in such settings. Throughout, the process of category evolution is coincident with apprenticeship in a particular culture. Consequently, it can only be correctly analyzed as a socially distributed process.

The study we will report in the section that follows was designed to address the network of themes introduced in prior sections of this chapter. In keeping with the Vygotsky-Wittgenstein heritage, we selected a joint picture-book reading task as an example of a commonly occurring language-game. Within the framework of that game, we varied exemplar typicality to test Mervis's claims and to help reveal the intradyadic processes involved in the social regulation of categorization. In addition, we manipulated the context of exemplar presentation to show how relatively minor variations in the structure of a particular language-game can lead to markedly different instructional strategies and labeling practices. We tested a broad age range of children to provide a differentiated picture of the transition between late infancy and early childhood, both in terms of changes in maternal labeling practices and associated shifts in children's pattern of word choice. Finally, we combined the cross-sectional with a minilongitudinal design and analyzed our data in a manner that allowed us to move toward a picture of how long-term and short-term social convergence processes operate in the development of word meaning.

An Illustrative Study

Method

The study involved a joint picture-book reading task, with multiple exposures to the materials. Picture-book reading is a common language-game with a highly predictable structure (Ninio & Bruner, 1978). Its natural role in vocabulary learning and memory training has been the subject of several recent investigations (e.g., DeLoache, 1983; Ninio, 1980, 1983). The structure of the task is readily understood by both parents and children, and the paradigm is flexible enough to accommodate a variety of content manipulations. In addition, since parent-child dyads typically read through the same books repeatedly, the task is naturally suited to a minilongitudinal training study.

Design and Procedure. The subjects were 36 mother-child dyads, with 12 children from each of three age groups: 14, 26, and 38 months. Upon coming to the laboratory, each dyad was presented with a picture-book containing 3 chapters. Chapter order was counterbalanced for each age and gender. Each mother was instructed to read through the book with her child as she would do normally at home, and each dyad was videotaped. Following the session, each mother was asked to take the book home and read it with her child daily. A follow-up session identical to the first was conducted 2 weeks after the initial visit. A standard posttest of how the mothers would label book items when conversing with another adult followed the second session.

Stimuli. Each picture-book, modeled on a photograph album format, contained almost equal-sized colored drawings of 9 different exemplars from each of six basic animal categories (*dog, cat, horse, bear, deer,* and *bird*). Each of the 54 exemplars appeared twice over the course of the book, and were selected to be representative of 3 exemplar types: basic level, typical, and atypical. By *basic level exemplar type* we mean highly prototypical exemplars that usually would be labeled at the basic level (e.g., a common black and white cat). Throughout the text we will adopt the phrase *generic, prototypical,* or *basic level* for these rather nondescript exemplars to distinguish them from more distinctive, yet still *typical* exemplars such as *Siamese* or *Persian*. Atypical exemplars are animals like penguins or leopards that are peripheral to their conventionalized adult categories *bird* or *cat*.[4]

---

[4]In keeping with our prior discussion, our stimuli were equated with Mervis's in terms of category structure (e.g., a leopard was considered an atypical exemplar of the category *cat* and a domestic cat was considered a basic level exemplar of the category). This structure also is compatible with the categories

Figure 7-1. Whole range.

Each book was divided into three six-array chapters bearing the names "Animal Friends," "Favorite Animals," and "Friendly Animals." To facilitate data coding, each array was preceded by a page with a brightly colored number (from 1-6); chapters were separated by a page with a set of three colored stripes. The last page of each book read, "The End." Within each picture-book, the three chapters provided five different contextual manipulations, illustrated in Figures 7-1–7-5.

In the first chapter, the *Whole Range* condition, each page presented an entire range of exemplars from a single category (see Figure 7-1). One generic (basic level), two typical, and three atypical exemplars appeared on the same page. For

---

used by Anglin (1977), Blewitt (1983), Rosch et al. (1976), and some of those used by White (1982). Because our stimuli were drawn from photographs of real animals, the range of typicality within each category was constrained by nature. Nonetheless, our results show that mothers' labeling practices agreed with our judgments about the identity and relative typicality of the exemplars. That is, the lion was labeled *lion*, the domestic cat *cat*, the calico cat *calico*, and so on.

Figure 7-2. Imported atypical.

example, in the case of the *cats* page, the exemplars presented were an average domestic cat, a Siamese cat, a Persian cat, a lion, a tiger, and a leopard.

The second chapter, the *Imported Atypical* condition, presented a single atypical exemplar from one category in a field of basic level, and atypical exemplars from a second category (see Figure 7-2). Thus, for example, a tiger appeared in the context of a black dog, a German shepherd, a collie, a terrier, and a Dalmatian.

In the third chapter, exemplars were arranged by exemplar type, yielding three separate two-page subconditions. In the first of these, referred to as *Basic Pages*, single prototypical exemplars from each of the six animal categories were presented together (see Figure 7-3).

In the second subcondition, *Atypical Pages*, each page presented one atypical exemplar from each category (see Figure 7-4). For example, one page presented a duck, a donkey, a dachshund, a lion, an antelope, and a polar bear.

Figure 7-3. Basic pages.

In the third subcondition, *Typical Pages*, each page presented one typical but distinguishable exemplar from each of the six animal categories (see Figure 7-5). One page, for example, presented a dove, an Appaloosa, a Dalmatian, a manx, a white-tailed deer, and a grizzly bear.

Patterns of Maternal Labeling

Typicality Effects. Based on the premise that word-type selection involves making a choice between potentially appropriate competing terms, data from the study first were analyzed in terms of the proportion of any particular word-type in mothers' (and children's) speech.[5] Figure 7-6 shows the proportions of different word-types in

---

[5]Proportions for each word-type were derived from the premise that word-type selection involves making choices between several potentially appropriate, but competing terms. For example, basic level terms can be selected over terms for both atypical and typical exemplars, since a basic term can be applied to

Figure 7-4. Atypical pages.

mothers' speech upon initial exposure to the picture-book, for each chapter. These results support our claim that atypical category members first are identified with their specific subordinate level names, rather than as members of the general class.

---

any member of the class. Therefore, in calculating the proportion of basic level terms we employed the formula: Basic/(Basic+Atypical+Typical). However, when selecting a label for an atypical exemplar the only true competitors are an atypical term or a basic level term: Typical labels, like *bluejay*, are not appropriately applied to atypical exemplars, like *penguin*, or vice-versa. (In our study, such errors occurred very rarely, as when a child called all members of the category *deer*, *reindeer*. These low-frequency errors are responsible for the occasional use of atypical terms in contexts where no atypical exemplars appeared or typical terms where no typical exemplars appeared, as occurs in the middle and lower graphs in Figure 7-6. Therefore, the proportion of atypical terms was calculated from the formula: Atypical/(Atypical+Basic). Our reasoning in calculating the proportion of typical terms was the same. In general, these formulas take the form: target terms/(target+competing terms) (see Bullock & Zare, 1980).

Figure 7-5. Typical pages.

That is, leopards generally were called *leopard* (not *cat*) and penguins were called *penguin* (not *bird*). The top two graphs show that, although basic level naming occurs at above-zero levels in contexts having only atypical exemplars (the *Atypical Pages* condition), even at 14 months, atypical exemplars are labeled with their more specific names over two-thirds of the time. On the other hand, the lower graph shows that, at 1 and 2 years of age, typical exemplars are treated in the manner predicted by Rosch and demonstrated by others: They first are labeled at the basic level. The introduction of more specific subordinate terms for these exemplars was delayed until 3 years of age. These results demonstrate that the proportion of any particular word-type in maternal speech is not related solely to the age of the child, as is sometimes implied, but also to the typicality of the exemplars and to the mix of particular exemplar types in the perceptual array. Thus, the differentiated patterns of word choice shown in Figure 7-6 caution against unconditional claims about "what mothers do" that overlook the nature of the stimuli, the structure of the task, and the capabilities of the child.

In the larger sense, these results demonstrate that immediate communicative concerns take precedence over technical concerns in the earliest phase of symbol formation. In word teaching, mothers ignore concerns that loom large in technical language-games (e.g., that penguins are birds), until after a baseline of shared referential practice is established on the basis of the child's innate perceptual operating characteristics. The situation is analogous to the often noted parental concern with content rather than syntactic form. Early on, concern with the practical efficacy of the message (i.e., with its level of usual utility) overrides concern with its formal correctness. Since penguins are perceptually distinctive enough (relative to other birds) to establish their own unique prototype, mothers tuned to label in accord with what is perceptually most natural, will naturally label penguins as such while labeling more typical exemplars as birds. Thus, pressures to quickly establish a baseline of shared referential practice lead to the observed pattern of usage. Note that an extension of the same process would be conscious editing out of remarks like "penguins are birds" until such time as the parent judges that there is little chance of confusion regarding basic referential practice (see below). These considerations begin to show in concrete detail how the child's ultimate convergence toward adult usage rests on social interactions.

Context Effects. As was noted above, the data presented in Figure 7-6 also demonstrate the influence of the particular context of exemplar presentation on the observed proportion of particular word-types in any sample of maternal speech. The most obvious point is that the proportion of a particular word-type is related, logically enough, to the proportion of particular exemplar types in the array. These results also corroborate empirical work by Blewitt (1983) and by Wales, Colman, & Patterson (1983), as well as our claim that the level of contrast inherent in any array is related to the level of specificity at which objects are labeled. Our data, however, having been compiled by book page and chapter, cannot determine whether word choice for a particular referent changed as a function of the context (i.e., structure of the stimulus array) in which it appeared. For example, we expected that an atypical exemplar was more likely to be identified as a member of the general class when it appeared in the company of exemplars from the same class (our *Whole Range* condition) than when it appeared in the context of a separate class (our *Imported Atypical* condition). For example, is a tiger more likely to be identified as a member of the cat family when it appears in an array of cats than when it appears in an array of dogs? Our preliminary analyses provide an affirmative answer to this question. In most cases, imported atypical exemplars were labeled with their specific subordinate names only (e.g., *tiger, duck*), whereas atypical exemplars embedded in their basic category are often identified as members of the general class as well (e.g., "A lion is a member of the cat family"), particularly at age three (see below).

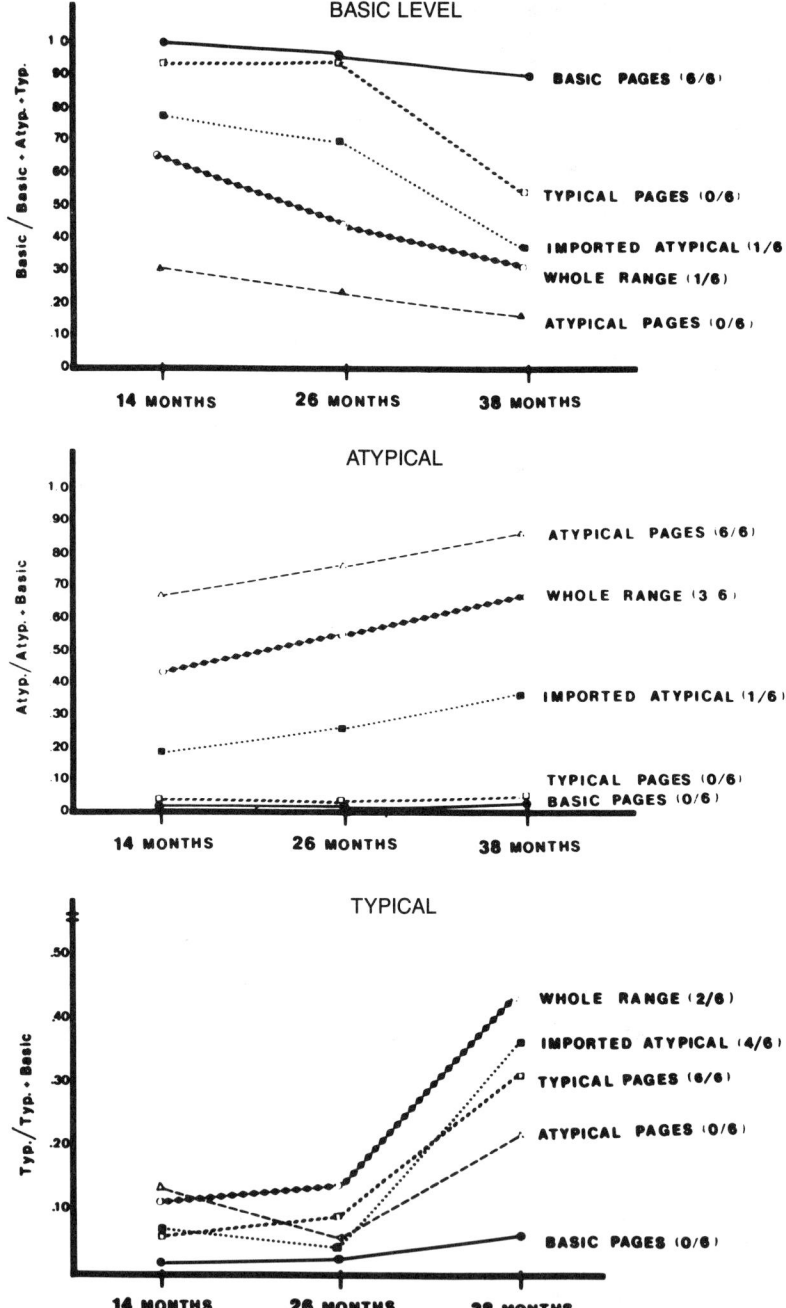

Figure 7-6. Typicality and context effects on mothers' choice of terms for each exemplar type during the first session. The ratios following each chapter manipulation indicate the proportion of target exemplars in each type of array.

An interesting exception to this pattern occurred on the one rather anomalous page in our *Imported Atypical* condition. Whereas the atypical exemplar stood out markedly in most arrays (as in the tiger/dogs example), in the fifth array we presented a Newfoundland in the company of bears—a configuration directly inspired by Greenberg and Kuczaj (1982). Given the physical similarity of the exemplars, genuine cross-category confusion is much more likely to occur on this page than on the others. Therefore, it is not surprising that, on array five, mothers did not make the category cut at the subordinate/basic level as on other pages ("This is a tiger, and these are dogs"), but made it instead at the basic/basic level ("These are bears, and this one is a dog"). Of course, the generalizability of this result remains to be seen, but it does suggest that a high likelihood of confusion based on perceptual similarity can lead to a shift in the level (within a Roschian hierarchy) of the label applied to the potentially confusable item—in this case from a preferred subordinate level name to a basic level name. Note that such shifts in categorical level of labeling are in fact responses to shifts in the communicative constraints framing the utterance. That is, on the basis of anticipated confusions, different judgments are made about which aspects of the objects are to be highlighted. If new data support the generality of such shifts, their existence will demonstrate additional ways in which socially-derived constraints shape word choice and parental instruction.

Posttest Results. Our simple posttest procedure yielded some surprising results we think may be of interest to other researchers. We employed the standard posttest characteristic of this type of research, namely asking mothers to name single instances of each exemplar (appearing in random order) as they would when conversing with another adult. Our assumption was that this procedure would allow us to exclude mothers who were insufficiently familiar with the animal types and, possibly, to verify mothers' simplification strategies. However, the procedure also produced the age trends depicted in Figure 7-7. These data show that relative to the other two ages, mothers of the 26-month-olds persisted in their speech simplifications by increasing their proportional usage of basic level names *even when asked to disengage from the task of speaking to a child* ($p < .001$). We interpret these data positively, as indices of a very high level of task-specific maternal involvement at an age when most children are beginning to show rapid gains in mastery of basic linguistic patterns. However, these results also caution against the assumption that such posttest results reflect adult usage independent of the child, and against research designs which depend on the idea that people are able to reproduce authentic adult-level or child-appropriate speech upon request. (See Fernald & Simon, 1984, for an empirical report of similar discrepancies in speech to an absent versus actual child in maternal speech to newborns.) As we will note below, the sensitive intercoordinations between mother's speech and child's response demands that data be collected on both members of the dyad and that some type of interactive analyses be undertaken.

Social Convergence in Labeling Practices

Age × Session Shifts. Other data from the study further illuminate the social-interactive nature of word teaching and word learning. By collapsing the data across chapter contexts, and charting mothers' and children's word choice in each session, we were able to detect shifts in usage for each word-type as a function of the child's age and the dyad's familiarity with the task (see Figure 7-8). These data also are reported in terms of proportional usage.

The upper left-hand graph in Figure 7-8 shows that proportional usage of basic level terms declines for both members of the dyad in relation to the child's age (dropping steadily from 1 to 3 years), and task familiarity (dropping between sessions one and two at all three ages). These macrolevel age trends are highly significant ($p < .001$), with a slight reduction in statistical significance ($p < .05$) for the difference between 14- and 26-month-old children on Session 1. (This slight reduction in significance level is due to lower levels of child speech at 14 months on the first session.) By comparison, between the first and follow-up sessions the proportions are *relatively* constant, although by 38 months the intersession decrements in proportional usage of basic level terms reach statistical significance for both mother and child ($p < .01$).

These changing patterns of basic level word use reflect temporal changes in children's skill on both the cross-sectional and on the minilongitudinal time scales. They also reflect mothers' sensitivity and adjustments to these changes in their children's abilities. In other words, these data capture the complementary nature of social and cognitive coordinations between mother and child, and point to the necessity of collecting data on both members of the dyad. Once mothers sense that their children have achieved a certain level of mastery in a given performance domain (e.g., that the use of basic level names in an adult-like manner is well-established), the focus of instruction shifts to a less well-established domain of expertise. The expert/parent's sensitivity in accommodating to these changing abilities of the apprentice/child is a hallmark of maternal speech to children and spontaneous parental teaching strategies (e.g., Snow & Ferguson, 1977). They also reflect adherence to a more general principle of language use—that the speaker be sensitive to the perspective and prior knowledge of the listener. Furthermore, these parallel declines in basic level word choice are indicative of dyadic agreement about what is deserving of comment. In other words, they represent agreement about what should be the focus of their joint activity. (See Bullock & Zare, 1980, for further discussion of the importance of such shared criteria of remarkability in normal language development.)

These themes are echoed in the pattern of shifts in proportional word use of terms for atypical and typical exemplar types, shown in the upper right-hand and lower left-hand panels of Figure 7-8. These graphs show progressive shifts in word choice as the focus of maternal instruction is directed to other areas of the semantic field. The lower left-hand graph, for example, shows proportional increases in the use of names for atypical exemplars that complement the simultaneous decrements in

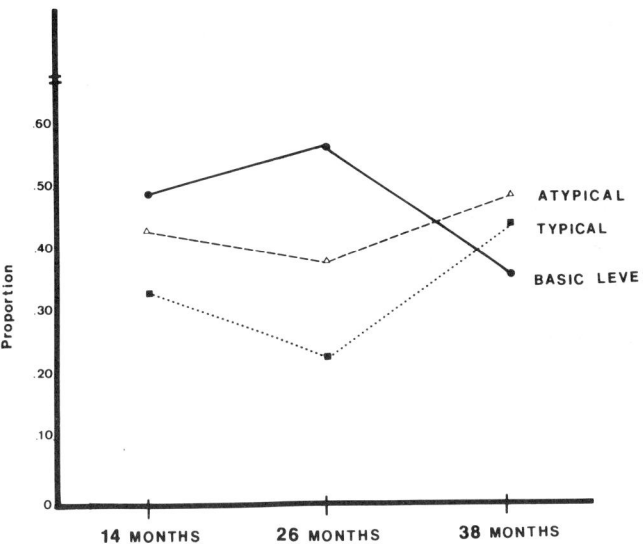

Figure 7-7. Mothers' posttest naming of each exemplar type as a function of child's age. Because the posttest procedure constrains labeling practices to one name per exemplar, the three lines in this graph are interdependent. This means increases in basic level labeling must also be manifested in reduced subordinate level naming of typical and atypical exemplars. This strong constraint does not operate in the other graphs presented in this chapter.

basic level usage that were shown in the upper left-hand graph. These age trends replicate the patterns of significance reported for basic names. In addition, the use of specific names for atypical exemplars does not change dramatically over the two-week time span, except at 26 months ($p < .05$). Again, we see that mothers and children largely are in agreement about the focus of the activity, in this case a shift towards increased labeling of more peripheral category members.

The right-hand graph, on the other hand, captures both the time period in which the focus of the task is renegotiated, and the subsequent convergence between child's and mother's use of terms for typical exemplars. At one and two years of age typical exemplars, such as *bluejay*, are not considered worthy of specific reference by either mother or child. The child, after all, is still mastering the names of basic level and atypical category members. Since, by definition, typical exemplars are quite adequately described by their basic level name, there is no reason to introduce their more specific names until the other two word-types are well-established. Thus, communicative pressures akin to those promoting the early introduction of subordinate names for atypical exemplars act to keep the subordinate level naming of typical exemplars relatively low on the maternal list of instructional priorities. By 3 years of age the situation has changed: Mothers now judge the child's labeling skills to be at a point where the introduction of subordinate level names for typical exemplars is

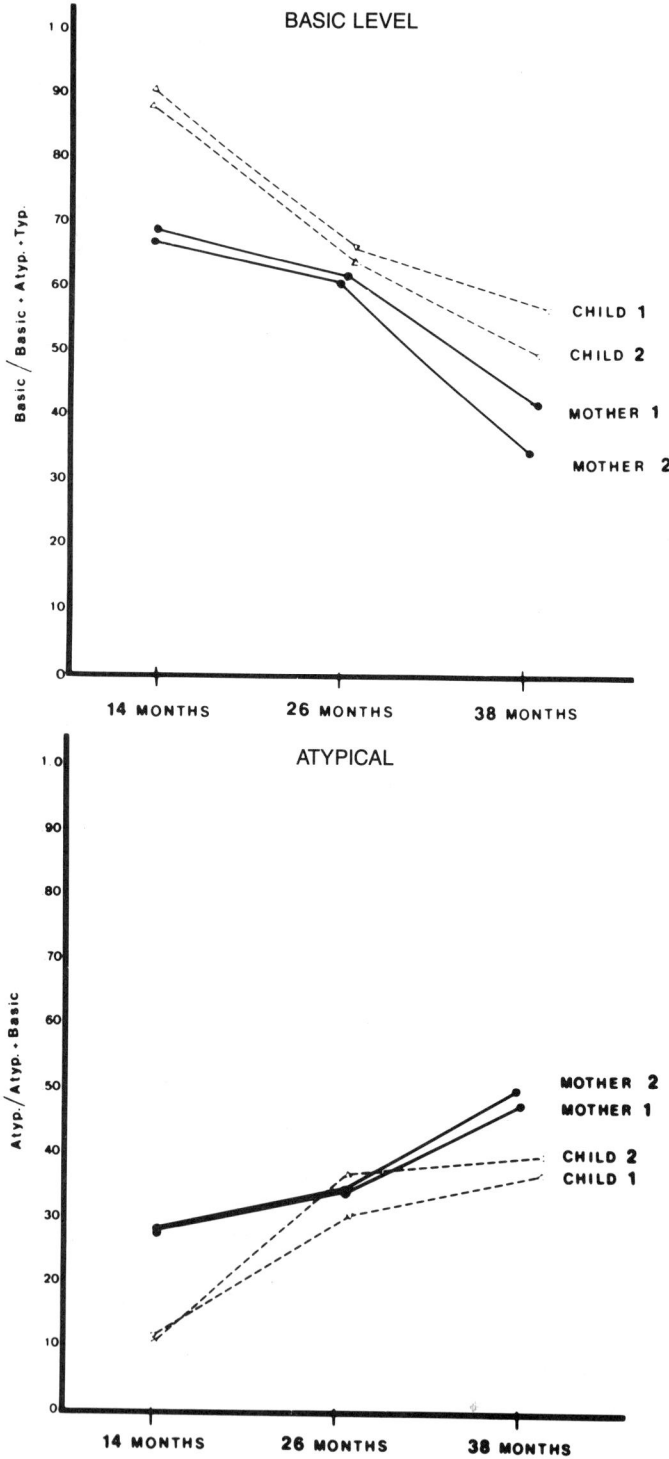

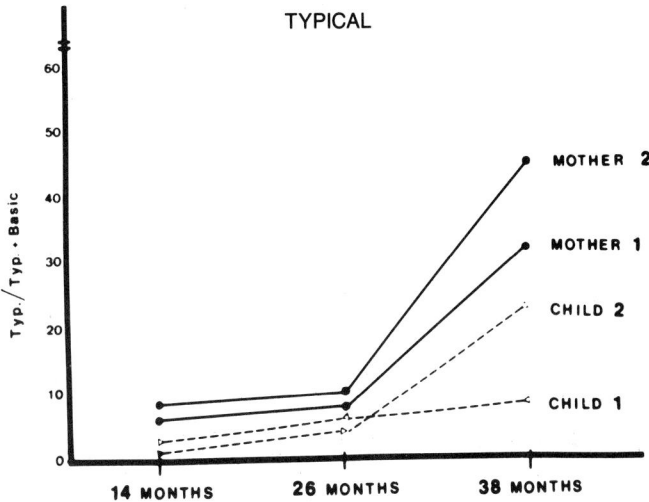

Figure 7-8. (Left and above). Overall covariation between mother and child in choice of terms for each exemplar type by age and session.

the next appropriate step. Therefore, on Session 1, mothers begin the process of helping the child differentiate the semantic field by dramatically increasing their use of subordinate names for these exemplars ($p < .001$). In fact, this tendency was so strong that mothers of 3-year-olds frequently invented names for our nondescript prototypical animals, imposing names like *hound dog*, *bay horse*, *alley cat*, and so on. Note, however, that the essentially flat curve for children on the first session indicates that they have not yet agreed to this redefinition of the task; their use of subordinate terms for typical exemplars remains virtually unchanged from what it was at one and two years. By the second laboratory session (after two weeks of home exposure) the renegotiation of the task demands is virtually complete. The children's pattern of word choice now reflects dramatically higher levels of subordinate level naming of typical category members ($p < .001$). This change in the pattern of word use shows convergence between mother's and child's naming practices in regard to typical exemplars within the time frame of the experiment. In addition, these results demonstrate that symbol formation—now involving secondary differentiation of the basic category—is a socially distributed process that involves mastery-contingent shifts in the current focus of the joint activity.

Contribution Shifts. Whereas the previous analyses were undertaken in order to examine more global shifts in mother-child word choice, those depicted in Figures 7-9 and 7-10 are aimed at specifying shifting patterns of interaction in the language-game itself. These analyses take the idea of *convergence* beyond the simple matching of performance patterns to a richer, more Vygotskyan understanding of the guided reinvention of cognitive skills. The clearest index of true mastery of any skill is the ability to perform that skill oneself, that is, to be able to assume responsibility for task components that were once beyond one's reach. Since any jointly performed activity or language-game depends on shared responsibility between collaborators, development in that domain can be thought of in terms of graduated shifts in responsibility for different aspects of the activity. These shifts in responsibility are indicative of the transition from the interpsychological to the intrapsychological plane, that is, of the transformation of a shared activity into an internalized activity. First asymmetrical performances, in which the parent carries most of the burden for the coherence and content of the activity, become more symmetrical. Then such equal collaborations shift to asymmetrical performances in which the *child* carries most of the burden, while the parent moves on to introduce further complexities (see also, Adams, 1984; Kaye & Charney, 1980; Wertsch et al., 1980).

Figure 7-9, then, illustrates this principle by presenting patterns of word choice in terms of age-related changes in mother's versus child's relative contribution to the total number of words of each type.[6] As the child moves from an apprentice to expert (adult) level in a given domain, such as basic level word usage, he or she assumes greater and greater responsibility for the use of words of that type. The important thing to keep in mind about these graphs is that points *above* the zero line indicate a greater relative contribution by the mother and points *below* the zero line indicate a greater relative contribution by the child. Therefore, falling lines indicate decreases in the mother's relative contribution and concomitant increases in the child's contribution to the labeling task. Thus, Figure 7-8 demonstrates that the closing of the gap between child and adult patterns of word use proceeds somewhat differently for word-types of varying complexity. Between 14 and 26 months the shift toward child-dominated responsibility for the use of all three word-types is parallel. However, between 26 and 38 months the pattern becomes more differentiated for different exemplar types. By 38 months, the child contributes well over half of all basic level names, such as *bird*, that occur in the reading sessions. For these simple names, the child's pattern of use has converged almost completely on full adult patterns of usage. On the other hand, subordinate level naming of atypical exemplars, like *penguin*, shows essentially equal contributions by mother and child. Here, the transition from the interpsychological to the intrapsychological plane has reached the point of symmetrical contribution to the labeling task.

Names for typical exemplars, such as *bluejay*, show a somewhat different pattern of convergence. Mothers of 38-month-olds continue to carry the greatest responsibility for such more specific names. However, they also have begun to promote the use of such names by their children—a fact hinted at by slight regression in relative contribution between 26 and 38 months.

The deeper layers of this change in maternal task demands in the joint activity are revealed by further specifying shifting patterns of participation in the picture-book language-game. In Figure 7-10 we see shifting patterns of responsibility for the

---

[6]Percent difference between mother and child calculated from the formula: $(x-y)/[(x+y)/2]$, where x=mothers' total words of that type and y=children's total words of that type.

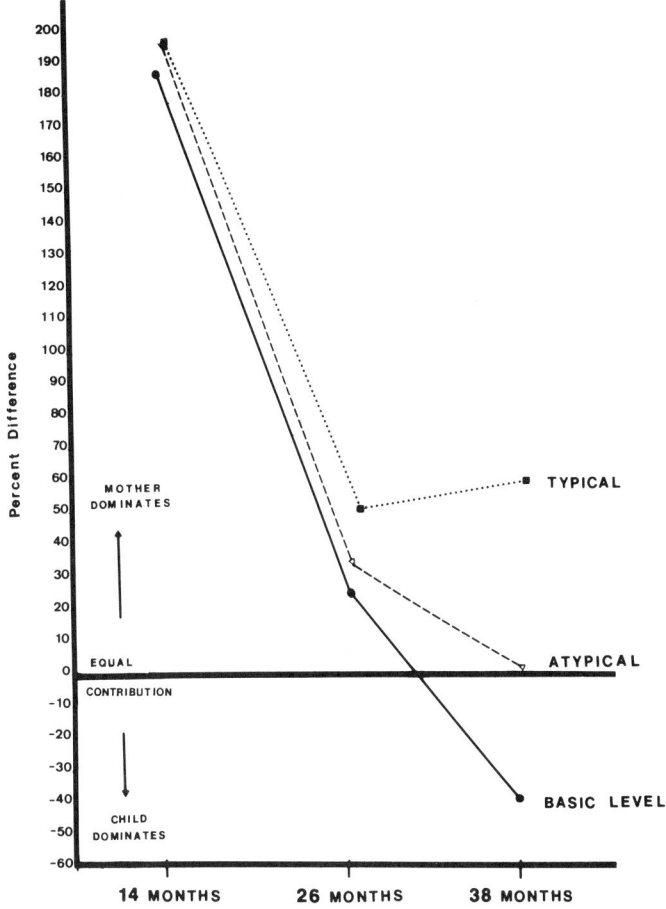

Figure 7-9. Overall changes with age in mother's versus child's relative contribution of terms for each exemplar type (sessions combined). Note that points above the zero line indicate a greater relative contribution by the mother and points below the zero line indicate a greater relative contribution by the child.

word-types by age and across the two-week training period. The left-most panel shows that, at 14 months, there is no meaningful change in relative contribution of any word-type across the two sessions. The middle panel, however, illustrates intradyadic shifts in word use across the two sessions at 26 months. As the child achieves greater skill in the conventional naming of prototypical and atypical category members—as indicated by falling lines between the two sessions—the mother begins to contribute a greater proportion of terms for typical exemplars. This upward shift in the mother's contribution marks a change in her expectations about the appropriate level of her child's performance. As convergence is achieved in one task

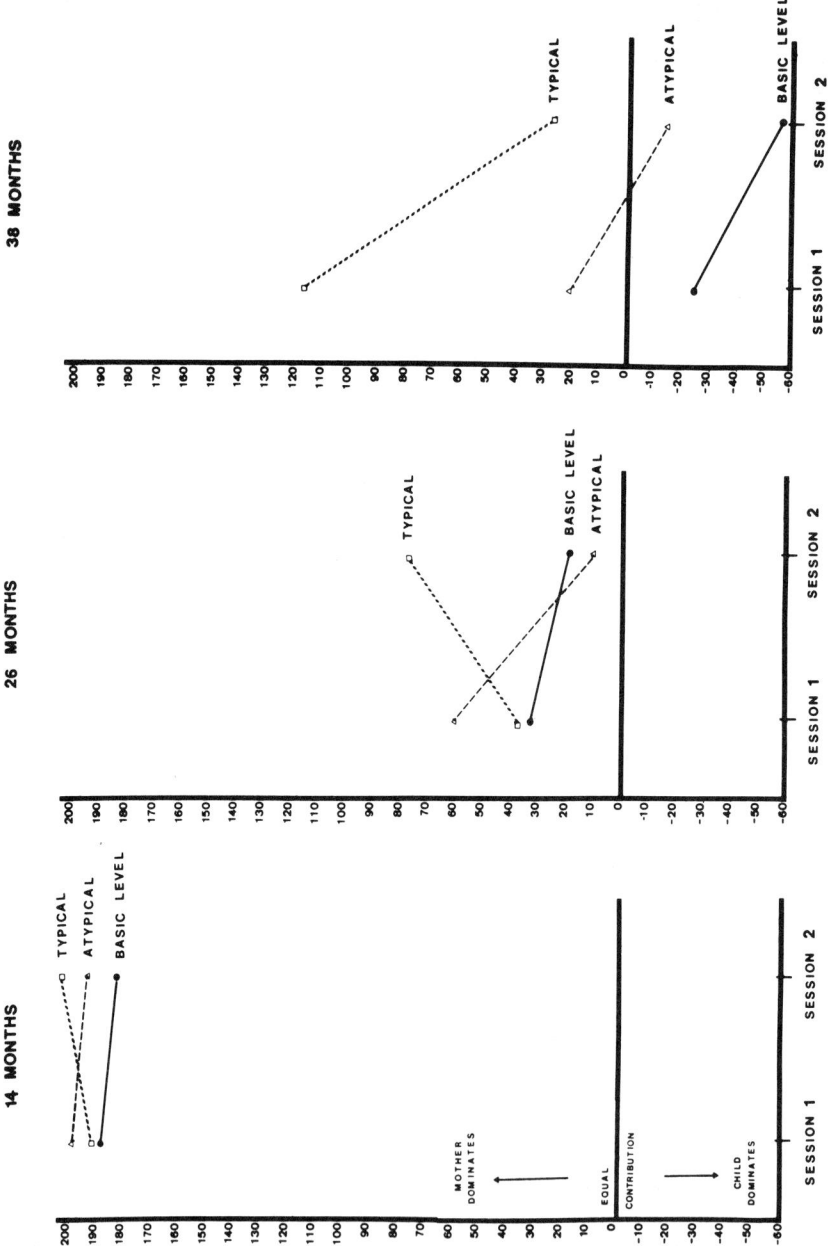

Figure 7-10. Age × exemplar-type interaction in name contribution across sessions.

domain, parents push for convergence in a slightly more complex domain. This shift away from equal contribution of names for typical exemplars in the second session also indicates that children have not yet begun to reproduce adult patterns of word use for this particular word-type.

The right-most panel, on the other hand, captures the successful renegotiation of task demands within the time-frame of the experiment. On the first session, children demonstrate largely adult-like patterns of word use for generic and atypical exemplars. Mothers implicitly sense this competence in their children and begin to emphasize more complex names for typical exemplars, leading to a large discrepancy between mother's and child's use of this word-type on the first session. By the second session, these three-year-olds have agreed to these more complex task demands and have markedly increased their own use of such subordinate names—as indicated by the rapid drop toward equal contribution of terms for typical exemplars. These shifts in relative contribution as a function of shifts in parental task demands and children's learning demonstrate that semantic convergence processes are so richly organized and so tightly regulated that we are forced to acknowledge that semantic development is essentially a socially-distributed process (see also Bullock, 1983, 1984, in press).

Mechanisms of Social Convergence

The analyses described in this chapter have provided us with a greater appreciation of the inherently social foundations of lexical development. However, they do not directly address the nature of maternal instructional strategies used to help children expand their category boundaries to include peripheral members or to help children differentiate the basic category into typical exemplars. Although the completed analyses offer insight into these strategies, our claims will have more weight when we are able to link particular strategies to specific exemplar types in specific arrays. However, we can say with confidence that, in addition to simple relabeling, these strategies include:

1. Hedges (e.g., "A penguin is a funny kind of bird");
2. Modifying phrases that identify critical physical features (e.g., "A zebra is a horse with stripes");
3. Discussions of more functional considerations, such as characteristic behaviors and habitats that distinguish the animal from other more typical members of the class (e.g., "Can penguins fly?" [child nods "yes"] "No, they swim. They live at the South Pole and they swim and they catch fish.").

The use of such strategies was observed in regard to both typical and atypical exemplars—that is, for differentiation of the category as well as expansion of the category's boundaries.

Hedges. The use of hedges in reference to peripheral category members has, of course, been noted by others (Lakoff, 1972; Rosch et al., 1976). Our work suggests that they also play an important role in semantic development through their use as tools in the instructional processes surrounding category development (see also Adam, 1984). By simultaneously identifying basic category membership and maintaining semantic distance from the prototype, hedges act to integrate atypical exemplars into the conventional adult category while continuing to mark their semi-independent status.

Modifiers. The second strategy, the addition of a modifier or modifying phrase to the basic level term, serves a somewhat similar function. Like a hedge, such phrases (e.g., *striped horsie*) identify basic category membership, with some degree of qualification. That is, some unusual feature is highlighted which prevents complete and instantaneous assimilation to the prototype. In lexical terms, the child learns that while the object is included in the extension of a particular term, the relationship is not one of equality. The importance of these modifier+noun constructions (e.g., *spotted kitty, striped horsie*) or the use of modifying phrases (e.g., *dog with spots*) is that they serve as a bridge to learning conventional adult names (e.g., *leopard, zebra, Dalmatian*). Their use should not be treated as a straightforward case of basic level labeling (and, indeed, in our study they were not), but instead should be considered a linguistically and/or cognitively intermediate step on the road to a morphemically less complex (and conceptually more opaque) name (e.g., *zebra*). Thus, the use of modifiers by both adults and children is an important mechanism governing the social regulation of category boundaries (cf. Merriman, this volume).

Identification of Functional Considerations. In addition to hedges and modifiers, mothers also spontaneously identified what might be called functional considerations, such as habitats or behaviors peculiar to particular animal types. Such explanations serve an important function in that they help the child override immediately salient, but misleading, perceptual similarities and dissimilarities. As described previously, such strategies speed the child's convergence on adult category structures by freeing the child from the necessity of autonomously reinventing the original adult language-game in which those functional considerations were relevant.

Mothers using this explanation mechanism also showed an interesting sensitivity to the age and experience of the child. For younger children, especially the 2-year-olds, mothers tended to provide explanations that were geared to particular events or experiences in the individual child's life. For example, in reference to a penguin, mothers would offer an explanation like: "That's a penguin. Do you remember when we saw him at the zoo? When you and Mommy and Daddy went to the zoo? And how funny he walked? He walked like this (imitates penguin's waddling gait), didn't he?" By 3 years of age the child was increasingly likely to hear an explanation that rested less on episodic and more on semantic information (cf. Tulving, 1983). That is, older children were more likely to be provided with an explanation like: "That's a polar bear. They live at the North Pole, don't they? Can they swim? (Child shakes his head "No") Sure they can. Polar bears swim." Thus, as the child matures, the nature of the mother's explanation shifts from a frame of reference idiosyncratic to the dyad (e.g., a particular trip to the zoo) to one that is more objective (i.e., conventional).

Negotiation. Maternal sensitivity also was reflected in mothers' willingness to negotiate the range of application of particular terms with her child. Occasionally, maternal pedagogical efforts met with resistance when the new information conflicted with the child's prior conceptual structure and understanding of a word's extension. For example, when her mother labeled the Appaloosa *horse*, one 3-year-old objected, declaring with great conviction, "Horsies don't have spots!" Her mother then patiently explained that some horses do have spots, and that such horses are called *Appaloosa*—an explanation skeptically accepted by her 3-year-old daughter. This exchange also shows that the fundamentally social process of intradyadic negotiation is an important mechanism in lexical development. Such negotiation also was observed in the direct anchoring of typical subordinate terms to basic level terms.[7] For example, when mothers reinterpreted our picture-book task as an opportunity to teach typical exemplar names, many children objected and insisted that the basic level name be appended to the new name (e.g., Mother: "Dalmatian"; Child: "Doggie!"; Mother: "Dalmatian doggie"; Child: "Dalamatian doggie"). In this case, the child initially has interpreted the range of application of the two terms to be mutually exclusive, which conflicts with the basic level name he or she knows for the object. Through instruction, he or she is taught that the range of application of the two words is overlapping, not disjoint. By a process of social agreement, the object becomes identifiable both by its subordinate name and as a member of its basic class. Our preliminary analyses did not reach such anchoring of atypical exemplars (e.g., *penguin bird*), which further supports Rosch's notion that such atypical category members are not readily identified as members of the basic class. The exception to this pattern occurred in cases such as *panda bear*, where the adult atypical term already is anchored, albeit incorrectly.[8] We anticipate that the by-referent analyses we have planned will enable us to differentiate child-initiated or

---

[7]Note that our definition of *anchoring* is stricter than that used by some other researchers. For us, *anchoring* is a strategy associated with labeling, in that a new (usually subordinate level) name is affixed to an old (usually basic level) name, as in the Dalmatian dog example. The *anchor* here implies equivalence in use of terms. The use of phrases like, *is a kind of* or *is a member of the X family* is an obviously related, but more complex strategy aimed at teaching part-whole relations. The latter strategy has been investigated most thoroughly by Callanan (1983) with regard to learning superordinate terms. Therefore, whereas one would explain a part-whole relation to a child with a sentence like, "A koala is a kind of animal," we would argue that the use of terms is not completely equivalent (e.g., one would not usually label a koala *animal* and nothing more), and that one therefore would not usually *anchor* the terms (e.g., *koala-animal*). The latter example shows that the two strategies serve somewhat different functions in the instructional process.

[8]Although we were fully aware that pandas (and koalas) technically are not bears, we used them as atypical exemplars of the *bear* category, hypothesizing that the distinction would be judged irrelevant for children in the age range we studied. Our subjects agreed; only one mother pointed out our error to her child (and none did to us).

parent-initiated anchoring from such conventional anchoring (see also Callanan, 1983; Merriman, this volume, Chapter 1). We also saw evidence suggestive of object name negotiation within the mother-father-child triad over the 2-week training period, especially with regard to names for typical exemplars or invented names for our nondescript exemplars. On several occasions the child was corrected, usually after using a basic level term, with a statement like, "No, Daddy says that one's an elk." These findings serve as a reminder that the conventionalization of category structure continues as an active social process throughout life.

Environmental Support of Particular Mechanisms. In addition to the context effects on maternal labeling practices described previously, it appears that different contexts of exemplar presentation (i.e., different chapter manipulations) had differential effects on the types and frequency of use of various maternal strategies of category differentiation and expansion. That is, the configuration of mechanisms supporting lexical growth is itself influenced by dimensions of the interactive environment. For example, in contexts having a high proportion of typical exemplars, mothers of 3-year-olds often used the question, "What kind of (basic level label) is that?" to set the stage for the choice of a more specific label. (As noted above, we do not think that the child's ability to respond appropriately to this question by supplying a more specific name indicates any true understanding of class inclusion. However, we do suspect that it helps the child understand that words have overlapping ranges of application, and that such understanding serves as the foundation from which an adult-like understanding or taxonomic relations later will be reconstructed.) Similarly, the use of hedges, with their implicit identification of basic category membership (e.g., "A penguin is a funny kind of bird"), occurred most often in our *Whole Range* condition, which highlighted basic category membership. In fact, some mothers of 3-year-olds used this *Whole Range* condition to discuss family membership explicitly, sometimes in charming detail (e.g., "These are all members of the horse family. You know how in our family we have Mommy and Daddy and David? And we're all kind of alike and we're all kind of different, aren't we? Well, this is a horse and his name is *mule*. And this is a horse and his name is *zebra* . . ."). Attention to taxonomically correct family membership appeared only in this condition and did not emerge until the dyad reached age three.

This result is made all the more noteworthy by the observation that many mothers spontaneously imposed alternate classification schemes on the stimulus arrays, such as big versus small, domestic versus wild, and zoo versus neighborhood animals. These results suggest that our structuralist preoccupation with taxonomic biological correctness may have caused us to fail to test for and to overlook the importance of alternate classification schemes more functionally relevant to young children. (See also, Storm, 1980, for a discussion of the preeminence of such nontaxonomic strategies for classifying animal types in children of various ages and in adult zoology doctoral students.) They also suggest that, at least in some settings, children are taught and learn multiple organizational schemes, which may be selected in relation to specific task demands, i.e., in relation to particular language-games.

Despite the strength of the evidence presented here, we recognize that our claims regarding the fundamental importance of social convergence mechanisms will prove even stronger when supported by individual difference data. First, it must be determined whether or not there exist demonstrable variations in particular strategies of maternal object labeling and description, as have been found in the syntactic domain (e.g., Barnes, Gutfreund, Satterly, & Wells, 1983; Cross, 1977; Moerk, 1983). Second, it must be determined whether or not such differences in patterns of maternal word choice and pedagogical strategies are linked to the child's level of lexical development. For example, we would expect that maternal individual differences in proportions of word-types selected, in the use of different differentiation and expansion strategies (e.g., hedges, identification of critical features, explicit and implicit anchoring), and in adaptation to the child's skill level (e.g., willingness to permit intersession role shifts as particular word-types are mastered) are linked to quantitative and qualitative differences in semantic development. Data demonstrating such a complex matrix of social-cognitive relations will, we hope, be forthcoming. With it, we expect that the autonomous invention view of early conceptual development finally will yield to one of guided reinvention.

Conclusion

The research described here supports the themes raised in the opening sections of this chapter. In accordance with Vygotsky and his contemporary proponents, we have shown that word meanings are socially constituted. Even in the domain of object categories, which have the clear support of environmental texture, both the differentiation of the semantic field into exemplar subtypes and the expansion of category boundaries to include peripheral members are socially guided processes that often involve active intradyadic negotiation. The choice of an object label was shown to be a highly fluid phenomenon, affected by the relationships between object features, the surrounding context, and the possibility of listener confusion. Object labeling also was shown to be sensitive to shifts in the child's level of mastery. Inspired by Wittgenstein, we have looked at how the common-noun language-game provides a microcosm in which the child learns the rules of word usage. In addition, we argued that learning normative patterns of word use is a precondition for, but does not by itself guarantee, an understanding of complex interrelations between concepts. Such an understanding depends upon a differently organized language-game.

The importance of social factors in lexical development demonstrates that the construction of a semantic system is a collaborative project. The joint efforts of parent and child ensure that the end product of their endeavor will be a conceptual system whose behavioral manifestations are shared, making communication between members of the culture possible. We predict that the socially distributed mechanisms underlying the process of reconstructive transfer from one member of the culture to another—mechanisms that may be collectively referred to as the system for guided reinvention—will be found to be species characteristic. By engaging children in organized activities and by explicitly directing children's attention to aspects of objects and events that might not be spontaneously noticed, parents systematically bias semantic network development and thereby ensure that their children develop conventionalized and functionally useful semantic systems.

A full appreciation of the ability of language-games and other symbolic processes to "create new perceptual centers" (Vygotsky, 1978/1934) by highlighting naturally nonsalient similarities and differences between objects and events, to overcome natural mnemonic barriers to the integration of superficially disparate phenomena (Fischer & Bullock, 1984), and to support later metacognitive and epistemic activities (Fischer & Bullock, 1984; Goody, 1977) is fundamental to understanding the development of word meaning. The critical importance of these richly patterned, shared activities warrants Wittgenstein's claim that language-games are primary engines of human conceptual growth. As noted in the introduction, we believe this point will become even better established when researchers go beyond relatively fine-grained convergence problems, like those covered in our study, to consider more coarse-grained semantic convergence problems, such as those involved in the acquisition of modern scientific concepts.

Acknowledgments. Preparation of this chapter would not have been possible without the cooperation and assistance of a number of people. We are indebted to Joe Campos, Donna Bradshaw, and Charlotte Henderson for help at the Center for Infant Studies. Marci Meeker and Jim Platt were the artists who provided us with the drawings used in the study. We also thank the army of friends who helped color the over 2,000 pictures that went into the 19 books. Kim Carpenter, Julia Gore, Cynthia Jaeger, and Pam Sartore provided invaluable assistance in the coding and analysis of the data. Dinah Fruth helped with the initial preparation of the graphs and Carol Bach with the preparation of the manuscript itself. We would like to thank Beth Byerly, Kurt Fischer, Gail Goodman, Marshall Haith, Bill Merriman, and Carolyn Mervis for their helpful comments on prior versions of the manuscript. We are also grateful to the editors of this volume, Stan Kuczaj and Martyn Barrett, for their assistance and support throughout this endeavor.

The research reported in this chapter was conducted during the time Adams was a National Science Foundation Predoctoral Fellow at the University of Denver. A prior report of the study was presented at the 1983 Biennial Meeting of the Society for Research in Child Development held in Detroit, Michigan.

References

Adams, A. K. (1984, March). *Methods for detecting dynamic regularities in parent-child verbal interaction.* Paper presented at the Biennial Meeting of the Southwestern Society for Research in Human Development, Denver, CO.

Adams, A. K. (1984). *Language and thought reconsidered: The role of linguistic tools in human cognitive activities*. Unpublished manuscript. University of Denver.

Anglin, J. M. (1977). *Word, object, and conceptual development*. New York: Norton.

Austin, J. L. (1962). *How to do things with words*. Cambridge, MA: Harvard University Press.

Barrett, M. D. (1978). Lexical development and overextension in child language. *Journal of Child Language, 5*, 205-219.

Barrett, M. D. (1982). Distinguishing between prototypes: The early acquisition of the meaning of object names. In S. A. Kuczaj (Ed.), *Language development, Vol. 1: Syntax and semantics*. Hillsdale, NJ: Erlbaum.

Barnes, S., Gutfreund, M., Satterly, D., & Wells, G. (1983). Characteristics of adult speech which predict children's language development. *Journal of Child Language, 10*, 65-84.

Bates, E., & MacWhinney, B. (1982). Functionalist approaches to grammar. In E. Wanner & L. R. Gleitman (Eds.), *Language acquisition: The state of the art*. Cambridge, MA: Cambridge University Press.

Blewitt, P. (1982). Word meaning acquisition in young children: A review of theory and research. *Advances in Child Development and Behavior, 17*, 139-195.

Blewitt, P. (1983). "Dog" vs. "Collie": Vocabulary in speech to young children. *Developmental Psychology, 19*, 602-609.

Blewitt, P. (1983, April). *What determines order of acquisition of object categories?* Paper presented at the Biennial Meeting of the Society for Research in Child Development, Detroit, MI.

Bloor, D. (1983). *Wittgenstein: A social theory of knowledge*. New York: Columbia University Press.

Bowerman, M. (1982). Reorganizational processes in lexical and syntactic development. In E. Wanner & L. R. Gleitman (Eds.), *Language acquisition: The state of the art*. Cambridge, MA: Cambridge University Press.

Brown, A. L., Bransford, J. D., Ferrara, R. A., & Campione, J. C. (1983). Learning, remembering, and understanding. In P. Mussen (Ed.), *Carmichael's manual of child psychology: Vol. 3. Cognitive Development* (pp. 77-166). New York: Wiley.

Brown, R. (1958). How shall the thing be called? *Psychological Review, 65*, 14-21.

Brown, R. (1976). Reference: In memorial tribute to Eric Lenneberg. *Cognition, 4*, 125-153.

Brown, R. (1978). A new paradigm of reference. In G. A. Miller & E. Lenneberg (Eds.), *Psychology and biology of language and thought: Essays in honor of Eric Lenneberg*. New York: Academic Press.

Bruner, J. S. (1975). From communication to language—A psychological perspective. *Cognition, 3*, 255-287.

Bullock, D. (1979). *Social coordination and children's learning of property words*. Unpublished doctoral dissertation, Stanford University.

Bullock, D. (1981). On the current and potential scope of generative theories of cognitive development. In K. W. Fischer (Ed.), *Cognitive development. New Directions for Child Development, No. 12*. San Francisco: Jossey-Bass.

Bullock, D. (1983). Seeking relations between cognitive and social-interactive transitions. In K. W. Fischer (Ed.), *Levels and transitions in children's development. New Directions for Child Development, No. 21*. San Francisco: Jossey-Bass.

Bullock, D. (1984, March). *Attentional dynamics and pattern completion processes as organizers of parent-child interaction*. Paper presented at the Biennial Meeting of the Southwestern Society for Research in Human Development, Denver, CO.

Bullock, D. (in press). Modes of interaction, language-games, and human-class intelligence. In M. Chapman & R. Dixon (Eds.), *Wittgenstein and developmental psychology*. New York: Academic Press.

Bullock, D., & Zare, S. (1980, September). *Determinants of word-choice in mothers' speech to three-year-olds*. Paper presented at the Annual Convention of the American Psychological Association, Montreal.

Callanan, M. (1983, April). *Parental input and young children's acquisition of hierarchically organized concepts*. Paper presented at the Biennial Meeting of the Society for Research in Child Development, Detroit.

Cross, T. G. (1977). Mothers' speech adjustments: The contribution of selected child listener variables. In C. E. Snow & C. Ferguson (Eds.), *Talking to children: Language input and acquisition*. Cambridge, MA: Cambridge University Press.

Danford, J. W. (1978). *Wittgenstein and political philosophy: A reexamination of the foundations of social science*. Chicago: University of Chicago Press.

Dennett, D. C. (1975). Why the law of effect will not go away. *Journal for the theory of social behavior, 5*, 169-187.

DeLoache, J. S. (1983). *Joint picture-book reading as memory training for toddlers*. Paper presented at the Biennial Meeting of the Society for Research in Child Development, Detroit.

Estes, W. K., & Suppes, P. (1974). Foundations of stimulus sampling theory. In D. H. Krantz et al. (Eds.), *Contemporary developments in mathematical psychology. Volume I: Learning, memory, and thinking*. San Francisco: W. H. Freeman & Co.

Fernald, A., & Mazzie, C. (1983, April). *Pitch-marking of new and old information in mothers' speech to infants*. Paper presented at the Biennial Meeting of the Society for Research in Child Development, Detroit.

Fernald, A., & Simon, T. (1984). Expanded intonation contours in mothers' speech to newborns. *Developmental Psychology, 20*, 104-113.

Fischer, K. W. (1980). A theory of cognitive development: The control and construction of hierarchies of skills. *Psychological Review, 87*, 477-531.

Fischer, K. W., & Bullock, D. (1984). Cognitive development in school-age children: Conclusions and new directions. In W. A. Collins (Ed.), *Development during middle childhood*. Washington, DC: National Academy Press.

Goody, J. (1977). *The domestication of the savage mind*. New York: Cambridge University Press.

Greenberg, J., & Kuczaj, S. A. (1982). Towards a theory of substantive word-meaning acquisition. In S. A. Kuczaj (Ed.), *Language development. Volume 1: Syntax and semantics*. Hillsdale, NJ: Erlbaum.

Grossberg, S. (1982). *Studies of mind and brain*. Boston: D. Reidel Publishing Co.

Guillaume, P. (1971). *Imitation in children*. Chicago: University of Chicago Press. (Original French edition 1926).

Hamburger, H., & Wexler, K. (1975). A mathematical theory of learning transformational grammar. *Journal of Mathematical Psychology, 12*, 321-351.

Hintikka, J. (1973). *Logic, language-games and information*. London: Oxford University Press.

Horton, M. S., & Markman, E. M. (1980). Developmental differences in the acquisition of basic and superordinate categories. *Child Development, 51*, 708-719.

Kaufmann, G. (1980). *Imagery, language and cognition*. Bergen: Universitetforlaget.

Kaye, K. (1982). *The mental and social life of babies*. Chicago: University of Chicago Press.

Kaye, K., & Charney, R. (1980). How mothers maintain "dialogue" with two-year-olds. In D. R. Olson (Ed.), *The social foundations of language and thought*. New York: Norton.

Laboratory of Comparative Human Cognition. (1983). Culture and cognitive development. In P. H. Mussen (Ed.), *Manual of child psychology: Vol. I. History, theories, and methods* (pp. 295-356). New York: Wiley.

Lakoff, G. (1972). Hedges: A study in meaning criteria and the logic of fuzzy concepts. *Pages from the Eighth Regional Meeting, Chicago Linguistics Society*. Chicago: University of Chicago.

Lock, A. (1980). *The guided reinvention of language*. New York: Academic Press.

Lucariello, J. (1983, April). *Is the basic level always basic?* Paper presented at the Biennial Meeting of the Society for Research in Child Development, Detroit.

MacWhinney, B. (1984). Commentary: Where do categories come from? In C. Sophian (Ed.), *Origins of cognitive skills*. Hillsdale, NJ: Erlbaum.

Mandler, J. M. (1983). Representation. In P. Mussen (Ed.), *Carmichael's manual of child psychology: Vol. 3. Cognitive development* (pp. 420-494). New York: Wiley.

Markman, E. M. (1981). Two different principles of conceptual organization. In M. E. Lamb & A. L. Brown (Eds.), *Advances in developmental psychology*. Hillsdale, NJ: Erlbaum.

Markman, E. M. (1984). The acquisition and hierarchical organization of categories by children. In C. Sophian (Ed.), *Origins of cognitive skills*. Hillsdale, NJ: Erlbaum.

Markman, E. M., & Hutchinson, J. E. (1984). Children's sensitivity to constraints on word meaning: Taxonomic vs. thematic relations. *Cognitive Psychology, 16*, 1-27.

Mervis, C. B. (1983). Acquisition of a lexicon. *Contemporary Educational Psychology, 8*, 210-236.

Mervis, C. B. (1984). Early lexical development: The contributions of mother and child. In C. Sophian (Ed.), *Origins of cognitive skill*. Hillsdale, NJ: Erlbaum.

Mervis, C. B., & Canada, K. (1983). On the existence of competence errors in early comprehension: A reply to Fremgen & Fay and Chapman & Thompson. *Journal of Child Language, 10*, 431-440.

Mervis, C. B., & Mervis, C. A. (1982). Leopards are kitty-cats: Object labeling by mothers for their thirteen-month-olds. *Child Development, 53*, 267-273.

Millikan, R. G. (1984). *Language, thought, and other biological categories: New foundations for realism*. Cambridge, MA: MIT Press.

Moerk, E. L. (1976). Processes of language teaching and training in the interactions of mother-child dyad. *Child Development, 47*, 1064-1078.

Moerk, E. L. (1983). A behavioral analysis of controversial topics in first language acquisition: Reinforcements, corrections, modeling, input frequencies, and the three-term contingency pattern. *Journal of Psycholinguistic Research, 12*, 129-155.

Nelson, K. (1979). Explorations in the development of a functional semantic system. In W. A. Collins (Ed.), *Children's language and communication. The Minnesota Symposia on Child Psychology, Vol. 12*. Hillsdale, NJ: Erlbaum.

Nelson, K. (1983). The derivation of concepts and categories from event representations. In E. K. Scholnick (Ed.), *New trends in conceptual representation: Challenges to Piaget's theory?* Hillsdale, NJ: Erlbaum.

Nelson, K., & Gruendel, J. (1981). Generalized event representations: Basic building blocks of cognitive development. In M. Lamb & A. Brown (Eds.), *Advances in developmental psychology, Vol. 1*. Hillsdale, NJ: Erlbaum.

Nelson, K. E., & Nelson, K. (1978). Cognitive pendulums and their linguistic realization. In K. E. Nelson (Ed.), *Children's language, Vol. 1*. New York: Halstead Press.

Ninio, A. (1980). Picture-book reading in mother-infant dyads belonging to two sub-groups in Israel. *Child Development, 51*, 587-590.

Ninio, A. (1983). Joint book reading as a multiple vocabulary acquisition device. *Developmental Psychology, 19*, 445-451.

Ninio, A., & Bruner, J. (1978). The achievement and antecedents of labelling. *Journal of Child Language, 5*, 1-15.

Piaget, J. (1955). *The language and thought of the child*. New York: Meridian Books. (Original work published 1923)

Posner, M. I., & Keele, S. W. (1968). On the genesis of abstract ideas. *Journal of Experimental Psychology, 77*, 353-363.

Posner, M. I., & Keele, S. W. (1970). Retention of abstract ideas. *Journal of Experimental Psychology, 83*, 304-308.

Ratner, N., & Bruner, J. (1978). Games, social exchange and the acquisition of language. *Journal of Child Language, 5*, 391-401.

Rescorla, L. A. (1981). Category development in early language. *Journal of Child Language, 8*, 225-238.

Rosch, E. (1978). Principles of categorization. In E. Rosch & B. B. Lloyd (Eds.), *Cognition and categorization*. Hillsdale, NJ: Erlbaum.

Rosch, E., & Mervis, C. B. (1975). Family resemblance: Studies in the internal structure of categories. *Cognitive Psychology, 8*, 573-605.

Rosch, E., Mervis, C. B., Gray, W. D., Johnson, D. M., & Boyes-Braem, P. (1976). Basic objects in natural categories. *Cognitive Psychology, 8*, 382-439.

Rogoff, B., & Wertsch, J. V. (1984). *Children's learning in the "Zone of Proximal Development." New Directions for Child Development, No. 23*. San Francisco: Jossey-Bass.

Sachs, J. (1983). Talking about the there and then: The emergence of displaced reference in parent-child discourse. In K. E. Nelson (Ed.), *Children's language, Vol. 4*. Hillsdale, NJ: Erlbaum.

Saxe, G. B., Gearhart, M., & Guberman, S. R. (1984). The social organization of early number development. In B. Rogoff & J. V. Wertsch (Eds.), *Children's learning in the "Zone of Proximal Development." New Directions for Child Development, No. 23*. San Francisco: Jossey-Bass.

Schlesinger, I. M. (1982). *Steps to language: Toward a theory of native language acquisition*. Hillsdale, NJ: Erlbaum.

Searle, J. R. (1969). *Speech acts: An essay in the philosophy of language*. Cambridge, MA: Cambridge University Press.

Snow, C. E. (1977). The development of conversation between mothers and babies. *Journal of Child Language, 4*, 1-22.

Snow, C. E. (1983). Saying it again: The role of expanded and deferred imitations in language acquisition. In K. E. Nelson (Ed.), *Children's language, Vol. 4*. Hillsdale, NJ: Erlbaum.

Snow, C. E., & Ferguson, C. A. (1977). *Talking to children: Language input and acquisition*. Cambridge, MA: Cambridge University Press.

Storm, C. (1980). The semantic structure of animal terms: A developmental study. *International Journal of Behavioral Development, 3*, 381-407.

Tulving, E. (1983). *Elements of episodic memory*. New York: Oxford University Press.

Vygotsky, L. S. (1962). *Thought and language*. Cambridge, MA: MIT Press. (Original work published in 1934)

Vygotsky, L. S. (1978). *Mind in society: The development of higher psychological processes*. Cambridge, MA: Harvard University Press. (Original work published in 1934)

Wales, R., Colman, M., & Patterson, P. (1983). How a thing is called—A study of mothers' and children's naming. *Journal of Experimental Child Psychology, 36*, 1-17.

Wertsch, J. V. (1979). From social interaction to higher psychological processes: A clarification and application of Vygotsky's theory. *Human Development, 22*, 1-22.

Wertsch, J. V., McNamee, G. D., McLane, J. B., & Budwig, N. A. (1980). The adult-child dyad as a problem solving system. *Child Development, 51*, 1215-1221.

White, T. G. (1982). Naming practices, typicality, and underextension in child language. *Journal of Experimental Child Psychology, 33*, 324-346.

Wittgenstein, L. (1953). *Philosophical investigations*. New York: Macmillan.

Wood, D. J. (1980). Teaching the young child: Some relationships between social interaction, language, and thought. New York: Norton.

Zimmerman, B. J. (1979). Concepts and classification. In G. Whitehurst & B. J. Zimmerman (Eds.), *The functions of language and cognition*. New York: Academic Press.

8. Words, Plans, Things, and Locations: Interactions Between Semantic and Cognitive Development in the One-Word Stage

Alison Gopnik and Andrew N. Meltzoff

If we want to understand the interaction between semantic and cognitive development, the one-word stage is a natural place to start. Since children only use one word at a time, we don't have to be too concerned about syntax. Fortunately, we know something about cognitive developments in this period and, even more fortunately, we have nonlinguistic ways of measuring these developments. Moreover, by looking at the very first words, we can hope to find out about the origins of meaning itself. We can witness the very first meeting of cognition and language, before they become hopelessly intertwined.

In this chapter we will describe the meanings of words in the one-word stage, the changes in those meanings during the one-word stage, and the relationship between semantic and cognitive developments in this period. We will also try to show that the data contradict most of the existing accounts of semantic development, particularly the Piagetian account. Finally, we will suggest an alternative account of semantic and cognitive development in this period. According to this account, children's early words encode the particular concepts that are challenging and problematic to them, concepts they are in the midst of developing. Moreover, the acquisition of these words may facilitate further cognitive developments.

There are several different kinds of evidence that can help us to understand these problems. The most important evidence comes from the child's spontaneous language. We can look at the context in which a child uses a word and try to discover what that word means to the child. Often, in fact usually, this meaning will turn out to be quite unlike the adult meaning of the word.

If a child consistently uses a certain word in a certain context, we may already infer something about the concepts he or she must have. We can also try to discover what children's concepts are like by looking at children's nonlinguistic behavior, particularly their problem-solving behavior. Investigators of cognitive development have made claims about the concepts of 15- to 21-month-old children on the basis of such evidence. We can compare these findings to the psycholinguistic findings and come to some tentative conclusions about which concepts children choose to encode when they begin to speak.

Finally, we can try to find empirical links between various kinds of linguistic and cognitive achievements, particularly links between the development of various types of meanings and the development of problem-solving skills that require certain concepts. We can ask whether there are general correlations between linguistic and cognitive develoments in this period, or more specific links between particular linguistic and cognitive achievements. We can also ask whether developments in one domain are prerequisite for developments in the other domain, or whether semantic developments and related conceptual developments occur in tandem. These empirical studies provide strong, direct evidence about the relationship between semantic and cognitive development in the one-word stage.

Meaning in the One-Word Stage

If we compare various descriptions of language in the one-word stage (e.g., Bloom, 1973; Carter, 1975a, 1975b, 1978, 1979; Nelson, 1973a; Halliday, 1975; McCune-Nicolich, 1981; Bowerman, 1978; & Gopnik, 1981, 1982), we are struck by the similarities in the kinds of meanings children express when they begin to speak. The children in all these studies seemed to encode similar concepts even when they used different words. We will classify early words into three categories: words about things; words about plans; and words about locations.

We will briefly describe the most significant early meanings based on the findings of the studies cited above (particularly those of Bloom and McCune-Nicolich), our own longitudinal recordings of the speech of 20 British and Canadian children, and our cross-sectional studies of 54 American children. (For details of the methodology of these recordings see Gopnik, 1981, 1982, 1984 and Gopnik & Meltzoff, 1983, 1984b).

Words About Things

Disappearance

Children consistently use an early word, usually *gone* or *all gone*, to talk about the fact that they cannot see an object. These words are often described as encoding *disappearance*—but this is too simple. Children do frequently use these words when objects disappear, especially if they have caused the disappearance themselves, but they also use these words when they believe or expect that an object should appear and it doesn't. For example, children may say *gone* when they search for hypothetical objects, objects they have never seen at all. For example, a child may say *gone* when searching for a cup that should go inside the smallest of a set of nesting cups, even if there is no such cup. *Disappearance* words seem to encode the fact that the child does not see an object, rather than the fact that the object has disappeared (Gopnik, 1984).

Notice

Children also frequently use a word that encodes the fact that they *do* see an object. In English, *that* and *there* are particularly common. Children use these words when they perceive or pay attention to an object; often the words are accompanied by pointing. In very early language, these words may be directed to other people. The child will point and say *that* to draw someone else's attention to an object (Bruner, 1983; Carter, 1975b). But later, children use *that* in ways that don't have this social character. In particular, children will use these words when they are acting on, or are about to act on an object themselves, or when an object simply interests them, regardless of the behavior of others (Gopnik, 1980).

Names

In addition to pointing out the fact that they see or don't see an object, children name objects. In fact, until Bloom's pioneering study (Bloom, 1973), investigators paid little attention to the many early words that do *not* simply name objects. Bloom pointed out that *relational* or *function* words, words like *no*, *more*, and *gone* were frequently used in early language, but until recently, names continued to receive most of the attention. In fact, it is still common to read claims that children begin using object names before they talk about actions or relationships (Gentner, 1982).

Names and Relational Words

Before we talk about what object names mean, we should consider why object names have had this privileged status. Part of the answer lies in the theoretical assumptions of most studies of early words. Object names fit associationist or ostensive definition theories of meaning more easily than relational words do. (Try to imagine giving an ostensive definition of *that*, *gone*, or *no*.) From St. Augustine on, these have been the most popular theories of the origin of meaning.

But part of the answer lies in the fact that children typically use many different names while they use the same small set of relational words. Most accounts of early language have been based on diaries, where the diarist is likely to list the child's new words. Names will seem to be disproportionately significant in such a study.

In a study of the spontaneous speech of nine children (Gopnik, 1980, 1981) we found that children did use more different names than relational words. By other measures, however, names were not more significant than other types of words. Children used individual names much less frequently than they used relational expressions. In fact, over all, only one of the children uttered names more frequently than relational words. For four children, more than two-thirds of their utterances did not name objects. Children were particularly likely to use relational words when they were younger. Two children used relational words before they used any names at all, and the rest began using both types of words in the same session. Moreover, if we compare the children's language before and after the midway point of the longitudinal study, we can see that a significantly greater proportion of relational words were uttered in the early period (see Table 8-1). Utterances of names became more frequent as the children grew older.

Relational words were also more likely than names to be used by several different children. For example, all nine children used *gone*, *down*, and *there*, while *mommy* was the only name used by all nine children. Children were also more likely to use relational words consistently over several months. Only 25% of the relational words only occurred in one recording session; 72% of the recorded names only occurred in one recording session.

In summary, the evidence suggests that relational words and names have different properties. Children use the same small set of relational words early and often. They use many different names but names tend to appear later and are used less frequently. Relational words seem to be just as important as names in early language.

It is worth noting that if we simply counted all the words in the dictionary, we might conclude that adult speakers were overwhelmingly concerned about naming objects, and were much less interested in talking about actions or relationships. This would be an inaccurate description of the adult language and it is an equally inaccurate description of meaning in the one-word stage. The evidence suggests that names are only one semantic category among many in the one-word stage, not the predominant category.

The Meaning of Early Names

The many investigations of early object names have raised almost as many questions as they have answered. Early accounts of object names (Clark, 1974; Nelson,

Table 8-1. Percentage of Nominal Utterances in First and Second Halves of the Recording Period.

	First half			Second half		
Child	Total utterances	Nominal utterances	%	Total utterances	Nominal utterances	%
Jonathan	364	13	3.6	1972	767	38.9
Henry	278	98	35.3	1824	763	41.8
Rachel	140	60	42.9	1352	931	68.9
John	263	89	33.8	179	70	39.1
Christian	208	68	32.7	288	152	52.8
Harriet	274	95	34.7	676	304	45.0
Paul	150	9	6.0	644	171	26.6
Hannah	232	56	24.1	721	234	32.5
Anna	428	153	35.7	763	219	28.7

1974) subscribed to feature theories of meaning. Such theories had been proposed to explain the semantic structure of adult language (Katz & Fodor, 1963; Bierswich, 1970). According to these accounts, names encode categories of objects, based on common properties of those objects. You can appropriately use a name to refer to an object if the object has the appropriate property or properties, and hence belongs to the appropriate category. These properties are represented as features in the semantic representation of the word.

According to this view, children should apply early names to groups of objects that have some property or properties in common. For example, the word *dog* might be applied to everything four-legged and medium-sized. The differences between the children's meanings and the adult meanings stem from the fact that the child attaches a different set of features to the word than the adult does. For example, a child who attached the features *four-legged* and *medium-sized* to the word *dog* might apply this word to cows and pigs as well as dogs. Clark suggests, more specifically, that the child's meaning consists of a subset of the features of the adult meaning. On this view, semantic development is a matter of acquiring more and more of the adult features.

More recent findings have tended to undermine these early accounts of the meaning of names. Kaye and Anglin (1981) report that underextensions and mismatches are as common as overextensions in early language. It seems that children do not simply have a subset of adult features. Moreover, when children do overextend names, they do not simply apply them to objects that have some property or properties in common. Instead, they are likely to apply the same name to many different objects with different properties in common. For example, Bowerman (1978) describes a child using the word *moon* to refer to an orange, a lamp, and a fingernail paring.

Bowerman (1978), Barrett (1982), and Kuczaj (1982) have suggested that early names encode categories that are organized in terms of prototypes rather than in terms of properties. Rosch and Mervis (1975) have argued that adult names are applied to objects that have different properties in common with each other. There are prototypical objects which are the best exemplars of a category. In addition, other objects which have some properties in common with the prototype may also fall into the category. However, there is no single property or set of properties that determines whether or not an object is a member of the category, or can be referred to by the category name. Children also seem to apply names to prototype-based categories. Anything that has some property or other in common with the prototypical *moon* (shape, color, luminance, etc.) may be called *moon*.

Changes in the Meaning of Names

A number of authors (Bloom, 1973; Nelson, 1975; Corrigan, 1978) have noted there is often a striking increase in the number of names children use during the one-word period. It's as if the child suddenly discovers that everything has a name. It's not uncommon to see an 18-month-old child point to every object in the room, giving each object a name. The names in this naming explosion have a rather different character from the earlier names. The very first names tend to refer to particularly important objects in the child's life, like *mommy*, *bottle*, or *teddy*. These early names are often underextended, and appear in a limited number of contexts (Barrett, 1982). In our observation, these names often have a strongly social or pragmatic quality. *Mommy* is used exclusively as a cry for help; *bottle* is used to request a bottle; and so on.

After the naming explosion, names are more likely to be overextended in the ways described above. Moreover, rather than simply naming salient objects, children start to name every object in sight. It's common to see an 18-month-old child point to every object in a room, giving each object a name. When children use names in this way, they seem to be more concerned about appropriately categorizing objects than they are about attaining some particular pragmatic goal.

Words About Plans

Relational words like *gone* and *that*, as well as names, seem to be primarily concerned about objects. Children use these words to comment on the fact that they do or do not perceive objects or that objects belong to prototype-based categories. Another group of relational words seem to be more concerned about actions. However, these words do not simply encode actions in the way that verbs like *walk* or *run* encode actions. Instead, children use these words to talk about actions that are performed on objects in order to bring about a particular consequence. Elsewhere, we have argued that these words encode aspects of plans (Gopnik, 1982).

When a child has a plan, he or she intends to bring about a certain event by performing a certain action. If a child simply acts, say, shaking a bookcase, that action is not a plan. If an event simply happens, say, a toy falls off a shelf, that is not a plan. If the child simply has a desire, say, to get the toy, but has no idea how to get that event to happen, that is not a plan. We can only say that the child has a plan when he or she wants the toy, and then shakes the bookshelf so that the toy will fall off; that is, when the child has a desire and then performs an action that causes an event that satisfies that desire. Plans involve desires, actions, and events in the world.

The term *plan* resembles other terms that have been used to describe events rather than objects, such as *script* and *sensorimotor schema*. However, *plan* is considerably more specific than these terms. Only a rather small number of all the possible sensorimotor schemas and scripts are also plans. This makes it all the more interesting that so many of the child's early meanings involve plans.

There are two rather different ways in which plans play an important role in early language. Children are particularly likely to use words to refer to events when those events are the consequences of the child's plans. For example, children are most likely to use *gone* when they themselves make an object disappear. Similarly, children are most likely to use spatial terms like *down* or *in* when they themselves make objects move (Gopnik, 1982; Farwell, 1977).

Another group of early words, however, refer to aspects of plans themselves rather than referring to the fact that a particular type of event occurs. For example, when children use a word to encode success or failure, they are talking about the nature of plans themselves. They mark the fact that plans may or may not work, rather than marking an event that is the consequence of a plan. We will now describe these words that encode abstract aspects of plans in more detail.

Success

Children are likely to use words when they try to do something and succeed. Different children use different words. *There* is common in English. While *there* is initially used to point out objects, many children use *there* later to mark success. We have recorded success uses of *hooray*, *did it*, and *good girl*. McCune-Nicolich (1981) and Farwell (1977) also report success uses of *there*. These words are applied to a wide variety of plans, from knocking down towers to completing jigsaw puzzles to appropriately using a potty.

Failure

Similarly, children are likely to use a word when they try to do something and fail. Again, a variety of words including *no*, *uh-oh*, *oh dear*, and memorably but briefly, *oh bugger* have been recorded. McCune-Nicolich describes a group of "mismatch" words which seem to be similar to what we have called *failure* words.

Success and failure words have been less commonly noted in the literature than other types of relational words. Nevertheless, these words are extremely common in early language. In our longitudinal studies, all 20 children used a word for success or failure before they reached age 2. In a recent cross-sectional study, 21 of 30 18-month-olds used a word for success or failure. These meanings may have been neglected in the literature because children use a variety of words to encode them. In fact, children may use rather unlikely words to encode success and failure. One of the children in the Gopnik (1980) study consistently used *come off* when she failed, and Bowerman's daughter seems to have used *heavy* in a similar way (Bowerman, 1978), whether or not the difficulty was caused by something coming off or being too heavy.

The fact that English-speaking children use such a variety of words to encode success and failure is interesting in itself. It's as if the children have a burning desire to express these particular concepts and will pick up whatever expressions are available in the adult language in order to do so.

Recurrence

Many observers have noted that children use *more* and *again* in their early language. The earliest use of *more* often involves requests for objects. It has been less commonly noted, however, that children use *more* later in the one-word stage when they repeat or try to repeat an action on an object. In this period, children use *more* to comment on the repetition of a plan. Later still, children use *more* to comment on the recurrence of an action or an object, whether or not the actions or objects are involved in plans (Gopnik, 1982). This may explain some of the difficulties children have in dealing with *more* in comprehension experiments where it is assumed that *more* refers to quantity (Donaldson & Balfour, 1968; Clark, 1979). Young children don't use *more* in this way in their spontaneous speech.

Refusal and Change of Heart

Finally, children in the one-word stage are likely to use a word, particularly *no*, to encode the fact that they do not intend to carry out a plan. The earliest and most common context is a social one: The child refuses to carry out an action suggested by someone else. But later, children also use these words in nonsocial ways. For example, children say *no* when they are about to do something and then have a change of heart, and do something else instead.

It seems then that children are at least as interested in talking about plans as they are in talking about objects. However, just as they talk about rather abstract aspects of objects (i.e., the appearance and disappearance of objects, the fact that objects belong in prototype-based categories), rather than particular features, children talk about abstract aspects of their plans rather than encoding particular types of actions or goals.

Words About Locations

Children are also likely to talk about space and spatial relationships when they begin to speak. Children talk about the general concept of movement and about three specific types of spatial relationships: relationships that involve gravity, containment, and attachment.

General Movement

While English-speaking children initially use *there* to point out objects, later they use *there* to point out the *location* of objects. Children use *there* when they move an object or when they point to the spot in which they intended to place an object. Still later in their development, children use *there* to point out the location of stationary objects (Gopnik, 1980; Gopnik & Meltzoff, in press).

Gravity

While some of the very earliest uses of *up* and *down* involve requests to climb up or get down, children use *up* and *down* early on when they themselves make an object move up or down (Gopnik, 1982; Farwell, 1977). In the Gopnik (1980) study, 89 of 182 uses of *down* were applied to movements that involved the effects of gravity. For example, children said *down* when removing the bottom block of a tower of blocks, or blowing on an unstable construction. Similarly, 54 of 97 uses of *up* involved relationships of support or equilibrium. Children would say *up* as they balanced a block on top of another block, or when they carefully placed a doll on the canopy of a toy four-poster bed. Children also used *down* and *up* when they moved downward and upwards themselves or when they simply moved objects upwards or downwards.

Containment

Children use *in* and *out* when they move objects into or out of containers (Gopnik, 1982; Farwell, 1977). Sometimes, the containers are really open enclosures, a child may say *in*, while putting a toy car inside a fence-off part of a toy ranch. But sometimes the container is closed and the object is not visible once it has been placed inside. A child may say *in* while pushing toy letters into a toy mailbox.

Attachment

Children use *on* and *off* most frequently when they make an object become physically attached to or detached from another object (Gopnik, 1982). Children commonly use *on* and *off* when they put on or take off pieces of clothing, but these words were also applied to lego blocks, magnets, train cars, and other objects that could be put together or taken apart. In the Gopnik (1980) study, occasionally children used *on* and *off* when two objects simply became contiguous. However, children never used *on* in the canonical adult sense, that is, to refer to a smaller object simply being placed on top of another larger object. Again, this may explain some of the difficulties children have in comprehension experiments which assume that this is the meaning of *on* (Clark, 1979).

It is rather surprising that children only encode this relatively small set of spatial relationships in their early speech. It would seem that the sorts of relationships encoded by *under*, *over*, *next*, *apart*, *near*, or *far* would be conceptually simpler than those that involve gravity, containment, or attachment. Moreover, the concept of a static spatial relationship might be considered to be simpler than the concept of a transformation from one spatial relationship to another. Yet children do not encode static spatial relationships until much later.

Other Early Words and Meanings

Most of the child's early utterances fall into one of the semantic categories described above. In the Gopnik (1980) study, which followed children until they were 24 months old and hence using some advanced language, 75% of all the recorded utterances belonged to one of these categories. Moreover, many other early words were closely related to these categories. For example, children said *look*, *this*, *here*, *see*, and *there* in contexts that were similar to the notice context of *that*. *Empty*, *where*, and *lost it* like "gone," occurred in disappearance context. *Top*, *open*, and *close* occurred when children commented on relationships that involved gravity or containment. A number of other early words, such as *another*, *ready*, *finish*, *do*, and *make* referred to aspects of plans. If we include utterances of these words, 89% of all the utterances belonged to these categories.

This relatively small set of semantic categories—disappearance, notice, naming, plans, and locations—accounts for almost all early language. Children use early words to encode a limited range of concepts. However, there were three other interesting types of words which occurred less frequently: social words, action words, and formal words.

One common group of early words established social relationships. These words are designed to influence other people in a particular way. For example, children often used *hello* and *bye-bye* as salutations, or used *hereyare* and *thank-you* when they exchanged objects with others. These words often occurred at a very early stage in the child's language.

Children did use some words to encode simple actions, for example, *drink*, *read*, and *jump*, but these words only appeared after other types of words. Seven of the nine children used these words only after they used words to encode aspects of plans. The other two children (who had already started to speak) used both types of words in their first session. The late emergence of simple action words may have contributed to the common belief that children talk about objects before they talk about actions.

Children also used some expressions such as *it*, *now*, and *one*, which might be called *formal* or even *syntactic*. These words were combined with other words to make two-word strings, but they did not seem to have any independent meaning. The formal words appeared during the transition to the two-word stage, and appeared to be similar to Allison Bloom's (Bloom, 1973) *wida* and to some of the expressions described by Dore, Franklin, Miller and Ramer (1977).

Changes in the Meaning of Early Words

So far we have emphasized the semantic structures of the child's language in the midst of the one-word period. But we have also seen that within the one-word stage there are a number of consistent changes in the meanings of words, both before and after the slice we have focused on.

From People to Plans

Some early words, such as *byebye* or *hereyare*, have a strongly social character. We have also seen that other early words, in particular *no*, *there*, *more*, and *down* are initially used to influence the behavior of others but are rapidly extended to non-social contexts.

Many, though not all children, begin using *no* exclusively to refuse other people's suggestions before they use *no* to indicate failure or a change of heart. Similarly, *more* sometimes begins as a request for the recurrence of an event before it is used to comment on the fact that the child intends to repeat a plan. *There* is used as a way of drawing the attention of other people to an object before it is used to indicate success or location, and *down* is sometimes used initially when the child wants to get down from a high place, such as a high chair or daddy's arms, before it is used when the child moves an object downwards (Gopnik & Meltzoff, in press). These very early uses of these words appear to be related to the prelinguistic communicative behaviors, such as the combination of a headshake and a nasal vocalization to reject food, a nasal and a stylized reach to request objects, and a d-initial sound and a point to draw attention to objects (described by Bruner, 1983; Bates et al., 1979; Carter, 1975b; & Halliday, 1975). These early utterances seem exclusively designed to get other people to behave in a particular way. However, once they begin to speak, children rapidly extend these words to nonsocial contexts, in particular, they use them to comment on their own plans.

From Plans to Propositions

At a later stage, children begin to use some words that originally refer to plans to refer to relationships between objects. In particular, children begin to use *no* to negate propositions as well as to indicate failure or refusal (Gopnik, 1982; Pea, 1980; McNeill & McNeill, 1968). Similarly, children begin to use *more* to refer to the similiarity or quantity of objects as well as to the recurrence of plans.

The early locative words undergo similar, though slightly more complicated, changes. Originally, they are used when children try to change the spatial relationship of objects; later they are used to refer to all such changes, whether or not children cause them; and finally, they are used to refer to static spatial relationships (Gopnik, 1980, 1982; Farwell, 1977).

In short, there appears to be a three-stage developmental progression in the meaning of some early relational words, such as *there*, *no*, *more*, and *down*. These words are used socially first, then they are used to encode plans, and finally, they are used to talk about relationships between objects.

Some of the changes in the meaning of early names may be analogous to these changes in the meaning of relational words. As we have mentioned, many of the earliest names seem to occur in particular social contexts; they talk about important people or are used to request important things. After the naming explosion, names seem to be used in a more cognitive way. They are used to sort the objects in the world into appropriate categories. This change may be analogous to the shift from social uses of relational words to uses of these words to encode relationships between objects. In this case, the intermediate stage, using words to talk about plans, does not occur.

Summary

There is some consistency, then, in the kinds of meanings children encode in the one-word stage. At the very beginning, children do not seem to use words to refer to the external world at all. Instead, they use words exclusively to influence other people's behavior in particular ways. Slightly later, children encode the fact that they do or do not perceive an object and they encode the fact that objects belong to categories. They also encode abstract aspects of plans, such as the success, failure, recurrence, or refusal of plans. They encode the fact that they have moved an object, in general, and they encode the specific fact that they have moved an object up or down, into or out of a container, or that they have caused an object to be attached to or detached from another object. At an even later stage, children begin to encode simple actions and static relationships between objects.

Conceptual Development and Early Meaning

A number of authors have noted the similarity between the kinds of meanings children encode in their early language and the kinds of concepts they develop in the first 2 years of life (Bloom, 1973; Brown, 1973; McCune-Nicolich, 1981; Gopnik, 1982, 1984; Gopnik & Meltzoff, 1984). It is certainly striking that the main areas of cognitive development in this period (understanding objects, the relationships between means and ends, and spatial relationships) seem to correspond to the most important semantic categories in early language.

It is not sufficient, however, simply to say that early words encode concepts that are developed in the first 2 years. During this period, children's concepts are rapidly changing. The 9-month-old's concept of the object is quite different from the 18-month-old's concept. Some authors (Bloom, 1973; Moore & Meltzoff, 1978) have suggested that some early words encode *Stage 4* concepts, concepts that are developed between around 9 months and 12 months of age. Others (McCune-Nicolich, 1981) have suggested that these words encode *Stage 5* concepts, developed between 12 months and 18 months. Still others (Clark, 1974) suggest that early words encode features which are innately determined. The question is, which of the concepts that emerge in the first 2 years are encoded by early words?

We have argued that at least two types of early words, *disappearance words* and *plan words*, actually encode rather sophisticated concepts, concepts that are only developed at around 18 months. In Piaget's terms, these words seem to encode *Stage 6* or *early preoperational* concepts rather than encoding sensorimotor schemas (Gopnik, 1982, 1984).

Disappearance Words and the Object Concept

When they are about 18 months old, children's ability to find hidden objects undergoes a striking change. Before this point, children can only find objects by using particular rules like, "Look for the object where you last found it," or "Look for the object where it disappeared." After this point, children seem to be able to generalize across all these rules and develop a general model of objects moving in space. This model allows them to deduce the location of objects that are hidden in complicated ways.

For example, 18-month-olds can find objects after they are hidden in someone's hand, the hand is placed under several cloths in succession, and the object is left under one of the cloths (the serial invisible displacement task). This task could not be solved if the child simply had a set of specific rules, such as, "Look for the object where it disappeared." The child must figure out that the object still exists at some location and deduce that location. After 18 months of age, children seem to believe that an object continues to exist and will reappear whenever it disappears. They also believe that all disappearances involve the same underlying process (Piaget, 1954; Bower, 1982).

Children apply the word *gone* to a wide variety of simple disappearances, but they also apply *gone* to more complicated events. In our studies, children consistently applied *gone* to serial invisible displacements (Gopnik, 1984). Moreover, as we have described above, children use *gone* when they search for *hypothetical* objects, such as the nonexistent cup that should fit in the smallest cup.

The fact that children say *gone* in all these contexts suggests that they recognize the underlying similarity between all the disappearances that are covered by their specific rules, and the similarity between all these disappearances and the disappearances that are not covered by their specific rules. *Gone* encodes the fact that the child does not see an object he or she has in mind. This general conflict between the child's conception of an object and the child's perception of an object is closely tied to the *Stage 6* or *early preoperational* object concept. The essence of this concept is that the child can conceive of an object at a location without perceiving the object at the location (see Gopnik, 1984).

Plan Words and Means-Ends Skills

There are also important changes in the child's understanding of plans at about 18 months. In particular, the child develops the ability to use insight to solve complex problems. Children figure out the right way to reach a particular end immediately, without a period of trial and error. For example, a child may immediately use a rake to pull an object, even if the child has never used a rake in this way before (Piaget, 1954; Bruner, 1973). Both Piaget and Bruner suggest that in order to use insight, the child must be able to consider, compare, and reflect on possible plans mentally, rather than simply executing those plans.

Similar abilities are necessary in order to use words to encode success, failure, recurrence, or a change of heart. Rather than encoding particular types of plans or goals, these words encode general features of all plans. In order to recognize that a number of very different plans have all succeeded, it is necessary to compare and reflect on those plans (see Gopnik, 1982).

Disappearance and plan words, then, seem to encode concepts that are just being developed in the 15- to 21-month-old period, when children first begin to use these words. What about other early semantic categories? Do these also encode difficult or problematic concepts?

Names and Classification Skills

In principle, names could encode two rather different kinds of concepts. Children could simply use names as labels for particular properties of the world. For example, a child could simply say *ball* everytime he or she noticed *roundness* in the environment. Alternatively, a child could use names to place objects in categories. When a child said *ball*, the child would be saying that this object belongs in the same category as other objects. In this second case, we might say that *ball* names a natural *kind* rather than naming a *property*.

If feature theories of naming are correct, we cannot tell which of these concepts names encode. If a child simply says *ball* at every round object, the child could be labelling the property *round* or saying that this object belongs in the category of round things.

However, prototype accounts are not ambiguous in this way. If a child applies a word to different objects that have different properties in common, the child can't simply be labelling the properties. If the child is using the word consistently at all, the child must be using it to place objects together in a category. When children use names in this way, they seem to think that objects must have some underlying similarity to other objects, the objects must belong to natural kinds, but the children don't know exactly which properties of the objects are going to be crucial in determining whether the objects belong to the category. For example, the children are trying to find out which properties are relevant to the category *ball*, rather than using *ball* to label a particular set of properties.

The philosophers Putnam (1975) and Kripke (1972) have argued that this sort of assumption underlies our adult use of names. When we use a name like *lemon* or *cat*, we know that we are referring to a category, and we can even point to some members of the category, but we do not know exactly which properties define members of the category. Putnam further argues that this is why adult categories are prototype-based. We suggest that children's names are similar to adult names in this respect.

There is some other evidence which supports this view of early naming. At least after the naming explosion, children don't just name objects with a particular set of properties. Instead, they name every object they see, and they rather compulsively request names for every object they see. This behavior also suggests that children are using names as a way of finding out how objects are sorted into categories, rather than using them to label properties.

We know that very young infants can recognize the common properties of objects. In fact, infants may even be able to recognize the complex combinations of features that a group of female faces or stuffed animals have in common (Fagan, 1976; Cohen & Strauss, 1979). Moreover, studies of infants' spontaneous sorting behavior suggest that infants as young as 9-months-old will pick out a group of objects with common properties from a larger group (Starkey, 1981). Clearly, young infants can produce a particular response when they see some property.

However, this doesn't mean that the infants are placing objects in categories. In the Starkey (1981) study, the infants always picked out the same objects from the group. This means that infants could simply have been reacting to the attractive properties of the object. However, between 12 months and 18 months, infants start to sort *all* the objects in a group into categories; all the dolls may go in one pile and all the cars in another (Ricutti, 1965; Nelson, 1973b; Sugarman, 1983). This kind of behavior looks more like genuine categorization. These children also seem to operate on the assumption that all objects should belong in categories, which may involve different properties, rather than simply responding to some set of properties. Thus, these more sophisticated classificatory behaviors seem to have the same conceptual underpinnings as the prototype-based names of the naming explosion (see Sugarman, 1983 for further discussion of this point).

We are not suggesting that children need to know the name of a category before they can sort objects into that category. That is clearly not true (see Nelson, 1973b). Instead, we arguing that the general idea that all objects can and should be sorted into categories seems to underlie both the changes in classificatory behavior at 18 months and the naming explosion. We suggest that the relationship between classificatory behavior and the naming explosion is analogous to the relationship between the acquisition of disappearance words and object-concept behavior, or between the development of plan words and the development of means-end skills. Like these words, names encode concepts the child is in the midst of developing.

Locative Words and Spatial Concepts

How about locative words? There is evidence which suggests that at least two of the spatial relationships encoded by early locative words, namely movement involving gravity and movements into and out of containers, are problematic for 15- to 21-month-old children.

Piaget (1954) reports several examples of children exploring the way objects fall or are balanced on top of each other. At 1;1, a child named Jacqueline initially pushes objects to the ground rather than simply letting them fall. Lucienne, at 1;3 and 1;4, studies the trajectory of falling objects and experiments with making objects fall. She also places objects on top of one another, investigating how one object can support another.

Uzgiris and Hunt (1975) have formalized these observations and include them in their scales of infant development. Common observation also suggests that infants of this age are intrigued by these relationships. For example, one of the most popular games for the infants in our home recordings was *build and bash*, a game in which the infant laboriously constructs a tower or blocks, and then immediately smashes it to the floor.

There are two interesting points about these observations. First, children are interested in these relationships and experiment with them. Second, children fail to understand these relationships completely until the end of this period. For example, Jacqueline only begins to drop objects, as opposed to throwing them to the ground, at 17 months of age. Similarly, Lucienne, at 17 months of age, fails to understand how objects are balanced on each other.

Piaget (1959) makes similar observations concerning containment relationships. From 1;2 to 1;4, Lucienne is preoccupied with filling and emptying containers, and placing containers, such as nested boxes, inside one another.

Piaget goes on to describe Jacqueline's behavior when at 1;3 (28) she sees the same nested boxes. She tries placing various boxes inside other boxes for several minutes. "Then comes a curious experiment; she takes one of the largest cubes which she tries to put into a smaller one; she gropes a moment and then gives up quite soon. Same reaction a second time" (Piaget, 1959, p. 194). Similar observations are described by Uzgiris and Hunt (1975) and Bower (1974). Again, infants in this period seem to be intrigued by these relationships but they fail to completely understand them, as when Jacqueline tries to put a larger cube inside a smaller one.

Piaget places the behaviors we have just described in *Stage 5* of the sensorimotor period. However, at least some of the later behaviors, in which the child actually does show some signs of understanding these relationships as opposed to simply exploring them, are, in fact, more closely contemporaneous with *Stage 6* behaviors in other domains. Lucienne, for example, is still throwing leaves to the ground and having trouble balancing objects at a time when she had solved the most difficult serial invisible displacement tasks, a hallmark of *Stage 6*. More significantly, from our point of view, the age at which children begin to solve these problems also seems to be about the age at which they acquire locative words such as *down*, *up*, *in*, and *out*.

We are suggesting, then, that names and expressions like *down*, *up*, *in*, and *out*, as well as disappearance and plan words, encode concepts that are developed in the 15- to 21-month period (i.e., at about the same time that children begin to use these words). If this suggestion is correct, most early words, not just a few relational words, encode concepts that are problematic for the child.

Relationships Between Semantic Development and Cognitive Development

The suggestions we have made in the previous section are based on rough correspondences between the age at which children typically begin to use certain words, and the age at which they typically solve certain types of problems. Given the variation in both these areas, these rough correspondences must remain merely suggestive. In order to demonstrate that children encode concepts they are in the course of developing, we would have to prove that there are strong and specific links between the development of specific types of words and the development of related cognitive abilities, links that are not simply due to age, intelligence, or some other general factor.

A number of recent studies point to two such relationships: a relationship between the acquisition of disappearance words and the solution of serial invisible displacement object-concept tasks; and a relationship between the acquisition of words that encode success and failure and the solution of means-ends tasks which require insight.

Corrigan (1978), McCune-Nicholich (1981), Gopnik (1984), Tomasello and Farrar (1984), and Gopnik and Meltzoff (1984b) all report a close relationship between the acquisition of words that encode disappearance, particularly *gone*, and the solution of *Stage 6* object-concept tasks. These results suggest that children acquire *gone* at about the same time that they solve serial invisible displacement tasks. Moreover, Gopnik (1984) and Tomasello and Farrar (1984) report that other early relational words such as *uh-oh* and *there* are not related to object-concept development in this way. Our studies also suggest that the acquisition of disappearance words is not related to other areas of cognitive development, particularly the development of means-ends abilities (Gopnik, 1984; Gopnik & Meltzoff, 1984b).

We have recently found a similar relationship between the acquisition of words that encode success and failure and the development of the ability to use insight to solve means-ends tasks (Gopnik & Meltzoff, 1984b). These linguistic and cognitive developments also seem to take place at about the same time. In our most recent study, we compared the cognitive and linguistic development of six children who were tested at two-week intervals. Children in this study always used a success/failure word within a month of their first use of insight to solve complex means-ends tasks, though either development could occur first. Significantly, however, the acquisition of these words was not this closely related to the solution of serial invisible displacement tasks. There were gaps of up to three months between these two developments (Gopnik & Meltzoff, 1984a). This suggests that there are two specific, independent relationships, one between disappearance words and object-concept tasks, and the other between success/failure words and means-ends tasks.

In another study, using a cross-sectional design, we again found evidence for the independence of these two specific relationships and for the independence of both these relationships from age. We asked mothers of 30 18-month-old infants to record whether their child used disappearance or success/failure words, and then tested the children on object-concept and means-ends tasks. There was a relationship between the use of disappearance words and the solution of *Stage 6* object-concept tasks, and a trend toward a relationship between the use of success/failure words and the solution of insight means-ends tasks. Strikingly, however, there was no such relationship between disappearance words and means-ends abilities or between success/failure words and object-concept abilities (Gopnik & Meltzoff, 1984a).

In all these studies, the acquisition of certain meanings, rather than certain words, was related to cognitive developments. For example, the early social uses of *no* and *there* to refuse suggestions or point out objects, were not related to the development of success and failure, while uses of *no* and *there* to encode success and failure were so related (Gopnik & Meltzoff, in press). Similarly, Tomasello and Farrar (1984) found that only words that encoded disappearance, such as *gone* and *away*, were related to object-concept development.

These findings take on even more importance since there is apparently little correlation between general linguistic and cognitive development in this period.

General measures of language development, such as Mean Length of Utterance (M.L.U.) or productive or receptive vocabulary size, seem to bear little relationship to performance on cognitive tasks (Bates et al., 1979; Miller, Chapman, Branston, & Reichele, 1980; McCune-Nicolich, 1981; Smolak, 1982; Corrigan, 1978, 1979). At the least, such relationships have proved difficult to demonstrate. In particular, several studies report that children are capable of using words productively well before they show signs of *Stage 6* behavior in other domains (Bates et al., 1979; Dihoff & Chapman, 1977; Tomasello & Farrar, in press; Gopnik & Meltzoff, in press), although there is often a notable increase in language during *Stage 6* (Corrigan, 1979).

Theories of Semantic Development in the One-Word Stage

The findings we have described so far do not fit any of the predominant theories of semantic devlopment in the one-word stage. Some recent theories have emphasized the social role of early language and its relationship to prelinguistic communication (Bruner, 1975, 1983; Lock, 1980; MacShane, 1980; Bates et al., 1979). While the earliest words may fit these models, by the middle of the one-word period, most of the child's language appears to be more closely related to cognitive concerns than to communicative needs.

These findings also do not fit the classical linguistic views of semantic development, such as those formulated by Clark (1974, 1979). The assumption behind these accounts is that the child's cognitive structures are similar to the adult's structures. The child's job is to map the adult linguistic system onto this common underlying cognitive system. According to these accounts, the child's meanings should be incomplete versions of adult meanings. Semantic development, on this view, involves the acquisition of more and more pieces of the adult semantic system.

The findings were have described here suggest that the child's meanings are not just incomplete versions of the adult's meanings. Rather, the child's cognitive structures are qualitatively different from the adult structures, and the child's language reflects these differences. Moreover, changes in children's meanings seem to be more closely related to changes in their concepts than to the acquisition of parts of the adult semantic system.

It might seem that these findings could be explained most easily by a Piagetian account, given Piaget's emphasis on the primacy of cognitive development and on the differences between the child's cognitive structures and the adult's. However, the picture that emerges from these findings is rather different from the classical Piagetian picture.

Piaget suggests that the first words encode sensorimotor schemes. "At this level the word does little more than translate the organization of sensorimotor schemes to which it is not indispensible" (Piaget, 1962, p. 222). This is in keeping with Piaget's general view that children must develop concepts behaviorally before they encode them in language (Piaget, 1952). Similarly, others (McCune-Nicolich, 1981; Sinclair, 1970; Bates et al., 1979) suggest that early words encode typical *Stage 5* concepts. More generally, this view was assumed by many of the classical cognitive accounts of early language (Nelson, 1973; Bloom, 1973; Slobin, 1973; McNamara, 1972). These accounts assume that the child can only encode concepts that have been developed previously. If this were true in the one-word stage, we would expect children's first words to encode concepts they had developed in infancy.

We have suggested, however, that rather than encoding simple and well-established concepts, early words encode concepts that the child is in the midst of developing at 18 months of age. In particular, many of these concepts involve rather abstract reflections on actions and experiences rather than being simple accompaniments to action. These early words do not simply encode sensorimotor schemas. Moreover, if Piaget's account were correct, we would expect that conceptual developments would be prerequisites for semantic developments. The empirical evidence suggests that conceptual and semantic development may occur concurrently.

There are other flaws in the Piagetian account of early language. Piaget stressed the formal similarities between linguistic and cognitive abilities. In particular, he suggested that the ability to use words productively was related to the ability to solve *Stage 6* object-concept and means-end problems, and to the development of symbolic play and deferred imitation. According to Piaget, all these developments reflect the same underlying cognitive change, the change from sensorimotor to preoperational or conceptual representation. Therefore, these developments should occur at about the same time.

It is sometimes claimed that Piaget was muddled or unclear about this, or that Piaget didn't make any claims about language. In fact, Piaget is as clear about this point as he is about anything. "The first verbal schemas" and "the first verbal signs" are "contemporaneous with Stage VI of sensorimotor intelligence" (Piaget, 1962, p. 219) and

> ... thus these first verbal schemas are merely sensori-motor schemas in process of becoming concepts: they are neither purely sensori-motor schemas nor clear concepts. They are still essentially sensori-motor, in that they are modes of action capable of generalization to an increasing number of objects, but they partake of the concept that there is already a partial dissociation from the child's own activity. Moreover, since they are expressed by verbal phonemes through which they are related to the actions of others, they involve the element of communication characteristic of the concept (Piaget, 1962, p. 220).

For Piaget, any *productive* use of a word is itself a sign that the child has passed beyond the sensorimotor stage, although the words themselves encode earlier sensorimotor schemas. The ability to refer at all is a *Stage 6* ability, but the first words refer to *Stage 5* concepts.

There is little empirical support for this formal claim. As we have mentioned previously, there is little correlation between general linguistic skill and cognitive development in this period. More seriously, children may use words productively well before they show signs of *Stage 6* abilities in other areas of development. In fact, as Ingram (1978) has pointed out, in Piaget's own observations, the first verbal schemas occur as much as six months before other signs of *Stage 6* intelligence.

Moreover, the findings we have discussed here undermine the notion that there is a single underlying relationship between linguistic development and cognitive development. The data suggest that there may be several independent, dissociable relationships between different areas of semantic and cognitive development. Disappearance words seem to be related to object-concept skills, but not to means-ends skills. Success and failure words, on the other hand, are related to means-ends skills but not to object-concept skills. We have suggested here that there may be similarly specific relationships between the naming explosion and the development of classificatory abilities, between *down* and *up* and the understanding of gravity, and between *in* and *out* and the understanding of containment. Several recent accounts have suggested similarly that there might be some independence between various types of *Stage 6* abilities and that linguistic developments might be related to some cognitive developments and not others (Bates & Snyder, in press; Fisher & Corrigan, 1981; Bloom, Lifter, & Broughton, 1981).

There are three areas, then, in which the recent findings contradict the Piagetian account. First, children appear to use early words to encode concepts they are in the midst of developing rather than concepts they have already developed. Second, children can use some words productively before they develop *Stage 6* abilities in other domains. Finally, there appear to be several independent dissociable relationships between various types of semantic developments and related cognitive developments, rather than a more general relationship between *Stage 6* cognition and language.

An Alternative Hypothesis

How, then, can these findings be explained? One intriguing possibility is that children begin to use language to help them to solve cognitive problems during the one-word stage.

By the time children are around 15 months old, they have developed a complex communicative system, a system that includes gestures and vocalizations (Bruner, 1983; Bates et al., 1979; Trevarthen & Hubley, 1978). As we have seen, many very early words seem to be an extension of this system. However, during the one-word stage, children begin to use words to encode cognitively significant concepts as well as to influence the behavior of other people. Halliday (1975) has described a shift from *pragmatic* to *mathetic* functions of language at about this point. Halliday suggests that the child begins to use languge to sort out his or her own experience of the world as well as to communicate that experience to other people. It is as if children suddenly realize that they can talk to themselves as well as to others.

We suggest that children apply this new-found ability to the cognitive problems that are particularly intriguing to them, that is, the cognitive problems they are on the verge of solving. An infant who is on the verge of solving the object-concept problem will be likely to pay attention to the appearances and disappearances of objects, and to acquire words like *gone* that occur in these contexts. An infant who is on the verge of sorting objects into categories will be likely to acquire object names. An infant who is concentrating on means-ends problems will be more likely to acquire words that encode success and failure. However, the cognitive concerns of all 18-month-olds are similar enough so that they will be likely to acquire the same sorts of meanings by the end of the one-word period.

This hypothesis can help to explain many puzzling features of early language. According to this account, the ability to use words productively is present well before the infant is 18 months old. In fact some ability to use arbitrary symbols is probably necessary to develop the most sophisticated prelinguistic communicative systems. It is not surprising, then, that there is little relationship between this aspect of language (that is, the ability to use words or gestures symbolically) and cognitive development in the one-word period. The great increase in the scope and complexity of language in the one-word stage is due to the new use to which this old ability is put. At around 18 months of age, the infant discovers a whole new world to talk about.

This account could also explain the following aspects of early language:

1. Children use relational words when they begin to speak because these words encode precisely the concepts children are trying to understand.
2. The naming explosion occurs because children move from using names to get what they want to using names to categorize all the objects they see.
3. Children acquire semantic categories at about the same time that they solve relevant cognitive problems because they choose to talk about problematic concepts.
4. There are several different independent relationships between different areas of semantic and cognitive development because of the different cognitive interests of particular children at particular stages of their development.
5. Finally, this account could explain some of the changes in the meanings of words during the one-word stage. As children develop, they face new problems and begin to apply the old words to these problems.

We are suggesting then that when children are around 18 months old, they begin to talk about their cognitive problems, and this explains many features of early language. But why do children do this? One explanation may simply be that these are the most significant, engaging, and fascinating phenomena in the 18-month-old's life. A more speculative explanation is that using linguistic symbols actually helps the child to solve cognitive problems. For example, the fact that adults apply *gone* to all sorts of disappearances, including complex serial invisible displacements, may help the child to figure out that all these events involve the same underlying phenomena. Similarly, the fact that adults apply words like *there* and *uh-oh* to a variety of plans may lead the child to compare those plans. The fact that *down* occurs when objects are moved downward, and in all the various circumstances in which gravity has an effect, may lead the infant to see the similarities in these events. The fact that *in* is applied to a wide variety of events involving containers, may help the child to see that all these events involve the same underlying spatial relationship. Finally, the fact that most objects have names, not just significant or salient objects, may lead the child to the idea that all objects belong in categories. There are two ways in which this might take place. First, the structure of adult speech may provide clues about how the infant should organize the world. Alternatively (or perhaps we should say, in addition), the fact that the infant has an explicit verbal symbol to use in all these circumstances may itself help the child to sort out his or her own concepts. We might draw an analogy here to mathematical notation systems. Mastering such a system allows a novice mathematician to take advantage of the elders' mathematical discoveries, it lets the mathematician understand what they're talking about. But more significantly, mastering such a system also allows the mathematician to put his or her own inchoate mathematical ideas in order and to make new mathematical discoveries.

Sometime ago, Schlesinger (1977) suggested a related view of how early language might facilitate cognitive development and, more recently, Bowerman (1980) and Kuczaj (in press) have suggested that semantic development might influence cognitive development at a later stage. We are suggesting that linguistic development influences cognitive development from the very beginning of language.

This view is similar in some respects to the classical Vygotskyan view of language (Vygotsky, 1962). Vygotsky suggested that children had to develop linguistic structures through social interaction before they could apply those structures to their cognitive problems. We are suggesting a more complex two-way interaction between linguistic and cognitive development. Children's cognitive concerns, rather than their communicative needs, may actually determine which aspects of language they will acquire. The acquisition of those aspects of language, however, may allow the child to make further cognitive advances. Infants use their knowledge of the world to help them understand language but they also use their knowledge of language to help them understand the world.

References

Barrett, M. (1982). Distinguishing between prototypes: The early acquisition of the meaning of object names. In S. Kuczaj (Ed.), *Language development, Vol. I, Syntax & sementics*. Hillsdale, NJ: Erlbaum.

Bates, E., Benigni, L., Bretherton, I., Camaioni, L., & Volterra, V. (1979). *The emergence of symbols*. New York: Academic Press.

Bates, E., & Snyder, L. (in press). The cognitive hypothesis in language development. In I. Uzgiris & J. Hunt (Eds.), *Research with scales of psychological development in infancy*. Champaign, Urbana: University of Illinois Press.

Bierwisch, M. (1970). Semantics. In J. Lyons (Ed.), *New horizons in linguistics* (pp. 161-185). Baltimore: Penguin Books.

Bloom, L. (1973). *One word at a time*. The Hague: Mouton.

Bloom, L., Lifter, K., & Broughton, J. (1981). What children say and what they know. In R. Stark (Ed.), *Language behavior in infancy and early childhood*. North Holland: Elsevier.

Bower, T. (1982). *Development in infancy, 2nd edition*. San Francisco: W. H. Freeman.

Bowerman, M. (1978). The acquisition of word meanings. In N. Waterson & C. Snow (Eds.), *The development of communication*. London: Wiley.

Bowerman, M. (1980). The structure and origin of semantic categories in the language-learning child. In M. Foster & S. Brandes (Eds.), *Symbol as sense*. New York: Academic Press.

Brown, R. (1973). *A first language: The early stages*. Cambridge, MA: Harvard University Press.
Bruner, J. (1973). The organization of early skilled action. *Child Development, 44*, 1-11.
Bruner, J. (1975). From communication to language-psychological perspective. *Cognition, 3*, 255-287.
Bruner, J. (1983). *Child's talk*. New York: Norton.
Carter, A. (1975a). The transformation of sensori-motor morphemes into words: A case study of the development of "more" and "mine." *Journal of Child Language, 2*, 233-250.
Carter, A. (1975b). The transformation of sensori-motor morphemes into words: A case study of the development of "here" and "there". *Papers and Reports on Child Language Development, II*, 31-48.
Carter, A. (1978). From sensori-motor vocalizations to words. In A. Lock (Ed.), *Action, gesture & symbol*. London: Academic Press.
Carter, A. (1979). The disappearance schema. In E. Keenan (Ed.), *Studies in developmental pragmatics*. New York: Academic Press.
Clark, E. (1974). Some aspects of the conceptual basis for first language acquisition. In R. L. Schiefelbusch & L. L. Lloyd (Eds.), *Language perspectives: Acquisition, retardation and intervention*. Baltimore, MD: University Park Press.
Clark, E. (1979). *The ontogenesis of meaning*. Weisbaden: Athenaion.
Cohen, L., & Strauss, M. (1979). Concept acquisition in the human infant. *Child Development, 50*, 419-424.
Corrigan, R. (1978). Language development as related to stage 6 object permanence development. *Journal of Child Language, 5*, 173-189.
Corrigan, R. (1979). Cognitive correlates of language. *Child Development* (50), 617-631.
Dihoff, A., & Chapman, R. (1977). First words: Their origins in action. *Papers and Reports on Child Language Development, 13*, 1-7.
Donaldson, M. S., & Balfour, G. (1968). Less is more: A study of language comprehension in children. *British Journal of Psychology, 39*, 461-472.
Dore, J., Franklin, M., Miller, R., & Ramer, A. (1976). Transitional phenomena in early language acquisition. *Journal of Child Language, 3*, 13-28.
Fagan, J. F. (1976). Infants recognition of invariant features of faces. *Child Development, 47*, 627-638.
Farwell, C. (1977). The primacy of goal in the description of motion and location. *Papers and Reports on Child Language Development*.
Fischer, K., & Corrigan, R. (1981). A skill approach to language development. In R. Stark (Ed.), *Language behavior in infancy and early childhood*. North Holland: Elsevier.
Gentner, D. (1982). Why nouns are learned before verbs. In S. Kuczaj (Ed.), *Language development: Vol. 2. Language, thought, and culture*. Hillsdale, NJ: Erlbaum.
Gopnik, A. (1980). *The development of non-nominal expressions in 12-24 month old children*. Unpublished doctoral dissertation, University of Oxford, Oxford, England.
Gopnik, A. (1981). The development of non-nominal expressions in 12-24 month olds. In P. Dale & D. Ingram (Eds.), *Child language: An international perspective*. Baltimore, MD: University Park Press.
Gopnik, A. (1982). Words and plans. *Journal of Child Language, 9*, 617-633.
Gopnik, A. (1984). The acquisition of *gone* and the development of the object concept. *Journal of Child Language, 11*, 273-292.
Gopnik, A., & Meltzoff, A. N. (April, 1983). *Semantic and conceptual development in 15-21 month-olds*. Paper presented at the Society for Research in Child Development, Detroit.

Gopnik, A., & Meltzoff, A. N. (July, 1984a). *Some specific relationships between semantic and cognitive development in the one-word stage.* Paper presented at the Third International Congress for the Study of Child Language. Austin, Texas.

Gopnik, A., & Meltzoff, A. N. (1984b). Semantic and cognitive development in 15-21 month-olds. *Journal of Child Language, 11,* 495-515.

Gopnik, A., & Meltzoff, A. N. (in press). From people to plans to objects. *Journal of Pragmatics.*

Halliday, M. (1975). *Learning how to mean: Explorations in the development of language.* London: Edwin Arnold.

Ingram, D. (1978). Sensorimotor intelligence and language development. In A. Lock (Ed.), *Action, gesture and symbol.* New York: Academic Press.

Katz, N., & Fodor, J. (1963). The structure of a semantic theory. *Language, 39,* 170-210.

Kay, D., & Anglin, J. (1981). Overextension and underextension in the child's expressive and receptive speech. *Journal of Child Language, 9,* 83-98.

Kripke, S. (1972). Naming and necessity. In G. Harman & D. Davidson (Eds.), *The semantics of natural language.* pp. 254-355. Boston: Reidel.

Kuczaj, S. (1982a). Acquisition of word meaning in the context of the development of the semantic system. In C. Brainerd & M. Pressley (Eds.), *Verbal processes in children.* New York: Springer-Verlag.

Kuczaj, S. (1982b). Young children's overextension of object words in comprehension and/or production: Support for a prototype theory of early word meaning. *First Language, 3,* 93-105.

Lock, A. (1980). *The guided reinvention of language.* London: Academic Press.

MacNamara, J. (1972). Cognitive basis of language learning in infants. *Psychological Review, 79,* 1-13.

MacShane, J. (1980). *Learning how to mean.* Cambridge: Cambridge University Press.

McCune-Nicolich, L. (1981). The cognitive bases of relational words in the single-word period. *Journal of Child Language, 8,* 15-34.

McNeill, D., & McNeill, N. (1968). What does a child mean when he says "no"? In E. M. Zale (Ed.), *Language and language behavior.* New York: Appleton Century Crofts.

Miller, J., Chapman, R., Branston, M., & Reichele, J. (1980). Language comprehension in sensorimotor stages V and VI. *Journal of Speech and Hearing Research, 23,* 284-311.

Moore, M. K., & Meltzoff, A. W. (1978). Object permanence imitation and language development in infancy. In F. Minifie & L. Lloyd (Eds.), *Communicative and cognitive abilities: Early behavioral assessment.* Baltimore, MD: University Park Press.

Nelson, K. (1973a). *Structure and strategy in learning to talk.* Monographs of the Society for Research in Child Development, 38.

Nelson, K. (1973b). Some evidence for the cognitive primacy of categorization and its functional basis. *Merrill-Palmer Quarterly, 19,* 21-39.

Nelson, K. (1974). Concept, word and sentence. Interrelations in acquisition and development. *Psychological Review, 81,* 267-285.

Nelson, K., (1975). The nominal shift in semantic-syntactic development. *Cognitive Psychology, 7,* 461-479.

Pea, R. (1980). The development of negation in early child language. In D. Olson (Ed.), *The social foundations of language and thought.* New York: Norton.

Piaget, J. (1952). *The origins of intelligence in children.* New York: Norton.

Piaget, J. (1954). *The construction of reality in the child.* New York: Basic Books.

Piaget, J. (1959). *The language and thought of the child.* London: Routledge and Kegan Paul.

Piaget, J. (1962). *Play dreams and imitation in childhood.* New York: Norton.

Putnam, H. (1975). *Mind, language and reality*. Cambridge: Cambridge University Press.

Riccuti, H. N. (1965). Object grouping and selective ordering behaviors in infants 12-24 months. *Merrill-Palmer Quarterly, 11*, 129-148.

Rosch, E., & Mervis, C. B. (1975). Family resemblances: Studies in the internal structure of categories: *Cognitive Psychology, 7*, 573-605.

Schlesinger, I. M. (1977). The role of cognitive development and linguistic input in language acquisition. *Journal of Child Language, 4*, 153-169.

Sinclair, H. (1970). The transition from sensorimotor to symbolic activity. *Interchange, 1*, 119-126.

Slobin, D. (1973). Cognitive prerequisites for the development of grammar. In C. Ferguson & D. Slobin (Eds.), *Studies of child language development*. New York: Holt, Rinehart & Winston.

Smolak, L. (1982). Cognitive precursors of receptive vs. expressive language. *Journal of Child Language, 9*, 13-22.

Starkey, D. (1981). The origins of concept formation. *Child Development, 52*, 489-497.

Sugarman, S. (1983). *Children's early thought: Development in classification*. Cambridge: Cambridge University Press.

Tomosello, M., & Farrar, M. (1984). Cognitive bases of lexical development. *Journal of Child Language,* , 477-495.

Trevarthen, C., & Hubley, P. (1978). Secondary intersubjectivity. Confidence, confiding and acts of meaning in the first year. In A. Lock (Ed.), *Action, gesture and symbol: The emergence of language*. London: Academic Press.

Uzgiris, I., & Hunt, J. (1975). Assessment in infancy. Urbana, IL: University of Illinois Press.

Vygotsky, L. (1962). *Thought and language*. Cambridge: MIT Press.

9. Actions and Things: What Adults Talk About to 1-Year-Olds

Allayne Bridges

Most texts on early child language state with some confidence that, as children approach their first birthdays, they utter their first words. They also typically describe how, in the next few months, the number of words in the children's productive vocabularies increases, slowly at first and then rapidly, such that by the time children are 18 months old, they command approximately 50 words. By the time their first two-word utterances appear, typically around their second birthday, children's productive repertoires have grown to about 200 words while their receptive vocabularies probably exceed 500 words.

Charting vocabulary growth is one of the oldest exercises in the history of child language research. Many of the early diarists (see Pollock, 1983) recorded the earliest efforts of their children to communicate verbally. More recently, there has been a renewed interest in this topic, which has given rise to more systematic attempts on larger samples to follow the progress of early language comprehension and/or production (e.g., Benedict, 1979; Goldin-Meadow, Seligman, & Gelman, 1976; Nelson, 1973; Rosenblatt, 1977; Snyder, Bates, & Bretherton, 1981). The results from these studies are striking in their similarity. As a group, it appears that 18-month-old children choose to talk about much the same sort of thing. Their vocabulary is restricted in quite predictable ways. The most common category among the first 50 words of children's vocabulary is nominals, defined by Nelson (1973) as "words used to refer to the 'thing' world (which) may be used in labelling or demanding, in extensive reference or relations involving agent or object" (p. 16). Thus, children typically talk about familiar people and pets (e.g., *daddy, nanny, Lassie*), objects upon which the children can act (e.g., *cookie, shoes, ball*), or objects which move or make a characteristic sound (e.g., *car, clock, duck*). General nominals account for nearly 50% of the first 50 words whereas specific nominals (i.e., the names of particular people and animals) account for about 15% of children's first 50 words. The next most common category (which accounts for about 33% of the first 50 words) is that of action words, defined by Nelson as "words that describe, demand or accompany action or that express attention or demand for attention" (p. 17), and which include words such as *down*, *out*, *throw*, *look*, *sit*, *bye-bye*, *brrm-brrm*, and *miaow*. Other non-nominals commonly found within the first 50 words are words such as *all gone*, *there*, *hot*, *dirty*, *pretty*, *no*, and *mine*.

Clearly, by 18 months, general nominals make up a large and important part of many children's lexicons. Perhaps as a result, the growth of children's early vocabulary has often been treated in the literature as though it were synonymous with the accumulation of names for objects, the acquisition of other non-nominal terms being relatively neglected. Much of the recent debate surrounding the acquisition of nominals in the one-word stage, for example, has centered on children's understanding of reference, that is, on establishing the point in development when children can be said to have grasped the idea that things can be named. Various measures have been taken as indicators of children achieving what Dore (1978) has termed the *nominal insight* (see Bloom, 1973; Nelson, 1981; Snyder, Bates, & Bretherton, 1981) . Despite theoretical differences, such accounts concentrate on the production of nominals. All of these accounts assume that learning the names of things is the focal activity of the one-word stage, and that object names will, quite naturally, come to constitute the largest class of words in a child's 50 word vocabulary.

Why should such a large part of so many children's lexicons comprise the names for objects? "Why," as Nelson (1982) puts it, "does not the child begin by naming the action instead of the object? If indeed action is all important to the child, why are there so few action words in the early vocabularies?" (p. 347).

Nominals are not always the first words to appear. Here, as elsewhere in language development (Braine, 1976; Bloom, Lightbown, & Hood, 1975), individual differences are rife. True, some children's early productions are dominated by nominals. A boy called Tadd (cited by Gentner, 1982), for example, had in the period from 11 to 18 months learned 11 nominals, 9 of which were general nominals, but only 2 non-nominals: *toot-toot*, a word he used when playing with a car; and *yuk*, a word he used when he encountered food he did not like. But there are examples in the literature of other children whose productions are almost exclusively non-nominal. Menn (1976; cited by Ingram, 1978) observed a boy called Jacob from the age of 12 months onwards. By 17 months of age, his productive vocabulary consisted of 10 non-nominals; the word *toast*, which had been used on one occasion only to request; the word *Jacob*, used in a game of peep-bo; and *doll*, a clear label. Similarly, Gopnik (1981) reports that there were children in her study who produced non-nominals before nominals. And if the grouped data of Nelson (1973) and Rosenblatt (1977) are compared, the major difference that emerges between the two sets of findings occurs in the composition of the 10-word vocabularies. General nominals are overwhelmingly the most common type of words reported by Nelson (41%); for Rosenblatt, general nominals are no more frequent than specific nominals or personal social words (26%, 25%, & 28%, respectively). Clearly, children can and do encode a variety of concepts from the outset of language production. Nonetheless, by the time the vocabulary has grown to 50 words, the average proportion of general nominals far exceeds the average proportion of personal social words and the average proportion of action words put together. This imbalance raises several fundamental questions. Why are there so few action words and verbs in children's 50 word lexicons? Why are there so many object names? When there is an explosion in vocabulary, why is it composed almost entirely of nominals?

Word class, of course, is not infallible, nor necessarily a good guide as to what 1-year-old children choose to talk about or what they seem to consider worthy of comment. If the contexts of early words are not examined in detail, there is always the danger of misrepresenting the children's achievement. In particular, there is the danger of assuming that whenever a child produces a noun, he or she is using that word to name objects. This is especially true during the earliest months of language development when children's productions tend to be contextually constrained and rather idiosyncratic. Thus, 9- to 12-month-old children may use conventional sounds, words, or phrases (possibly in conjunction with formalized gestures), but the precise words that the children acquire and the meanings which these early words seem to have for the children owe much to the repeated, routine, and possibly ritualized nature of the social and verbal interactions between caregivers and children. Many authors (e.g., Ratner & Bruner, 1978; Ferrier, 1978) have argued that it is within the familiarity of such frameworks that children come to attend to speech and meaning is first given to words. Within such frameworks, the link between what is most salient situationally and the accompanying language is highlighted for the child listener. Words come to accompany actions (e.g., *bang* as a tower of bricks is knocked down), occupy certain positions within exchanges (e.g., *ta* as the child gives or receives a toy), and can be associated with particular individuals, objects, events, or settings.

Sometimes, though, children misconstrue what is conventionally meant by a particular word, and it may not be until they attempt to apply the term to new, similar but different situations that the discrepancy between intended and perceived meaning becomes apparent. So, for example, Ferrier (1978) describes how her daughter came to use the word *phew* (originally used as a comment about the offensive smell that emanated from her baby daughter's diaper each morning) as a general social greeting. Mistakes such as this are particularly obvious early on in a child's language development but can occur at any time during language development. There can be no guarantee that words from one class will always be used appropriately by young children in their own spontaneous speech. Examples of nominals being used nonreferentially are not difficult to find in the literature. For instance, Piaget's daughter, Jacqueline, used *panana* (her word for grandfather) to express any desire or need, regardless of the presence or absence of the grandfather himself (1962, p. 211). Huttenlocher (1974) cites the case of a child, Wendy, who at the age of 10 months used the word *fish* to direct attention towards any object. Slightly older children have been reported to use the word *door* to request the assistance of adults in unblocking an opening or disentangling two toys (Griffiths & Atkinson, 1978).

Edwards (1978) has suggested that the word *mummy's* may be used by children not to label the possessor, but in recognition of prohibition or social constraint—in the same way *no* or *hot* are sometimes used. What is a nominal for an adult (picking out the agent, possessor, or object of an action) may appear in the speech of young children, but it would be simpleminded to assume that all such productions by young children are attempts to name objects.

Leaving aside the issue of what children use particular words to mean, we are still left with the question of why the vocal fragments 9- to 18-month-old children isolate from a stream of speech are so often the words which adults would categorize as nouns. This is true both for children's receptive vocabulary and children's productive vocabulary (Benedict, 1979; Snyder, Bates, & Bretherton, 1981).

There are at least two ways to explain this nominal advantage in early lexicons. Firstly, one could suggest that the mental representation of objects differs from the mental representation of action concepts in ways which lead to object words being learned more easily (Nelson, 1982; Gentner, 1982). There is little experimental evidence to support this hypothesis. Oviatt (1980) compared the ability of 10-, 13-, and 16-month-old children to retain for 15 minutes the name for an animate object (e.g., a live hamster) and the name of a simple action (e.g., pressing a lever to activate a toy). There was a marked improvement in the number of children responding to each of the words over the age range studied. In addition, while children were much more likely to vocalize spontaneously on trials involving the object word than on trials involving the action word, there was no significant difference in the number of children showing comprehension of the two types of word. How then are we to account for the high proportion of nominals in young children's lexicons? If there is nothing fundamentally different about the way in which object concepts and action concepts are acquired, then we have to look for an alternative explanation for why there are so few action words in children's productive vocabularies during the one-word period.

The second explanation of the nominal advantage stems from the suggestion that the high proportion of object words in early lexicons reflects the formal and functional characteristics of the speech which accompanies parent-infant interaction. Simply, the nature of the speech input to children during the one-word period may be that there are more opportunities to learn the names for objects than to learn the names for actions. Without in any way ignoring or diminishing the children's contribution to conversational exchanges and the importance of the constraints imposed by children's mental processes for the task of language learning (see Hoff-Ginsburg & Shatz, 1982; Shatz, 1982; Bates, 1983), I shall argue that there is a close relationship between child-directed speech and children's early lexical acquisition. In particular, I suggest that the way in which nominals are encountered and received is very different from children's experience with action words.

This chapter will explore this possibility by considering four main areas of the linguistic environment: (a) the surface features of child-directed speech; (b) topics of child-directed conversation; (c) maternal speech styles; and (d) the task demands of communicative exchanges during the one-word period.

Speech Input Characteristics

A considerable and growing body of evidence exists about the prosodic and linguistic features of maternal speech to infants. Although a few studies have examined the characteristics of child-directed speech to babies less than 6 months old (Sherrod, Friedman, Crawley, Drake, & Devieux, 1977; Stern, Spieker, Barnett, & MacKain, 1983), most have concentrated on the language environment of children older than 6 months. Speech to language-learning children has been described as perceptibly different from speech addressed to more mature language-users. Higher pitch, exaggerated prosodic contour, a slower rate of delivery, shorter utterances, and the presence of well-defined pause boundaries all serve to direct attention to speech and make segmentation of the speech stream easier (Snow, 1972; Broen, 1972; Cross, 1977; Newport, Gleitman, & Gleitman, 1977).

To what extent though, could such features of mothers' speech to young children determine the types of words individual children pick up? Chapman (1981) suggests that the repertoire of a child at the one-word stage might simply be a matter of segmentation, a matter of which parts of the stream of speech are distinctive enough to attract attention and be retained in memory long enough to become familiar. If this is so, names for objects should be especially noticeable in the speech that young children hear. To examine this possibility in more detail, let us consider the speech addressed to children in the very earliest stages of lexical acquisition and explore the extent to which the phonological characteristics, stress, and the position of a word within an utterance might encourage the early preferential acquisition of nominals.

The sounds that make up specific words do have an influence on whether or not particular words appear early in children's productive vocabularies. There is evidence in the literature to support the notion that children are selective about the phonological characteristics of the words they attempt to produce (Ferguson & Farwell, 1975; Kiparsky & Menn, 1977; Schwartz & Leonard, 1982). Rosenblatt (1977) has noted that the availability of an easy, acceptable phonemic variant may lead to the earlier inclusion of a word/concept than might otherwise be the case. For example, for many English-speaking families in Britain but not in the United States, *ta* operates as an alternative to *thank-you*. *Hi* may serve in place of *hello* in the United States but is unlikely to be used in Britain. It is difficult, however, to extend this type of consideration far into the period of language development: phonological constraints lessen considerably by the time the children have acquired 50 words (Leonard, Schwartz, Folgen, & Wilcox, 1978). Moreover, there is no data to suggest that non-nominals are adversely affected to a greater extent by phonological constraints than are nominals.

The importance of the relative frequency of occurrence of a particular word within child-directed speech has been investigated by Schwartz and Terrell (1983). They presented 12 children (who were 12 to 15 months of age at the beginning of the study and each of whom had fewer than five words in his or her productive vocabulary) with 16 names during the course of 10 home visits carried out over 4 months. Some names were presented frequently (twice during each of the 10 sessions), and some were presented infrequently (only once during each session). Half the names referred to objects (e.g., things that dangle from the end of a string or chain) and half referred to actions (e.g., slow, vertical, downward movements). The mean number of presentations before these exemplars were named by the children was very similar for both object concepts (7.59 and 12.77 for infrequent and frequent exemplars, respectively) and action concepts (7.33 and 12.19, respectively), but more object words were produced than action words. Nonetheless, it seems that there is no essential difference in children's ability to comprehend and produce action words and object words during the one-word period.

Stress may be a critical factor, for the names of objects are often stressed within sentences. Messer (1981) carried out a study of mothers' speech to their 14-month-old infants during free-play sessions, and reported that the loudest word within an utterance was most likely to be the name of a toy. Verbs, although they were the second most frequent class of words (364 instances of verbs compared with 511 instances of names for toys), were three times less likely to be the loudest vocalization within the sentence. Some other non-nominal expressions (e.g., *brrm-brrm*) fared better and were quite often the loudest part of an utterance, despite the fact that non-nominal expressions occurred less frequently. These types of utterances do appear in children's early lexicons.

Not altogether separate from the issue of stress is the contribution of the position of a word or phrase within the total utterance. Whether or not a word appears in utterance initial position or utterance final position has also been suggested as an important parameter (Chapman, 1981). Slobin (1973) has postulated a number of operating principles that are supposed to govern children's language learning. One of these is *pay attention to the ends of words*. Data from cross-linguistic studies show that children find postpositions easier to learn than prepositions (Slobin, 1973) and suffixes easier to learn than prefixes (Kuczaj, 1979). Could it be that a similar principle—*pay attention to the ends of utterances*—is at work for children in the early one-word stage? Benedict reported that even when words were only just beginning to become decontextualized in their meaning, there was no evidence that the children responded exclusively to particular types of words (e.g., object names as opposed to action words) or to word position within a verbal command. "The difficulty appeared to reside in attending and/or responding to, through an organized motor response, more than one unit, nor the form or position of the unit itself" (p. 83). However, there was evidence of individual response preferences even during this period. When presented with verbal commands specially constructed to contain only words which had generalized meaning, six of the eight children responded more accurately to general nominals; the other two children more often responded correctly to action words. When the children were older, a distinct pattern emerged: For four- and five-unit utterances, words in initial or final position were responded to more accurately than words in intermediate positions. All these findings unfortunately confound semantic class, prosodic cues, and word position, but the suggestion that children's dynamic sentence processing may influence language interpretations is surely worthy of further investigation (Tyler, 1981).

One cannot go far discussing segmentation problems for children without realizing the very special significance of single-word utterances. Several writers have remarked on the possible perceptual salience for language-learning children of single word utterances, for they combine features of stress, prosody, and are bounded by pauses. Carter (1979), reporting her study of 1-year-old David, comments that "most of (David's) new acquisitions were primitive imitations of certain words which could themselves legitimately be used in isolation or in short phrases by adults and were, in fact, frequently so used by his mother" (p. 85). Chapman (1981) also notes that those words which occur early in a child's productive vocabulary often occur as single-word utterances or in utterance final position in adult speech, whereas "all the late developing words (which are incidentally mostly verbs) are unlikely to do so" (p. 220). She goes on to argue that "most verbs and many other parts of speech, by virtue of their failure to occur singly or in utterance final position, are less accessible, perceptually, to the child" (p. 221). Significantly, where action words do occur singly or as isolated phrases, they are learned by children. Words such as *no*, *bye*, *see*, *up*, and *more* occur again and again in the records of 10- to 19-months-old children's speech (Nelson, 1973; McCune-Nicolich, 1981).

What can be concluded about the influence of the prosodic characteristics of child-directed speech on early lexical acquisition? Surface features of the linguistic input to children may account for the appearance of *night-night* before *sleep* or *lie down*, *round and round* before *turn*, and *brrm-brrm* before *drive* or *go along*. However, it is still unclear why the proportion of action words as a whole should be so low in comparison to the proportion of nominal words in children's 50-word vocabularies. We must explore other possibilities.

What Is the Topic of Conversation: Action or Object?

Most child-directed speech occurs during either the child's activities, the mother's activities, or in situations of joint attention. There is no reason why children should discuss objects and people more often than actions. Whether the mother is the principal actor (e.g., caretaking or demonstrating an action), or whether she is commenting on her child's current focus of attention or participating in the child's play activities, there is usually ample opportunity to remark on either object, action, or both. There is certainly more than one way to describe building a tower of blocks, eating a banana, or the antics of the presenters of "Playschool." What do parents choose to talk about in such situations?

All child-directed utterances in Nelson's (1973) study were coded in terms of whether they related to an object or to the child. Object-related utterances were defined as being those that named or described attributes or actions of an object or those that related the child and the object. Child-related utterances were described as requests, descriptions of actions, and utterances containing references to the child's behavior or person. The average ratio of object-related to child-related utterances was found to be 1.15. In other words, references to actions were about as frequent as references to objects in the speech addressed to these 13-month-old children.

The results from several recent studies bear on the question of whether adults deliberately concentrate on talking about objects rather than actions when addressing young children in free-play sessions. Schnur and Shatz (1984) videotaped four 16-month-old children (vocabulary range 2-50 words, MLU range 1.0-1.15), while they and their mothers engaged in play with toys. The study was designed to examine the extent to which there was any relationship between mothers' gestural cues and their use of utterance-type words to address children. Transcripts of the play sessions were segmented into episodes of interaction, termed *cycles*. Each cycle consisted of one or more maternal utterances related to a single, naturally occurring topic of conversation. There were two categories: *reference* cycles and *activity* cycles. A reference cycle was defined as a sequence of utterances in which a mother named an object, talked about its attributes, or tried to elicit naming from her child (e.g., "What is that? Is that a ball? Yeah, that's a ball!"). An activity cycle was defined as a segment of interaction during which a mother talked about an action on an object as she or her child performed the activity, or when the mother was trying to get her child to carry out a particular action (e.g., "Can you make them swing? That's right. Push them. Make them swing."). Taken together, reference and activity cycles were found to account for approximately 80% of all cycles in the transcripts, and within that, the ratio of reference cycles to activity cycles averaged 0.82.

In another recent study of 16 children, Schaffer, Hepburn, and Collis (1983) explicitly asked mothers to get their children to carry out certain actions (e.g., to build a tower of bricks, to put a hat on a teddy bear, to scribble with a crayon). Action directives in this study were defined as utterances containing a specific verb (e.g., *draw*, *push*) or a general action verb (e.g., *try*, *do*). Attention directives were defined as other utterances containing either the child's name, *look/see*, locatives, or nonverbal vocalizations. Significantly more specific action directives were addressed to the 8- to 18-month-old children per minute than to the 8- to 10-month-old children, but there was no significant difference between the rate at which either attention directives or general action directives were addressed to the two age groups of child-listeners. Clearly, adults do *not* avoid talking about actions with their 1-year-old-children. Indeed, the topic of conversation (during free-play sessions, at least) seems to be distributed evenly between talk about the toys themselves and talk about the actions be performed.

Attention cycles and action cycles are not always independent or mutually exclusive. In practice, as close examination of transcripts of mother-child pairs during free-play sessions with toys reveals, action cycles and attention cycles are often embedded within each other or closely linked as complementary parts of a developing game or conversation. Consider the following episode taken from the recording of Sean, one of the children being studied by the Bristol Language Development Project (see Wells, 1985). The recording was made in the child's home when he was 18 months old. Note how Sean's mother first establishes the game of building a tower (action directives) but then, within the framework of the continuing tower-building game, introduces references to the attributes of the objects (attention directives).

Sample 1

Time 9.51   Location: Sitting room
Activity: Free-play with adult participation—M(other) and C(hild) playing with building bricks

	M: Come on build these bricks up
C: (Laughs)	M: One (slowly)
	M: Two
C: There	
C: There there there	
C: There	M: That's it
	M: Oops it fell off
	M: Go on you put that one on
	M: That's it
	M: And this one
C: (noises)	
C: (noises)	
	M: Good
	M: And that one
	M: Bump
C: (laughs)	M: See if you can put that one on
	M: Wheee!
	M: It fell off [didn't it]?
C: [Brick]	M: Try again
	M: Oh there's a clever boy (approval)
	M: Now here's a red one
	M: Try and knock it over
	M: Oh there it fell over
C: There	M: And again
	M: Oops!
	M: Put the yellow one on there
	M: Put the yellow (emphasis) one on there
	M: Yellow
	M: And the green
C: (Look)	

Sample 2 is another episode taken from the same day's recording with the same mother-child pair. This time the mother begins the session by commenting on the attributes of the object she is handling. She later converts the discussion into a request for action.

Sample 2

Time 11.03   Location: Sitting room
Activity: Free-play with adult participation—M and C are playing on floor with a toy bus
Asterisks indicate unintelligible speech.

	M: Look at the big bus
	M: The bus
	M: Brr (* *) mind your finger
C: (Laughs)	M: (Coming)
C: (Laughs)	M: (Brrm brm) (making bus noises)
C: (Laughs)	M: Brm brm brm brm brm brm brm
	M: It's a big bus look
	M: Oh he's getting up speed
	M: Brm brm brm brm brrr he's gone
C: (Laughs)	M: (Get) the bus
	M: Go and get the bus
C: (Laughs)	M: Get the bus
	M: That's my boy
(C brings the bus back to M)	
	M: *you do it back to me
	M: That's right weeee!
	(5 secs. pause)
	M: Brrrr
	M: Brm
	(7 secs. pause)
	M: The bus is coming
	M: The bus is coming
C: Brrr (bus noises)	
	(7 secs. pause)
	M: Zoom

In both samples, Sean's mother plays a dominant role in the conversations. She initiates, she maintains, and directs the interchanges. She is working hard to involve her child in the activities and to keep him amused and there is an unmistakable tutorial quality to both episodes. The mother starts by demonstrating the action and explicitly instructing the child. She then continues to direct the child's activities and attention closely throughout the rest of the recorded sequence.

Most mothers reserve the right to become forceful or demand certain types of behavior from their children at some time or another. Equally, most mothers are also prepared, at least for some of the time, to play a supportive role and allow their children's own interests and behavior to suggest the next move. On these occasions, it would be unlikely for a mother to deliberately make a concerted effort to restrict or divert the direction in which a conversation is heading.

The question therefore arises as to whether mothers as a group differ significantly among themselves in how they choose to adopt the role of director or commentator when talking to their young children. If so, we need to determine whether such differences influence the type of words individual children acquire during the one-word period.

Mother Speech Styles

Maternal speech styles and their association with observed differences in the relative proportion of nominals in the early vocabularies of individual children has recently been the subject of a considerable amount of attention. Much of the present interest in the relationship between maternal style and lexical acquisition derives from Nelson's (1973) longitudinal study of the lexical development during the one-word period of 18 children. She found that differences existed in terms of types of words and short phrases the children learned. By the time the children had learned 50 words, the majority of them had productive vocabularies featuring a high proportion of general nominals. This group was termed the *referential* group. However, a large minority of children (the *expressive* group) had more diverse vocabularies which included in addition to some nominals, adjectives, and action terms, many social routines or formulaic phrases (e.g., "I want it", "Do it"). These differences, Nelson reported, were loosely associated with the position of the child within a family (i.e., birth order) and the level of education achieved by the child's mother. Moreover, the differences between the two groups in terms of vocabulary size and the use of pronominalization (though not MLU) persisted into their third year of life.

As part of her study, Nelson investigated the quality of mother-child interaction, particularly the topics of converation chosen by mothers when they were seeking to engage their children in play with toys. To this end, she recorded a toy-play session with each of the mother-child pairs in her sample. This took place during one of the home visits when the median age of the children was 13 months. Each mother was presented with a group of toys and household objects and asked to show them to her child and encourage the child to play with them. In general, there were no significant differences between the speech addressed to children in the referential group and the speech addressed to children in the expressive group. There were, however, two variables within the mothers' talk which correlated with measures of the children's language development. These were the proportion of utterances which commented on the child and the child's activities (as opposed to references to the toys or other objects in the environment) and the proportion of utterances which served as directions, instructions, commands, and requests for action. Both of these variables were negatively correlated with the rate of lexical acquisition. Only one adult speech variant—the proportion of positive directives in a mother's speech—was found to be significantly correlated with the proportion of object names in a child's vocabulary. The fewer the relative number of directives, the higher the proportion of object words in the child's productive vocabulary. No other features—not even object labeling—correlated significantly with the type of words the child had otherwise learned.

Since the publication of Nelson's 1973 monograph, there have been several other investigations which have reported significant relationships between features of maternal speech style and children's language development. Della Corte, Benedict, and Klein (1983) studied mothers' speech to 15- to 19-month-old children in three caretaking situations: dressing, bathing, and diapering. Few differences were found between the speech of the mothers of the five most referential children and the speech of the mothers of the five most expressive children. The mothers of the referential children spoke more, and described aspects of the environments and the ongoing events more often. However, they directed their children's behavior less often than did the mothers of the expressive children. When the data from the entire sample of 16 children were considered, the number of general nominals in the children's 50-word vocabularies correlated positively with their mothers' use of description and negatively with their use of directive prescription. The more general nominals in a child's vocabulary, the more description and the less prescription the child's mother used. Mothers whose children had relatively few nominals in their 50-word vocabularies used description and prescription equally. Mothers of referential children used many more descriptive utterances and many fewer prescriptive utterances. Indeed, these mothers were about three times more likely to describe an object, event, or a person's behavior than request an action or verbalization from their children.

Similar findings have been reported for older children. McDonald and Pien (1982) examined the utterances of 11 mothers while they were engaged with their 29- to 36-month-old children in free-play with toys. They reported intercorrelations among the data which revealed two polarized patterns of conversational interaction: one pattern reflected a mother's intention to control her child's physical actions; the other pattern revealed the mother's elicitation of the child's conversational participation (see also Olsen-Fulero, 1982). Barnes, Gutfreund, Satterly, and Wells (1983) analyzed the speech of adults who addressed 32 2-year-old children. Data regarding syntactic, semantic, pragmatic, and discourse features of the child-directed speech were subjected to a principal components analysis and nine principal factors extracted, the first six of which accounted for 86% of the variance. Included among these six factors were the number of direct requests made to control the child's behavior and the number of utterances which extended, elaborated, or added to the meaning just contributed by the child. The amount of adult speech, the number of extending utterances, and the number of questions which called for the child to comment were all found to correlate positively and significantly with the semantic and pragmatic range exhibited by the children in their own speech. In contrast, the number of directives used to control the child's behavior tended to be negatively correlated with a child's Mean Length of Utterance measured in morphemes (though this did not reach significance). When the extent of the children's language development over the subsequent 9 months was considered, it was found that gains in the children's MLU were significantly associated with (among the other measures) both the number of extending utterances and the number of controlling directives.

Conversational Demands and Child-Directed Speech

The preceding sections have concentrated on two characteristics of mothers' speech and their possible relationship to the proportion of nominals in young children's lexicons. Firstly, we asked what adults choose to talk about with their 1-year-old children. In particular, we addressed the issue of whether or not adults deliberately avoid talking about actions, preferring instead to talk about objects. A review of the literature relating to mothers' speech during free-play sessions did not indicate that there was any overwhelming preference to do so. Mothers were as likely to mention actions as objects. Next, we addressed the relationship between mothers' speech style and the composition of young children's lexicons. Evidence was presented which suggested a correlation between the relative number of directives a mother used and the proportion of non-nominals in her child's early lexicon and rate of later language development.

Thus far, no attempt has been made to go beyond a description of the content and type of utterances used by the mothers. Mothers' speech has been examined as an isolated body of data with no consideration given to the children's contributions to and influence on what is said. The fact that the mothers' speech occurs within the framework of social interaction and mutual involvement should not be neglected, however. Mothers are not independent operators producing monologues, deaf and blind to the behavior of the children they are addressing. Their speech is influenced by the language children use as well as by children's general social responsiveness and communicative initiative (Lieven, 1978). The reciprocal nature of the conversations from which maternal speech data come is a matter which Barnes et al. (1983) have stressed. They write:

> For example, it seems probable that the frequency with which a child receives extending utterances will depend, in part, on the frequency with which he himself produces utterances with propositional content that is of interest to the adults with whom he interacts and which is susceptible to being extended (p. 91).

It is also important to consider the conversational demands various types of utterance make on child-listeners. Directives and descriptive comments are not equivalent in this respect. Directives demand considerably more of child-listeners in terms of an appropriate response than do running commentaries. To provide a description, an adult need only comment on an already existing state of affairs, the focus of the child's attention, the child's current activity, or extend the child's incomplete utterances. There is no demand, no conversational necessity, for a response from the child-listeners. The children need do nothing, not even change their fixation point. Furthermore, within the limits of conversational demands, the rules of the game, and the level of their own general involvement, whether the adult intervenes at a particular moment is neither crucial to the maintenance of the children's interest in playing nor necessary for the achievement of a goal. The descriptions of events, comments, and suggestions provided by the adult may be accepted or ignored by the child without prejudice to the relationship between adult and child or the satisfactoriness of the interaction as a whole. In direct contrast, an instruction (whether a request for action, an attempt to direct attention, or a call for vocalization) always involves the child as a necessary and active participant. The child's behavior or focus of attention is meant to change as a result of what has been said.

As children grow older, mothers become gradually more demanding in the type of responses and the compliance they expect of their children. However, changes in conversational demands and elocutionary force do not always show up formally as different sentence types in mothers' speech. Snow (1977) examined the speech of two mothers during the period when their children were 3 months to 18 months old. She identified five commonly occurring questions and showed how they were used to elicit increasingly more complex behavior from the children. For example, at 3 months, the question "What's that?" was used to comment on a child's visual fixation on a particular object. Saying "What's that?" required no further action from the child; the utterance merely served to mark the moment when mother and child were both paying attention to the same object. Later "What's that?" was used to get the child to pay attention to novel objects (that is, to encourage the child to change the focus of attention). Once the child began to produce recognizable words, however, "What's that?" became a request for the child to produce the name of the indicated object.

The success of the communicative exchange depends on the adults asking the question at the right level for the child-listeners. Clearly, adults are not free agents as regards what they can demand or expect from their young addressees. Cultural factors may influence what adults consider to be appropriate or inappropriate games to play with one-year-old children (Schieffelin, 1979), but children's compliance, cooperativeness, interest in engaging in social interaction, and general attentiveness and initiative will all affect the likelihood of a particular style of interaction being successful and enjoyable.

The remainder of this chapter will trace the changes that occur in adults' descriptive and directive speech to children during the one-word period and the extent to which adults' tendency to talk about objects and actions is a reflection of changes in their children's spontaneous play and imitative behavior.

Descriptive Comments About Objects and Actions

Whether they like it or not, most young babies find themselves confronted by a steady stream of curious, enthusiastic, and sympathetic admirers, all eager to engage them in conversation-like exchanges. Doting grandparents, next door neighbors, and even casual acquaintances try to attract the baby's attention and pass the time of day in bouts of mutual distraction. Inevitably, these encounters are suffused with language. The adults talk to the infants, ask them questions, exclaim and comment on their behavior, express mock admiration, show disappointment, and punctuate their games with vocal and verbal outbursts.

Infants play a central role in all this. Firstly, the perceived sociability of the baby (amount of positive regard toward the speaker, smiling, contented or excited vocalization) influences adult speech even in the early prelingual period (Sylvester-Bradley & Trevarthen, 1978). Later, gestures—such as pointing—may elicit object-naming in nearby adults (Masur, 1982). Secondly, from the beginning, it is the child who unwittingly chooses the topics of conversation. A change of facial expression, a change in direction of gaze, an indication of impending crying or incipient drowsiness may all serve to change the topic. In short, given generally responsive child-listeners, most western English-speaking adults are prepared to turn the conversation to whatever the infant seems to be interested in or whatever the infant's behavior seems to suggest is of greatest importance at that moment. Typically, the overall impression is one of open-endedness, with the mothers allowing themselves to be influenced by their children's curiosity and perhaps providing no more than commentary. Thus, much of maternal speech to very young children reflects the infants' own spontaneous interests and activities (Penman, Cross, Milgrom-Friedman, & Meares, 1983; Sherrod, Crawley, Peterson, & Bennett, 1978). Given this observation, we might expect to find that as the infants' interests and activities change with increasing age, there will be a corresponding change in what mothers talk about to their children.

Snow (1977) studied the conversations of two mother-infant dyads longitudinally and noted a striking change in the nature of conversational topics when the children reached approximately 6 months of age. The mothers began to comment much less on the infants' internal states and feelings and began to comment more about activities and events in the external world (see also Harris, 1983). Penman et al. (1983) studied the functional (affective vs. informational) and referential (infant's actions and feelings, mother's behavior) changes in mothers' speech in 19 dyads during free-play sessions when the children were 3 months and 6 months old. Penman et al. reported a significant increase in the mothers' tendency to use information-oriented speech. References to the external environment increased and there was a small rise in the frequency of references to the infants' activities. Cross and Morris (1980) compared mothers' speech to 1- and 2-year-olds and found that the proportion of references to the children's actions continued to increase in the second year. Indeed, a sudden increase in the number of references made to children's activities to about 50% of mothers' utterances has been reported to occur when the children reach 18 to 24 months of age (Cross, 1977; Ellis & Wells, 1980). The overall picture therefore is one of a gradual and continuing shift in what mothers talk about to their children. At 3 months, much (though not the majority) of infant-directed speech comprises idiomatic, nonpropositional, context-dependent utterances which serve to attract and maintain the children's attention and to accompany actions and events. By 6 months, nonpropositional speech has become less frequent and information-salient utterances are in the ascendancy. Questioning the children's intentions, providing descriptions of objects, activities and events, and directing the children's attention or actions all significantly increase in mean relative frequency between the ages of 3 months and 6 months according to the data of Penman et al. (1983). The indications are that this trend continues such that by the second half of the second year, the majority of mothers' utterances refer to aspects of the child's activities or interests. Data from a longitudinal study of 8 mother-child pairs by Harris (1983), however, reveal that the vast majority of mothers' utterances during free-play sessions referred to the object which was the current focus of the children's attention rather than to some ongoing action. This was true when the children were 9 months old and when they were 16 months old. Actions were talked about, but mothers tended to suggest possible actions rather than comment on current activities.

How does the emergence of talk about children's activities fit in with changes in the children's attentional and behavioral repertoires and the amount of time and interest children spend in various activities? At 6 months, infants have just become interested in reaching for and playing with objects. Penman et al. (1983) report that the 6-month-olds in their study spent nearly two thirds of their time attending to objects whereas at 3 months these same children had spent only one quarter of their time holding and looking at toys. Studies of young children's spontaneous play with objects (e.g., Fenson & Ramsay, 1980; Fenson, Kagan, Kearsley, & Zelazo, 1976; Lowe, 1975; Rosenblatt, 1977) have described how the play of children under 12 months of age is restricted almost entirely to close visual or tactile examination (fingering, turning) and indiscriminate actions (banging, mouthing, waving) in which toys are used without regard for their specific qualities or associated functions. Representational play in which toys are handled in socially appropriate ways (e.g., cuddling a doll, brushing one's hair) appears toward the end of the first year of life and develops rapidly over the next 6 months to become the predominant type of spontaneous play with toys. Gradually, the actions become less stereotyped and more imaginative. At first, play involves only one toy; later, two toys are used in conjunction and play emerges in which other animate or lifelike toys act as the patients or recipients of the children's own actions (e.g., combing a doll's hair or mock-feeding a doll).

What evidence is there that individual children's style of play is at all related to the types of words and phrases those children acquire during the one-word period? Rosenblatt (1977) studied the interrelationship between development of play behavior, language, and cognitive skills in 20 children. She found that early language learners tended to engage more in social play and demonstrate less mouthing of objects, even at 9 months of age. The frequency and range of appropriate representational play (i.e., responses which demonstrated knowledge of the specific function or physical properties of the object such as building a tower of bricks or brushing hair) and the amount of imitation and gesture during mother-child play sessions were significantly associated with rate of vocabulary acquisition. More crucially for the present discussion, Rosenblatt reported:

> Children with a certain style of play were more likely to learn particular types of words, i.e. they encoded a personal set of experiences in language. Those whose 50-word vocabulary contained mainly object words (book, car) were from the beginning more toy-oriented and more investigative in their play. Children who were more socially oriented and had

greater appropriate and varied toy play tended to learn action words (up, down, whoops-a-daisy) first and object words later. A greater number of personal-social words (bye-bye, ta, yes, oh dear) was not related to early play behaviour (9 to 13 months) but occurred oftener in children whose play became more socially ritualised between 15 and 24 months (1977, pp. 39-40).

It seems that children's spontaneous focus of attention and level of social responsiveness play an important part in shaping the nature and content of their own linguistic environment during the first 2 years of life. Adults take their cue about what is an appropriate conversational topic from the children's current focus of attention and provide forms of vocal and verbal accompaniment to match the nonverbal interactional context.

The discussion so far has concentrated on the adult descriptions of objects, people, and events. But, as was mentioned earlier, mothers sometimes choose to be more directive in their dealings with their young children. Rather than simply commenting on whatever it is the child seems to be interested in (thereby relying on the children's initiative), an adult will commonly make suggestions, request particular actions, and issue commands and instructions. Sometimes this is done to draw the child's attention to a new or different object, sometimes it is to encourage the child to perform a new or different action, and sometimes it may be an attempt to elicit a specific vocalization from the child. Whichever it is, when adult speakers decide to take the initiative and urge particular responses from children, they have to contend with and allow for a range of immature conversational skills.

Adults do, of course, make demands of their children from an early age. Shaking a rattle, jiggling a doll, or holding up a spoonful of food may all be intended to bring about specific actions in children, and often such gestures and nonverbal acts will be accompanied by appropriate verbal requests for action (e.g., "Look at the rattle," "Are you going to play with the dolly now?," "Open your mouth."). Children are not unresponsive to these overtures. Deeply embedded within well-established routines of caretaking, mothers often produce questions and requests for action which are met with seeming compliance from the children addressed. However, closer inspection of these episodes of interaction reveal that the accompanying speech is more akin to a running commentary than to true requests for action (Hepburn & Schaffer, 1984; Trevarthen & Hubley, 1978). The illusion of the child's conversational involvement is achieved by extremely deft timing and good anticipation on the part of the mother. In reality, children around the age of 6 months cannot be relied on to pay much attention to the efforts of others who are directing their behavior by verbal means alone. Listening to speech is an extremely challenging activity, even for 9- to 12-month-olds. Children of this age are considerably limited in their attention and responsiveness to language. Indeed, if they are repeatedly asked to carry out various tasks, they may become so tired and annoyed that they cease to show any reaction at all to language, even to normally salient suggestions (e.g., "Do you want a cookie?"). This condition (which Benedict, (1982) has labeled *mock deafness*) has been remarked upon by others (e.g., Huttenlocher, 1974) and illustrates the severe constraints imposed by children's attentional capacities on mothers' attempts to direct their behavior. How, then, are mothers capable of directing their children's attention and behavior?

Directing Visual Attention

Directing a child's visual attention seems to be easier than directing a child's activity. In a study by Schaffer, Hepburn, and Collis (1983), mothers showed that they were able to successfully orient their children's visual attention to target toys without fail, although this took somewhat longer to achieve in the younger (10 month old) group than in the older (18 month old) group. Much more significant, however, was the difference in the likelihood of success in terms of time taken to get a child to carry out a specified action. Ten-month-old children only completed 66% of the tasks and took, on average, 75.3 seconds; the 18-month-old children completed 87% of the tasks and took just under 42 seconds to carry out the instructions. Clearly, the older children were not only more successful at producing the action demanded but also produced it more quickly. There are several possible explanations for this. Mothers of 18-month-old children might be more practiced at giving instructions than mothers of 10-month-olds and therefore provide their children with better messages. Or, alternatively, it could be argued that 10-month-olds are poor imitators or show little interest in anything but the most stereotypic, repetitive actions.

The idea that the mothers were timing directives differently for the two groups of children can be disregarded. Both groups of mothers timed action directives to coincide with points in the interaction when their children were already looking at or touching the relevant object rather than when the child's attention was engaged elsewhere. The greater success of the older children cannot be attributed to better stage management on the part of their mothers.

Perhaps mothers of 18- to 24-month-old children are more efficient than mothers of 9- to 12-month old children in terms of deploying gestures to support their verbal messages. Approximately 85% of utterances were accompanied by gestures in the Schaffer et al. study. This was true for both the 18-month-old group and the 10-month-old group. There were age-related differences, however, in the extent to which verbal and nonverbal means of communication were coordinated for the two types of directives. A clear pattern of association was detected for the 18-month-old group between the two major verbal categories (attention directives and action directives) and the most commonly occurring nonverbal gestures (manipulating, modeling, and pointing). Calls for visual attention were positively associated with manipulation of the object by the mother (e.g., jiggling) and negatively associated with explicit modeling of an action. Action directives were positively associated with pointing toward the target object and with modeling the action. In contrast, as a group, the mothers of 10-month-olds showed no sign of systematically organizing their verbal and nonverbal messages. The group figures concealed considerable individual variation within the group. An investigation of the extent to which individual mothers of 10-month-old children organized their verbal and nonverbal behavior found that there was a correlation between the degree to which each mother's presentation resembled that of the mothers of older children and the likelihood of her child successfully carrying out the task. "The more (the mother) packaged verbal and nonverbal into the combinations described, the more likely she was to obtain compliance from her child" (Schaffer et al., 1983, p. 350). Verbal and nonverbal means of communication are not always well-coordinated for children early on in the one-word stage. Some children, however, who do receive coherently presented messages, can use the information to successfully complete the task. For the remaining children, the link between verbal and nonverbal direction is rather weak, particularly for action directives. Schnur and Shatz (1984) have found that, while gesturing on reference cycles does seem to have a considerable beneficial effect on directing visual attention, gesturing on action cycles does not seem to facilitate task completion. Moreover, there is evidence to suggest that ungestured action cycles are as likely to be successful as action cycles accompanied by gesture (Schnur & Shatz, 1984; Shatz & Grave cited in Shatz, 1982). Findings such as these have led Shatz to argue (see also Schaffer & Crook, 1980) that gesture functions primarily to capture a child's attention rather than to direct him or her toward a particular activity. The extent to which this is true for children beyond the one-word stage has still to be determined.

What significance can be attached to the continued if disorganized attempts by mothers of 9- to 18-month-olds to provide gestural support for action directives? From the point of view of a language-learning child, the message presentation makes one-to-one mapping between gesture and the function or formal characteristics of utterance types virtually impossible. So why do mothers do it? Shatz (1984) has argued that mothers are relatively unconcerned about the efficiency of gestural cueing, that mothers of young children do not detect the difference in effectiveness of gesture on reference cycles and action cycles (or that, if they do detect the difference, it is not considered to be crucial), that mothers offer gestural cues regardless of outcome, and that gesturing is a response to general features of child-listeners (such as their age and not their demonstrated linguistic maturity). On the other hand, one could argue that the problem is not so much a matter of gross insensitivity on the part of the mothers as unreliability on the part of the children. Viewed in this way, the high level of gesturing exhibited by mothers is a sign of desperation in the face of listeners whose powers of concentration and comprehension are limited and whose responses are unpredictable. In circumstances such as these, gesturing may seem to be the most forceful, least ambiguous way of conveying what is intended. The fact that a high percentage of utterances are accompanied by gestures is testimony to the patience and optimism shown by mothers during such exchanges, a sign that they are willing to offer all the help they possibly can to get their message across. With the younger child-listeners, though, even this is not always enough, especially if the mother is trying to direct the child's activities.

Ultimately, of course, the extent to which gesturing makes an appropriate response from a child-listener more likely depends on the child's capacity to imitate a mimed or demonstrated action and the child's ability to interpret gestures such as pointing or headshaking appropriately. Perhaps a 10-month-old child's understanding of pointing as a gesture to direct visual attention is more advanced and reliable than the child's understanding of demonstration as an invitation to copy, or the child's interest in imitating a modeled action. If so, this might explain why gestured attention directives are more likely than action directives to be successful. Ten-month-old children may be such poor imitators of mimed or modeled behavior that, even when their attention is already focused on the target object, they cannot be relied upon to perform the demonstrated action.

How competent are 9- to 18-month-olds at making sense of communicative gestures? There have been several experimental investigations of children's comprehension of pointing (Churcher & Scaife, 1982). For example, Murphy and Messer (1977) found that 9-month-old children were able to follow a pointing gesture and look toward the indicated object, but this only happened when the mother's hand and the target object were in the same visual field. By 14 months of age, however, the children were capable of following points which required them to extrapolate direction beyond their immediate field of vision, turn their heads, and direct their attention in a completely new direction. Macnamara (1977) found that 12- month-olds were unable to respond appropriately if confronted by an adult who simultaneously extended an object toward the child but looked elsewhere. By 17 months of age, though, children could attend to these two divergent signals and coordinate them meaningfully. This general progression has been found also in studies of looking (Butterworth & Cochran, 1980; Butterworth & Jarrett, 1980). Clearly, the ability to follow a point or someone's line of sight is not a sudden achievement; it develops throughout the one-word period. Nevertheless, it is sufficiently developed by the time children reach 9 months of age for mothers to feel justifiably confident about drawing their children's attention toward objects, especially if the objects are small, movable, and not too far away. In contrast, mothers of 9-month-olds may feel considerably less sure about how to get their children to carry out particular actions. Much depends on the willingness and ability of individual children to participate in communicative interchanges with other people and the child's interest in imitating the sounds and actions of those around him or her.

Directing Actions

Imitation is not common among 9-month-old children. Those actions which are imitated closely resemble the types of activities characteristic of children's spontaneous behavior at this age. Opening and closing the mouth, putting tongues out, and looking toward the ceiling are all actions which are readily reproduced by children in response to a model (Abravanel, Levan-Goldschmidt, & Stevenson, 1976). All of these activities are common in the spontaneous behavior of 6- to 9-month-old children.

The same limitations are evident in children's imitations of object-related actions. Types of action which are frequent in children's spontaneous behavior, but only these types of actions, are imitated by 6- to 9-month-old children. So, for example, nonspecific actions such as banging with a stick or making a noise by scratching on the bottom of an upturned cup will be produced in imitation of an adult's action. However, actions that involve conventional acts with socially appropriate objects (such as pushing a toy car along or drinking from a cup) are not imitated (Killen & Uzgiris, 1981).

Children change, and in the last quarter of their first year they become noticeably more attentive to the behavior of adults, more cooperative, more sociable, and more amenable to being directed (Trevarthen & Hubley, 1978; Lempers, 1979). The children will now watch an adult model an activity and they will imitate conventional acts with appropriate objects. They will, for example, put a toy telephone to their ear or drink from a cup. With increasing age, children can imitate a wider range of activities with much greater reliability and accuracy (McCall, Parke, & Kavanaugh, 1977; Uzgiris, 1972). Stacking cubes, squeezing a toy duck to produce a sound, putting beads into a cup, and stirring a cup with a spoon are all more likely to be imitated by 12- and 15-month-olds than by younger children (Abravanel et al., 1976). Faced with cooperative, responsive, conversational partners, mothers may be encouraged to adopt a more directive role, which will be reflected in the utterances they address to the children. No longer can the mothers' speech be characterized as a running commentary on the essentially independent activities of their children. Instead, the mothers seek to guide their children's attention and behavior through explicit suggestion, instruction, and rhetorical questioning. This is the period in which ritual question-and-answer action games break out in profusion (e.g., "Where's your nose?", "Can you dance?", "Show me your shoe.", "Kiss the dolly.", "Point to the clock.").

Nonetheless, there is a limit to a 1-year-old child's ability or willingness to imitate. Significantly less attention is paid to simple gestures and other actions that do not involve objects than to object-related actions. The superiority of infants' imitative performance of object-based actions compared with vocal or gestural actions has been remarked upon by several researchers (Abravanel et al., 1976; McCall et al., 1977; Uzgiris, 1972; Rodgon & Kurdek, 1977). For example, Abravanel et al. found that 9- to 18-month-old children were much less likely to imitate clapping their hands together in the style of pat-a-cake than clapping two blocks together. Furthermore, despite their interest in imitating acts involving socially appropriate objects, 9- to 18-month-old children will not readily imitate acts with inappropriate or counter-conventional objects. "The 10-month-olds clearly differentiated between the types of actions modeled. During modeling of acts with inappropriate objects the infants closely followed the demonstration, yet the only response made afterwards was a blank stare at the E or a return to using the object in a socially appropriate way" (Killen & Uzgiris, 1981, p. 227). Young children are selective and discriminating about what they are prepared to imitate: They are not equally willing to imitate any action on any object. In other words, actions are not independent of the objects on which they are to be performed. Not until the children are nearer 24 months of age does imitation develop into a game in its own right (Killen & Uzgiris, 1981). Before this age, the likelihood of an action being imitated (with or without an object) seems to depend on the extent to which the modeled action is seen to resemble a play activity that the child has already established with other people. The objects used in Killen and Uzgiris' experiment were all familiar to the children; so were the actions to be imitated. The problem for the younger children, therefore, was one of massive perceived incongruity given previous experience, rather than absolute strangeness. In his study, Schwartz (1983) presented children with opportunities to watch and then imitate novel actions being performed on familiar objects, and familiar actions being performed on novel objects. The results indicate that the children were interested in the novel objects rather than the novel actions. The children imitated a significantly greater number of actions when the (novel) target object was the labeled entity than when the action itself (carried out on familiar objects) was labeled. However, while the degree of interest shown may have influenced the total number of object or action words that were learned, it did not affect the speed with which any particular word (labeling object or action) was acquired and used. Given interest in the event as a whole, therefore, we may conclude that both the action to be performed and the presence and nature of the toys being handled influence the likelihood of compliance and task completion. Any object is better than none: an action-appropriate object is better than an inappropriate object; but a novel object is better than a familiar object if the action to be imitated is not a ritual one.

For all sorts of reasons, adults may find it easier to direct the attention of 9- to 18-month-old children to objects than to direct or promote the actions of the children. It may be no coincidence that mothers tend to spend time chatting and looking at and labeling pictures in books for their 1-year-olds, but leave the children to explore the range of actions on activity centers in the privacy and solitude of their early morning cots.

Promoting Verbal Responses

The third way in which adults seek to direct their children's behavior is to invite them, explicitly, to produce the name for an indicated object. Verbal games and ritual question-and-answer sessions between parents and 1-year-old children are common in many households. Looking at picture books, especially, generates "What's that?" routines. This is the most obvious example of verbal direction by parents, but it is not the only one that can be cited. One-year-old children may also find themselves being asked, "What does the cat (dog, bee, pig) say?", "How does the clock (car, telephone) go?", "Who's that?" (of a reflection in a mirror or a photograph), and "Can you say 'Happy birthday'?" Looking at picture books is a routine unlike any other. Not only does it maximize joint visual attention between adults and children, but it affords a situation within which adults can legitimately and intensively supply the names for, or otherwise discuss, a wide range of objects from a wide range of categories which, under normal circumstances, would be an unusual juxtaposition. It is within such a setting that the more cooperative and responsive children can be encouraged to become attentive to language alone and to adopt the role of verbal participant (Ninio & Bruner, 1978; Murphy, 1978). The following example is taken from Bruner (1983). The child, Richard, was 1; 1.1 at the time of recording.

M: Look!
C: (touches picture)
M: What are those?
C: (vocalizes and smiles)
M: Yes, they are rabbits
C: (vocalizes, smiles and looks up at mother)
M: (Laughs) Yes, rabbit

The appearance of word-like sounds and standard lexical labels led on for this mother and child to other "what" questions.

M: What's that? (falling intonation)
C: Fishy
M: Yes, and what's he doing? (rising intonation)

Initially, children's vocal contribution may be extremely limited in nature, stereotyped, and idiosyncratic: Only certain books or wall friezes may be used for the book reading; only certain elements (pictures, pages, characters) may be selected for comment; only certain questions posed (and only certain answers expected). The characteristics of the particular conventional routine or questioning style that is played will generate different types of verbal responses from different children. Giving the names for things may be the way in which some children learn to take part in request-for-verbalization games; others may play a game in which they have to reply by providing people's names; yet others may play at making animal noises. The appropriateness of the verbal response for the particular question asked may not be appreciated by the children early on, however. Their understanding of the entire exchange may simply be one of vocal turn-taking ("You ask a question and I'll say my part."). When the question is the well-practiced one, the response type will match it and the child may demonstrate seeming comprehension. If the question is different from the one he or she has become accustomed to, the child may still be prepared to join in the question-and-answer game, but the answer will be inappropriate. Precisely what children say, therefore, when strange adults pose questions may turn out to be more a function of a particular question-and-answer routine they are used to playing than of the question they have actually been asked.

A study by Allen and Shatz (1983) reported that 16- to 18-month-old children's responses to questions such as "What does the cat say?" and "What do you wear on your head?" were crucially dependent on the children's past experience of engaging in linguistic routines of a particular sort. Faced with a "What?" question, four of the five children in the study responded as though the question posed was of the form they were used to encountering during conversational routines with their mothers. Thus, one child (whose mother reported only occasional use of "What's this?" questions) offered no verbal responses to the experimenter's questioning despite having the vocabulary to do so. Another child (MLU 1.15, lexicon=50 words) was found to exhibit two patterns of vocalization in response to "What?": naming a salient object and verbal imitation. This same child never offered an action response or an animal noise. "What's this?" was a common question-and-answer routine for this child with his mother; indeed for some time it had been their only regular verbal game.

Experience and expectation of a particular conversational routine therefore can significantly affect the likelihood and appropriateness of a 1-year-old child's responses—a fact worth remembering when we consider experimental attempts to elicit verbal productions from young children. After all, the formulation "What's this?" is precisely the prompt used by most investigators of early vocabulary development. Parenthetically we may wonder, given the fact that the corresponding experimental question, "What am I doing?" is rarely encountered, what can be concluded from such experiments about the ease of acquisition of action words and object words. Perhaps if video versions of children's board books ever become a reality, we may find that nonstatic characteristics, activities, and events become question-and-answer fodder in the same way as objects are now. In the meantime, the superiority of some children in supplying the names for objects in response to the question "What's this?" may be as much a sign that ritual naming games have developed at home with adult interlocutors as it is an indicator of the size of the children's productive vocabulary. This point has been made by McShane (1979) in connection with Nelson's (1973) referential-expressive categorization of speakers.

> ... The referential speakers may be the children who have played ritual naming games and the expressive speakers those who have not. This not to say that expressive speakers learn to talk by bypassing the concept of naming but rather that the achievement of that concept will be slower and its manifestation less dramatic than in referential speakers (McShane, 1979, p. 891).

Nor is playing ritualized 'What's this?' games the only way of learning about naming. There are at least three different forms of the naming game, including an early version played by some children when they first begin to point, where the children initiate one- or two-turn bouts of attention to object behavior (pointing toward or holding out an object, visually fixating the object concerned and uttering a protodeclarative, or indicative performative such as *da* to which the adult responds with the name of the indicated objects). (See Bates, 1976; Greenfield & Smith, 1976.)

Smolak and Weinraub (1983) compared the speech of five mothers whose own two-year-old daughters were relatively advanced in terms of language development (vocabulary size = 100 + words, 3 + word utterances) with the speech of five mothers of similarly aged daughters who were still producing only single-word utterances and had vocabularies of less than 60 words. Each mother (in addition to being recorded playing with her own daughter) was recorded in a 10-minute toy-playing session with another 2-year-old girl, Marlyce, whose own speech production was at the level of the less advanced group. A comparison of the speech style of the two groups of mothers when in conversation with Marlyce yielded few differences, but the differences that were found are revealing and relevant to the present discussion. In particular, the mothers of the more advanced group of children made significantly fewer comments about Marlyce and her activities and made significantly more calls for attention than did the other group of mothers, suggesting that the latter were less prepared to discuss, in either a prescriptive or descriptive way, any ongoing activities to which Marlyce might already be attending, and expected her, instead, to be alert to the speaker and prepared and willing to direct her attention with ease to new foci of attention.

Conclusion

Briefly I would argue that there are four main contributing factors to consider in regard to the questions with which I have attempted to deal in this chapter. In places the evidence is sparse, and so, in the absence of firm, direct evidence, I shall take this opportunity to indulge in well-intentioned speculation.

Firstly, 1-year-old children seem to be capable of comprehending, representing, and reproducing words referring to a wide variety of aspects of scripted events. Exactly how those words are represented mentally is not a question which is within the scope of this chapter. Suffice it to say, merely, that as children approach their first birthdays there is a noticeable increase in their social responsiveness and in their attentiveness to words and patterns of speech, and that, in establishing a meaning for some of the words and phrases they hear, children are clearly willing to entertain a wide range of aspects of their social and physical world. In this scheme of things, objects per se are no more or no less worthy of comment than many other interesting experiences. They are just part of the fabric of day-to-day living in much the same way as are people, activities, settings, sounds, expectations, and achievements. Sometimes, objects are prominent in children's event representations, sometimes they are not. Sometimes they are topical, sometimes they are not. Insofar as 9- to 12-month-old children can be said to have a generalized concept of objects, I doubt whether objects are seen as being natural, obvious, or especially conspicuous targets for language, separate from other noticeable features. Instead, as Nelson (1983) has recently argued, "when children begin to understand and use a few words themselves, they do not yet have well-formulated ideas about either the uses or structure of language" (p. 184). She writes, "at least the following kinds of prelexical language forms appear to be used during the first part of the second year: words and phrases in social interaction within scripts; naming routines; words to refer to scripts; and words attached to general action schemes" (p. 184). In theory, naming games, script labels and words that are part of general action schemes could all involve action words and yet, in practice, they rarely do. We are forced back to the original question: Why are there so many nominals and so few action words in children's early vocabularies?

I have argued in this chapter that the answer to this question rests with what adults choose to talk about with their children, and this, in turn, depends on what adults judge to be the child's primary topics of interest and intentions and on the extent to which the child is cooperative, compliant, and prepared to be directed by another person.

My second point, therefore, is that much of 9- to 18-month-olds' behavior is interpreted by parents as indicating that the child has a special interest in objects. Close visual examination and manipulative exploration of toys in spontaneous play is a clear example. Since adult commentaries reflect what adults believe to be the matter of most immediate interest or concern to the child, the speech which commonly accompanies such play could hardly fail to mention the objects in their grasp (e.g., "Now what have you found? Mummy's purse?"). Reaching, holding something up and, later, pointing—especially when accompanied either by vocalization or a look toward the adult—are also particularly potent at encouraging object-talk from obliging adults (e.g., "What do you want? A biscuit?", "And that's the other sock, isn't it?" "Yes, that's nanny.") Actions are not excluded from discussion, but the emphasis is more often on describing or identifying toys, people, foods, articles of clothing, household objects, and so forth. Any apparent interest in watching television or turning the pages of books is similarly acknowledged by naming: "And look, there's a tractor." Object-naming, at least for many mothers in Western cultures, is seen as an appropriate response to supply for a 1-year-old. It seems natural, the response of least effort. Perhaps this nominal tendency alone is enough to explain the predominance of nominals in the vocabularies of even expressive children.

Some 1-year-old children, however, get drawn into a special interactive situation, such as book reading, which increases their vocabulary rapidly and selectively. The activity of book reading is an extremely powerful one for several reasons:

1. Naming games of this sort present the child-reader with repeated opportunities to be told a large number of names for widely differing entities which otherwise might be relatively infrequent in their lives (e.g., *Christmas tree, doctor*), or which they might not otherwise encounter for several years (e.g., *teacher, trumpet, elephant, ship*), or which might otherwise be very difficult to demonstrate (e.g., *snowflake, London, angel*).
2. Book reading naming games give children the opportunity to become familiar with the "What's that?" routine, which, itself, may influence performance in any test of vocabulary.
3. Naming games give the child the opportunity to discover a specialized use for language and to establish a scripted framework that, with insight, will give rise to the concept of naming.

But (and this is my third point), naming games cannot be imposed on every child. The whole activity depends on the child being spontaneously interested in engaging in object-oriented activities and, in the case of book reading, being prepared to have his or her attention directed from one place to another in quick succession by another person. Children differ in the extent to which they are interested in engaging in such allocentric exchanges. A child whose powers of concentration are low, whose responsiveness to adults is minimal, or whose mock deafness is profound and prolonged is unlikely to prove an active participant in a naming game. Rosenblatt (1975) found that the amount of time which individual children spent doing things other than playing with toys in free-play sessions was negatively related to the onset and rate of early lexical acquisition. "The important factor," Rosenblatt suggests, "is not that these infants (usually boys) do not play with the toys, but that they are more distractible, and active, and thus less 'capturable' by the mothers for interaction" (1975, p. 10). We should remind ourselves, too, that mothers do not avoid mentioning actions when they are talking to their one-year-olds. But when they do so, they are likely to be making a suggestion or giving an instruction about a future activity or describing the children's own ongoing activity—none of which will allow the child the luxury of detached observation of the referent action. In the first two cases, the talked about action is not presently available—and may never be. In all three cases, the child's involvement in responding at all to the adult's speech or the child's concentration in planning a particular manipulation of his or her own may be so overwhelming that the child pays little heed to what is actually said.

My final comment is that the availability of suitable specific, descriptive verbs in the language being learned fuels the imbalance between the number of nominals and the number of non-nominals in children's 50-word vocabularies. Children who are keen pointers do not point only at objects; they spontaneously indicate interest in events and activities as well (e.g., falling snow, the flashing of Christmas tree lights, laundry going around in a washing machine, windscreen wipers going back and forth, a clock pendulum swinging). Sudden quieting and pausing in play also occurs as children attend to sounds (e.g., a dog's barking, the chiming of a clock, the sound of a motorcycle roaring by, a sudden burst of music on the radio). And what do adults do? How adults typically respond to these indications of shifts of attention is by naming—not naming the action but naming the object (e.g., "Brr, snow", "pretty lights"). For those parents who seek to provide action terms, there is often an embarrassing moment of realization when they find themselves stuck for an appropriate verb to use from their own vocabularies and are obliged to make do with non-specific action terms such as *working*, *going*, and *putting*. The nominal advantage problem clearly is not just about children's attentional or conceptual preferences, but is instead a problem shared by all users of a particular language. The characteristics of the mother tongue begin to make their mark very early in language development.

References

Abravanel, E., Levan-Goldschmidt, E., & Stevenson, M. B. (1976). Action imitation: The early phrase of infancy. *Child Development, 47*, 1032-1044.

Allen, R., & Shatz, M. (1983). "What says meow?": The role of context and linguistic experience in very young children's responses to what-questions. *Journal of Child Language, 10*, 321-325.

Barnes, S., Gutfreund, M., Satterly, D., & Wells, G. (1983). Characteristics of adult speech which predict children's language development. *Journal of Child Language, 10*, 65-84.

Bates, E. (1976). *Language and context: The acquisition of pragmatics*. New York: Academic Press.

Benedict, H. (1979). Early lexical development: Comprehension and production. *Journal of Child Language, 6*, 183-200.

Benedict, H. (1982). *Learning to understand: The structure of early language comprehension*. Unpublished manuscript, Michigan State University.

Bloom, L. (1973). *One word at a time*. Monton: The Hague.

Bloom, L., Lightbown, P., & Hood, L. (1975). Structure and variation in child language. *Monographs of the Society of Research in Child Development, 40*(2, Serial No. 160).

Braine, M. D. S. (1976). Children's first word combinations. *Monographs of the Society of Research in Child Development, 41* (No. 1 Serial No. 164.

Broen, P. (1972). The verbal environment of the language-learning child. *ASHA Monograph, 17*.

Bruner, J. S. (1983). *Child's talk: Learning to use language*. Oxford: Oxford University Press.

Butterworth, G., & Jarrett, N. (1980). The geometry of pre-verbal communication. Paper presented at the Annual Meeting of the Developmental Section of the British Psychological Society, Edinburgh.

Butterworth, G., & Cochran, E. (1980). Towards a mechanism of joint visual attention in human infancy. *International Journal of Behavioural Development, 3*, 253-270.

Carter, A. L. (1979). Prespeech meaning relations: An outline of one infant's sensorimotor morpheme development. In P. Fletcher & M. Garman (Eds.), *Language acquisition*. Cambridge: Cambridge University Press.

Chapman, R. S. (1981). Exploring children's communicative intents. In J. F. Miller (Ed.), *Assessing language production in children: Experimental procedures*. London: Edward Arnold.

Churcher, J., & Scaife, M. (1982). How infants see the point. In G. Butterworth & P. Light (Eds.), *Social cognition*. Chichester: Harvester.

Cross, T. G. (1977). Mothers' speech adjustments: The contribution of selected child listener variables. In C. E. Snow & C. E. Ferguson (Eds.), *Talking to children: Language input and acquisition*. Cambridge: Cambridge University Press.

Cross, T. G., & Morris, J. E. (1980). Linguistic feedback and maternal speech: Comparisons of mothers addressing infants, one-year-olds and two-year-olds. *First Language, 1*, 98-121.

Della Corte, M., Benedict, H., & Klein, D. (1983). The relationship of pragmatic dimensions of mothers' speech to the referential-expressive distinction. *Journal of Child Language, 10*, 35-43.

Dore, J. (1978). Conversation and preschool language development. In P. Fletcher & M. Garman (Eds.), *Language acquisition: Studies in first language development*. Cambridge: Cambridge University Press.

Edwards, D. (1978). Social relations and early language. In A. Lock (Ed.), *Action, gesture & symbol: The emergence of language*. London: Academic Press.

Ellis, R., & Wells, G. (1980). Enabling factors in adult-child discourse. *First Language, 1*, 46-62.

Fenson, L., Kagan, J., Kearsley, R. B., & Zelazo, P. R. (1976). The developmental progression of manipulative play in the first two years. *Child Development, 47*, 232-236.

Fenson, L., & Ramsay, D. S. (1980). Decentration and integration of the child's play in the second year. *Child Development, 51*, 171-178.

Ferguson, C. A., & Farwell, C. (1975). Words and sounds in early language acquisition: English initial consonants in the first 50 words. *Language, 51*, 419-439.

Ferrier, L. (1978). Word, context and imitation. In A. Lock (Ed.), *Action, gesture & symbol: The emergence of language*. London: Academic Press.

Gentner, D. (1982). Why nouns are learned before verbs: Linguistic relativity versus natural partitioning. In S. A. Kuczaj II (Ed.), *Language development (Vol. 2): Language, thought and culture*. Hillsdale, NJ: Erlbaum.

Goldin-Meadow, S., Seligman, M., & Gelman, R. (1976). Language in the two-year-old. *Cognition, 4*, 189-202.

Gopnik, A. (1981). Development of non-nominal expressions in 1-2 year olds: Why the first words aren't about things. In P. S. Dale & D. Ingram (Eds.), *Child language: An international perspective*. Baltimore, MD: University Park Press.

Greenfield, P., & Smith, J. (1976). *The structure of communication in early language development*. New York: Academic Press.

Griffiths, P. D., & Atkinson, M. (1978). A 'door' to verbs. In N. Waterson & C. Snow (Eds.), *The development of communication*. London: Wiley.

Harris, M. (1983). Early linguistic experience and early lexical development. Paper presented to British Psychological Society Conference, London.

Hepburn, A., & Schaffer, H. R. (1983). Les contrôles maternels dans la prime enfance. *Enfance*, *1-2*, 117-127.

Huttenlocher, J. (1974). The origins of language comprehension. In R. L. Solso (Ed.), *Theories in cognitive psychology: The Loyola Symposium*. Potomac, MD: Erlbaum.

Ingram, D. (1978). Sensorimotor intelligence and language development. In A. Lock (Ed.), *Action, gesture and symbol: The emergence of language*. London: Academic Press.

Kiparsky, P., & Menn, L. (1977). On the acquisition of phonology. In J. MacNamara (Ed.), *Language learning and thought*. New York: Academic Press.

Killen, M., & Uzgiris, I. C. (1981). Imitation of actions with objects: The role of social meaning. *Journal of Genetic Psychology*, *138*, 219-229.

Kuczaj, S. (1979). Evidence for a language learning strategy: On the relative ease of acquisition of prefixes and suffixes. *Child Development*, *50*, 1-13.

Lempers, J. D. (1979). Young children's production and comprehension of nonverbal deictic behaviors. *Journal of Genetic Psychology*, *135*, 93-102.

Leonard, L. B., Schwartz, P. G., Folger, M., & Wilcox, M. (1978). Some aspects of child phonology in imitative and spontaneous speech. *Journal of Child Language*, *5*, 403-417.

Lieven, E. (1978). Conversations between mothers and young children: Individual differences and their possible implications for the study of language learning. In N. Waterson & C. Snow. (Eds.), *The development of communication*. London: Wiley.

Macnamara, J. (1977). From sign to language. In J. Macnamara (Ed.), *Language, learning and thought*. New York: Academic Press.

Masur, E. F. (1982). Mothers' responses to infants' object-related gestures: Influences on lexical development. *Journal of Child Language*, *9*, 23-30.

McCall, R. B., Parke, R. D., & Kavanaugh, R. D. (1977). Imitation of live and televised models by children 1-3 years of age. *Monographs of the Society of Research in Child Development*, *42* (5, Serial No. 173).

McCune-Nicolich, L. (1981). The cognitive bases of relational words in the single word period. *Journal of Child Language*, *8*, 15-34.

McDonald, L., & Pien, D. (1982). Mother conversational behaviour as a function of interactional intent. *Journal of Child Language*, 337-358.

McShane, J. (1979). The development of naming. *Linguistics*, *17*, 879-905.

Menn, L. (1976). *Pattern, control, and contrast in beginning speech: A case study in the development of word form and word function*. Unpublished doctoral dissertation, University of Illinois.

Messer, D. (1981). Non-linguistic information which could assist the young child's interpretation of adults speech. In W. P. Robinson (Ed.), *Communication in development*. London: Academic Press.

Murphy, C. M., & Messer, D. J. (1977). Mothers, infants and pointing: A study of a gesture. In H. R. Schaffer (Ed.), *Studies in mother-infant interaction*. London: Academic Press.

Murphy, C. M. (1978). Pointing in the context of a shared activity. *Child Development*, *49*, 371-380.

Nelson, K. (1973). Structure and strategy in learning to talk. *Monographs of the Society of Research in Child Development*, *38* (1-2, Serial No. 149).

Nelson, K. (1981). Individual differences in language development, implications for development and language. *Develomental Psychology, 17*(2), 170-187.

Nelson, K. (1982). The syntagmatics and paradigmatics of conceptual developments. In S. A. Kuczaj II (Ed.), *Language development (Vol. 2): Language, thought & culture*. Hillsdale, NJ: Erlbaum.

Nelson, K. (1983). The conceptual basis for language. In T. B. Seiler & W. Waunenmacher (Eds.), *Concept development and the development of word meaning*. Berlin: Springer-Verlag.

Newport, E., Gleitman, H., & Gleitman, L. R. (1977). Mother, I'd rather do it myself: Some effects and non-effects of maternal speech style. In C. E. Snow & C. A. Ferguson (Eds.), *Talking to children: Language input and acquisition*. Cambridge: Cambridge University Press.

Ninio, A., & Bruner, J. S. (1978). The achievement and antecedents of labeling. *Journal of Child Language, 5*, 1-5.

Olsen-Fulero, L. (1982). Style and stability in mother conversational behaviours: A study of individual differences. *Journal of Child Language, 9*, 543-564.

Oviatt, S. (1980). The emerging ability to comprehend language: An experimental approach. *Child Development, 51*, 97-106.

Penman, R., Cross, T., Milogrom-Friedman, J., & Meares, R. (1983). Mothers' speech to prelingual infants: A pragmatic analysis. *Journal of Child Language, 10*, 17-34.

Piaget, J. (1962). *Play, dreams, and imitation in childhood*. New York: Norton.

Piaget, J. (1963). *The origins of intelligence in children*. New York: Norton.

Pollock, L. A. (1983). *Forgotten children: Parent-child relations from 1500 to 1900*. Cambridge: Cambridge University Press.

Rodgon, M. M., Jankowski, W., & Alenskas, L. (1977). A multifunctional approach to single word usage. *Journal of Child Language, 4*, 23-43.

Rodgon, M. M., & Kurdek, L. A. (1977). Vocal & gestural imitation in 8-, 14-, and 20-month-old children. *Journal of Genetic Psychololgy, 131*, 115-123.

Rosenblatt, D. (1975). *Learning how to mean: The development of representation in play and language*. Paper presented to Conference on the Biology of Play, Farnham.

Rosenblatt, D. (1977). Developmental trends in infant play. In B. Tizard & D. Harvey (Eds.), *The biology of play*. London: Heinemann Medical Publications.

Schaffer, H. R., & Crook, C. K. (1980). Child compliance and maternal control techniques. *Developmental Psychology, 16*, 54-61.

Schaffer, H. R., Hepburn, A., & Collis, G. M. (1983). Verbal and non-verbal aspects of mothers' directive. *Journal of Child Language, 10*.

Schieffelin, B. B. (1979). Getting it together: An ethnographic approach to the study of the development of communicative competence. In E. Ochs & B. B. Schieffelin (Eds.), *Developmental pragmatics*. New York: Academic Press.

Schnur, E., & Shatz, M. (1984). The role of maternal gesturing in conversations with one-year-olds. *Journal of Child Language, 11*, 29-41.

Schwartz, R. G., & Leonard, L. B. (1982). Do children pick and choose? An examination of phonological selection and avoidance in early lexical acquisition. *Journal of Child Language, 9*, 319-336.

Schwartz, R. G. (1983). The role of action in early lexical acquisition. *First Language, 4*, 5-20.

Schwartz, R. G., & Terrell, B. Y. (1983). The role of input frequency in lexical acquisition. *Journal of Child Language, 10*, 57-64.

Shatz, M. (1982). Our mechanisms of language acquisition: Can features of communicative environment account for development? In L. Gleitman & E. Wanner (Eds.), *Language acquisition: The state of the art*. Cambridge: Cambridge University Press.

Shatz, M. (1984). Contributions of Mother and Mind to the development of communicative competence: A status report. In M. Perlmutter (Ed.), *Minnesota Symposium on Child Psychology* (Vol. 17). Hillsdale, NJ: Erlbaum.

Sherrod, K. B., Crawley, S., Petersen, G., & Bennett, P. (1978). Maternal language to prelinguistic infants. *Infant Behavior and Development*, *1*, 335-345.

Sherrod, K., Friedman, C. S., Crawley, S., Drake, D., & Devieux, J. (1977). Maternal language to prelinguistic infants: Syntactic aspects. *Child Development*, *48*, 1662-1665.

Slobin, D. I. (1973). Cognitive prerequisites for the development of grammar. In C. A. Ferguson & D. I. Slobin (Eds.), *Studies of child language development*. New York: Holt, Rinehart & Winston.

Smolak, L., & Weinraub, M. (1983). Maternal speech: Strategy or response? *Journal of Child Language*, *10*, 369-380.

Snow, C. (1972). Mothers' speech to children learning language. *Child Development*, *43*, 549-565.

Snow, C. E. (1977). The development of conversation between mothers and babies. *Journal of Child Language*, *4*, 1-11.

Snyder, L. S., Bates, E., & Bretherton, I. (1981). Content and context in early lexical development. *Journal of Child Language*, *8*, 565-582.

Stern, D. N., Spieker, S., Barnett, R. K., & MacKain, K. (1983). The prosody of maternal speech, infant age and context related changes. *Journal of Child Language*, *10*, 1-15.

Sylvester-Bradley, B., & Trevarthen, C. (1978). Baby talk as an adaptation to the infants' communication. In N. Waterson & C. Snow (Eds.), *The development of communication*. Chichester: Wiley.

Trevarthen, C., & Hubley, P. (1978). Secondary intersubjectivity: Confidence, confiding and acts of meaning in the first year of life. In A. Lock (Ed.), *Action, gesture & symbol: The emergence of language*. London: Academic Press.

Tyler, L. K. (1981). Syntactic and interpretative factors in the development of language comprehension. In W. Deutsch (Ed.), *The child's construction of language*. London: Academic Press.

Uzgiris, I. C. (1972). Patterns of vocal and gestural imitation in infants. In F. J. Monks, W. W. Hartup, & J. de Witt (Eds.), *Determinants of behavioral development*. New York: Academic Press.

Wells, G. (1985). *Language development in preschool children*. Cambridge: Cambridge University Press.

10. Action Words and Pragmatic Function in Early Language

Derek Edwards and Roger Goodwin

The authors of linguistic texts seem unwilling to offer any precise definition of the concept of a *verb*. Despite this, they would almost certainly all agree that verbs can be notionally characterized as words referring to actions, states, processes, or relations. Typical examples include *play*, *eat*, *hold*, *fix*, *sit*, *stand*, *fall*, and *move*—all of which have been reported in the speech of two-year-old children (see Bloom & Lahey, 1978, p. 153)—and *explore*, *arrive*, *expand*, and *exceed*—none of which have been reported in the speech of very young children. Given this notional characterization of verbs, we can then ask various types of question concerning the development of verb meaning. These include the following questions about reference, grammatical role structure, and temporal expression:

What sorts of actions, states, processes, and relations do children *refer* to at the various stages of their development? Initially, children seem to talk about the physical events taking place around them, particularly if they themselves are directly involved, but which aspects of these events can and do they talk about at this initial stage? How is this referential range subsequently extended? For example, when do they start to talk about mental as well as physical events?

What are the *grammatical contexts* in which children's early verbs first appear? How do these contexts develop over time? For example, assuming that it is necessary for the adult verb *open* to take an obligatory Objective noun phrase and that this verb may also take optional agentive and instrumental noun phrases (see Fillmore, 1968), we can ask when and how this type of information concerning grammatical role structure was first acquired by the child, and how this information develops with time.

How do children master the system of auxiliary verbs and verb inflections which express the *temporal relations* of past, nonpast, and future, and the notions of completion or otherwise of an event (i.e., tense and aspect, respectively)?

This chapter will examine the origins of certain verbs which, for adults, refer either to simple movements (e.g., *walk*) or to changes of state of objects (e.g., *open*). Our interest will be focused primarily on the issue of reference. This will also involve us in a discussion of grammatical role structure since, in practice, these two questions cannot be rigidly separated. (For a discussion of temporal expressions see McShane, Whittaker, & Dockrell, this volume.)

Huttenlocher, Smiley, and Charney (1983) have argued, on the basis of studies of both production and comprehension, that the early development of such verbs, that is, *action words*, can be understood as a direct reflection of the development of children's understanding first their own actions and subsequently those of other people. The predominant direction in the growth of this conceptual understanding is one of decentration from the self in which children first categorize and verbally encode their own action and then perceive that a similar analysis can be applied to the actions of others. Thus, while motor development may occur through imitation of the actions of others, the conceptualization of actions seems to develop through a process of *anti-imitation* in which actions of others are interpreted using the child's own actions as models. Huttenlocher et al.'s cognitive theory of the early language of action can be summarized in the following propositions:

1. Individual action words are initially used to refer either to action by the self or to the observed actions of others, but not to both.
2. Action-by-self is verbally encoded before action-by-another. The latter develops via a process in which parallels are noted between the self and other people.
3. The movements (e.g., *walk*) of others are encoded earlier than other people's initiations of changes of state (e.g., *open*). This is because the latter requires not only observations of movements in the physical world but also an understanding of goal-directed actions and causality.
4. Correspondingly, children's mental verbs (*want*, *need*, etc.) are initially self-descriptive rather than other-descriptive, since the latter require inferential judgments as to the intentions and mental states of others.

We shall examine the basis of these claims, and suggest re-interpretations of the early language of action founded on a pragmatic analysis rather than one essentially tied to referential semantics.

Action Words: Classes and Contexts

Any proper classification of early action words must include two sorts of information. First, it must establish the conceptual distinctions—for instance, between movements and changes of state, or between intentional and nonintentional acts—which underlie the semantic content of the children's words. Secondly, the classification must be able to take account of the details of children's individual usages of action words in different situations. There is no point in listing all of a child's movement words classified according to their adult meaning if the child is using many of them only in particular contexts, seemingly with individual, idiosyncratic meanings. Unfortunately, few studies have yet made serious attempts to provide these two sorts of information.

Let us first consider the conceptual distinctions. Action words may be subdivided either according to the types of actions involved, that is, defined referentially, or by case-grammatical criteria, such as the word's *case frame* (see Fillmore, 1968). Thus, Huttenlocher et al. (1983), employing referential criteria, distinguish between movements which specify some sort of physical activity (e.g., *walk*, *run*), and those which specify some change of state of an entity without clearly specifying the nature of any actions bringing about that change of state (e.g., *open*, *bring*, *cook*). In fact, it is arguable (cf. Edwards, 1973) that this latter group of words, in their adult meanings, do not specify *actions* at all, but refer only to *changes of state*. It is important that we begin at least with the possibility that adults and children may have words that encode stative change independently of performed action. Indeed, there is evidence that this is the case for a set of locative words that occurred in the early speech of several children (see Edwards, 1978a).

Action words may also be subdivided according to case-grammatical criteria. However, these criteria must be employed with care. For example, one must be careful not to equate *persons* with *case roles*. Persons, either as physical entities in events or as named elements in sentences, do not have to be *agents* of actions, *possessors* of objects, or *experiencers* of mental processes. Persons can be the objects acted upon, possessed or experienced, the locations where things are situated, or the things located somewhere. In case-grammatical terms, agent, object, and location are roles within processes and activities specified by verbs. Persons can be in places, but agents cannot be in locations. Consequently, one cannot have "a change in location of an initiator" (Huttenlocher et al., 1983, p. 74); one can only have a change in location of an object. That object may be anything at all—a book, a car, or a person. Its location may be changed by an agent, that is, someone moving the book, table, or car. The agent and object roles may be played by the same person, though not necessarily. For example, contrast *John got onto the table* and *John lifted Mary onto the table* (see Edwards, 1973 for a fuller discussion). The source of these confusions is a failure to distinguish between the stative information in sentences involving the case roles (locative, goal, beneficiary, etc.) and their causal information (concerning agents and instruments). A given entity may have a role on both the stative and causal dimensions.

These distinctions take on a special importance when one seeks to classify children's meanings. An utterance such as *daddy chair* may have a larger number of possible readings than are commonly allowed for, even assuming that the individual words are close to their adult meanings. For example:

Agent + Object (e.g., *daddy* is moving the *chair*)
Agent + Location (e.g., *daddy* is putting something on the *chair*)
Object + Location (e.g., *daddy* is on the *chair*)
(Agent and Object) + Location (e.g., *daddy* is getting onto the *chair*)
Possessor + Object (e.g., that's *daddy's chair*)

Clearly, case-grammatical distinctions are useful in elaborating the range of possible meanings of utterances. However, they are not sufficient to establish just what meanings individual utterances actually have. We shall argue that the situation-specific usage of children's early words necessitates a careful pragmatic analysis in order to uncover their real meanings. We do not have the luxury of simply checking against contexts and ticking off preformed case-grammatical categories appropriate to adult speech as they occur. Unfortunately, many researchers have acted as if we do have this easy option. Context of use became a significant factor in the analysis of children's language with Bloom's (1970) demonstration of the importance of meaning for an understanding of early grammar. Compatible observations by Schlesinger (1971) and Slobin (1970) culminated in Brown's (1973) influential synthesis of the interpretations of two- and three-word speech in terms of case grammar. This interpretation gained added plausibility with Edwards's (1973) detailed demonstration, based on evidence from nonlinguistic behavior, that children possessed the cognitive prerequisites, largely in the form of Piagetian sensorimotor intelligence, which were presumed by the case-grammatical interpretation of their speech. The procedure of assigning contextually inferred relational meanings to words and word combinations has since been used in many studies of early speech, including that of Huttenlocher et al. (1983). Unfortunately, much of this work has had a tendency to present these semantic interpretations as a *fait accompli*. The early uses of contextual information were as rather casual aids in a process of semantic interpretation based on analyses of the adult grammar and lexicon and this was duly criticized by Howe (1976). Nonetheless, many studies have treated the establishment of children's meanings as so uncontroversial that little or no supportive evidence (i.e., contextualized examples) is quoted at all. This is the case with Brown (1973) and with Huttenlocher et al. (1983) among others. It is important to realize that it has been demonstrated only that young children have the cognitive capacity to express some of the meanings described by case grammar. Nobody has yet shown with convincing supporting evidence that children do indeed express those meanings. The interpretations of early speech using case grammar still remain essentially a matter of imposing preordained categories on children's meanings.

In some cases, even the context information is of doubtful status. Some researchers (e.g., Bloom, 1970; Wells, 1985) are content to rely on reconstructed accounts of the ongoing situation by participants several hours or even days after the sound recordings were made. Such reconstructions are presumably open to the usual mnemonic distortions (Bartlett, 1932; Bransford, 1979) and must inevitably be prompted by an adult reading of the children's words. Indeed, it is quite possible that the reports of the extralinguistic contexts are reconstructed from interpretations of the words spoken, rather than vice versa.

Accurate semantic interpretation of early language requires more than a superficial matching of words to context. Consider, for example, a child who says *fall down* on occasions when the child allows himself or herself to fall down. According to Huttenlocher et al. (1983) this is a "one entity" verb involving "action of only an initiator," and an unintentional one at that (p. 75). No possibility is envisaged that the term *fall (down)* has any meaning differing from that of standard adult usages.

However, in adult language, the expression specifies the change of location of an object, which is not necessarily the action of an initiator (or agent). Also, in adult usage the expression is not bound to any particular object or pragmatic context. However, if a child only says *fall down* in a particular situational context, then presumably the expression has a particular, idiosyncratic meaning related to that context.

Let us assume for the moment that we have good conceptual and empirical grounds for distinguishing a class of *movement* words from a class of *state change* words, as implied in Huttenlocher's proposition. Huttenlocher et al. postulate (and claim to have demonstrated) the earlier development of movement verbs (e.g., *cough, walk, run, sing*) than of causative stative change verbs (e.g., *bring, buy, clean, fix, give*) in situations where reference is extended to both actions by self and by others. The suggested explanation is that the conceptual prerequisites for the use of state-change verbs are more complex, requiring identification of the intentionality and goal-directedness of other people's behavior over and above parallels between the bodily actions of the self and others. One problem with such an explanation is the obvious alternative noted but not incorporated into the theory: The state change words label events which "are also perceptually complex for an observer" (Huttenlocher, 1983, p. 79). *Cleaning, fixing, buying,* and *cooking* all involve complex transactions and events whose identification poses problems irrespective of the possible involvement of mental states such as intentionality. The young child's putative self-awareness of mental processes and the mental processes of others may have little to do with the primacy of movement words.

The possibility also exists that children's movement words and state-change words may not correspond with those of adults. Words such as *clean, fix,* and *cook*—presumably acquired from observations of adult use, may well have meanings for children that, despite a superficial situational appropriateness, actually refer not to changes but to particular sorts of actions. For example, *clean* may be the sort of motion one does with a cloth or sponge; *fix* may be a certain sort of tinkering one does with particular objects; and *cook* may be an activity involving playing around with pots, pans, and food. The implication is that *for the child* these would not be stative change verbs at all, but rather, movement words, or even less general words constrained to very specific sorts of practical activity. Even the simpler sorts of stative change words, such as, *open, shut,* and *pick up* may, on closer examination, be found to refer to particular sorts of bodily movements or grasping actions. Clearly, semantic classifications are premature unless based on a close comparison of the consistencies and constraints in word usage across different contexts.

Data: Actions and State Changes

If we assume that some apparent state-change verbs might label actions, and that some state-change verbs appear later in development as a result of the cognitive difficulty of recognizing the named process rather than the agent's intentionality, then the following empirical consequences can be explored. First, we would expect to find evidence in early contextual usage for the more complex state-change verbs being used with idiosyncratic, action-specific meanings. Second, we would expect to find earlier adult-like usage of words for the simpler sorts of state change, such as perceivable locative changes (*open, go, pick up, fall*, etc.), in contrast to the more complex transformations (*clean, fix, cook*, etc.).

The data we shall draw on to explore these two points is a fortnightly series of recordings of the situated speech of "Alice," at 16 through 20 months (younger than the subjects in Huttenlocher et al.'s study—whose age range was 22 to 42 months). Concentrating on a single child is justifiable because it is necessary to examine individual instances of contextual usage rather than tables of precoded data, even if the data come from several children. Additional virtues of our method and data include Alice's age (which rules out any suggestion that her accomplishments are merely the result of developmental maturity), and the principle that a single good exception is sufficient to upset any universal rule.

Some of Alice's early language has been described elsewhere (Edwards, 1978a; 1978b; Edwards & Goodwin, in press). The relevant parts of these earlier analyses are the demonstration of an early appreciation of locative change distinct from types of action (Edwards, 1978a), and the argument concerning the action-basis of apparently experiential verbs (Edwards, 1978b; Edwards & Goodwin, in press). We shall concentrate here on Alice's use of words for actions and state changes.

Locative State Changes

Alice, like the other children studied by Bloom (1973), and Greenfield and Smith (1976), appeared to use locative change expressions independently of the actions involved in bringing about such changes, from as early as the single-word period (Edwards, 1978a). Although actions were being performed when these words were used, it was clear, from an examination of the variety of contexts in which the words were used, that these actions were very variable, not always present at all, and that the one consistency of usage was the proximate occurrence of a locative change by some entity. As well as the terms *up* and *down*, which in adult word classes would be prepositions, Alice used adult verbs to express locative change; her vocabulary at 16-18 months included the terms *all-fall (down)*, *dropped-it* and *(all) gone*. The expression *all-fall (down)* clearly derived from frequent uses by S (Sheila, Alice's caretaker) in contexts where objects or Alice herself fell over. (It is, of course, derived from the nursery game Ring o' Roses, at the end of which "we all fall down.") Contexts of use were as follows:

Alice aged 16;1 (Months;weeks)
(1) *all-fall* A has stumbled and fallen to the floor.
(2) *fall, all-fall* A repeatedly and deliberately slips from her feet to her bottom, on a seat cushion.

Alice aged 16;3
(3) *all-fall* A walking to S, having just stumbled and fallen over.

(4) *all-fall down* A has just (accidentally) knocked some of her parents' books onto the floor, and stands looking at them.

All uses of *fall* involve Alice's personal involvement, though she is not necessarily the falling object. The word occurs in both intentional and unintentional contexts with different sorts of action (e.g., letting herself fall is unlike knocking objects over). The use of *all-fall (down)* is comparable therefore to *down*, which replaced it from age 17;3 onwards.

Alice also used the term *dropped-it* in this period, but only in the following types of contexts:

Alice, aged 17;1
(5) *dropped-it* A has accidentally dropped her teddy bear onto the floor and is bending down to pick it up.
(6) /ə/*dropped-it* A has accidentally dropped her toy dog onto the floor, stands looking at it.
(7) *dropped-it* A has been trying to fit two lego bricks together; one falls to the floor; A looking at it.

Alice, aged 18;3
(8) *dropped-it* A was offering toy rabbit to S; it has fallen to the floor as S was reaching for it.

In the above examples, the expression *dropped-it* is clearly context-specific (used only for objects falling from being hand-held by Alice). Unlike *all-fall* and *down*, *dropped-it* was not used for Alice's own body, nor for objects not held; its use was constrained to accidents and defined by criteria similar to an adult's. While limited to Alice herself dropping things, it should be noted that whatever her situational or case-grammatical role, it was neither that of *agent* (intentional initiator of an action), nor that of *object* (the object falling). Indeed, since she was a young child still acquiring motor coordination, and therefore by far the clumsiest person around, it would not be surprising if Alice appeared for this reason alone to be the only person who kept dropping things.

Young children's presyntactic and syntactic uses of *all-gone* or *gone* are among the best known features of early child language. They are characterized by Bloom (1970, 1973) and by Brown (1973) as denoting *nonexistence*, although by the definition of the term given by these authors, and in accordance with the examples of data which they cite, a more accurate term would be *absence* (cf. Clark, 1975). Alice's early use of *gone* and of *all-gone* occurred in the following contexts:

Alice, aged 16;3
(9) looking out of the window for a bus whose engine noise she heard.
(10) looking around the room for a toy tortoise.
(11) having put her pencils into their case and shut the case.
(12) after finishing her dinner.

Alice, aged 17; 1
(13) after S has left the room.

(14) when A was hiding from S under a table.

Alice, aged 17;3
(15) when A was hiding from S behind a curtain.

We shall not dwell on these uses here since they are comparable to similar ones reported throughout the child language literature. However, two points deserve emphasis. First, *gone* and *all-gone* are used to express the locative sense of *absence* (state) or *disappearance* (state change), not to label any sort of action, movement, or state of nonexistence. Second, examples (14) and (15) show that Alice was capable, even at 17 months, of extending the term *all-gone* to include her own disappearance from S's view as well as the disappearance of S and other objects from her own view. Of course, the delight that young children take in playing peek-a-boo is well known. The point here is that Alice appears to be taking account of her own and other people's perceptions.

It seems clear then that Alice, even at the single-word stage, was quite capable of using words to refer to stative change, as long as this change was conceptually and perceptually simple. Moreover, there appears to be no rigid restriction on either the agent or the object of change—it does not have to be Alice herself or any other particular person or object for her to apply the expressions *fall*, *drop*, or *all-gone*.

Having distinguished locative change from types of action, we need now to consider action-words themselves.

Distinguishing Between Actions and State Changes

It was apparent from the first recorded session that Alice had a particular predilection for shutting doors, invariably accompanying such acts with the utterance *shut* (or *shut door*). On face value this could be an utterance describing a particular sort of action (e.g., *push*), a particular sort of state (e.g., being *closed*), or perhaps a particular sort of movement undergone by the door (e.g., swinging shut), or even a label for the door itself. The following are the variety of Alice's usage of this expression.

Alice, aged 16;1
(16) *shut*   A walking toward an open bedroom door; pushes it shut.
(17) *shut*   A pushing washing machine door shut.

Alice, aged 16;3
(18) *shut* / / ə A pushing kitchen door shut.
(19) *shut door*   A walking toward a half-open door. A pulls door wide open and walks through.
(20) *shut door*   A watching as DE (author) closes tape recorder lid.
(21) *shut door*   A pushing playroom door shut.
(22) *shut door*   A picking up a pencil case with its flap open. A closes the flap.
(23) *shut door*   A pushing a kitchen drawer shut.
(24) *shut door*   A pushing an oven door shut (occurred twice).
(25) *shut door*   A folding a multihinged picture book.

Alice, aged 17;1
(26) /ə/*shut* A closing a purse, using fingers and thumbs to press either side of the catch.
(27) *shut* A slamming living room door shut with a two-handed push.
(28) *shut* A folding up a multihinged picture book.
(29) *shut* S has just left the room, pulling the door shut.

The word *door* did not appear by itself until age 17;1, and was then uttered in the context of the door being opened. It seems reasonable, therefore, to treat Alice's earlier utterances as *shut (door)*, with *door* optional and possibly nonmorphemic. Its use with a variety of objects (e.g., doors, lids, folding books, and pencil case flaps) suggests, at best, the general meaning of *thing being shut*. As for *shut* itself, it would appear (at least by age 16;3) that it had a variety of uses comparable to the adult word *shut*; its usage was not restricted to self action—*performative* in Greenfield and Smith's (1976) sense—since the action did not have to be done by Alice herself. The word *shut* occurred across a variety of types of actions, such as pushing, lifting, pressing between the fingers, and so on. Utterance (19) was unique; rather than allowing it to destroy the obvious coherence and sensibility of all the other uses, we may interpret it as consistent. It would seem that Alice saw the half-open door and immediately set off with her intention of shutting it. On reaching the door, however, she simply changed her mind, or was distracted, and walked through. The utterance *shut door* occurred as she set off towards the door, a few seconds before reaching it.

Again, although the variety of actions involved in shutting things was rather dominated by *pushing* doors shut, it can be argued that the use of *shut* was in reference not to the action of pushing, but to the consistent type of change of state undergone by the object. First, this change of state (becoming *closed* in the adult sense) was indeed more consistent than the sort of actions performed by Alice, S and D in closing things. Second, the most frequent recorded uses of the term for pushing doors shut was probably an artifact of Alice's physical environment; she spent much of the time following S from room to room, and all of the rooms involved (as is typical of English houses) had inward-opening doors, which, once inside a room, required pushing rather than pulling shut. Even so, utterance (29) occurred when S *pulled* the door shut from the other side; it is unlikely that Alice thought the door was being pushed. Alice's expression *shut (door)* was therefore descriptive of an event rather than of a particular object, and was descriptive not of a type of action performed, but of a type of change of state undergone by objects that *close*, this change of state invariably being *causative*, that is, instigated by the agency of some person. Thus, contrary to the pattern claimed by Huttenlocher et al. (1983), we have very early evidence of word usage to refer to state changes, both self-initiated and effected by others.

The fact that Alice did not show a similarly productive early use of the word *open* was probably due to the fact that she generally found things much more difficult to open than to close. Despite S's many attempts to encourage Alice both to open things (having previously shut them), and to say the word *open*, Alice remained stubbornly uncooperative in both matters. An examination of how Alice came to use the word *open* reveals some important features of early word-learning.

Alice, aged 16;1
(30) S: Ópen it. Leave it ópen. Ópen the door. (A has just shut the bathroom door.)
(31) S: Alice ópen. Alice ópen. Ópen the door. (A has just shut the bedroom door.)
A: *ópen*. (A standing with back to door, looking at S. S walks past A and opens the door.)
(32) S: I didn't want that door shut, Alice. It's hot in here. Hot. Go and open the door. Ópen. Alice ópen the door. Alice can't. (A has just shut playroom door. A reaches up, grasps doorknob, tries and fails to turn it.)
(33) (A has closed oven door as S was trying to clean it.)
S: Alice open it. Go on. Open. Go on. (A standing looking at S. S opens oven door herself.)

Alice, aged 17;1
(34) A: *door* A walking towards door which has clicked open in draught.
/ s/ *door*
open A, pulling door wide open, walks through.

Alice, aged 18;3
(35) A: *open dóor* A standing by door, eye contact with S.
open dóor
S: No. Sheila musn't.

At ages 16;1 and 16;3 Alice's uses of *open* are imitations of S, preserving the same rising intonation contour and said while looking back at S (with no sign of comprehension or compliance). In sequence (32) Alice does appear to comprehend, but is physically unable to open the door. From age 17;1 Alice's uses of the expressions *open* and *open door* all accompany the successful opening of the door, or else a request that S open the door. Alice appears to have eventually learned what S had been trying to teach her, namely the word *open*. Interestingly, Alice's comprehension and use of the term seemed to be a function of her ability to perform the action required. When trying *un*successfully to open the door, she used another word instead, as we shall see in the following data sequences. Moreover, unlike *shut*, the word *open* remained restricted, for several months, to the successful or requested opening of doors.

These constraints—*successful* or *requested*—are of general importance. It appears from this and other studies, that early word usage is a function of what a child can do, and what a child can get other people to do. Underlying the apparent distinctions between reference to self-initiated and observed action, are powerful pragmatic constraints derived from physical capability and social cooperation. Alice's usage of *shut* and *open* did show some early patterning related to self-action (*shut*) and other-action (*open*). However, the patterning was a matter of predominance rather than exclusivity. Rather than justifying any notion that Alice was unable to generalize between her own and other people's intended actions or goals, it would appear that the asymmetry between self-reference and other-reference is due more to the fact that there are differences between what a young child and his or her caretaker are capable of doing.

Alice's early usage of *open* and *shut* were, as they are for adults, labels for state changes rather than for bodily actions. Early words do not necessarily follow adult usage in this respect. In adult usage, *pull* is an action-verb and *stuck* is an attributive state. As noted briefly by Edwards (1978a), these words in Alice's early vocabulary had more idiosyncratic meanings. A proper examination of them here will reveal both the value of detailed contextual information, and also the importance of the child's practical capabilities in determining word usage. It is instructive to examine both the contexts in which *pull* was used, and also the contexts in which Alice was pulling but did not utter the word. It was not until age 19;1 that the meaning of *pull* as a type of bodily action on things started to become distinguishable from the meaning of *stuck*.

Alice, aged 17;1
(36) A: *pull*   A pulling in vain at the handled of a closed door.
(37) A: *oh*   A pulling string out of a box; it keeps coming and coming. A gives up before pulling it all out. (The vocalization and expression suggest frustration.)
(38) S: You want it ópen, say ópen. Go on. Say ópen.
A: *pull*   A trying in vain to pull her purse open.
S: Open. (A eventually succeeds in opening purse and shuts it again.)
A: /ə/ *shut*
S: Open. Say open. (A pulling again at purse.)
A: *pull*
S: Pull. Say open. (A eventually succeeds again in opening the purse.)
(39) A: *pull*   A trying to pull a book out of a plastic bag, but it is caught and A cannot do it.
pull
S: Pull.
A: *pull* (A eventually manages to extricate the book.)
(40) A: *door*   A trying in vain to pull door open by the handle.
pull
door
(41) A: *door*   A walking towards door which has clicked open in a draught.
/əs/ *door*
ópen   A pulling door wide open, walking through.

Alice, aged 17;3
(42) A: *door*   A pulling door open by the handle; it was not properly shut.
(43) A: /I/ *stuck*   A pulling vainly at handle of toy brush, trying to pull it out of string bag from which it protrudes; A moans and wails.
A: /I/ *stuck*   A eye contact with D. D extricates brush, gives it to A.

Alice, aged 18;1
(44) A: /I/ *stuck*   A is turning a plastic carrier bag around in her hands, pulling at it (apparently trying to get it open.)
A: /ʔɔ/   A drops the bag (frustrated).
/I/ *stuck*

/ʔɔwI/ *stuck*   A pushing bag into S's lap, stands, makes eye contact with S.
S: What's the matter? What's stuck? . . . Want your book?   S opens the bag, gets the book out, gives it to A who reads it.

Alice, aged 18;3
(45) A: *pull*   S gently and absentmindedly pulling at the hair at the back of A's head.
S: Mm?
A: *pull*
S: Oh! (laughing) (S letting go of A's hair.)
(46) A: *stuck*   A vainly trying to pull xylophone striker out of a string bag while the head of striker is caught in the mesh.
S: Mm. Stuck.
A: *pull*
pull
S: Pull. It won't come out that way. Put your hand in. That's it, go on, put your hand in. (A letting go of striker, turning bag around, does not find an opening.)
S: No (laughing). Put your hand in the bag.
A: *stuck*   A pulling at striker again.
S: It's still stuck, yes.
A: *pull*   A still pulling. A starts unfolding the bag and has the striker almost out. A starts pulling again, but it remains stuck.
S: Ah, she's got it.
A: /I/ *stuck*

Alice, aged 19;1
(47) A: *pull*   A looking down at her bib, trying to pull it off.
pull   S pulling A's bib off for her.
(48) A: *pull*   A pulling at part of a toy which is supposed to detach. Eventually it comes off.
S: You got it stuck? Pull. (A pulling at another similar part.)
A: *pull pull*
stuck   A, letting go of the toy, sits back looking at it.

Alice's early uses of *pull*, at 17;1 and 17;3, were always in the context of pulling at objects which were stuck fast and would not move. She never said *pull* when pulling at something which freely came, for example, when pulling a wheeled toy dog along the floor (at 18;1), and in the examples cited above: in (37) pulling string out of a box; and in (41) pulling the door open. Sequence (41) is particularly interesting. Alice had only a minute or two earlier (40) uttered *pull* when pulling in vain at the handle of the closed door. When the door later became free to move, her expressions on pulling it open were *door* and *open*. As we noted earlier, Alice's uses of *open* came in contexts in which things would freely open. At ages 17;3 and 18;1 Alice started to use the word *stuck* in similar situations where she had been using *pull*, when trying in vain to open bags, and to extricate entangled objects from a string bag.

At 18;3 we see the two terms starting to become dissociated. *Stuck* remains in its former usage, based on some physical constraint on Alice's attempts to pull things open or free. *Pull* is similarly used, but also, in (45), Alice uses the term in the context of S gently pulling at her hair (which Alice could feel but not see). It is unlikely here that Alice thought S was trying to tug her hair out of her head! In (46) we see the two words used typically and together in the same context. At age *19;1* the dissociation continues; Alice says *pull* not only when vainly pulling at her bib, but when S easily pulls it free for her. Again, in (48) *stuck* is used at the end when, having pulled vainly at the toy, Alice sits back and has given up pulling. In later transcriptions, *stuck* is used in contexts where Alice need not be pulling, but still where she experiences a physical constraint on her intended action. For example, at age 22;1 she said *stuck* when trying vainly to push a brick to fit onto a construction she was making. While free of its restriction to pulling, the word *stuck* is still not in its adult usage; the brick was not really stuck, but free to move. Alice was simply unable to put it where she wanted to.

Physical constraints imposed by the world on a child's freedom of action and intent are clearly a source not just of knowledge of the nature of the world, but also of early word-meanings. Such meanings can be idiosyncratic, as Alice's were: *Pull* was restricted to pulling in vain; *stuck* was initially restricted to pulling. A casual interpretation would probably assign *pull* to the class of verbs (or *action words*), and *stuck* to the class of adjectives (or *attributives*), each with its usual adult meanings. Such interpretations would be consistent with each context of use—Alice was pulling when she said *pull*, and things were stuck when she said *stuck*. However, our examination of cross-contextual consistency and variation has revealed idiosyncratic usages which were closely linked to physical action and capabilities.

Pull and *stuck* were used exclusively for Alice's own actions. However, contrary to the predictions of Huttenlocher et al. (1983), the state-change terms *shut* and *open* were not similarly constrained. How should we interpret this? The contingencies of physical action seem to be the key factor. It was only Alice herself who had any discernible difficulty in opening doors, purses and bags, or removing detachable objects. Alice's usage of *pull* and *stuck* was restricted to self-reference because only she pulled on various things that seemed stuck. Indeed, it is clear that she had no problem in conceiving of other people's capabilities for action, since she would sometimes resort to other people for help when she was in difficulty—as shown in sequences (43) and (44). Alice's use of words was a reflection of her physical and pragmatic capabilities—what she could do, could not do, or get someone else to do for her.

The Pragmatics of Early Action Words

The data we have examined do not support the hypothesis that difficulties in conceptualizing other people's mental processes and intentions hinder the description of the change-of-state of objects. The verbal description of state-changes posed no problem for Alice so long as the events themselves (shutting doors, moving things) were perceptually and conceptually simple and occurred as part of the practical activities in which Alice was directly involved. The predominance of self-description in early usage of action and state-change terms is accounted for by three factors, none of which imply any solipsism or egocentrism in the young child's understanding of his or her own or other people's mental processes. The determining factors are: (a) The child's attention is largely directed by his or her own activities; (b) There are substantial and systmatic differences between what the child can do and what the child's caretakers can do; (c) The pattern of self-reference and other-reference is affected by the communicative needs of the child. That is, there are particular sorts of activities that the child has to request to perform, seek assistance from others in performing for himself or herself, or cooperate with others to accomplish.

As soon as it is appreciated that the use of action words is rooted in the practicalities of physical actions and transactions with other people, then the observed asymmetry in the pattern of reference to actions by the self and by others falls naturally into place. Many words in early speech are performatively self-directive, or encode practical difficulties, physical constraints, or prohibitions on freedom of action. Other words are used to direct and coordinate joint attention to or action upon the physical world, or to request actions from others. It is these pragmatic aims which underlie the patterning of children's early reference to self actions and the actions of others.

In seeking to maintain a sharp distinction between self-reference and observed action, on the one hand, and state-change and movement verbs on the other, Huttenlocher et al. (1983) are led into some questionable interpretations of their data. For example, *come* and *go* (and presumably *gone*) were excluded from their categories of change-verbs or movement-verbs referring to observed actions by other people. This was done not because these words did not occur in utterances which referred to some person other than the speaker as agent, but on the grounds that the child, as speaker, was always situationally involved as the source or goal of the movement. That is to say, the movement was always being made toward or away from the child. This exclusion seems arbitrary not only because the same condition would also hold for many adult uses of the verbs but also because it is clearly the agent who is responsible for the intentional movement. The verb *do* is similarly excluded from the analysis because it "is a dummy verb that can stand in for action verbs with any number or type of semantic roles" (p. 85). This exclusion removes some potentially embarrassing data: 22% of the uses of *do* encoded observed actions; 28% encoded action requests; and 50% encoded self-action. Huttenlocher et al. justify the exclusion on the grounds that

> While the percentage of descriptions of observed actions using *do* is higher than the overall percentage of verbs used to encode observed action, it is similar to the percentage of single-entity verbs used to encode observed actions (23%). Thus the children may have noted simply that people were moving in a particular way when they used *do* and not that they were achieving a goal (p. 85).

But this is just an admission that they are giving themselves the benefit of the doubt. In adult speech, the verb *do* can function as an auxiliary or (*dummy verb*), but it can also function as a main verb which refers to an intentional action of an unspecified type, that is, as a *general action word* or *pro-verb*. Clark (1978) notes that young children often rely upon *general purpose verbs* such as *do*, *make*, *put*, and *go*, since they do not yet know the specific verbs referring to different types of actions, however, "the specific actions picked out by the general purpose verbs seem very obvious with the context supplied" (p. 957). According to Clark (1978)

> General purpose verbs are similar in function, then, to the deictic terms *this* and *that* used for talking about objects. Both play an important communicative role in the early stages of language acquisition. Both constitute devices whereby children can stretch their resources to the uttermost (pp. 957-958).

Clearly, the importance of such verbs calls for their being given a separate analysis rather than merely excluded for dubious grammatical reasons.

Mental Process Verbs

Our basic findings extend to the development of mental as well as physical verbs. Shatz, Wellman, and Silber (1983) present a careful study of the acquisition of mental verbs by children aged two to four years based on a functional coding system. They conclude that

> Mental verbs are not first used to refer to internal mental states or processes, however. Our functional analysis revealed that all seven children who ultimately produced a mental process reference had previously used mental verbs with at least the Directing of Interaction functions (p. 317).

Examples of this function included seeking to introduce information (*know what?*) and introducing activities (*I guess I'll go for a ride*). Many of these expressions seemed to be stereotypic forms of which the children could not have had a full adult-like understanding.

The initial use of *mental verbs* to direct the attention of a caretaker, rather than to refer to mental states, is also described by Edwards and Goodwin (in press). Alice initially used *see*, accompanied by manual gestures and directed gaze, as a deictic term, within the context of Sheila asking her to find named objects. The use of *see* was then extended to situations in which vision is either difficult or novel, such as suddenly seeing a reflection on the screen of a switched-off television. It seems probable that children do not start to understand *see* as a mental verb until they experience situations in which either their caretaker can see something but they cannot, or vice versa.

Thus, mental as well as physical verbs first appear in the speech of young children only in particular contexts. A careful examination of these contexts reveals that many of the verbs are not being used with their standard adult meanings. Because of this we are not entitled to ascribe either the full adult meanings to the children's words, or even a sub-set of the semantic features thereof. The only way in which we can hope to infer what meanings children do give to their words is by searching for commonalities in the contexts in which individuals words are used. Shatz et al. (1983) have made a start on exploring the development of mental verbs by this means but much remains to be done. For example, they admit that their data do not show definitely whether or not mental verbs are initially used only with reference to the self.

Conclusions

The study which we have reported here is small in range and draws its data from a single child. Nonetheless, it permits two important conclusions to be drawn. Firstly, this study has shown that semantic analyses which are derived from the study of adult language should be extended to child language only with caution. This is because we cannot simply assume that such analyses will necessarily apply to the semantic system of the child, which may be quite idiosyncratic. Instead, it seems that the most suitable way to study semantic development is by means of a careful and systematic examination of children's utterances in context. Secondly, this study has shown that what young children say is influenced by their communicative needs. In particular, the pragmatics of physical capability and of the need to request assistance probably underlie the apparent asymmetry of early references to the actions of self and others. It is our contention that if we are to make any serious progress in understanding the early acquisition of verb meaning, it is necessary to pay far greater attention to the examination of children's utterances in context, and to the exploration of the possible interactions between the pragmatics and the semantics of children's early verbs.

References

Bartlett, F. C. (1932). *Remembering: A study in experimental and social psychology*. Cambridge: Cambridge University Press.
Bloom, L. (1970). *Language development: Form and function in emerging grammars*. Cambridge, MA: MIT Press.
Bloom, L. (1973). *One word at a time: The use of single word utterances before syntax*. The Hague: Mouton.
Bloom, L., & Lahey, M. (1978). *Language development and language disorders*. New York: Wiley.
Bransford, J. D. (1979). *Human cognition: Learning, understanding and remembering*. Belmont, CA: Wadsworth.
Brown, R. W. (1973). *A first language: The early stages*. London: Allen & Unwin Ltd.

Clark, E. V. (1978). Strategies for communicating. *Child Development*, *49*, 953-959.
Clark, R. (1975). Review of Lois Bloom, "One word at a time." *Journal of Child Language*, *2*, 169-183.
Edwards, D. (1973). Sensory-motor development and semantic relations in early child grammar. *Cognition*, *2*, 395-434.
Edwards, D. (1978a). The sources of children's early meanings. In I. Markova (Ed.), *The social context of language*. Chichester: Wiley.
Edwards, D. (1978b). Social relations and early language. In A. J. Lock (Ed.), *Action, gesture and symbol: The emergence of language*. London: Academic Press.
Edwards, D., & Goodwin, R. Q. (in press). The language of shared attention and visual experience: A functional study of early nomination. *Journal of Pragmatics*, *4*(9).
Fillmore, C. J. (1968). The case for case. In E. Bach & R. T. Harms (Eds.), *Universals in linguistic theory*. New York: Holt, Rinehart & Winston.
Greenfield, P. M., & Smith, J. H. (1976). *The structure of communication in early language development*. New York: Academic Press.
Howe, C. J. (1976). The meaning of two-word utterances in the speech of children. *Journal of Child Language*, *3*, 29-47.
Huttenlocher, J., Smiley, P., & Charney, R. (1983). Emergence of action categories in the child: Evidence from verb meanings. *Psychological Review*, *90*, 1, 72-93.
Schlesinger, I. M. (1971). Production of utterances and language acquisition. In D. I. Slobin (Ed.), *The ontogenesis of grammar*. New York: Academic Press.
Shatz, M., Wellman, H. M., & Silber, S. (1983). The acquisition of mental verbs: A systematic investigation of the first reference to mental state. *Cognition*, *14*, 301-321.
Slobin, D. I. (1970). Universals of grammatical development in children. In G. B. Flores d'Arcais & W. M. Levelt (Eds.), *Advances in psycholinguistics*. Amsterdam: North-Holland.
Wells, G. (1985). *Language development in the pre-school years*. Cambridge: Cambridge University Press.

11. Verbs and Time

John McShane, Stephen Whittaker, and Julie Dockrell

Cutting Up Verbs

Possibly no other area of the lexicon is as complex as verbs. They not only convey information about events and states but also about motives, intentions, causality—to mention but a few dimensions. In addition, verbs can be inflected for tense and aspect and thus are the major means of conveying temporal information. An account of how the child masters the verb system would necessarily play a central role in a complete account of language development.

Among the questions that require answering are at least the following: In the early stages of language acquisition, what types of verbs are learned first? Are certain types of verbs acquired earliest as a result of input frequency or as a result of conceptual limitations on what events can be encoded by the young child? What is the developmental course of establishing the accurate denotation of a verb? Are the earliest learned verbs organized in a single category or in several subcategories? If there is subcategorical organization, as some have argued, does this affect the way in which inflections are learned? What types of reorganization does the system undergo over time? How do children learn the principles of grammatical agreements that govern the relation between verbs and other parts of speech?

All of these questions, and the list is by no means exhaustive, raise their own set of finer theoretical and methodological issues. The verb lexicon poses a considerable challenge; one to which all too little attention has been devoted. Our primary aim is to map out some of the issues that have concerned us in our recent research and to show, as far as possible, how these issues are related. We shall have little to say here about what might be called the first level of the lexicon: the way in which the denotation of individual verbs is established. Howver, we have been concerned with the next level of organization: the way in which verbs are treated by the child as being of a particular *type*. The major dimensions of verb typology are concerned with time. Thus, in order to explore the organization of the verb lexicon, it is necessary to consider the complex relations between verbs and time. These relations are encoded by various inflectional modifications of the verb stem, and so, the child's use and understanding of verb inflections will be of central importance to this issue.

During development, a child must learn a large number of words that can be used to refer to events and states; the child must learn about the many interrelations among these words; and the child must learn how to modify any particular word in order to convey temporal information. Some of the problems that the child faces are familiar problems in learning any substantive word, but some are also more specific to verbs. Among the familiar classification problems are the denotation of a particular word and its sense relations with other words. Questions about precisely what action *walk* denotes and what the differences are between walking and other forms of motion are similar in outline to questions about learning the denotation of *dog* and the distinctions between dogs and other animals (see McShane & Dockrell, 1983, for a review of the latter issues). However, the familiarity of this issue should not lead to the supposition that the lexical classification of verbs is analogous to that of nouns. We shall argue that there are considerable differences between the two, especially in hierarchical organization.

Subcategories for Verbs

There are many ways in which one can explore the internal organization of the verb lexicon. Attempts have been made to construct adult verb taxonomies on the basis of semantic primitives and alternatively on the basis of communicative intent. Miller and Johnson-Laird (1976), for example, use procedural semantics as their basis for subdividing verbs among the categories of motion, posssession, vision, and communication. Dixon (1971) has offered a more detailed semantically based system that distinguishes among position (including rest and motion), affect, giving, attention, speaking and gesturing, other bodily activities, and metaverbs of breaking off some state or action. Among pragmatic theorists the pioneering work was carried out by Austin (1962) who distinguished five general types of illocutionary act: verdictives, exercitives, commissives, behabitives, and expositives. Austin's taxonomy was a preliminary attempt at classification and was avowedly not intended as definitive. Several later works have attempted to improve on Austin's efforts, most notably Searle (1975) and Bach and Harnish (1979).

The semantic and the pragmatic categories divide verbs in quite different ways. While this is not especially surprising, it is important to note that either a semantic or a pragmatic approach can be adopted to categorization. There is no similar duality with the categorization of nominals. The fact that there is such a duality with verbs suggests that the mental organization of the verb lexicon will be complex and multidimensional, based both upon semantic similarities and pragmatic equivalences. To date, the ways in which these factors interact in conceptual organization have been relatively neglected. Ultimately, it is an important task to uncover the principles by which verbs are related in the adult lexicon. However, the present state of affairs of this area suggests that there is little that can be used at present to cast light on developmental issues.

An alternative approach is to create a taxonomy of children's verbs without reference to adult taxonomies. Bloom, Lightbown, and Hood (1975), for example, identified seven categories of verb relations in the speech of a sample of four children aged between 19 and 26 months. The categories, which are essentially semantic, were action, locative action, locative state, notice, state, intention, and causality. The question of interest to us here is whether these categories reflect principles of semantic organization used by the child as opposed to an organization of the data by the adult theorist. The issue is, of course, a notoriously difficult one, because of the complex problem of devising a criterion of mental organization in young children. Bloom et al. used a criterion of productivity—five or more utterance types in a category in a given speech sample—and found certain relations in the order of emergence of the categories: Actions were encoded before states and nonlocative relations were encoded before locative relations. Whether or not this reflects a primitive semantic segmentation of verbs is a moot point. Bowerman (1975) has pointed out that using a fixed criterion of productivity as a measure of acquisition causes the more frequently used constructions to appear to become productive earlier than the less frequently used constructions. This argument, however, addresses itself to the issue of sequence only; it presupposes that the categories reflect organizational principles used by the child. An alternative possibility is that the words have been learned item-by-item as encodings of particular situations about which children and caretakers communicate. If communication is biased (for whatever reason) toward certain types of situations, then these types of situations will appear productive before other types. In sum, it must be concluded that productivity on its own is insufficient as a criterion either for the existence of categories or for the order of acquisition of categories.

If some taxonomic division is psychologically real for the child, this will be reflected in selective differences between the categories with respect to some facet of the child's linguistic behavior. The concern of this paper is whether there are principles of semantic subcategorization that affect the way in which verb inflections are learned. When children begin to learn inflections, do they simply add these to every verb they already know (and this begs the question of how they know to which words the inflections should be added), or do they add them to selected subcategories of verbs? A further issue concerns the meaning encoded by the inflections. But all of this in time.

Terminology

There is a peculiar difficulty in using the terms *noun*, *verb*, and *adjective* in developmental studies of language. The terms denote grammatical categories but the developmentalist frequently wants to draw attention to the lexical word-object relation—not a grammatical word-form-class relation. It is important not to conflate these two relations. Understanding that *dog* denotes a certain class of entities is not the same as understanding that *dog* is a member of a grammatical category with all the privileges and restrictions of that category. It would be convenient to have one categorical label to signify a word-object relation and another to signify a word-form-class relation. In the case of words like *dog* there is little problem. The terms *name* or *nominal* can be used for the word-entity relation and the term *noun* can be used for the word-form-class relation. However, in the case of *verb* (and *adjective* and *adverb*), there is no accepted alternative to the form-class label for the lexical relation. The term *verbal* does not function easily as an equivalent of *nominal* because the term itself has other connotations. Consequently, we shall use the term *verb* both as a form-class label and as a lexical label. The ambiguity is regrettable but, short of coining is neologism, it is inevitable.

Verbs can be divided into two broad types: those that denote *dynamic* and those that denote *static* situations. The term *situation* has been adopted by a number of writers (e.g., Comrie, 1976; Lyons, 1977; Miller & Johnson-Laird, 1976) as the superordinate term and we follow this practice here. Static situations allow the convenient term *state* but dynamic situations have no similarly convenient term. However, it has been common, if unsystematic, practice to use the term *event* to signify all nonstates (e.g., Bull, 1960) and we shall adopt this practice. Later, we shall have occasion to draw further distinctions.

Time Talk

Much of discourse is about situations that are remote in time from the present. A language must have a means of dealing with the different types of remoteness that are possible and of ordering situations relative to one another. The major means by which this is done is by modification of the verb (either by inflection or the addition of auxiliaries) to denote temporal ordering. This is the tense system of a language. But, taken on its own terms without reference to any other situation, each individual situation has its own temporal contour: at some point it begins, continues for some time, then ends. In referring to a situation, a speaker might wish to draw attention to some feature of the temporal contour of a situation (e.g., to describe a point "in the middle" at which the situation has begun but not yet ended). The way in which a language encodes the situation's temporal contour is called its aspectual system. Languages differ in their aspectual systems but modifications of the verb are the major means of encoding aspect. In this section we shall discuss first the conceptual basis of tense and aspect and then some developmental issues that relate to these concepts.

In our treatment of the topics of tense and aspect we shall begin with an analysis of the distinctions underlying the domain of time talk and examine what cognitive and communicative skills are necessary for their operation. We shall then examine how these distinctions are realized in language, that is, we shall investigate how the semantics of time map onto the system of verb inflections.

Tense and aspect are concerned with the various temporal relations that hold within and between situations. Any analysis of these relations must therefore begin at the level of situations and their properties. The most important property of situations is that they occur in *sequences*. That is, for any two situations it is possible to order them in time. A second property of situations is that they possess internal temporal contour. Most situations can be conceived of as having a beginning, a middle, and an end. This second property is not true of all situations, however, a fact that has implications for the use of aspectual distinctions.

We may represent time as a line of infinite extent stretching from left to right. If situations are represented as points then, in Figure 11-1, S_1 occurs before S_2 and S_3; S_2 occurs after S_1 and before S_3; and S_3 occurs after S_2 and S_1.

Tense

As we have represented situations to this point, the observer has been outside the frame of reference. If we now place the observer on the time line in Figure 11-1, we introduce the necessary dynamic element for an understanding of tense. Consider the passage of time as an imaginary observer travelling from left to right on the time line. As the observer travels, the observer's relation to the situations S_1, S_2, and S_3 changes. If we represent the observer's situation as S_0 and let $<$ represent before and $>$ after, then at some point t_0

$$S_0 < (S_1, S_2, S_3)$$

while later after the observer has passed S_1 but not yet reached S_2

$$S_0 > (S_1), < (S_2, S_3)$$

while later still after S_3 has been reached

$$S_0 > (S_1, S_2), = (S_3).$$

As McTaggart (1927) observed "an event, which is now present, was future, and will be past."

The observer who wishes to communicate about his or her experiences will need to establish some situation that serves to fix his or her relation with S_1, S_2, and S_3. Further, if a situation is to serve this function for an audience, then it must be readily identifiable as a situation that the audience can locate in time. One situation that uniquely fixes the temporal relations for both speaker and audience is the act of talking (S_t) itself. The act of talking occurs in the present for both speaker and audience and is the basis of the simple tenses. If we designate as S_d the situation to which reference is made, then the relative ordering of situations that give rise to the past,

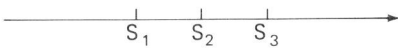

Figure 11-1. Time line with three discrete situations.

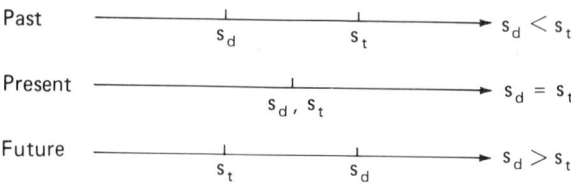

Figure 11-2. The temporal relation between S_d and S_t in the past, present, and future.

present, and future can be represented as in Figure 11-2. If we next examine how these temporal relations are realized in language, we find that in English there is not a simple mapping between the temporal relations outlined in Figure 11-2 and the tense system. As Miller and Johnson-Laird remark:

> The basic distinction in the English tense system is twofold, not threefold. It can distinguish past from nonpast; it cannot distinguish the nonpast present from the nonpast future. The trouble begins to appear when we stop to realize that the simple present, as in "he arrives," is more often than not understood as habitual or future, not as "He arrives right now".... When people want to communicate the "right now" sense, they generally use the present progressive, "He is arriving" (1976, p. 437).

However, if the tense system of English is twofold, it does not mean that there are only two temporal relations in English. The regular past tense in English is denoted by the addition of *-ed* to the verb stem, as in *he walked*. The simple present is denoted by the use of the nonpast tense, as in *he walks*, and the future is denoted either by the modal auxiliary *shall/will* with the verb stem as in *he will walk*, or by the nonpast tense as in *he walks (in the parade tomorrow)*. Contextually, there is rarely any ambiguity about whether the nonpast tense refers to the present or the future.

To summarize, the location of situations in time requires a number of conceptual and linguistic skills. The conceptual skills involve the construction of the various relations of sequence between situations and the communicative skills lie in the selection of an appropriate reference point to meet the needs of the audience and an appropriate method of linguistic encoding.

Aspect

Thus far, we have represented situations as points. However, if we allow that each individual situation may have its own internal temporal contour, then a variety of further relations among situations becomes possible, especially simultaneity, overlap, and inclusion. Whereas tense is concerned with the relations between situations, aspect is concerned with the temporal contour of one individual situation. The major general distinction here is between perfective and imperfective aspects (Comrie, 1976). In English, the specific distinction is between the nonprogressive and the progressive.

In the examples *I was walking* and *I walked* the tense is the same as can be seen in (a) and (b) in Figure 11-3. In both, we have absolute past tense denoted respec-

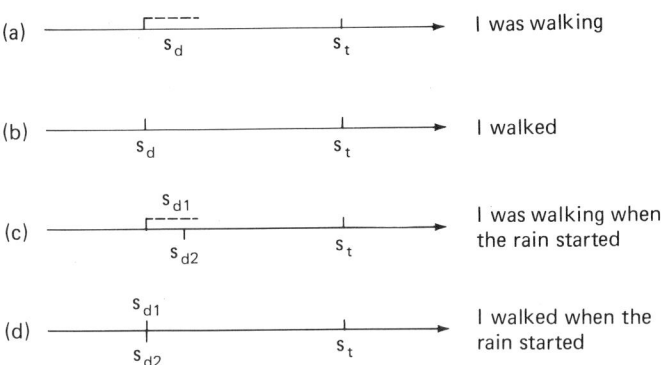

Figure 11-3. The temporal realtions between S_d and S_t described by different utterances.

tively by the irregular past *was* and the *-ed* inflection. The difference between the sentences is one of aspect. In *I was walking*, which has imperfective or progressive aspect, the situation is described as evolving, and it is easy to see how other situations that occurred simultaneously with that of walking could be described within such a framework as in *I was walking when the rain started* [see (c) in Figure 11-3]. In *I walked*, which has perfective or nonprogressive aspect, the situation is described without any reference to its evolution and it is not possible to describe other situations that occurred simultaneously without further scene-setting. If, for example, I wish to describe the co-occurrence of walking and raining I cannot say *I walked when the rain started*, whose meaning is quite different from *I was walking when the rain started* as can be seen by comparing (c) and (d) in Figure 11-3. Instead, I must say something like *I walked and while I was walking the rain started*, which is a combination of (b) and (c) in Figure 11-3.

Figure 11-3, represents the distinction between perfective and imperfective aspect: situations can either be represented as point-like or as extended in time. When a situation is represented as extended in time, the aspectual description is not of the complete extension but rather, it draws attention to some portion of the temporal contour, whether this be its inception, its ongoing nature, or its termination. This figure is an outline only of some of the concepts of time and time talk. Let's now turn to a consideration of the issues relevant to the development of time talk.

Stative Verbs and the English Progressive

A deep-rooted aspectual distinction in linguistic and psychological writing on verbs is that between events and states. The distinction is especially relevant to the learning of inflections because Brown (1973) has remarked that at Stage 1 none of his subjects ever used the progressive *-ing* with a stative verb and comments that "this is surprising because all the other inflections, the past and present indicative on the verb, the plural and possessive on the noun, were overgeneralized to unsuitable stems" (p. 172). Brown argues that the invulnerability of statives to over-generalization is due to a primitive, possibly innate, categorical distinction by the child between states and events. He adds "consequently the distributional break in the inflection following the lines of these covert classes would be easily learned and followed" (p. 172). This claim is powerful in two respects: it suggests a very fundamental psychological division of verbs and it suggests that this division resists an error of overgeneralization that might be expected from the distribution of other errors. Before examining the validity of Brown's claims, it will first be necessary to establish what is meant by the terms *state* and *event*.

What sets of situations do stative verbs denote? Most linguists find little difficulty in providing lists of stative verbs (Comrie, 1976; Leech, 1971; Lyons, 1977; Palmer, 1965; Vendler, 1957). Palmer identifies the following verbs of state: *contain, belong, matter, deserve, consist, please, depend, own* and includes what he calls a rather special subgroup—verbs which indicate the quality of creating sensations (e.g., *smell* and *taste*). Leech (1971) draws up the following list: *be, live, belong, last, like, stand, know, have,* and *contain*. Lyons (1968) suggests that we may use the term *state* to refer to location, quality, condition, and possession, while Leech (1971) offers a more detailed subdivision of states: (1) verbs of inert perception, for example, *feel*; (2) verbs of inert cognition, for example, *know*; (3) verbs of having and being, for example, *contain*; and verbs of bodily sensation, for example, *ache*. Leech's framework fails to account for a number of verbs that are commonly taken to denote states, for example, *sit* and *stand*—an intersting omission given that *stand* is viewed as a prototypical state verb by Leech himself (1971, p. 5).

Two different sets of criteria have been offered to distinguish stative from nonstative verbs: *language external* and *language internal*. Language external criteria appeal to objective differences between a state and an event. Language internal criteria appeal to differences in grammatical privileges as a distinguishing criterion between stative and dynamic verbs. The criteria are not exclusive; it would not be surprising to find a language external criterion mirrored in a language internal one, but there is, on the other hand, no necessity for this to be the case.

Language Internal Criteria for Stative Verbs. The usual linguistic test for a stative verb, as Comrie (1976), Lyons (1968), and Miller and Johnson-Laird (1976) all point out, is that it does not freely take the progressive form. However, a good deal hinges here on *freely* because the condition is very much a matter of degree. Verbs such as *know* seem to resist the progressive in all contexts, but verbs such as *stand* or *live* take the progressive with relative ease. The complexities of the progressive and its uses are considerable (see Comrie, 1976), but it is enough to observe here that whether or not a verb takes the progressive is not a sufficient criterion of distinction between stative and nonstative verbs.

Other language internal criteria have been proposed to distinguish stative and nonstative verbs. It has been argued that stative verbs cannot appropriately be used to answer questions of the form *What is X doing?* (Lyons, 1977), or *What's happening?* (Chafe, 1970). The former question would appear to be a rephrasing of the argument that stative verbs cannot take the progressive. Appropriate responses to the question *What is Charles doing?* are *Charles is standing* or *dying* or *looking* (all the progressive of verbs characterized as stative). Similarly, responses to *What's happening?* produce acceptable uses of stative verbs.

It has also been argued that the imperative cannot be used with stative verbs (cf. Miller & Johnson-Laird, 1976). This criterion is derived from Allen's (1955) suggestion that these verbs are not strictly under human control. If states are not under human control, it is logically impossible to respond to a command requiring the implementation of a particular state. However, with many stative verbs the imperative can be used, for example, *Stand to attention*, *Sit down*, *Go to sleep*, and so on. Equally, there are numerous nonstative verbs that are odd in the imperative; *digest* for example.

We may conclude that there are no satisfactory language-internal criteria to identify stative verbs. In each instance we can see that there are many exceptions to the proposed general rule. Nonetheless, intuitively, states do seem to differ from nonstates. Leech, for example, argues that "the choice between 'state' and 'event' is inherent in all verbal usage in English" (1971, p. 4). Since the distinction between states and nonstates is essentially semantic, it may be preferable to seek the basis of the distinction in language external criteria.

Language External Criteria for States. A number of objective criteria have been proposed to distinguish *states* from *events*. The majority of these, in one form or another, refer to the duration and nature of the situation. Palmer (1965) notes that a sense of duration is integral to the notion of states. But states need not last for an extended period of time. It is possible to sleep, stand, own, or live for relatively short periods of time. Conversely, many events can be of extended duration; one can walk all day, spend weeks making a chair, and so on. Duration by itself cannot suffice to differentiate static from dynamic situations.

Lyons (1977) offers a slightly different characterization of states, which does not rest completely on the notion of duration. He argues that static situations are ones that are conceived of as existing rather than happening, and as being homogeneous, continuous, and unchanging throughout their duration. The notion of homogeneity is further developed by Leech (1971) who views a state as undifferentiated and lacking in defined limits. It is not at all clear how these notions do distinguish between static and dynamic situations. As far as defined limits are concerned, many states start and end as do events, for example, I will die after living, wake up after sleeping, stand after sitting. It is equally difficult to see how sleeping differs from running in terms of either continuity or homogeneity throughout the specific period of time. Vendler (1957) tries to capture the distinction by noting that events consist of successive phases following one another in time while states do not. Comrie (1976) argues that for *states*, we shall find exactly the same situation whichever point in time we choose to cut in on, whereas for *events*, different phases of the situation will be different. However, it is unclear how one might objectively identify the phases in certain nonstates, for example, winning and arriving. Alternatively, one can imagine phase-like components of some states, for example, sleeping.

Comrie (1976) offers an alternative characterization where the critical issue is energy input.

With a state, unless something happens to change that state, then the state will continue: this applies equally to standing and to knowing. With a dynamic situation, on the other hand, the situation will only continue if it is continually subject to a new input of energy: this applies equally to running and to emitting a pure tone, since if John stops putting any effort into running, he will come to a stop and if the oscilloscope is cut off from its source of power it will no longer emit a sound (p. 49).

The key issue here is to operationalize the concept of energy input, and it is unclear how this might be done. However, input of energy presumably results in some behavioral manifestation in the situation, for example, the sound continues or the legs continue to rise for running. It may, therefore, be possible to distinguish states from events on the basis of the presence or absence of related action criteria. Such a definition avoids bringing into play assumptions that rely on concepts that are difficult to operationalize. How might this work?

None of the state verbs identified by Leech as prototypical involve action that is related to the said state. For example, that my hands might be in constant motion while I am sitting has no bearing on my state of sitting. The same is true for believing, standing, knowing, and seeing. On the other hand, dynamic verbs necessarily involve overt action that is related to the particular situation. We cannot run without moving our legs, *sing* without moving our mouths, or *buy* without involving ourselves in some transaction. This distinction also helps us to deal with some of the cases where verbs can be used to denote both static and dynamic situations. It is not the case that stative and dynamic verbs are mutually disjoint categories (cf. Vendler, 1957; Joos, 1964). Rather, it would appear to be the case that when stative verbs like *smell* and *feel* are used in a dynamic way they refer to active rather than inert perception (cf. Leech, 1971). Nonetheless, this is not a completely satisfactory definition to distinguish between static and dynamic situations, though it appears to be the best we have. There are instances of events, for example, digesting, observing, for which it is difficult to identify a relevant observable action. At best it is possible to identify prototypical dynamic and static situations with the present criteria. It seems more than likely that the distinction between static and dynamic situations is a relative rather than an absolute one.

We have argued that there are no clear language-internal criteria to distinguish stative from dynamic verbs and we have only been able to formulate a fuzzy language-external criterion. Since we are dealing with a semantic category, the fuzziness is hardly surprising; the boundaries of the majority of semantic categories are fuzzy (Labov, 1973; Lehrer, 1970).

Is There Evidence for a Distinction Between Stative and Dynamic Verbs in the Language of Young Children? We return now to the question of whether children distinguish categorically between static and dynamic situations. As we have seen, Brown (1973) notes that at Stage 1 none of his subjects ever used the progressive with a stative verb and he argued that the invulnerability of statives to overgeneralization is due to a primitive, categorical distinction by the child between states and events.

There is reason for caution in accepting Brown's claim. No direct evidence is presented that young children make a categorical distinction between states and events. The evidence in favor of the distinction is based on Brown's examination of the data collected in his longitudinal study. However, it is difficult to know whether the evidence is derived from a detailed examination of the child's use of inflections or whether it relies on the absence of overt errors. A detailed examination of inflections could be conducted by grouping together all the verbs used with the progressive inflection and then examining whether there were any stative verbs among these. If no stative verbs were found in this grouping, then it might reasonably be concluded that children distinguish categorically between stative and dynamic verbs. The conclusion would be strengthened by the fact that although the combination of stative verb and progressive inflection is possible, this combination is, apparently, resisted. However, if the evidence for the claim advanced derives instead from an absence of overt errors, such as *knowing*, then the conclusion is weak in the extreme because, as we have shown, very many stative verbs do take the progressive (cf. also Brown, 1973) and these verbs, presumably, would not have been classified as errors. Thus, error analysis would not establish whether or not the progressive is used selectively with nonstative verbs.

If it is the case that children draw a distinction between states and events, then it ought to be possible to obtain direct evidence for this. Accordingly, we designed an experiment to test: (a) whether children can draw a distinction between *situations* commonly described as static and those commonly described as dynamic; (b) whether children can draw a distinction between *verbs* commonly described as stative and those commonly described as nonstative; and (c) whether there is any development in these categorization processes with age. The experiment used a technique devised by Braine and Wells (1978). They developed a method for exploring the semantic concepts of 4- and 5-year-old children. In their experiment, children were shown pictures of scenes accompanied by simple descriptive sentences, for example, *The big bear is washing the little bear with a washcloth*. During the training phase, the children learned to place tokens of different shapes on the objects in the pictures according to the role the objects played in the scene. The reasoning behind the experiment was as follows: If 4-year-olds actually possess concepts like *actor* or *agent* then they should associate the tokens with the roles that they perceive the objects to be playing in the pictured scenes. On the other hand, if 4-year-olds do not possess these concepts, then with this training procedure they should find it difficult if not impossible to learn these concepts. Our reasoning was that if the distinction between static and dynamic situations is psychologically real, then children should have no difficulty in learning the distinction using the Braine and Wells technique.

In our study, we began by introducing the children to a collection of small, identical teddy bears. The child was told that the bears were going on a picnic. The child was told that each bear would engage in one situation on the picnic and the child was required to assign the bear either a red or blue badge depending on whether the situation was a state or an event. The procedure for allocating badges (described below) constituted the training phase of the experiment.

We tested 96 children. There were three different age groups with mean ages of 4;0, 5;6, and 6;7. The experiment consisted of four stages: a pretest, an introduction, training, and, for some children, a test of generalization, which will not be reported here.

The pretest established that the child could understand the denotation of the eight verbs to be used. In the introduction, the experimenter told the child which of the two badges to associate with each of the two types of situation. In the training phase, the child had to allocate to each bear a badge of the correct color. There were two conditions in this phase: demonstration and verbal. In the demonstration condition the child was told that four of the bears would engage in static situations (such as sleeping, sitting, etc.) and four would engage in dynamic situations (such as running, jumping, etc.). Each situation was demonstrated to the child as it was described and the bear was given a badge. In the verbal condition, the situations were described to the child without demonstration. For each child, one color badge was associated with static situations and the other color with dynamic situations. The color was varied randomly as was the order in which the situations were described. The child was taught to award the correct color badge to each bear. Training continued until either all eight bears were given the correct badge or five complete trials of eight situations had been conducted. A pilot study had shown that if children failed correctly to allocate the badges on the fifth trial (approximately 45 minutes of testing), they failed to learn the distinction.

In Braine and Wells' study, learning in the training sessions was essentially errorless. They argue that "the extremely rapid learning suggested that these meaning categories were ones that the children brought with them to the experiment" (p. 102). In contrast, in our experiment only one child (2%) in the verbal condition and nine children (19%) in the demonstration condition produced errorless learning. Despite the children's initial difficulties, the distinction was learnable, but not with equal facility in the two conditions.

Table 11-1 shows the number of children who succeeded in learning the distinction by the fifth trial. It is evident that the youngest children found the verbal condition significantly harder than the demonstration condition ($\chi^2 = 11.13$, $p < .01$) whereas there is no such difference for the older children. Further, while there is no difference among the age groups for success in the demonstration condition ($\chi^2 = 3.4$) there is a significant difference across the three age groups for the verbal condition ($\chi^2 = 10.30$, $p < .01$), with the older children being increasingly more successful in the verbal condition.

It is evident from this preliminary study that, although children can learn the

Table 11-1. Number of Children Who Learned the Distinction Between States and Events

Mean age	Condition	
	Demonstration	Verbal
4;0	13	3
5;6	9	7
6;7	13	12

Note: We tested 16 children in each condition.

distinction between states and nonstates, it does not come easily to them and this would suggest that there is little basis to the claim that this distinction is one that is innate. This conclusion is strengthened by the demonstration of age trends in the learning of the distinction. Further, the mapping from a situational distinction to a semantic one is not automatic: younger children could master the distinction in the demonstration but not in the verbal condition. There is little evidence here to suggest that there are semantic cases of state and nonstate that the child deploys initially in the organization of lexical and grammatical knowledge. Even if it is the case that the progressive is initially restricted to dynamic verbs, the explanation of this phenomenon is not to be found in a natural categorical division of the situations denoted by verbs.

Dynamic Events and the English Progressive

Thus far, the only language-external aspectual distinction we have considered is that between states and events. There are, however, many different types of event. In this section we shall draw out the distinctions that might be made among them on objective grounds and then examine how the major language-internal aspectual distinction in English, that between the progressive and the nonprogressive, can be applied. We shall be chiefly concerned with situations in the past. The reason for this will be evident when we consider the developmental evidence. Figure 11-4 shows the distinctions to which we shall refer.

We may divide events into those that are nondurative and those that are durative. An event that is nondurative has no meaningful extent in time and thus can-

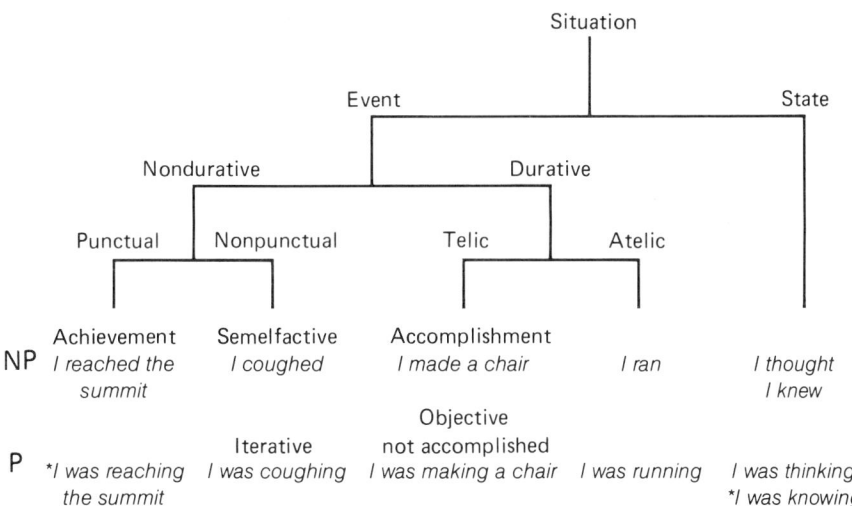

Figure 11-4. Interaction between language-external aspectual criteria and the past nonprogressive (NP) and progressive (P).

not be considered imperfectively; that is, such an event cannot have progressive aspect. There are two types of nondurative event: those that are *inherently* nondurative and those that are *perceptually* nondurative. Vendler's (1957) category of *achievements*—such as reaching the summit of a mountain or winning a race—are inherently nondurative: There is an instant at which these events occur but the instant cannot be divided into component instants. Examples of perceptually nondurative events are coughing and sneezing. An individual act of coughing occurs too quickly to allow progressive reference while it is in progress. However, these events are often repeated in quick succession and in such cases the progressive can be used with iterative meaning. Thus, *he was coughing* indicates a bout of repeated coughs, not a single cough.

Durative events constitutive, by far, the largest category of situations. These events are extended for some finite period of time and include the vast majority of actions done by or to animate agents. There is one major subdivision here that imposes constraints on the use of the progressive: that between *telic* and *atelic* events. In general, the progressive may be used to denote either telic or atelic situations but the implication is different in each case.

A *telic* event possesses a natural goal or end-point and when the goal is reached the event is concluded; an *atelic* event does not possess a natural end-point, although it may end. As an example, consider the difference between running a mile and running. The former is telic; the latter atelic. If one is running a mile, the event is completed when a certain distance has been completed; if one stops before that distance has been completed one has not run a mile. By contrast, if one is running, when one stops one has run. The difference can be brought out further by considering a runner who has run a mile and continues. The answer to whether the runner has finished a mile is *yes*; the answer to whether the runner has finished running is *no*.

It is clear from these examples that it is the situation described by the verb phrase, not the verb itself, that is inherently telic or atelic. However, some durative verbs are inherently (lexically) telic or atelic. One example of a lexically telic verb is *make*: one cannot be *making*, one has to be *making something*. As far as the progressive is concerned, its use to describe a telic situation implies that the objective has been accomplished; its use to describe an atelic situation carries no such implication (because no objective was involved). The use of the nonprogressive (*-ed* in the past in English) implies that the objective of a telic situation was reached. Vendler (1957) calls these situations *accomplishments*. With atelic situations, the nonprogressive carries no implication about objectives. Thus, atelic situations are the only situations about which either the progressive or nonprogressive form may be freely used without any constraints imposed by the situation. The choice of which form is used is, of course, determined by the speaker's communicative purpose.

Do Verb Inflections Mark Aspect? In recent years, a number of studies have investigated the relations between tense and aspect, on the one hand, and verb inflections, on the other. A number of writers have suggested that aspectual distinctions play a particularly important role in the acquisition of verb inflections (Antinucci & Miller, 1976; Bloom, Lifter, & Hafitz, 1980; Bronckart & Sinclair, 1973). The claims made by different writers vary, so we shall consider the various arguments as our discussion progresses. It must also be borne in mind that in English, as in many other languages, the morphology of tense and aspect are intertwined: the regular past tense suffix in English is *-ed*, which also indicates perfective aspect. For this reason it will be important to pay particular attention to the methodology employed to disentangle tense and aspect.

Two types of evidence have been advanced in favor of aspect before tense: *naturalistic* and *experimental*. The major piece of naturalistic evidence is a study by Bloom, Lifter, and Hafitz (1980), which reports the initial acquisition of verb inflections by four American children between the ages of 1;0 and 2;4. Bloom et al. claim that only verbs of a certain *inherent lexical aspect* co-occurred with particular inflections.

In order to support such a claim, it would be necessary first to divide verbs according to their aspectual character on a priori grounds and then to examine the co-occurrence of inflections within the aspectual categories. To some extent it is possible to divide verbs according to their inherent lexical character but, as we have described above, the largest aspectual category of verbs (those that refer to durative events) consists of verbs that do not, for the most part, have inherent lexical aspect. As the vast majority of verbs used by Bloom et al.'s subjects fall within this category, it is necessary to go beyond the verb used, to the situation itself, in order to determine whether aspect controls inflections. It might be possible to do this to some extent by categorizing the situations referred to as either telic or atelic, for example, but this is not the method adopted by Bloom et al. Instead, they categorized verbs on the basis of the inflection used and then examined the categories formed to see whether the verbs within a category shared a common aspectual feature. Bloom et al. argue that this, indeed, was the case. However, in view of the fact that many of the verbs produced by their subjects do not actually have inherent lexical aspect, it is difficult to see how they arrived at this conclusion. Consequently, it is difficult to evaluate Bloom et al.'s intuition that inflections encode aspectual distinctions. This issue remains to be resolved.

The major piece of experimental evidence in favor of aspect before tense in children's use of verb inflections has been reported by Bronckart and Sinclair (1973) for French-speaking children. Although aspect is not equivalent in French and English, the claim advanced by Bronckart and Sinclair is that properties of *situations* (not of *verbs*, as argued by Bloom et al.) determine the inflection used, so the study may suggest possible lines of investigation with English-speaking children. The difference between the Bronckart and Sinclair claim and the Bloom et al. claim is small but important. Bronckart and Sinclair claim that there is a direct relation between situational properties and inflectional encoding. Bloom et al. claim that there is a relation between categories of verbs and inflections used. This latter claim presupposes subcategorical organization of the verb lexicon, which the Bronckart and Sinclair claim does not.

Bronckart and Sinclair used toys to act out a series of different situations to five age-groups of children aged between 3 and 9 years old. The children observed the situations and, when the action was completed, were required to describe what had occurred. Bronckart and Sinclair manipulated three dimensions of situations. The first dimension differentiated between perfective, imperfective, and aperfective situations. As we have discussed above, the distinction between perfective and imperfective is a languge-internal distinction not an objective distinction between situations. Thus, it is not possible to manipulate directly perfective and imperfective aspect although it is possible to manipulate situations that require either one or the other aspectual expression. In fact, Bronckart and Sinclair's experimental manipulation approximates to the situational distinction between telic and atelic events.

The second dimension manipulated was between durative and nondurative events. Here again, the distinction is not equivalent to the aspectual distinction. Bronckart and Sinclair's nondurative events were not instantaneous events but events of short duration. The events could legitimately have had a longer duration had the experimenter chosen. This is not true of aspectually nondurative events. However, it may be that children do distinguish between events of long and short duration and that they encode this distinction by the use of different inflections for the two types of event.

The third dimension manipulated was the division of durative situations into those that were iterative (*frequentative* is their term) and those that were continuous.

If we consider first the dimension of telicity, Bronckart and Sinclair's results suggested that telic situations produced different inflections from those that were atelic. In encoding telic situations, children's descriptions were mainly in the passé composé, whereas in encoding atelic situations their descriptions were mainly in the présent.

The data that relates to the dimensions of duration and interativity are shown in Table 11-2 (derived from Bronckart and Sinclair's results). It would seem that there is no overall difference in the encoding of situations of long and short duration. Based on a subsample of these data, Bronckart and Sinclair report that there was no developmental trend in the use of inflections for situations of short duration but that, for situations longer in duration, 3-year-old children produce the same proportion of passé composé and présent and thereafter the use of the présent diminishes with age, whereas that of the passé composé increases. Table 11-2 shows that durative situations that are non-iterative elicit fewer passés composés and more présent responses than other situations. However, this result must be treated with caution for the present because it is strongly affected by the extreme results of one situation in which a duck swam for 15 seconds.

Table 11-2. Mean Number of Responses by Children in Brockhart and Sinclair (1973) Experiment

Aspect	Tense		
	Passé composé	Présent	Imparfait
Durative & iterative	48	22	1
Durative & noniterative	26	38	7
Nondurative	48	21	2

In view of the limited number of situations sampled, these results cannot be taken as conclusive evidence of a relation between situations and the inflections children use. At best, the results suggest the need for further investigation to test whether Bronckart and Sinclair are correct in their conclusions that there is a relation between situations and inflections, and that children use inflections and auxiliaries that normally encode tense to mark these situational differences.

Experiments on Aspect and Inflection. We have conducted three experiments to investigate the relation between the properties of situations and the verb inflections children use in their descriptions of those situations. We shall briefly report the method and results here.

We modified three dimensions of situations: duration, telicity, and iterativity. We elicited descriptions from 3-, 4-, and 5-year-old children in the same manner as Bronckart and Sinclair. Children observed each situation being acted out with toys before them and were then asked to describe what they had seen.

In the first study, we examined whether the duration of a situation influenced the inflection used in the children's descriptions. There were six different situations consisting of an agent engaging in some action (such as a duck swimming). Each situation was presented twice. In one presentation the action lasted three seconds; in the other presentation it lasted twelve seconds. The question of interest was whether children would use different inflections depending upon the duration of the situation. Overall, there was little indication that duration had a significant effect on the verb inflection used. In 81% of cases, the same inflection was used for both situations. The remaining 19% of responses did not conform to any obvious pattern but were distributed throughout the various response categories.

We next examined the inflections children used when the results from the two versions of the situations were combined, and found 63% were past progressive (*was -ing*) and 25% were simple past (*-ed*) endings. The remaining 12% of responses were either present tense or uninflected verbs. There was no evidence for age trends in children's sensitivity to the dimension of duration: Older children were as likely as younger ones to use the same inflection in the two versions of the situation. There was also no evidence for any age trend in the inflections used by the three age groups. Overall, the data suggest that modifying the duration of an action has little effect on the inflections children use to describe that action.

In the next study we examined whether telicity influenced the inflections children use. Again, we asked children to describe two versions of six situations. In one version the action of the agent was directed toward a goal (a monkey climbing a tree to get a banana). This was contrasted with a situation in which the action was not goal-directed (the monkey climbing around the tree).

Again, in the majority of cases, 68% of the children produced different inflections in the two conditions. Of the remaining cases, however, one type of responding was most prevalent. This consisted of past-tense endings to telic events and past-progressive to atelic events. This accounted for 17% of the responses. The final 14% of responses did not seem to conform to any pattern.

Overall, when the descriptions from the two versions of the situations were combined, 51% of inflections were simple past, 38% were past progressive, and 11% were simple present, present progressive, or uninflected verbs. Although the age groups did not differ in their use of the simple past, there was a significant trend toward increasing use of the past progressive when the Jonckheere test (see Leach, 1979) was employed ($Z=1.97$, $p<.05$). The relative percentages of past progressives for the 3-, 4-, and 5-year-old children were 19, 42, and 54 respectively. The experiment suggests that the goal-directedness of the action does not directly influence the inflections children use in their descriptions, but there is some evidence that overall the type of inflections children use may change with age.

In the final experiment we investigated whether the repetition of an action influenced the inflection used. We compared descriptions in two versions of a situation. In the first, the action occurred once (a bear banged on a table with a hammer). This was contrasted with a situation in which the bear hammered several times. Again, there was little evidence that inflections were different in the two versions of the situation, with 69% of cases having the same inflection in both conditions. When the remaining co-occurrences were examined, it was found that 18% of responses were past-progressive for iterative and simple past for noniterative events. When we examined the overall distribution of inflections we found that 50% were simple past, 34% were past progressive, and 16% simple present, present progressive, and uninflected verbs combined. There was some evidence of a change with age in the inflections used. The frequency of past progressives increased significantly with age ($Z=5.37$, $p<.001$, Jonckheere test) with the percentage at each age level being 18%, 35%, and 50%. Of further interest was the fact that there was a significant trend ($Z=2.68$, $p<.01$, Jonckheere test) toward the use of the simple past for a single action and the past progressive for an iterated action. Only 9% of the responses from 3-year-old children were co-occurrences of this sort but the proportion rose to 18% for the 4-year-old children, and 26% for the 5-year-old children.

We are currently conducting more detailed analyses of the data reported above, but a number of tentative conclusions can be drawn at this time. There was no evidence that the aspectual variables were the sole or major determinants of the inflection children used as might be inferred from the study of Bronckart and Sinclair (1973). The vast majority of responses were in the past tense, as was appropriate in the circumstances. Nevertheless, there were differences in whether the simple past or the past progressive was used. In the first experiment, which explored the effects of durativity, the children in general, and the 3-year-olds in particular, were more likely to use the past progressive than the simple past. In the remaining two experiments, there was a trend with age to favor the use of the past progressive to the simple past and, in the iterativity experiment, to use selectively the simple past for a noniterated action and the past progressive for an iterated action.

In this section we have discussed production data from a number of studies that examined the relationship between tense and aspect. Both the Bronckart and Sinclair study and our own research suggest a weak relation between situations and inflections. However, the data cannot be taken as suggesting that the exclusive function of inflections initially is to encode aspectual distinctions. Aspect would appear to be a contributing factor to *selecting* one inflection rather than another, but not a rigid determiner of the choice. A second feature of our results was that, in contrast to Bronckart and Sinclair, we found few examples of children using tense inflections inappropriately to mark aspect-related differences among situations. These findings reinforce those of Smith (1980) and Harner (1981).

None of the above studies addressed the question of aspect by gathering comprehension data. Comprehension data may afford a more direct method of disentangling the complex interrelations between tense and aspect. As we have already noted, one crucial aspectual distinction is that between *perfective* and *imperfective* aspect. Such a distinction is language internal and signaled by the use of simple and progressive inflections. One problem with the available production data is that there is no means of inferring the child's representation of the situation independently of the inflections used. This makes it difficult to determine whether inflections are being used in the adult manner. Comprehension data would enable this issue to be addressed. If it could be shown that young children interpreted utterances containing simple and progressive inflections as representing different aspects of a situation, this would be strong evidence that children have mastered this distinction.

The Category *Verb*

Thus far we have considered whether there is any subcategorical organization of the verb lexicon that determines an initial selective use of inflections with particular verbs. We have not yet considered how children arrive at the knowledge that certain words belong to the category *verb*. Let us consider it here.

From about the age of 18 months, children are unequivocally aware that words can be used as representational symbols (McShane, 1980; McShane & Whittaker, 1983). From this age on, they can name objects and they can combine an object's name with a property of that object, usually an action or an attribute. The ontological categories of object, action and attribute form the rudimentary basis of the grammatical categories noun, verb, and adjective. However, children do not initially seem to organize either the world or their language into such macrocategories. Their initial word combinations reflect limited-scope formulae (Braine, 1976) rather than a grammar based on more general categories. Accepting this position as a starting point, the developmental issue becomes: How do general grammatical categories develop? Two possible types of answer have been offered. First, general conceptual categories develop initially and these categories then become the basis of grammatical categories. Such an account can be found in Bates and McWhinney (1982). Second, linguistic categories develop autonomously without any input from an independent cognitive system. Such an account can be found in Maratsos and Chalkley (1980). These positions, as we have outlined them, are skeleton extremes. The act of fleshing out either account could easily lead to a modified position, but, of course, it need not. Let us consider, briefly, what the implications are of the extreme positions.

Two Positions on the Category *Verb*

There are at least two major requirements of the *cognitive origins* account: (a) it must provide a clear, rigorous, and language-independent account of how the relevant conceptual category develops; and (b) the mechanism by which the conceptual category gives rise to the linguistic category must be clearly described. It is crucial for such an account, in its extreme form, that the linguistic category be rigorously related to a nonlinguistic category. A less extreme and, perhaps, more plausible version of the account would be that the conceptual category provides an approximation to the linguistic category with the remaining fine tuning done by specifically linguistic processes. Whether or not grammatical categories are formed in this way can be tested by stating what the initial approximation is; working out the implications of such an approximation in terms of errors, selective constructions, and so forth; and testing the model against developmental data.

The *autonomous origins* position can be represented in two ways. The first of these assumes that the grammatical categories are innate. Two major requirements can also be imposed on such a position: (a) the innateness assumption be justified; and (b) the mechanisms by which category members are instantiated be specified. The technicalities of this debate are too complex to pursue in this chapter.

A second *autonomous origins* position assumes that regularities in the words that children learn provide the basis of grammatical categories. The requirements on this position is a model of (a) regularities that are sufficient to give rise to the grammatical categories, and (b) the mechanisms that detect such regularities and then generate a grammatical category from them. Like the *cognitive origins* positions, once the implications of the model have been worked out, it can be tested against a developmental data base. It can be remarked, in passing, that the innatist position is much less amenable to this standard method of testing. For a discussion of these issues, see Pylyshyn (1973).

Let's examine, in more detail, what is involved in the construction of a verb category.

The standard account of how verb inflections are learned is approximately as follows: Children initially learn inflected forms as separate lexical entries. Thus, words such as *walked*, *walks*, and *walking* are initially unanalyzed wholes for the child and not the product of rules that combine the verb stem with an inflection. During this period, irregular forms are used correctly by the child, for example, *caught*, *ran*, and *thought*. However, in time the child discovers regularities: When reference is to the past, the word ends in *-ed*; when the action is in progress, the word ends in *-ing*. The child adopts these regularities as rules. In the case of the past tense, the child overgeneralizes the rule to previously correct forms to produce *catched*, *runned*, and *thinked*. The process, in detail, might be something like the following: The first step is the item-by-item learning of inflected forms as unanalyzed wholes. The absence, at this point, of overregularization errors and their presence at some later point, suggest that the child does indeed learn the initial past-tense forms on an item-by-item basis. To proceed from a list of items to a productive rule, the child must be capable of segmenting words in such a way that the inflectional ending is a recognizable morpheme in its own right. To do this, the child must be capable of morphological segmentation—an ability that must get primed at a particular point so that a productive rule is induced. How and why this ability gets primed must be explained. If the child does pay attention to the end of words as Slobin (1973) has argued, this might give some slight hold on recognizing morphemes as independent grammatical units. However, there is much about the process of morphological segmentation that remains ill understood, in particular, whether the data base on which the child works is the input speech that he or she hears or the child's output of the unanalyzed form.

Having segmented a word, the child must recognize the similarity between the result of the segmentation and the result of other segmentations carried out at other times. This means that some permanent memory record must be kept. There are two ways in which such a record could be kept. First, the segmented words already belong to a common store, implying that the child has already grouped together words such as *run/talk/think*, *see/ran/saw*, *running/walking/seeing*, and *runs/walks/sees* according to some principle. As a result of segmentation *running* becomes *run+-ing*, *walked* becomes *walk+-ed*, *sees* becomes *see+-s*, and so forth. As each of the stems already exist in the store in their own right, the store can be reorganized into stems and optional inflections so that, for example, *walked*, *walking*, and *walks* become *walk+-ed, +-ing, +-s*.

Next, the child must derive the general rules (presumably by induction) that the past tense is formed by adding *-ed* to the root of the verb, the progressive is formed by adding *-ing*, and the third person present singular is formed by adding *-s*. When the first of these rules is applied, overregularization errors occur.

The second possibility is that prior to segmentation, there is no substantial categorical organization among the words segmented but stores are created labeled *words that take* -ed, *words that take* -ing, and *words that take* -s. For the sake of simplicity, we assume that at this stage the inflectional morphemes have the semantic roles of pastness, progressiveness, and presentness respectively.

Following this, the child must derive the rule (presumably by induction) that the same stems take *-ed*, *-ing*, and *-s* as inflections. A common store of stems can now be created—all of which take the optional inflections *-ed*, *-ing*, *-s*. Entry of a stem can now be made on the basis of any of the inflections. When stems that do not take *-ed* to denote pastness are entered on the basis of their co-occurrence with *-ing* or *-s*, then overregularization errors will occur when the general rule of pastness is applied.

In either case, the next step is to learn the complex exceptions for denoting pastness (in English), and thereby eliminate overregularization errors (see Bybee & Slobin, 1982).

Let us now consider the way in which empirical data could help clarify these issues. Toward the end of their second year, children begin to use recognizable verbs to denote actions, usually in combination with a word denoting the agent of the action (McShane, 1980). Prior to this, children do use action words in a more limited fashion (see Barrett, 1983, for a discussion). It is difficult to know at this stage to what extent the words used to denote actions have a common categorical status. The major problem in addressing this issue is the absence of a suitable methodological tool. Production data simply reveal what words and word combinations the child uses. As most, action-words are uninflected at this stage there are no grammatical clues to indicate the categorical constraints with which the child is operating. It is entirely possible that action words have simply been learned as individual items that denote individual actions and are not yet encoded in a particular grammatical category. (Clearly, we are not claiming that no categorical work is necessary at this stage. If a child learns action words individually, this implies a recognition that actions require labels independently of agents and that appropriate distinctions can be drawn among different actions. This requires considerable categorical abilities, but not the ability to categorize words as belonging to a particular form-class.) For production data, the most relevant evidence comes from the child's overregularization of verb inflections. For comprehension data, the most relevant evidence comes from the child's ability to use inflections as a criterion for choosing actions as the appropriate referent. Showing that a child can match a given word with an appropriate action simply shows an ability to perform word-action mappings. What is required in both production data and comprehension data is evidence that some feature of a form-class is being manipulated by the child. We shall consider each case separately.

Production Data on Verbs

When children first use inflected words (such as *walked*, *walking*, and *walks*) it is probable that these are learned as individual words rather than as a root combined with an inflectional morpheme. The major piece of evidence in favor of this argument is that the irregular past of verbs (such as *think*, *see*, *run*, etc.) is often used correctly for a time only to be replaced later by overregularized forms (such as *thinked*, *seed*, *runned*). It is evident in the latter case that the child is using a productive form-class rule. How has the rule been made?

One possible answer is that the child has (a) already categorized all the relevant words together, (b) discovered that there is a regularity in certain endings, (c) detached these endings as separate morphemes, and (d) added the morpheme to the class as a whole rather than simply to the subclass from which the initial regularity was derived. For such an answer to be plausible it must be possible to articulate a basis on which the words were initially categorized. A criterion of action might seem appropriate but a little reflection reveals that the verb category is not comprised exclusively of action words. There is very little of an active nature associated with verbs such as *think*, *like*, and many others which are productively used by children. These words are, however, evidently treated as verbs by children during the overregularization phase. Thus, it does not appear that a simple concept of action lies behind the category *verb*. In general, previous attempts to define the category on semantic grounds have been largely unsuccessful.

An alternative argument advanced by Maratsos and Chalkley (1980) is that the inflections themselves are the basis on which the category is formed. The argument assumes that inflected forms are learned initially on an item-by-item basis. At some point, the child becomes aware that the inflected form can be divided into a component root and an inflectional morpheme. In general, a root that takes -*ed* as an inflection will also take -*ing* and -*s* as inflections. Thus, one inflection can be used to predict another: they have "correlated privileges of occurrence" (Maratsos & Chalkley, 1980). Overregularizations occur because verbs that have an irregular past nevertheless have a regular present and progressive and, thus, these latter are used by the child to predict the incorrect form.

In favor of this proposal, Maratsos points to the relative lack of form-class errors in children's speech. He argues that it would be difficult for a semantic categorization system to account for this relative paucity of errors given the overlap of stative adjectives and stative verbs. However, the argument that the child constructs the form-class category on distributional grounds has no such difficulty because only words that partake of the distributional privileges are treated as category members and partaking of the distributional privileges is, of course, the criterion for membership. A problem with such a developmental sequence is that it contains too little semantics. This is illustrated by the case of the inflection -*s*—which denotes third person present singular when used with a verb and plural when used with a noun. If a strict version of the argument outlined were to apply, many nouns might be added to the verb store because of their plural inflection. The fact that they are not, suggests that the child has some grounds for distinguishing one type of meaning from another when -*s* is the suffix. This implies that meaning plays a role in the development of the system. Note, however, that for the case outlined, the crucial role for meaning is in the interpretation of the role of the inflection, not of the root. The evidence of comprehension will help to explicate what may be involved here.

Comprehension Data on Verbs

As far as comprehension is concerned, the main source of evidence for a form-class category comes from the ability to infer that a particular inflection implies a particular form-class. It is not possible to carry out the relevant experiments using words commonly produced by children because the fact that a child correctly identifies walking, say, on hearing *walking*, does not imply that the inflection was the basis of identification. In order to overcome this difficulty, researchers have traditionally used syllabic nonsense words and added normal inflections to these words. If a child can, under these conditions, choose the correct form-class, then it might seem reasonable to presume that the inflection was the basis of the child's choice and thus, that the child understands the form-class inflectional relation.

The classic experiment in this area was carried out by Brown (1957). Brown showed children pictures that contained three elements: an action, a mass quantity, and a container. One picture showed a pair of hands performing a kneading sort of motion, with a mass of red confetti-like material piled into and overflowing a blue and white round container. The picture was described to the child who might be told (in the case of a verb test): "In this picture you can see sibbing; now show me another picture of sibbing." The child was then shown a set of pictures, one of which contained the mass alone, one the container alone, and one the motion being carried out on a mass of different color into a container of different size, shape, and color.

Brown reported that 10 out of 16 children aged 3 to 5 years selected the action picture under these circumstances. This result has frequently been interpreted as showing that children in this age-range understand the form-class inflectional relation. However, there are considerable difficulties with this interpretation. Apart from the less-than-overwhelming distribution of responses, the picture of the action was the only picture of the choice set that contained three elements; the responses could have been the product of some gross-matching strategy. In order to explore this issue further we recently conducted a version of this experiment and shall report here the relevant results for verbs.

We tested children's comprehension of the progressive form and the third person present simple form of the verb (the inflections -ing and -s, respectively). Children were shown a picture that contained three elements: an action, an object or objects, and a context. The action was depicted by a stick-like figure performing an unknown action (a bodily movement that did not involve any objects and for which there was no available word in the adult lexicon). Before showing a picture, the experimenter asked "Do you know what Xing is?" or "Do you know what it is to X?" X was a nonsense syllable. On showing the picture, the experimenter said "In this picture you can see Xing." or "In this picture he Xs." The child was then shown the remaining pictures and asked "Can you show me another picture with Xing in it?" or "Can you show me another picture with someone who Xs in it?"

Table 11-3 shows that 56% of the 3-year-olds' choices to -s and 46% of their choices to -ing were of the picture depicting the action. Analysis by the Friedman test showed that there was no significant difference among the pictures in the choices of the 3-year-olds for either -s or -ing. (However, the result for -s did not fall far short of significance, $(\chi^2_r = 5.65, 2$ d.f., $p = 0.059)$. For the 4-year-old children, there was a significant tendency to choose the action picture for the -s inflection $(\chi^2_r = 13.72, 2$ d.f., $p < 0.01)$, and to choose the object picture for the -ing inflection $(\chi^2_r = 9.78, 2$ d.f., $p < 0.01)$.

The results of this experiment do not support Brown's (1957) conclusion that 3- to 5-year-old children can make form-class assignment purely on the basis of the -ing inflection. In fact, the 4-year-old children when faced with this task chose the object

Table 11-3. Distribution of Responses to -s and -ing Inflections by 3- and 4-year-old Children

Age	Inflection	Picture chosen		
		Object	Action	Context
3	-s	15	27	6
	-ing	17	22	9
4	-s	10	36	2
	-ing	28	14	6

Note: We tested 16 children at each age. Each child made three choices for each inflection.

picture 58% of the time. However, for -s, the story is different: 3-year-old children chose the correct picture 56% of the time (although the preference marginally failed to reach significance); 4-year-olds chose the correct picture 75% of the time.

Why should there be this difference between the responses to -s and the responses to -ing? The difference, it seemed to us, was due to the differing linguistic context of the two inflections. The linguistic context provided for -s was *paradigmatic*. That is, the verb occurred at a place in the sentence at which a verb would be naturally expected. It was preceded by an animate agent (someone), and it was appropriately inflected. By contrast, the linguistic context provided for -ing was distinctly *nonparadigmatic*. There was no agent specified and the sentence-type ("In this picture you can see _____.") is more naturally reserved for nouns (especially plural nouns, which do not require an article). In fact, as we have shown, the 4-year-olds did have a significant preference for the object picture and the responses from the 3-year-olds were essentially random.

The conclusion suggested by these experiments is that children make form-class assignment not primarily on the basis of inflections but on the basis of paradigmatic sentence-frames. To test whether this was the case (and not due to some peculiarity of -ing), we repeated the experiment with a different group of children. This time, the linguistic context was "In this picture you can see someone *X*ing" and the child was asked "Can you show me another picture with someone *X*ing in it?" For the 16 children tested, all but 4 of the 24 choices of the 3-year-olds were of the action picture; the 4-year-olds chose the action picture with 100% accuracy.

These results support our contention that during comprehension, children use a paradigmatic sentence-frame to make decisions about the part of speech. The ability to allow inflections to override this paradigm (as in the case of "Can you show me another picture with *X*ing in it?") is obviously one that develops after the age of 5. However, the results should not be interpreted as showing that children ignore inflections. They do show, however, that inflections are not the primary means by which part-of-speech assignment is carried out in comprehension.

Conclusion

This chapter has been concerned with the cognitive organization of the verb lexicon and the relation between such organization and verb inflections. We have examined several claims about organizational factors that influence the acquisition and use of inflections and have reported some preliminary data of our own on these issues. More detailed analysis of these data and further experiments remain to be done before definite conclusions can be drawn. Accordingly, we shall not attempt a premature conclusion but simply summarize the issues and the current balance of the evidence.

Much remains to be done with adults and children on different approaches to the subdivision of the verb lexicon. The popular division between states and events appears to have the status of a fuzzy semantic division rather than the clear bipolar distinction that is sometimes supposed. Further, it would appear that the distinction is one that is less than obvious to young children. There does not appear to be overwhelming evidence, either direct or indirect, to suggest that stative and dynamic verbs represent a categorical subdivision that is used by the child as a determining principle for the co-occurrence of *-ing* with particular verbs. We view both the claims—that there is such a psychological division and that children do not use the progressive inflection *-ing* with stative verbs—with scepticism.

There has been much discussion in recent years about whether inflections first encode tense or aspect. There is little evidence, in our view, that the child exclusively encodes aspectual features initially. Our tentative interpretation of our own data is that children encode both tense and aspect from the beginning of their use of inflections. However, there is much that remains to be discovered about the factors that influence the choice, for English-speaking children, of encoding perfective or imperfective aspect when referring to the past. In our view, a comparative analysis—both among children and between children and adults—of the factors that determine aspectual choice would be a more profitable line of inquiry than the all-or-none tense or aspect choice.

Finally, there is the issue of how a large number of words cohere in a particular syntactic category. There are reasons for resisting the suggestion that the category *verb* is simply a semantic category of actions and states. *States* cause most embarrassment for such an argument because many statives are adjectives rather than verbs. Consequently, if the category is semantically based, some confusion might be expected on the categorical status of statives. Yet, there is little evidence of such confusion as Maratsos and Chalkley (1980) have argued. An alternative argument is that distributional privileges of inflections (rather than reflect) define membership of a verb category. However, such an argument has to incorporate some semantics, albeit in a secondary role, to eliminate potential confusions from similar inflections performing different functions (such as plural nouns and third person present singular verbs). We have argued that, in comprehension, such potential confusions are resolved by the use of a paradigmatic sentence-frame to predict what type of word is expected. When such information is degraded, as it was in one of the experiments reported, then performance deteriorates. We interpret such evidence as suggesting a role for paradigmatic frames in comprehension. In more general terms, we suspect that children make use of any available and comprehensible information—information about reference, word order, and inflections. The task remains to explicate in more detail the developmental balance of these and other cues on the route to mastery of the adult language.

References

Allen, W. S. (1955). *Living English structure*. London: Longman.
Antinucci, F., & Miller, R. (1976). How children talk about what happened. *Journal of Child Language*, 3, 167-189.
Austin, J. L. (1962). *How to do things with words*. Oxford: Oxford University Press.

Bach, K., & Harnish, R. M. (1979). *Linguistic communication and speech acts*. Cambridge, MA: MIT Press.

Barrett, M. D. (1983). The early acquisition and development of the meanings of action-related words. In T. B. Seiler & W. Wannenmacher (Eds.), *Concept development and the development of word meaning*. Berlin: Springer-Verlag.

Bates, E., & MacWhinney, B. (1982). Functionalist approaches to grammar. In E. Wanner & L. R. Gleitman (Eds.), *Language acquisition: The state of the art*. Cambridge: Cambridge University Press.

Bloom, L., Lifter, K., & Hafitz, J. (1980). Semantics of verbs and the development of verb inflection in child language. *Language, 56*, 386-412.

Bloom, L., Lightbown, P., & Hood, L. (1975). Structure and variation in child language. *Monographs of the Society for Research on Child Development, 40* (2, Serial No. 160).

Bowerman, M. (1975). Commentary on Bloom, Lightbown, and Hood's structure and variation in child language. *Monographs of the Society for Research in Child Development, 40* (2, Serial No. 160).

Braine, M. D. S. (1976). Children's first word combinations. *Monographs of the Society for Research in Child Development, 41* (1, Serial No. 164).

Braine, M. D. S., & Wells, R. S. (1978). Case-like categories in children: The actor and some related categories. *Cognitive Psychology, 10*, 100-122.

Bronckart, J. P., & Sinclair, H. (1973). Time, tense, and aspect. *Cognition, 2*, 107-130.

Brown, R. (1957). Linguistic determinism and the part of speech. *Journal of Abnormal and Social Psychology, 55*, 1-5.

Brown, R. (1973). *A first language*. Cambridge, MA: Harvard University Press.

Bull, W. E. (1960). *Time, tense, and the verb*. Berkeley: University of California Press.

Bybee, J. L., & Slobin, D. I. (1982). Rules and schemes in the development and use of the English past tense. *Language, 58*, 265-289.

Chafe, W. (1970). *Meaning and the structure of language*. Chicago: University of Chicago Press.

Comrie, B. (1976). *Aspect*. Cambridge: Cambridge University Press.

Dixon, R. M. W. (1971). A method of semantic description. In D. D. Steinberg & L. A. Jakobovits (Eds.), *Semantics: An interdisciplinary reader in philosophy, linguistics, and psychology*. Cambridge: Cambridge University Press.

Harner, L. (1981). Children talk about the time and aspect of actions. *Child Development, 52*, 498-506.

Joos, M. (1964). *The English verb: Form and meanings*. Madison: University of Wisconsin Press.

Labov, W. (1973). The boundaries of words and their meanings. In C. J. N. Bailey & R. W. Shuy (Eds.), *New ways of analyzing variation in English*. Washington, DC: Georgetown University Press.

Leach, C. (1979). *Introduction to statistics*. New York: Wiley.

Leech, G. N. (1971). *Meaning and the English verb*. Harlow: Longman.

Lehrer, A. (1970). Indeterminacy in semantic description. *Glossa, 4*, 87-110.

Lyons, J. (1977). *Semantics* (Vols. 1 and 2). Cambridge: Cambridge University Press.

Maratsos, M. P., & Chalkley, M. A. (1980). The internal language of children's syntax: The ontogenesis and representation of syntactic categories. In K. E. Nelson (Ed.), *Children's language* (Vol. 2). New York: Gardner Press.

McShane, J. (1980). *Learning to talk*. Cambridge: Cambridge University Press.

McShane, J., & Dockrell, J. (1983). Lexical and grammatical development. In B. Butterworth (Ed.), *Speech production* (Vol. 2). London: Academic Press.

McShane, J., & Whittaker, S. (1983). The role of symbolic thought in language development. In D. R. Rogers & J. A. Sloboda (Eds.), *The acquisition of symbolic skills*. New York: Plenum Press.

McTaggart, J. M. E. (1927). *The nature of existence*. Cambridge: Cambridge University Press.

Miller, G. A., & Johnson-Laird, P. N. (1976). *Language and perception*. Cambridge: Cambridge University Press.

Palmer, F. R. (1965). *A linguistic study of the English verb*. London: Longman.

Pylyshyn, Z. (1973). The role of competence theories in cognitive psychology. *Journal of Psycholinguistic Research, 21*, 21-50.

Searle, J. (1975). A taxonomy of illocutionary acts. In K. Gunderson (Ed.), *Language, mind and knowledge*. Minneapolis: University of Minnesota Press.

Slobin, D. I. (1973). Cognitive prerequisites for the development of grammar. In C. A. Ferguson & D. I. Slobin (Eds.), *Studies of child language development*. New York: Holt, Rinehart & Winston.

Smith, C. S. (1980). The acquisition of time talk: Relations between child and adult grammars. *Journal of Child Language, 7*, 263-278.

Vendler, Z. (1957). Verbs and times. *The Philosophical Review, LXVI*, 143-160.

12. Acquiring and Using Words to Express Logical Relationships

Lucia A. French

This chapter considers children's understanding of a small set of terms (*before*, *after*, *because*, *so*, *if*, *but*, and *or*) that function to express relationships between propositions. Because these terms permit the linguistic expression of the logical structures central to human cognition, their acquisition has been of concern to investigators with a variety of interests, including language acquisition, the development of logical reasoning, and general cognitive development. Understanding how these terms are acquired ultimately contributes to our knowledge of the relationships among language, logic, and cognitive development by indicating the ways in which nonlinguistic representations are integrated with linguistic knowledge to produce descriptions of logical relationships.

In the past ten to fifteen years, there has been a great deal of research addressing children's acquisition and understanding of these terms, and this interest shows little sign of abating. Despite the long history of research on children's understanding of relational terms, the relevant literature is fragmented and by and large uninterpretable. A discussion of the problems that arise in attempting to interpret the literature constitutes a major portion of this chapter. The problem of fragmentation can be described more briefly. There are several aspects to the fragmentation: the terms studied, the questions being addressed, the definition of the terms, and the nature of the data believed to bear on the issue of "understanding." By and large, there are quite separate, nonoverlapping literatures for different terms or pairs of terms. This arises in part because different investigators have had specific questions (e.g., the development of causal understanding) which could best be addressed through a consideration of children's understanding of particular terms. The question of the terms' definitions arises because those terms used in both natural language and formal logic (*if*, *or*, and *but*) have overlapping, but not identical, meanings in the two domains. Some confusion has arisen due to investigators' lack of sensitivity to these differences. Finally, individual investigators have tended to rely on either comprehension or production data in assessing children's understanding of a particular term, and there has been little attempt to coordinate the conclusions resulting from these different approaches.

Although the research on the relational terms under consideration here does not form a cohesive body of literature, similar methodologies and similar conclusions are apparent across the different literatures, and presumably similar processes underlie children's acquisition of the terms. This makes it both possible and desirable to attempt an integrative review and critique of the literature as a whole.[1] The goals of this chapter are to provide an overview of the literature on children's understanding of relational terms, to discuss some of the problems involved in interpreting this literature, and to propose a general model of children's understanding of relational terms that may be useful in guiding future research in this area.

Before proceeding, certain issues need to be clarified regarding the boundaries of the literature to be considered, the distinction between knowing the "definitions" versus the "functions" of relational terms, and the general theoretical orientation from which the question of the extent of children's understanding of relational terms will be approached.

Since the primary issue of interest here is in children's understanding of the natural language meanings of relational terms, there will be little reference to two closely related areas of research, children's "extralinguistic" understanding of logical relationships and their understanding of the meanings the terms may assume in formal logic. While an understanding of the natural language meanings of *before*, *after*, *because*, *so*, *if*, *but*, and *or* necessarily presupposes an understanding of the logical relationships the terms express, the converse is not true. That is, children may have an understanding of logical relationships without yet having acquired the linguistic means for expressing those concepts. Similarly, children may know the natural language meanings of relational terms without yet knowing the meanings these terms assume in formal logic. There is an extensive literature on children's extralinguistic understanding of temporal and causal relationships (e.g., Baillargeon, Gelman & Meck, 1981; Brown, 1976; Brown & French, 1976; Brown & Murphy, 1975; Bullock, 1981; Bullock & Gelman, 1979; Kun, 1978; Schmidt & Paris, 1978; Shultz, 1982; Siegler, 1976; Sommerville & Bryant, 1983) and on children's understanding of formal logic propositions (e.g., Braine & Rumain, 1983; Braine & Rumain, 1981; Ennis, 1976; Hill, 1961; Shapiro & O'Brien, 1970; Suppes & Feldman, 1971). Both are clearly related to the issues that will be discussed but will not be addressed in this chapter.

The relational terms to be discussed function in ordinary language to express logical relationships among propositions. In describing the function of an individual term, one comes up with something that could pass for a definition of the term. For

---

[1]No attempt will be made to exhaustively review all the articles dealing with particular terms. Rather, the literature will be reviewed selectively, focusing on articles that either have been very influential, or that illustrate a particular method or point especially well.

example, Clark (1971) paraphrases *before* as "At a time preceding the time at which" (p. 273). However, such definitions seem somewhat awkward and are unlikely to be generated, or perhaps even recognized, by adult speakers who can be assumed to know the meaning of the terms. The focus of this chapter will be on children's understanding of the *functions* rather than *definitions* of the terms. Thus, when we say that children "know the meaning" of a relational term, we generally mean that in speaking they can use it appropriately to establish relationships and that in listening they can form a representation of the relationship that it establishes. This definition of "knowing the meaning" of a term does not conflict with the usual standard used by investigators in determining whether a child knows relational terms, and is made explicit primarily because the distinction between functional and definitional knowledge of a term is important from a theoretical perspective (e.g., Katz & Brent, 1968).

The theoretical orientation to the study of children's understanding of relational terms expressed in this chapter is based more firmly in the cognitive development literature than in that of language development. In the past few years, the study of cognitive development has undergone a striking change as researchers dissatisfied with the generally negative terms in which Piaget characterized the abilities of preschool children have attempted to develop a more positive characterization of young children's cognitive abilities. A major outcome of this effort has been an emphasis on the role of contextual factors in cognitive development. In a number of areas, it has been found that the careful manipulation of context reveals cognitive abilities among preschoolers that remain undetected using more traditional measures (Donaldson, 1978, and Gelman, 1978, review much of this context sensitive research). A primary result of the emphasis upon context sensitive research has been a shift from showing that various abilities do not exist prior to a given age, to assuming that they are present very early and attempting to determine how they can be elicited and used at various ages.

In studies of language development, investigators have long recognized the necessity of attending to the context of children's statements in order to interpret them appropriately (e.g., Bloom, 1970). There has also been some recognition that the experimental context, that is, the situation or task in which evidence of language understanding is elicited, may influence the level of linguistic competence displayed by the child (e.g., Brown, 1973; Dale, 1976; Karmiloff-Smith, 1979; Maratsos, 1983; Richards, 1979; Tanz, 1980). However, context has been less widely recognized as a variable of interest *in its own right* in the study of language acquisition than in the study of cognitive development, and there has been virtually no attention given to the possibility that the *semantic* context in which terms appear may affect whether or not they are comprehended (although, see Carey, 1982, and French & Brown, 1977).

Following a review and critique of the relevant literature, a context sensitive model of the acquisition and understanding of relational terms will be outlined. This model gives central importance to the semantic content being "related" by relational terms in determining whether they are understood and used appropriately by young children. The essence of the proposed model is that knowledge of the meaning of relational terms first emerges, and can first be displayed, with regard to relationships that are already well-represented by the child. With time, the child decontextualizes his knowledge of relational terms and understands these terms when they function to establish unfamiliar relationships.

Two factors make the proposal of a new model particularly timely. First, the prevalent model invoked to explain the course of acquisition of relational terms, Clark's (1971, 1973) semantic feature hypothesis, has recently been rejected as inadequate by Clark herself (e.g., Clark, 1983). Second, our research suggests both that prior research has seriously overestimated the age at which children acquire relational terms, and that the standard procedures for assessing children's understanding of these terms may be systematically biased so as to fail to tap into a theoretically central aspect of the developmental course of acquisition (e.g., Carni & French, 1984; French & Nelson, 1981, in press).

In addition to being able to incorporate most of the existing literature, the proposed model offers a viable, theoretically motivated framework for further research in the area of children's acquisition and understanding of relational terms. It thus offers an alternative to the deadlock which seems to have been reached in this area of research, that is, endlessly reinventing, or disputing the validity of, the semantic feature model.

The sections that follow include: (1) an overview of the literature on the various terms being considered; (2) a discussion of the two basic approaches to studying children's knowledge of relational terms—production and comprehension—and an examination of the problems that arise in interpreting the data from these two approaches; and (3) an explication of the context-sensitive model that is being proposed to account for the development of children's understanding of relational terms.

Selective Review of the Literature Concerning Children's Understanding of the Terms *Before, After, Because, So, If, But,* and *Or*

Studies of children's knowledge of relational terms usually involve measures of either comprehension or production, but not both. Most studies rely upon comprehension paradigms. With some variation, depending upon the particular term and particular procedure used to assess comprehension, the typical conclusion has been that the meanings of relational terms are not acquired until age five, eight, or even later. These ages are considerably higher than the ages at which various investigators have found children to produce the same terms appropriately. The wide disparity between the ages at which competence with the various terms is displayed in production and comprehension situations has by and large been ignored. Those attempts that have been made to account for the disparity between comprehension and production have tended to be methodologically rather than theoretically oriented, and typically involve challenging the validity of the data obtained using the nonfavored method (e.g., Maratsos, 1983; Clark, 1983). In this section, an overview of the literature reporting studies of preschoolers' comprehension of relational terms is followed by a description of the literature on children's productions of relational terms. It is noted that the literature is in conflict at a theoretical level; the models of acquisition that have been proposed on the basis of comprehension studies yield certain predictions about production which are in fact not substantiated by the literature on children's productions.

Studies of the Comprehension of Relational Terms

Of the terms being considered here, *before* and *after* have been the focus of the greatest number of studies. The temporal relationship *X followed by Y* can be expressed in four different ways using these two terms: (1) X before Y; (2) before Y, X; (3) after X, Y; and (4) Y after X.

In sentences containing *before*, it is the second event (Y) that is subordinated, whereas in sentences containing *after* the first even is subordinated. In sentence forms 1 and 3, the order in which the events are mentioned preserves the order of occurrence, whereas in sentence forms 2 and 4, the order of mention violates the order of occurrence.

The attention given the terms *before* and *after* derives from a highly influential article by Eve Clark (1971). Clark's analysis of children's comprehension of *before* and *after* formed an important basis for her proposal that lexical acquisition generally could be accounted for in terms of a semantic feature model. Many investigators interested in assessing the validity of this model have continued to work with *before* and *after* (e.g., Amidon & Carey, 1972; Carni & French, 1984; Coker, 1978; French & Brown, 1977; Goodz, 1982; Kavanaugh, 1979; Keller-Cohen, 1974). Because Clark's article has been so influential, it will be described in some detail.

Clark's (1971) stimuli consisted of small toys and sentences that could be acted out using those toys. All subjects (N=40, age range 3;0-5;0) participated in two conditions: they responded to eight *when* questions about pairs of events acted out by the experimenter; then they acted out 16 *before* and *after* statements (balanced across the four sentence types described above) made by the experimenter.

Clark divided the subjects into three levels as a function of their enactment of the *before* and *after* statements. At Level 1, the subjects tended to follow the order of mention in enacting the sentences, so were incorrect on approximately half of the statements containing each term. At Level 2, the subjects enacted the *before* statements correctly. Subjects at this level fell into two subcategories in terms of their enactments of *after* statements: some continued to follow the order of mention in enacting *after* statements and some responded as if *after* meant *before*. Level 3 subjects responded correctly to both *before* and *after* statements. The classification of children according to these three levels correlated highly with age and with whether or not the children gave relational responses to the *when* questions.

Clark used the results from this study as an important basis for proposing the semantic feature hypothesis to account for lexical acquisition (e.g., 1971, 1973). According to this hypothesis, word meanings consist of various semantic components that are acquired individually over time. For words consisting of hierarchically ordered features, general features are acquired before specific features, and a feature's positive value is acquired before its negative value. The relevant features for temporal terms are +*Time*, ±*Simultaneous* and ±*Prior*. *Before* contains the features +*Time*, −*Simultaneous*, and +*Prior*; *after* differs from *before* in having a negative value of *Prior*.

Clark interpreted the three levels of performance she found in children's enactment of *before* and *after* statements in terms of the sequential acquisition of the features comprising the meanings of *before* and *after*. Children judged to be at Level 1 were said to have not yet learned any words to express −*Simultaneous*. Children at Level 2 had acquired the feature +*Prior* and applied it to *before*. This feature was extended to *after* by those children who responded to *after* statements as if they were *before* statements and not by those children who continued to follow the order of mention in enacting *after* statements. Children at Level 3 had acquired all the relevant features for both *before* and *after* and so responded appropriately to statements containing either term.

Clark's (1971) study analyzing the various patterns evident in children's responses to *before* and *after* statements offered an elegant and credible account of the course of acquisition of these terms. Also, since *before* and *after* were acquired at a later age than much of the lexicon—at a time when children's knowledge of the meanings of the terms could be assessed experimentally—Clark's (1971) data on age-related changes in children's understanding of *before* and *after* provided an important source of support for the semantic feature hypothesis as a general account of lexical acquisition.

However, subsequent investigators failed to consistently support Clark's conclusions, which depended crucially upon two patterns in the data. First, comprehension of *before* must precede comprehension of *after*. Second, errors in enactment must involve reversals of the two events (rather than the omission of one) in order to support the conclusion that the children's errors involve, for example, following the order of mention or interpreting *after* as if it means *before*. Although subsequent investigators using the enactment paradigm consistently replicated Clark's basic finding that preschoolers perform poorly when asked to act out sentences containing *before* and *after*, some found no difference between the levels of performance for *before* and *after* (e.g., Amidon & Carey, 1972; French & Brown, 1977), and some reported a substantial number of omission errors, particularly of the event in the subordinate clause (e.g., Amidon & Carey, 1972; French & Brown, 1977; Johnson, 1975). While such inconsistencies presumably arise from variations in procedures across studies (e.g., Johnson, 1975), they do suggest that an interpretation of children's acquisition of *before* and *after* in terms of the semantic feature hypothesis is not as straightforward as it appeared on the basis of Clark's initial study.

As an illustration of the way procedural variations may affect the occurrence of the pattern of data supporting the semantic feature model, consider Clark's data in conjunction with other investigators' findings that errors of omission generally involve the event in the subordinate clause. If children making reversal errors and those making omission errors are drawn from the same population, then perhaps many reversal errors can be assumed to be "corrected" omission errors. That is, perhaps the child initially omits one event, then adds it on in response to a reminder—self-generated or provided by the experimenter—that he or she is expected to act out *two* events. If the child making reversal errors is generally adding on the event in the subordinate clause, this would result in correct enactments of *before* statements and reversed enactments of *after* statements, a data pattern central to Clark's claims that *before* is learned earlier than *after* and that there is a period during which *after* is treated as if it is synonymous with *before*. Amidon and Carey (1972) suggest that the elicited production task, which always preceded the comprehension task, cued Clark's subjects that they were expected to act out two events for each statement. This apparently minor procedural difference may account, in part, for the differences in error types found by Clark and other investigators, as well as for the data pattern crucial for supporting the semantic feature hypothesis.

Clark's semantic feature model is a highly refined version of a general class of componential models of lexical acquisition. Such models hold that word meanings consist of discrete components acquired individually over time. Componential models have also been proposed to account for the acquisition of three other terms being considered here: *but*, *because*, and *if*.

Kail (1980) studied French-speaking children's understanding of *mais*, a word more or less synonymous with English *but*. Kail's subjects were from the first through fourth grade, with mean ages of 6;8, 7;11, 8;6, and 9;5. They were asked to judge the acceptability of three types of sentences containing *but*. The three types are exemplified by the following sentences.

1. The pen is new, but it writes poorly.
*2. The pen is new, but it writes well.
*3. The pen is red, but it writes well.

The word *but* has an adversative function, signaling that what is to follow is unexpected on the basis of either prior presuppositions or an inference that might be drawn from a prior statement. New pens ordinarily write well, and *but* appropriately introduces information that denies rather than confirms this presupposition. Thus, Sentence (1) is considered appropriate, while Sentence (2) is considered inappropriate. Sentence (3) is considered inappropriate because the information contained in the two clauses is unrelated.

Kail's first-grade subjects judged the anomalous Type 2 sentences to be correct over 90% of the time, the anomalous Type 3 sentences to be correct about 60% of the time, and the correct Type 1 sentences to be correct only 20% of the time. Second graders rated the Type 3 sentences, in which the two propositions were unrelated, as correct 35% of the time, and the other two sentence types as correct about 60% of the time. Subjects in the two older groups gave the highest acceptability ratings to the correct sentences and the lowest acceptability ratings to the sentences containing unrelated propositions. They did not, however, consistently reject the two inappropriate sentence types. This patterning of the data led Kail to conclude that *but* is first believed to be synonymous with *and*, and that it is then misinterpreted as functioning to *support* rather than *deny* a prior implication or presupposition. Such an analysis is easily translated into a componential model of lexical acquisition, with the youngest children understanding only the conjunctive component of *but*, the intermediate children attaching +*Supportive* to *but*, and the oldest children attaching −*Supportive*.

Emerson studied children's judgments of the grammaticality of *because* and *if* statements (1979, and 1980, respectively). Her basic paradigm involved asking children to attribute appropriately or inappropriately formed *because* and *if* statements to either a sensible *teacher* who always said sensible things or to a silly *clown* who always said silly things that couldn't be true. Children asked to make attributions of *if* statements ranged from 4;10 to 8;7, while those asked to make attributions of *because* statements ranged from 5;8 to 10;11. A sensible *if* statement would be "The dog barked, if someone walked by the house," while a silly *if* statement would involve reversing which clause was introduced by *if*, as in "If the dog barked, someone walked by the house." Similar sentences containing *because* were constructed. After judging a sentence as either *silly* or *sensible*, the child was asked to change it so that it would have the opposite characteristic (i.e., asked to make sentences judged *silly* to be *sensible*, and vice versa).

If, *because*, and *so* can each be considered to involve at least two meaning components: one expressing a causal or conditional relationship between propositions; the other expressing the order of the propositions. It is the order component that distinguishes *because* from *so*, and that was violated to create the *silly* sentences used as stimuli. Emerson's conclusions regarding the course of acquisition of *because* and *if* were that while children understand the causal or conditional component of the terms by about age five, they do not acquire the order component until age eight or later. These conclusions are in accord with Piaget (1928), who asked children to complete sentences such as "The boy fell off his bicycle because..." and found that although preoperational children generally mention a causally related event, it is likely to be a consequent rather than an antecedent of the event described in the main clause. An important pattern emerging in Emerson's studies was a positive response bias, with children more likely to judge *silly* sentences as *sensible* than vice versa.

A recent study by Bebout, Segalowitz, and White (1980) also suggests that the order component of *because* is not well understood by children under nine. These investigators assessed the ability of children in kindergarten through fourth grade to act out sentences taking three forms: (1) X so Y; (2) because X, Y; (3) Y because X.

Sentence content was very simple; four objects were referred to, and only the verb *moved* was used. A sample sentence would be "The ruler moved because the car moved," for which the correct response would involve using the car to push the ruler. The actual (antecedent-consequent) order of occurrence of events X and Y is preserved by Sentence Forms 1 and 2, and reversed by Sentence Form 3. Subjects at all ages were above chance on the two sentence forms in which order of mention preserved order of occurrence. On the Y because X sentences, kindergarteners' performance was at chance, first and second graders were systematically incorrect, third graders were at chance, and fourth graders responded accurately. Bebout et al. interpreted these findings as indicating that kindergarteners have no particular strategy for responding to sentences taking this form, and that older children adopt a systematic, but incorrect order-of-mention strategy that is gradually replaced with a full understanding of the meaning of *because*. While noting that their findings do not indicate that children do not understand or use sentences containing *because* before age nine, the authors claim that "many children under 9 do not pick up the syntactic cues provided by *because* when given a task where all semantic and contextual cues are deliberately removed" (1980, p. 567).

Some of the first studies assessing children's understanding of the word *or* were carried out by Neimark (1970; Neimark & Slotnick, 1970), who assessed the ability of subjects from third grade to college-age to comprehend *or* statements. One task Neimark used involved presenting subjects with pictures of black birds, white birds, black flowers, and white flowers, and then asking them to select all the elements represented by *or* statements, such as "Things that are black or birds." The only response considered correct for this example involved selecting all the black birds, white birds, and black flowers. Subjects made two major types of errors. One involved selecting the intersection of the two sets (e.g., black birds). The other error involved selecting only one of the two sets mentioned (e.g., only black things, or only birds). The relative frequency of these error types varied somewhat across age, but both were common. Neimark (1970) concluded that the ability to comprehend *or* does not develop until the high-school years, and is dependent upon the attainment of formal operations. There is also a suggestion in her discussion of the data that prior to the high-school years, *or* is often misinterpreted as meaning *and*. Other investigators, including Suppes and Feldman (1971) and Paris (1973), also found that *or* statements were often interpreted as if they were conjunctive, rather than disjunctive. Although these authors did not discuss it in these terms, their conclusion that *or* was often misinterpreted as if it meant *and* would fit a componential model of the acquisition of word meaning, with children learning fairly early that both *or* and *and* have an iterative function (e.g., Braine, 1978), but failing to attach the meanings of joint and alternative iteration to *and* and *or*, respectively, until adolescence.

The idea that the concept expressed by *or* is so complex that it depends upon the attainment of formal operations is counterintuitive, and the conclusion that young children do not understand the meaning of *or* appears to result from a failure to respect the different meanings or functions *or* assumes in natural language compared to formal logic. Ford (1976) describes three presuppositions that underlie the use of *or* in natural language, but are not relevant to the function of this term in formal logic. First, *or* implies a choice between elements; second, these elements are mutually exclusive; third, these elements are members, at equivalent levels of specificity, of the same category. One or more of these presuppositions have been violated in a number of experiments designed to measure children's comprehension of *or*. In the studies by Neimark, described above, all three presuppositions were violated. First, to be credited with responding correctly, subjects were required to select *all* of the items that could satisfy the *or* statement, rather than choosing among them. (Note that both error types prevalent in Neimark's data involved selecting *a* correct choice, rather than exhaustively selecting *all possible* correct choices). Second, sets such as *black* and *bird* are intersecting rather than mutually exclusive, which also means that, third, they are not members of the same category. Similar violations of the presuppositions associated with the use of *or* in natural language occurred in other studies that were interpreted as indicating that young children do not understand the term *or* (e.g., Paris, 1973; Suppes & Feldman, 1971).

Ford (1976) and Braine and Rumain (1981) presented children and adults with multiple tasks assessing the comprehension of *or*. These tasks varied in the extent to which they tapped knowledge of either the natural language or formal logic meanings of *or*. Both studies found age-related changes in the ability to comprehend *or*, with those uses of *or* most closely related to its natural language meaning being understood first, and those uses most closely related to formal logic such as set union, being understood much later. Ford (1976) found little difference between the ability of five-year-old children and adults to respond appropriately to *or* statements whose content was in accord with the presuppositions governing the use of *or* in natural language, and found that compared to their performance in response to these natural language statements, even adults were slower and made more errors when asked to deal with *or* statements that were well-formed according to the conventions of formal logic but violated those of natural language.

Studies of the Production of Relational Terms

While it is by no means exhaustive, the above review of the literature of the majority of the research in this area in terms of both the methods used and conclusions reached. Many of the studies reviewed either explicitly or implicitly propose versions of a componential model of lexical acquisition to account for age-related changes in response patterns on the various comprehension tasks. If these componential models accurately reflect stages through which children progress in acquiring the meaning of particular terms, then it is possible to derive quite specific predictions about the types of errors they would be expected to make when producing the terms.

As noted earlier, fewer studies of young children's acquisition of relational terms have involved production measures than comprehension measures. However, there are several reports based upon production data, and these suggest both that comprehension measures overestimate the age at which the various relational terms are acquired and that componential models developed to account for the acquisition of these terms are inaccurate.

The most extensive study of the production of relational terms has been carried out by Lois Bloom and her colleagues (e.g., Bittetti-Capatides, Fiess & Bloom, 1980; Bloom, Lahey, Hood, Lifter, & Fiess, 1980; Fiess, Bittetti-Capatides & Bloom, 1979; Hood & Bloom, 1979). Bloom recorded children's spontaneous speech in their home longitudinally over approximately the 24 to 41 month age-range. Bloom et al. (1980) report the appropriate production of *if*, *so*, *because*, and *but* during this period. Eisenburg (1980) also recorded spontaneous speech across approximately the same age-range, and reports appropriate productions of *because* and *so*. McCabe, Evely, Abramovitch, Corter, and Pepler (1983) found that the *if* statements three- to seven-year-old children directed toward their siblings were syntactically and semantically appropriate. Gallivan (1982) considered productions of *but* that occurred while interviewing three- to seven-year-olds about verb meanings. This term was used appropriately by children spanning the entire age-range. Johannson and Sjölin (1975) reported that all productions of *or* by their two- to seven-year-old subjects were appropriate. French (1981, 1983, in press; French & Nelson, 1981, 1982, 1983, in press) analyzed transcripts obtained by interviewing three- to five-year-old children about familiar events, and found that the children produced all the terms being considered here (i.e., *before, after, because, so, if, but,* and *or*). In most cases, the children's productions were correct, and their occasional errors were not ones that would be predicted on the basis of the various componential models developed to describe stages of lexical acquisition.

Production and Comprehension Measures

As noted earlier, there are disagreements among investigators as to whether production or comprehension measures provide more valid means of assessing what children know about a term's meaning. To further complicate matters, there are different types of production and comprehension. In this section, various approaches to studying children's production and comprehension of relational terms are described, and problems that arise in interpeting the results of these various approaches are discussed. The following quotes provide a context within which to consider the relative benefits and drawbacks of each approach.

> The results from the two types of study sometimes conflict, with the observational studies of production attributing more to children than comprehension studies do. This is because of a tendency to assume that anything said by a child has the adult value for the words used. But production alone, however adultlike it *sounds*, is not necessarily a good guide to what children know about the meanings in question. (Clark, 1983, p. 811)

> The most straightforward problem with comprehension studies that has emerged over the last decade or so is that these studies seem easily to underestimate children's knowledge when comparisons with rigorously analyzed naturalistic findings can be made.... After all, the child spontaneously speaks only if interested but may give some kind of comprehension response to a construction because of experimenter pressure, not from interest. (Maratsos, 1983, p. 774)

Naturalistic Contexts

In "naturalistic" settings in which a child is observed engaging in spontaneous conversation with an adult or another child, the child may use relational terms or respond in various ways (appropriately, inappropriately, indeterminantly) to the other's use of the terms. Except for the inevitable demand characteristics associated with the observer's presence (e.g., Orne, 1970; Graves, 1981), such settings are very similar to those in which children typically learn and use language, and so in many ways are ideal for studying the child's linguistic knowledge. The speakers' utterances can be assumed to arise solely from communicative intent. The child's responses to the partner's utterances are likewise motivated by voluntary engagement in a (usually) socially meaningful interaction.

However, although collecting data in naturalistic settings avoids the pitfalls of more contrived contexts for studying language understanding, it is often difficult to draw unequivocal conclusions about what children really understand about a term from their productions and responses to other's productions in such a situation. For example, a listener may be able to use the extralinguistic context to reach a plausible interpretation of a child's use of a particular term despite the fact that the child does not understand its meaning and did not intend the interpretation reached (e.g., Clark, 1983). Similarly, what appears to be an appropriate production of a term may actually be a formulaic, unanalyzed string of words that the child has memorized. Rather than reflecting an understanding of a particular term's meaning, the child's appropriate responses to the other's utterances may rely either upon the child's general world knowledge or upon cues provided by the extralinguistic setting. For example, a child who correctly acts out a mother's suggestion to brush a doll's hair before putting on its hat may be relying on knowledge of the typical order of these events rather than on an understanding of the meaning of the word *before*.

It is in an effort to alleviate these sorts of problems of interpretation, and also because of the low incidence of production of relational terms in children's spontaneous speech (e.g., Ford, 1976), that many investigators prefer experimental means of assessing production and comprehension of relational terms. Experimental approaches allow the investigator a great deal of control over the extralinguistic context, and thus often permit less ambiguous determinations that a child comprehends or produces a term appropriately.

Experimental Contexts: Production

There are two primary ways investigators have elicited production in experimental settings: asking the child to imitate a statement containing the term of interest, and asking questions whose correct answers are likely to contain the target term (e.g., asking *why* questions to elicit responses containing *because* or *so*, and asking *when* questions to elicit responses containing *before* or *after*). Two less commonly used measures are hybrid tasks involving both comprehension and production—*sentence completion* and *sentence repair*. Sentence completion is illustrated by Piaget's (1928) task in which children are asked to complete sentences such as "The boy fell off his bicycle because . . . ." Sentence repair is illustrated by Emerson's (1979, 1980) task in which children are asked to make *silly* sentences *sensible* (e.g., "If I put up my umbrella, it starts to rain"), and vice versa.

Elicited production is by no means a foolproof way of determining whether a child knows the meaning of a term. Whichever means of elicitation is used, the child's failure to produce a particular term clearly does not permit a conclusion that he or she *cannot* use the term. Conversely, it is entirely possible for a child to imitate a statement without actually understanding the meanings of the individual terms it contains. There also seem to be marked individual differences in children's willingness or ability to imitate (e.g., Maratsos, 1983).

Appropriate responses to *why* and *when* questions often provide a strong basis for concluding that a child knows the meanings of words such as *because*, *so*, *before*, and *after*. However, failures to respond, nonlinguistic responses such as pointing to a picture of the queried event in response to a *when* qustion (Carni & French, 1984), and nonrelational responses such as answering "just now" in response to *when* questions asked about one of two events just enacted (Clark, 1971) do not permit conclusions that the child does not know the term the investigator is attempting to elicit.

Successful repairs of anomalous sentences (e.g., changing "If I put up my umbrella it starts to rain" to "I put up my umbrella if it starts to rain") may provide strong evidence that a child knows the meaning of the target term, but again it is generally inappropriate to interpret unsuccessful performance as indicating that the child does not know the term. Repairing anomalous sentences requires several steps, and children may understand the target term perfectly well, but fail to understand what they are expected to do, or fail to successfully execute one or more of the steps necessary to effect a repair.

Experimental Contexts: Comprehension

Most research on children's understanding of relational terms involves experimental assessments of comprehension, and a variety of different comprehension paradigms have been developed. In these paradigms the child is required to do or say something in response to a series of statements containing the target term(s). A judgment is then made regarding the child's understanding of the term(s) on the basis of the pattern of responses. Comprehension paradigms include asking children questions that contain the target term, asking them to act out a statement containing the term, asking them to judge the grammaticality of a statement, asking them to select a picture depicting the statement, and so forth. In this section, several general concerns that apply to comprehension paradigms are raised, then discussed with reference to the particular paradigms or particular stimuli used in the studies reviewed above.

A centrally important point when considering investigations of children's lexical development is that both task and child variables prevent any direct or pure measures of comprehension. All comprehension tasks involve secondary task demands in addition to the primary (to the investigator) demand of comprehending a particular term. For example, successful performance within a grammaticality judgment paradigm requires metalinguistic skills (i.e., conscious reflection upon the language) in addition to knowledge of the meaning of the target term. Successful performance on an enactment task designed to assess comprehension of *before* and *after* typically involves enacting the events described in both clauses, rather than enacting the first event, then awaiting approval or further instructions prior to carrying out the second event (e.g., French & Brown, 1977). Poor performance on comprehension tasks may result from failure to understand or comply with secondary task demands, as well as from lack of understanding of the target term. That is, a child who understands the meaning of a term may nevertheless perform poorly if he or she does not understand the secondary task demands.

When working with preschoolers, an important child variable is that they are unlikely to have learned test-taking conventions (e.g., attending closely to the questions being asked, trying to understand fully what the test-giver expects, asking questions to clarify things they do not understand, being committed to getting the right answer to the question being asked, etc.). Preschoolers do, however, understand some fairly elementary aspects of assessment situations, such as that they are expected to provide a response to every question the experimenter asks, and that they will receive positive feedback, and be allowed to move on, only when they do so. The speed and confidence with which preschoolers often respond to an experimenter's questions should not necessarily be taken as evidence that their responses are governed by the stimuli sentences the experimenter presents. For example, a common response pattern for two- and three-year-olds in a two-choice picture selection task is to alternate between the left and right positions. That this is systematic, suffices to move on to the next item, and—except in training studies—is typically met with nods, smiles, and words of encouragement from the experimenter.

Young children are committed strategy users, which means that they often produce systematic rather than random error patterns. Such systematicness can lend spurious support to certain models of acquisition. Some patterns of response, such as the left-right alternation just mentioned, are easily detectable as nonlinguistic response strategies. Other systematic patterns of responding are more subtle, and it may be difficult to determine whether they are lexically relevant. Systematic error patterns within a single paradigm form the basis for many of the componential models proposed to account for the acquisition of particular relational terms. A crucial question is whether such support is spurious or genuine. For example, if children fail to distinguish between *silly* and *sensible* sentences containing *if*, declaring all to be *sensible*, does this reflect a failure to appreciate the order component of *if*, or is it a lexically irrelevant response bias? A particular task affords only a restricted set of lexically irrelevant response patterns, and the choice among these may vary with age as the child becomes sensitive to different aspects of the task. For example, in enacting two-clause *before* and *after* sentences, it appears that younger children tend to follow an order-of-mention strategy, while older children tend to follow a main-clause-first strategy.

It is often assumed that lexically irrelevant response strategies compensate for lack of appropriate lexical knowledge, and so are used by children only when they do not know the meaning of the term being assessed. This is not necessarily the case. The factors governing the use of a particular strategy may be too powerful to be counteracted by lexical knowledge alone, and so a lexically irrelevant response strategy may persist even when the child has the relevant lexical knowledge. For example, Goodz (1982) offers an excellent demonstration that syntactically determined response strategies evoked by the enactment task traditionally used to assess comprehension of *before* and *after* may mask genuine comprehension of these terms.

Finally, a point implicit in much of the above discussion that should be made explicit concerns the appropriate interpretation of poor performance. On a carefully designed comprehension measure, successful performance generally provides a strong basis for concluding that a child knows the term in question. The converse conclusion—that is, that poor performance reflects lack of knowledge of the target term—is simply not logically supportable. Despite underlying knowledge of the term, a child may exhibit poor performance for a variety of reasons, including adoption of a lexically irrelevant response strategy, lack of attention or motivation, failure to understand the task demands, inability to comply with one of the secondary task demands, and so forth.

The logical fallacy of concluding lack of specific underlying knowledge on the basis of potentially multiply determined performance failure is easy to appreciate in the abstract. However, when an investigator has carefully designed a task on which successful performance necessarily indicates the presence of certain knowledge, the conclusion that unsuccessful performance indicates the absence of that knowledge is very inviting. Investigators have been particularly susceptible to this fallacy when their subjects produce systematic error patterns that can be interpreted as indicating partial knowledge of a term's meaning.

Many of these critiques of comprehension paradigms apply to the specific studies reviewed above. The results of many of these studies were interpreted as supporting componential models of lexical acquisition, with the components constituting a term's meaning being acquired individually over a several year period. While Carey (1977) is undoubtedly correct in stating that the rapid rate of preschoolers' vocabulary acquisition must mean that they operate with incomplete lexical entries much of the time, some of the claims regarding the length of time between the acquisition of two components seem improbable. For example, why should there be a three-year lag between the time children acquire the causal or conditional component of *because* and *if*, and the time they acquire the order component of these terms (Emerson, 1979, 1980), especially since there is no a priori reason to expect that *order* is a more difficult concept than *causality*? While this analysis of the subjects' performance seems improbable, it is quite plausible that lexically irrelevant response strategies subjects brought to the task, failure or inability to comply with the task demands, the experimental stimuli, or some interaction among these, yielded the results Emerson interpreted as indicating the sequential acquisition of the meaning components. It is generally the case that children display a positive response bias and agree that *everything* sounds sensible. In addition, a number of Emerson's *silly* sentences were actually sensible, elliptical sentences. For example, the sentence "If the dog barks, someone walks by the house" is an elliptical and only slightly syntactically deviant version of the evidential usage of *if* in the sentence "If the dog barks, [I take it as evidence that] someone has walked by the house." People keep watchdogs precisely because they believe that if the dog barks, they can draw an inference about someone being nearby. More to the point, children undoubtedly hear a large number of elliptical evidential *if* statements, and the requirement that they judge such sentences as inappropriate in order to be credited with understanding the meaning of the word *if* seems overly stringent.

Similar questions about stimuli arise with regard to Kail's (1980) study of children's understanding of *but*. The stimulus sentences regarded as anomalous (e.g., "The pen is new, but it writes well" and "The pen is red, but it writes well") can be regarded as perfectly acceptable given certain assumptions (e.g., that the speakers had just been expressing their preference for old pens, or that one had just requested a black pen). To the extent that the anomalous sentences used by Emerson and Kail were really more or less acceptable, then subjects in these studies were faced with the very complex secondary task demand of determining what rules of acceptability held in the experimental context that did not necessarily hold in ordinary discourse. Experienced test-takers develop skill in figuring out teachers' and experimenters' often opaque intent, but this skill is unlikely to be well-developed in preschoolers.

Bebout et al.'s (1980) claim that children under nine "do not pick up the syntactic cues provided by *because* when given a task where all semantic and contextual cues are deliberately removed" (p. 562) is a plausible interpretation of their data. This claim may be interpreted either as meaning that young children lack knowledge of the *order* component inherent in the meaning of *because*, or as meaning that children succumb to a syntactically based but lexically irrelevant response strategy involving beginning their enactment with the first object mentioned. The latter interpretation seems the more feasible since, in their spontaneous speech, children frequently produce semantically appropriate *because* statements of the form "Y because X" (e.g., French & Nelson, 1983). Under this interpretation however, Bebout et al.'s (1980) results are less relevant to the question of the extent of children's lexical knowledge than to the question of whether children can display their lexical knowledge in a particular experimental context. This general point is discussed further below.

Conclusion and Implications

The above discussion should make it clear that in studying the acquisition of relational terms there are no self-evident solutions to the questions of whether to rely on naturalistic or experimental procedures, and whether comprehension or production data are preferable. Each method has its own benefits and drawbacks, and investigators relying on only one measure almost inevitably run the risk of either overestimating or underestimating their subjects' understanding of a term. The fact that most investigations of children's understanding of relational terms rely upon experimentally generated comprehension data reflects (a) the low incidence of relational terms in spontaneous speech, and (b) the fact that experimental approaches to studying comprehension offer greater control over the linguistic and extralinguistic stimuli, thus permitting greater confidence in conclusions that accurate performance reflects genuine understanding of the terms. However, reliance on comprehension paradigms becomes problematic in the face of the comprehension-production disparity, and the propensity of young children to adopt systematic, but possibly lexically irrelevant strategies in responding to comprehension tasks.

In a critique of the semantic feedback account of lexical acquisition, Richards (1979) suggests employing converging operations to address the recurrent problem that "children's comprehension task performance is confounded with their response biases which are specific to the linguistic and nonlinguistic contexts in which the lexical items are presented" (p. 1). Assessing production and comprehension in both naturalistic and experimental settings, and particularly using various comprehension paradigms in assessing children's understanding of the same term, would appear to be an obvious first step toward resolving some of the issues that have been raised regarding the appropriate interpretation of various studies of children's acquisition of relational terms.

While converging measures offer the obvious, "textbook" solution to the question of how best to account for children's understanding of relational terms, such an approach would require great care. Different assessment paradigms afford different lexically irrelevant response biases, so it would be extremely difficult to develop a complete picture of children's understanding of a particular term on the basis of their pattern of response across a variety of tasks. Rather than yielding a clear picture of children's understanding of a given term, using a variety of different assessment procedures would be likely to yield a relatively confusing picture interpretable primarily in terms of idiosyncratic or age-related response strategies evoked by various tasks.

On the other hand, using different paradigms offers an ideal means of assessing the validity of models of acquisition based upon an analysis of error patterns. If instead of reflecting lexically irrelevant response biases, error patterns genuinely arise from children's understanding of the terms themselves, then similar errors should arise across different assessment contexts. Thus, converging methods can offer a check against overinterpreting paradigm-generated error patterns as indicating stages of partial understanding. For example, Clark's (1971) conclusion that *before* is acquired earlier than *after* was based on her finding that children correctly enacted sentences containing *before* more often than sentences containing *after*. If children really acquire *before* earlier than *after*, then they would be expected to show this pattern across tasks, despite changes in various aspects of the assessment procedure. However, using a different task, Carni and French (1984) found that children of approximately the same age as the children in Clark's study made more errors in response to *before* questions than in response to *after* questions. For each task, it is possible to explain the superior performance on one or the other of the words in terms of lexically irrelevant response strategies (Carni & French, 1984), and there is therefore no basis for concluding that either task validly indicates that one of the terms is acquired earlier than the other. In short, while the indiscriminant use of converging measures is likely to yield uninterpretable data, converging measures offer an invaluable and necessary means of assessing the validity of specific models of acquisition.

The preceding review of research addressing children's acquisition of relational terms indicated that most of this research has been interpreted as supporting a componential model of lexical acquisition, whereby words are assumed to consist of a set of meaning components that are acquired and attached to the word individually over some period of time. Similar conclusions about acquisition have emerged for different relational terms despite the fact that investigators with quite different interests and theoretical orientations have used a variety of different methods to investigate children's understanding of the various terms, and have in some cases been unaware of research addressing the acquisition of the other terms. This would seem to offer strong converging support for the validity of a componential model as an account of lexical acquisition within this semantic domain.

It can be argued, however, that such support is spurious and artifactual, and that the various lines of research have converged for several reasons, all having little to do with the process of lexical acquisition. These reasons include the following: (1) Children are committed strategy users and so tend to make systematic rather than random errors when they do not understand either the target term or the task demands. (2) It is often possible (although perhaps erroneous) to interpret systematic error patterns as indicating partial knowledge of the components constituting a word's meaning. (3) Investigators have succumbed to the logical fallacy of concluding that poor performance on a task designed to measure comprehension of a target term necessarily indicates lack of knowledge of the target term. They have rarely considered that poor performance may arise from lexically irrelevant factors such as compliance with a powerful but lexically irrelevant response strategy, or failure to understand and/or comply with secondary task demands. (4) After deriving models on the basis of a single study, investigators have rarely attempted to *test* these models using different tasks or different stimuli; it is noteworthy that in those cases where models have been tested by other investigators, the models have often not received support (e.g., Ford's, 1976, assessment of the model developed to account for the acquisition of *or*, and numerous investigators' assessments of the model developed to account for the acquisition of *before* and *after*).

Content as a Context for Comprehending Relational Terms

This section proposes a model of children's understanding of relational terms which offers several advantages over the current collection of componential models. This model is congruent with current views of cognitive development, can account for the existing literature (including the problematic disparity between the ages at which children appear to use relational terms appropriately and the ages at which they appear to comprehend them), and can support the generation of testable predictions. The theoretical orientation underlying the model is described first, followed by a description of how this orientation translates into a model of developmental change in the understanding of relational terms.

Characteristics of Context-Sensitive Research

As noted in the introduction, the study of cognitive development during the preschool years has recently undergone a substantial change in focus. Following Piaget's lead, for many years researchers simply used preschool-aged subjects as a foil against which to display the more advanced cognitive competencies of older children. As developmental psychologists began to seek a more positive characterization of the abilities of preschoolers, they found that careful manipulation of the experimental context could reveal the existence of a number of cognitive competencies previously believed to be beyond the capacity of very young children.

When investigators initially began attempting to devise context-sensitive approaches to studying cognitive development, it was sufficient to simply challenge the traditional view of preschoolers' ability by showing that manipulations of the experimental context could significantly lower the ages at which certain competencies could be displayed. In the past ten years, it has become increasingly clear that the traditional Piagetian view seriously underestimates preschoolers' cognitive abilities.

As the area of context-sensitive research has become more established and sophisticated, there has been an increasing attempt to go beyond simple demonstrations that context makes a difference, and to explain why this should be the case and why careful attention to contextual variables becomes less important in eliciting displays of cognitive competence with increasing age. In other words, instead of simply using the results of context-sensitive research as a basis for challenging Piagetian claims, investigators have begun to use these results as the basis for developing alternative models of cognitive development.

Models of development based on context-sensitive research are not yet well-developed, but their essential outlines are becoming apparent. Currently, several major developmental theorists seem to be suggesting that cognitive development may be characterized, in large part, as the *gradual decontextualization* of cognitive abilities (e.g, Brown, 1976, 1977; Brown, Bransford, Ferrara, & Campione, 1983; Donaldson, 1978; Gelman, 1978; Mandler, 1983; Nelson, 1977; Nelson & Gruendel, 1981). Despite the fact that these investigators study quite different domains within cognitive development, make different assumptions about the origins of particular cognitive abilities, and describe their results in different terms, they are in basic agreement about the importance of contextual factors in both the acquisition and display of cognitive abilities. Their essential premise is that cognitive competence initially arises within, is embedded within, and is practiced within particular contexts. The child then gradually becomes able to separate the competence from the particular context and apply it more widely. Eventually, although not inevitably (depending upon the skill and its importance within a particular culture), the child may be able to separate the competence from any particular context and apply it in a relatively context-independent manner. The process just described is often referred to as the *gradual decontextualization* of cognitive abilities.[2]

The expression *context-sensitive* has been coined to serve as an umbrella term capturing commonalities among quite varied research issues and orientations. As one way of attempting to define this vague expression more precisely, and capture some important differences among the various context-sensitive approaches investigators have developed, it is useful to think of context as referring to both *external* (experi-

---

[2]The term "decontextualization" is sometimes misunderstood as suggesting an assumption that cognitive abilities can be used or displayed in the absence of *any* context; this is of course impossible, and the expressions "context-independent" and "decontextualized" should be taken as indicating that an ability is not tied to any *particular* context, but rather may be applied in a variety of different contexts.

mental) and *internal* (cognitive) factors. In study of both language and cognitive development, context has generally been considered in terms of *external* factors, such as experimental setting, procedure, and stimuli. One might, for example, vary the setting (home or laboratory) in which a particular ability is assessed, adjust the response required so that it is simpler or more in accord with the child's habitual behavior, and/or devise stimuli that are of inherent interest to the child, and therefore highly motivating. These various approaches may be seen in numerous studies by investigators seeking ways to maximize opportunities for young children to display their emerging cognitive competencies. DeLoache (1980) provides an excellent discussion of context-sensitive approaches to working with very young children, and has used these approaches successfully in studying the development of memory for object location.

Manipulations of the experimental context are, of course, undertaken in accord with assumptions about *internal* characteristics of the child (e.g., what constitutes a motivating task or a simpler response mode). However, a more powerful way of conceiving of context as an internal variable has been proposed by Nelson and Gruendel (1981). These authors suggest that the child's *knowledge base* constitutes an important context for cognitive activity. This suggestion was made specifically with regard to children's general event representations, or scripts, but can be considered to apply more widely. The claim is essentially that children will display more sophisticated performance across a variety of cognitive domains when they are operating with familiar, well-represented content. While Nelson and Gruendel were the first to frame such a suggestion in terms of scripts as an important cognitive context, the general point is in accord with positions taken by Shatz (1978) in terms of information processing load, and by Bremner (1982) in terms of the interplay between the child's ever-changing representation of the environment and the child's ability to act intelligently within that environment.

Toward a Context-Sensitive Model of Relational Term Usage

With regard to the understanding of relational terms, Nelson and Gruendel's (1981) suggestion of the importance of the child's knowledge base as a context central to the display of cognitive competencies can be translated into a concern with the *content* of the sentences in which relational terms are embedded. Sentence content is not a variable that has been considered extensively in the research on children's comprehension of relational terms, yet would seem to be an important factor in children's ability to acquire and understand relational terms. Macnamara (1972) claimed that it was only by having access to an extralinguistic context redundant with the linguistic context, that the child could conceivably learn which syntactic variations were semantically relevant and which were not. French and Brown (1977) made a similar point regarding the acquisition of relational terms, claiming that it was only through independent knowledge of the relationship being described that the child could induce the meanings of terms such as *before* and *after*. Redundancy between extralinguistic knowledge and linguistic input may be achieved in several ways, including matching the linguistic input to an observable event (e.g., "Look, Dad dropped the keys before he got in the car"), or matching the linguistic input to an already known relationship (e.g., "Get into bed after you put on your pajamas").

French and Brown's (1977) general point regarding the importance of matching linguistic input to extralinguistic context is in accord with generally accepted views on how children come to establish word-meaning correspondence. The acquisition of relational terms differs from vocabulary acquisition in that there are no concrete, observable referents for the terms themselves. Whereas objects and actions can be labeled directly for the child, the "meaning" of relational terms can be displayed only when they are embedded within semantic content the child understands.

The essential premise of the model being proposed is that in addition to being a crucial factor in the initial acquisition of relational terms, the semantic content of statements containing relational terms remains an important factor in children's ability to comprehend them for some time after the period of initial acquisition. The relationship expressed by a statement containing a relational term may be one that is already familiar to the child, or it may be unfamiliar. Consider for example the following sentences:

1. Raggedy Ann took the dog for a walk before she fed the baby.
2. Raggedy Ann filled the baby's bottle before she fed the baby.

There is no inherent temporal constraint upon the order in which babies are fed and dogs walked. On the other hand, there is an inherent temporal constraint upon the order in which bottles are filled and babies fed. An individual with general cultural knowledge about the care of babies is likely to be familiar with the relationship expressed in the second sentence. Relationships such as that expressed in the first sentence, which are not constrained by cultural convention of logical necessity, are unlikely to be widely familiar.

It is proposed that the distinction between using or comprehending relational terms when they refer to an already known relationship, versus when they establish an essentially arbitrary relationship, is of developmental significance. Comprehension involves generating a mental representation on the basis of linguistic input. To comprehend statements reporting *familiar* relationships, the listener need only use the linguistic input to access an already existing mental representation of the relevant relationship. To comprehend statements reporting *unfamiliar* relationships, the listener must use the linguistic input to generate a mental representation of a previously unknown relationship. Comprehension of these two different types of statements would seem to place quite different demands on the listener.[3] These differing demands can be characterized in terms of information processing load (e.g., Shatz, 1978), in terms of the distinction between using linguistic input as a guide rather than the sole source of meaning (e.g., Olson & Nickerson, 1978), in terms of the facilitating effect of easily represented content on cognitive processing (e.g., Wason & Johnson-Laird, 1972; Nelson & Gruendel, 1981), and so forth. Whichever

---

[3]Degree of familiarity is obviously a continuous rather than dichotomous variable, and so talking about "two different types" of statements is something of a simplification.

of these overlapping orientations is adopted to describe the difference between the comprehension of statements expressing familiar versus unfamiliar relationships, the ability to comprehend statements reporting known relationships can be expected to be a developmental precursor of the ability to comprehend statements that require *establishing representations of unfamiliar relationships*. Such a developmental progression in terms of the ease of comprehending the two types of statements would not reflect a change from *partial* to *full* knowledge of the lexical terms expressing the relationships but, rather, an extension of the contexts in which knowledge of the meaning of the terms can be called upon.

Most studies designed to assess children's comprehension of relational terms have used sentences reporting arbitrary (and thus unfamiliar) relationships as stimuli.[4] Most of the existing literature is therefore systematically biased against the possibility of detecting a developmental stage at which children can understand relatilar terms when they express familar relationships but experience difficulty in using relational terms as the basis for establishing representations of novel relationships.

There seem to be two reasons that most studies of children's comprehension of relational terms use stimuli in which the propositions in the two clauses have no particular relationship to one another beyond the fleeting one established by the target term. Within some paradigms, confidence that correct responses reflect understanding of the target term is possible only if the individual propositions have no real-world relationship with one another. For example, within an enactment paradigm, children could respond correctly to sentences describing temporally constrained events (e.g., filling bottles and feeding babies) on the basis of their general knowledge, without understanding the relational term. Although it has rarely been made explicit (cf. Bebout et al., 1980), it is likely that a second reason for using statements that contain propositions having no inherent relationship with one another as stimuli derives from the assumption that "true comprehension" or "full understanding" of lexical items is necessarily context and/or content independent.

These reasons for relying solely on statements expressing arbitrary relationships to assess children's understanding of relational terms are inappropriate. First, it is possible to devise assessment paradigms that permit confidence that correct responses to statements expressing either familiar or unfamiliar relationships do, in fact, depend on correct interpretation of the target term. Second, it can be argued that the transition from being able to comprehend relational terms when they refer to familiar relationships to being able to comprehend relational terms regardless of the semantic content being related does not reflect lexical development per se. Third, even if it is maintained that comprehending relational terms when they are used to express familiar relationships does not indicate "full comprehension" of the term, the finding that young children's understanding of relational terms is initially sensitive to the semantic context in which they occur would nevertheless be of developmental significance. Finally, insistence that the child demonstrate full

---

[4]The exceptions to this claim in the literature we have reviewed include Kail's (1980) and Emerson's (1979, 1980) grammaticality judgment studies.

understanding before being credited with lexical acquisition is a stringent criterion rarely applied to other terms.

Evidence Supporting the Proposed Developmental Progression

French and Brown (1977) and later Kavanaugh (1979) proposed variants of the contextual model several years ago, based on their findings that young children correctly enacted logically constrained sentences containing *before* and *after* (e.g., "Raggedy Ann fed the baby after she filled the bottle") earlier than they correctly enacted sentences in which the temporal ordering of the events was arbitrary (e.g., "The dog ran away after Raggedy Ann fed the baby"). However, such data cannot be interpreted as strong support for the contextual model since, as noted above, correct responses to the logically constrained sentences could have been achieved without comprehending, or even attending to, the temporal terms.

In a recent study, Carni and French (1984) used a comprehension paradigm that enabled a more adequate test of the contextual model. In this study, three- and four-year-old children heard 16 five-event stories about topics familiar to young children. Half of the stories (*invariant*) were about topics having a culturally or logically constrained ordering of events (e.g., eating at a restaurant) and half (*arbitrary*) were about topics for which there was no necessary or conventional order to the composite events (e.g., taking a walk in a park). Each story was illustrated with five pictures, which were placed in order in front of the child as the story was read. After hearing the story, the child was asked what happened *before* or *after* the third (i.e., central) event. The child was then asked *when* one of the events happened. The pictures, still sequenced, remained present while the children responded to the questions.

In this paradigm, above-chance discrimination between *before* and *after* questions referrring to either the invariant or arbitrary stories necessarily depends on comprehension of the temporal term. Furthermore, syntactic factors are held constant so that despite any lexically irrelevant response strategies elicited by the task, differences across story types can be attributed solely to the content of the stories. The paradigm thus offers a valid means of assessing the possibility that children are able to respond appropriately to temporal terms earlier when they refer to familiar, compared to unfamiliar, sequences.

Using correct responses to *before* and *after* questions as the dependent variable, the main effects for age and story type, as well as the interaction between these variables, were significant (F $(1,30)=8.41$, $p<.01$; F $(1,30)=11.20$, $p<.005$; F $(1,30)=4.47$, $p<.05$ respectively). In responding to questions referring to the invariant stories, the performance of the three- and four-year-olds was not significantly different, and was significantly above chance. Four-year-olds showed no difference in responding to questions referring to the invariant and arbitrary stories; three-year-olds responded at chance to questions referring to arbitrary stories.

This pattern of results was interpreted as indicating that children are able to demonstrate comprehension of *before* and *after* when these terms refer to relatively familiar, temporal relationships at an earlier age than they can understand the same terms when they refer to relatively unfamiliar, temporal relationships. In discussing these findings, it was noted that in responding to the questions about the invariant stories, the three-year-old children demonstrated *basic comprehension* of the "full" lexical meaning of the terms *before* and *after*. They did not, for example, demonstrate the sorts of partial comprehension of the terms suggested by Clark's (1971) semantic feature account. It was argued that the increase with age in the ability to deal successfully with the terms when they referred to arbitrary sequences should not be considered as indicating *lexical* development but, rather, that the change observed with age reflected the *extension* of the basic lexical knowledge to a wider range of situations (e.g., those in which the terms referred to novel, rather than simply familiar, relationships).

Because production generally involves formulating a statement to describe an already existing mental representation, the ability to produce relational terms appropriately would seem to be more closely related to the ability to comprehend statements reporting familiar, compared to unfamiliar, relationships. However, children may sometimes have occasion to talk about relationships that are not well-represented. The *when* questions asked by Carni and French represented an attempt to elicit *before* and *after* responses referring to both familiar and novel sequences. However, the children tended to respond to these *when* questions by pointing to the picture depicting the queried event—a correct, but nonrelational response. While responses containing *before* and *after* were too infrequent and produced by too few subjects to permit statistical analysis, an interesting pattern emerged. Of the 16 subjects at each age, 7 three-year-olds and 8 four-year-olds used *before*, *after*, or both. Table 12-1 shows the distribution of these productions by age, story type, and correctness.

The four-year-olds never used the terms incorrectly. The three-year-olds almost always used the terms accurately (95%) when they responded to questions about the invariant sequences, but were accurate less than half the time (43%) when they responded to questions about the arbitrary sequences. The finding that the familiarity of the sequences being referred to influences the accuracy with which temporal

Table 12-1. *Before* and *After* Responses to *When* Questions

	Story type			
	Invariant		Arbitrary	
	Correct	Incorrect	Correct	Incorrect
Three-year-olds				
Before	6	0	3	6
After	16	1	7	7
Four-year-olds				
Before	10	0	6	0
After	19	0	33	0

terms are used is in accord with the contextual model being proposed. These data are too sparse to be more than suggestive, however.

In the study just described, the productions of *before* and *after* were elicited by *when* questions, and so are not directly comparable to spontaneous production. As noted earlier, we also have extensive data on young children's spontaneous productions of relational terms (e.g., French, 1981, 1983, in press; French & Nelson, 1981, 1982, in press). These production data were culled from protocols obtained by asking 43 children (age range: 2;11 to 5;6) to describe six familiar activities: getting dressed, going to the grocery store, having a birthday party, having a fire drill, making cookies, and eating at a restaurant. Each child was asked to describe each event two or three times, yielding a total of 687 protocols. These event descriptions were elicited following a relatively standardized procedure in which the investigator first asked a general question such as "What happens when you . . .?" or "Can you tell me about . . .?" then followed up with nondirective probes such as "Anything else . . .?" and "Can you tell me more . . .?" until the children indicated that they had nothing more to say about a particular activity. It is important to note that these probes did not provide any suggestion that the children describe temporal, causal, or other relationships holding within a particular activity. Figure 12-1 shows examples of productions of the terms *before*, *after*, *because*, *so*, *if*, *but*, and *or*.

As various investigators have noted (e.g., Clark, 1983; Emerson, 1980), it is often difficult to judge whether a term produced by a child is really being used appropriately to convey the child's underlying communicative intent. The adult may be able to impose an appropriate meaning the child did not intend, the child may be using the word in an unanalyzed routine heard used by others, or the child may have randomly hit upon the correct word or correct placement. These problems of interpretation are minimized in this data base for the following reasons.

Because the children in this study were describing widely familiar cultural activities, it was possible to judge whether their descriptions were accurate in general, as well as whether the relationships they expressed through the use of relational terms were veridical. Various syntactic features, and the fact that the descriptions were typically organized in a sequential manner, often provided secondary support for our judgments that the terms were used correctly.

When the child describing a birthday party says "We eat cake *after* we play," it is impossible to know whether the child really means that play precedes or follows eating cake. This problem of interpretation is of limited significance in respect to our data since the children were describing events for which we have independent (cultural) knowledge of many of the relationships holding among the elements being described. For example, it is not problematic to determine that the child who says "First, you have to put on some underwear. Then short-sleeve shirt or a long-sleeve shirt" (S#39, 5;4) is appropriately expressing a disjunctive relationship, and contrasting it with the conjuctive relationship holding between underwear and outer clothing.

The probability that a substantial proportion of the children's productions were unanalyzed routines is low for several reasons. First, formulaic productions are

And *before* I eat it, I just take out all the candles. (Birthday Party, S#17, 4;1)

Make the dough. And then you put it in the oven. But *before* you put it in the oven, you make the cookie shapes, and then you put it in the oven. (Making Cookies, S#24, 4;7)

After I'm done making them, I just eat them. And that's all. (Making Cookies, S#17, 4;1)

And then *after* we got all our stuff, we go to the counter and then we head home. (Going to the Grocery, S#43, 5;6)

You walk fast but you can't put your coats on *'cause* you need to hurry. (Fire Drill, S#19, 4;2)

Then when we're finished eating the salad that we ordered we get to eat our pizza when it's done, *because* we get the salad *before* the pizza's ready. (Going to a Restaurant, S#34, 4;10)

You need to make them brown, *so, so* you can eat them. (Making Cookies, S#11, 3;9)

Sometimes, um, you find a cart that, you need a cart and all the cart, carts, are outside, caught in the rain sometimes, *so* you can't take them shopping. (S#42, 5;6)

Sometimes *if* you're so hungry, go to a restaurant that gives ya a lot of stuff. (Going to a Restaurant, S#16, 4;0)

But sometimes Thursday you don't go to school. All you do is just eat breakfast and get dressed *if* you want, but you could stay in pajamas too. (Getting Dressed, S#28, 4;8)

I putted on my green pants, and one of my socks is blue, one of my socks is brown, *but* I couldn't find the other one . . . (Getting Dressed, S#15, 4;0)

I never cooked them, *but* I'll try cooking them *if* my mommy buys it. (Making Cookies, S#20, 4;3)

You could, you could—get on dresses, *or* you can get in pants *or* shorts *or* skirts. (Getting Dressed, S#38, 5;4)

You use, um, ah, a mixer, ah, eggs, sometimes butter *or* margarine. Crisco sometimes, instead of butter. (Making Cookies, S#41, 5;6)

Figure 12-1. Productions of relational terms in children's descriptions of familiar events.

uncommon among children of this age. Second, the children often made statements such as ". . . what you do is put them in the oven to bake (Yeah) because they have to be hot when you eat them" (S#42, 5;6), which they were unlikely to have heard, and which revealed a child-like attempt to make sense of an activity they did not fully understand. Finally, subtle changes in the same child's descriptions yielded similar but not identical verbalizations, indicating productive use of the terms. For example, a child describing what happens at a grocery store expressed roughly the same conditional concept in two ways:

1. Sometimes, if you have a child or a baby you put it in the cart.
2. And sometimes if you don't have the cart you have to carry a person, because it's a baby. (S#42, 5;6)

Because the proportion of errors to correct productions was extremely low, the possibility that correct productions were generated randomly could be ruled out. In considering the productions judged to be incorrect, a question of central concern was whether the children would make the specific types of errors that would be predicted on the basis of the various componential models of lexical acquisition proposed for particular terms. These errors include using *after* as if it means *before* (Clark, 1971), introducing consequent as well as antecedent clauses by *because* and *if* (Emerson, 1979, 1980), failing to distinguish between *because* and *so* (Bebout et al., 1980), using *but* where *and* would be more appropriate (Kail, 1980), and using *or* as if it referred to conjunction rather than disjunction (Neimark, 1970; Neimark & Slotnick, 1970; Paris, 1973). Despite every attempt to make very conservative judgments, very few of the productions could be considered to represent these particular types of errors. Instead, the productions classified as errors tended to be either false starts or semantically uninterpretable, as in the following examples.

Uh—you eat—uh—well, you see, after, if you eat your food up, ya get dessert. (S#16, 4;0).
Buy food, or if you wanna, you return something what you don't want. If you don't wanna, if you don't need anything. (S#38, 5;4)

There was only one case (of 33 productions) in which *after* was used where *before* would have been more appropriate (i.e., "this week after this"); no case (of 124 productions) in which *because* and *if* introduced consequent clauses, or *so* introduced an antecedent clause; 15 cases (of 96 productions) in which *or* could have been appropriately replaced by *and*; and no cases (of 81 productions) in which it was judged that *but* statements would have been better formulated using *and* (see French & Nelson, in press, for a full description of these data). In short, when the children were describing familiar activities, their productions of *before*, *after*, *because*, *so*, *if*, *but*, and *or* were generally accurate, and their occasional errors were not interpretable as supporting the componential models proposed to describe the acquisition of relational terms.

It is important to note that the children in this sample were younger than the age at which investigators using comprehension paradigms have concluded that children have acquired the "full" set of components of the various relational terms. For example, Emerson (1979, 1980), Kail (1980), and Bebout et al. (1980) all claimed that children have incomplete knowledge of the terms they assessed until age eight or nine.

As discussed above, componential models are derived from the error patterns children produce when responding to experimental paradigms designed to assess comprehension. If such error patterns genuinely reflect partial knowledge of the lexical components of the terms, then children below the age at which the full meaning of a term is acquired would be expected to make specific types of errors when producing the terms. Our failure to find production errors which support the componential models cannot be taken as *conclusive* evidence against the validity of these models, however. Since not all the children in our sample used the various terms, it is possible that children simply do not produce the terms until they have acquired their "full" meaning. This way of accounting for our finding that children use relational terms appropriately earlier than the age at which they are typically judged to comprehend them is implausible from several perspectives, however. First, not only do children frequently misuse words (e.g., overextensions), but it seems unlikely that they could know they had acquired only a partial set of the relevant lexical components of a relational term and so delay using it until they knew they knew all the components. Second, even if there is variation across children in the age at which relational terms are acquired, it seems unlikely that many children would appropriately produce relational terms *several years* earlier than their peers could comprehend them. Finally, the children observed longitudinally by Bloom and her colleagues (e.g., Bloom et al., 1980) appropriately produced some of these terms (i.e., *but, because, so, if*) at a younger age than the children in our sample. This suggests that the proportion of children in our sample who happened to use a particular relational term in their event descriptions offers a conservative estimate of the proportion of the children *able* to use each term.

Production data alone are inherently incapable of disproving componential models of lexical acquisition. However, such data can be more or less in accord with predictions generated by different models of lexical acquisition. Our data on children's spontaneous productions are decidedly contradictory to what would be predicted on the basis of componential models, and our data on children's responses to *when* questions referring to highly familiar and novel sequences are in accord with what would be expected on the basis of the proposed contextual model.

Despite the fact that the literature does not contain a corpus of incorrect productions of relational terms, investigators who use data from comprehension paradigms to argue that children below a certain age have not acquired all the lexical components of a term quite freely call upon the "common knowledge" that children often misuse these terms. Actually, there are only occasional reports in the literature of children using relational terms inappropriately, and these reports are subject to two criticisms. First, they tend to be selective, and it is likely that investigators notice occasional erroneous statements while not noticing correct statements. Second, some of the erroneous productions, such as those offered by Menyuk (1969) (e.g., "If they put him in between he wants to go there", p. 93), are ambiguous or perhaps elliptical, rather than clearly erroneous. In light of our data, as well as that of other investigators (e.g., Bloom et al., 1980; Eisenberg, 1980; Gallivan, 1982; McCabe et al., 1983) showing that young children do by and large use relational terms appropriately, it appears that the widely accepted assumption that relational terms are often misused is in err.

Nevertheless, it is true that children sometimes misuse relational terms. For example, the first time we presented our data showing the production of relational terms to be almost always accurate, a member of the audience noted that her young son had recently said "I have a stomachache because I'm going to the doctor." As the child's mother, she presumably had independent knowledge that the child was going to the doctor because of the stomachache rather than developing the stomachache in anticipation of the visit. Such a misstatement is in accord with either the claim that children do not know which clause (antecedent or consequent) should be introduced by *because* (Emerson, 1979) or the claim that they fail to distinguish between *because* and *so* (Bebout et al., 1980).

Such a misstatement may also be accounted for within the framework of the proposed model, however. It is quite probable that the child making this statement did not have well-established knowledge about the relationship between stomachaches and visits to doctors. While production generally involves selecting the appropriate linguistic means to express an underlying mental representation, erroneous productions would be expected if a child had an erroneous, or simply unclear, representation of the activity being described. Talking about a poorly represented, or novel, relationship is conceptually similar to comprehending statements about unfamiliar relationships; each involves additional cognitive effort beyond simply matching the linguistic means of expressing a relationship onto a well-established mental representation of the relationship.

Thus, one prediction that can be derived from the contextual model is that young children's accuracy in using relational terms will depend upon their level of familiarity with the relationship (i.e., semantic content) being expressed. Carni and French's (1984) data on elicited productions are in accord with this prediction, but too sparse to offer strong support. This study is currently being replicated with the further control that subjects are discouraged from giving nonrelational, pointing responses. Our more extensive production data, obtained by eliciting event descriptions, are only tangentially relevant to this prediction, since the events the children described were highly familiar. If it were possible to collect a representative sample of young children's spontaneous productions of relational terms across contexts and to adequately judge whether or not they were used appropriately, then the contextual model being proposed would predict (1) that most productions would be accurate since children typically talk about things they know about, and appear quite able to select the appropriate term to express a well-established representation, and (2) that erroneous productions would occur primarily when children were attempting to express relatively unfamiliar relationships.

Conclusions

As described, the proposed contextual model refers more to children's deployment of knowledge about the meanings of relational terms than to the process of initial acquisition. French and Brown's (1977) initial research on children's understanding of *before* and *after* was based on the premise that the extralinguistic context (either physical or mental) must necessarily play a major role in the initial acquisition of relational terms. While this still seems indisputable, evidence on the *acquisition* as opposed to the *deployment* of knowledge about relational terms is difficult to obtain experimentally. It remains possible, in principle, that a componential model may eventually be found to offer the best account of the initial acquisition of these terms. However, as described above, the existing literature on relational terms does not support such a model.

As an account of children's understanding of relational terms, the contextual model has several advantages over the componential models previously proposed. It is in accord with current theories of cognitive development, it can account for the large disparity in the ages at which the literature attributes to children's competency in the production and comprehension of relational terms, and is not derived from error patterns, which are potentially multiply determined. At this point, however, the model is underdetermined by data. That is, while it does not directly conflict with any available data, only a few studies directly supporting the model are available.

However, some clear predictions can be generated from the model and assessed empirically. The prediction that young children will be more likely to make production errors when referring to relatively unfamiliar relationships is one example. Another example is illustrated by a study currently underway, in which children overlearn three-event causal chains (i.e., X causes Y causes Z), and then are asked to complete sentences "Y because . . ." "Because Y . . ." and "Y so . . ." Our prediction that preschoolers will perform well on this task is contrary to the prediction that can be drawn from prior literature (e.g., Piaget, 1928; Emerson, 1979; Bebout et al., 1980) that young children will not respect the order component of *because* and *so*.

While componential models are clearly models of lexical acquisition per se, the contextual model is not. Rather, the contextual model essentially provides a cognitively based account of the conditions under which children will be able to display their lexical knowledge. Because relational terms are quite different from most of the lexicon (e.g., have no observable referents, express quite complex concepts), there is no necessary reason to expect that a model designed to account for children's understanding of relational terms will be applicable to other words. While the contextual model may not be broadly applicable to lexical acquisition and development, it does have the potential of having a significant impact on psycholinguistic research more generally, by pointing out that the semantic context within which variables of interest (syntactic, lexical, or pragmatic) are embedded may critically affect children's performance in experimental settings (e.g., Olson & Nickerson, 1977). The more important goal in proposing the contextual model, however, is that it provides a viable theoretical framework within which to collect more sensitive measures of how children develop an understanding of logical relationships and the linguistic means for expressing them.

Summary

Interest in how children acquire the lexical means for expressing logical relationships has been strong for a number of years and shows no sign of abating. In reviewing the literature on children's acquisition and understanding of *before*, *after*, *because, so, if, but,* and *or,* it was argued that this body of literature is by and large inadequate to support any conclusions regarding either the process or course of acquisition of these terms.

Both methodological and theoretical issues were raised as being central to the uninterpretability of much of the literature. The major methodological issue involves the appropriate interpretation of performance failure on tasks designed to assess comprehension. The major theoretical issues are closely related to this methodological issue and concern the status of componential models for the acquisition of relational terms, and the possibility that a major developmental stage in the acquisition and understanding of relational terms has been systematically overlooked due to the methods and stimuli selected to assess their comprehension.

Componential models have been the primary means of describing the acquisition of relational terms. Such models assume that (1) the meaning of a term consists of various components, (2) these components may be acquired separately over a period of time, and (3) the child who has acquired only a partial set of the components of a term will systematically misuse and misinterpret that term. Such models arise and gain support from the systematic error patterns children produce in response to comprehension paradigms. The fact that componential models provide a theoretical account for systematic error patterns has perhaps led investigators to take less seriously than they normally would the fallacy of interpreting poor performance on comprehension measures as indicative of lack of knowledge. However, systematic error patterns may arise due to lexically irrelevant response strategies afforded by a particular comprehension paradigm. In this case, systematic error patterns cannot legitimately be interpreted as indicating anything about the child's level of understanding of a particular term.

Componential models of lexical acquisition are essentially context independent in that no consideration is given to the possibility that a term may be understood in some semantic contexts but not in others. The alternative model proposed here to describe children's understanding of relational terms is in accord with developmental psychologists' current emphasis upon context in accounting for cognitive development. This contextual model recognizes that two distinct types of comprehension may be involved in understanding statements containing relational terms. Such statements may report relationships which either are or are not already known to the listener. In the first case, the statement serves as a means of eliciting a preexisting representation of the known relationship. In the second case, the statement serves as a means of establishing a representation of a novel relationship. These two different types of statements would seem to make quite different cognitive demands upon the listener.

The contextual model is essentially a proposal that children first understand relational terms when they function to express a relationship that is already known, and only later are able to use relational terms as the basis for establishing representations of previously unknown relationships. This model accounts readily for the commonly found comprehension-production disparity, as well as for demonstrations that children's success or task assessing the comprehension of relational terms varies as a function of the semantic context in which these terms occur (e.g., Carni & French, 1984; Ford, 1976).

In summary, the advantages of the contextual model are:

1. It relates the acquisition of relational terms to current views of cognitive development.
2. It can account for existing data on both children's production and comprehension of relational terms.
3. It generates predictions about the development of children's understanding of relational terms which can be, and in some cases have been, assessed empirically.

While there has been a consistently high level of interest in children's acquisition and understanding of relational terms throughout the last decade, research has done little to advance our understanding of the process or course of development in this area. The reason seems to be that for a number of years researchers have tended to focus either on discrediting the validity of the semantic feature model as an account of the acquisition of *before* and *after*, or on proposing similar componential models to account for the acquisition of other relational terms. The contextual model proposed here offers an alternative to endlessly disputing and/or reinventing various versions of a semantic feature model. By offering a testable and viable alternative account of the acquisition and development of the understanding of relational terms, the contextual model provides a framework to support the collection of more sensitive data on the development of children's understanding of relational terms.

References

Amidon, A., & Carey, P. (1972). Why five-year-olds cannot understand *before* and *after*. *Journal of Verbal Learning and Verbal Behavior, 11*, 417-423.

Baillargeon, R., Gelman, R., & Meck, B. (1981). *Are preschoolers truly indifferent to causal mechanisms?* Paper presented at the Biennial Meeting of the Society for Research in Child Development, Boston.

Bebout, L. J., Segalowitz, S. J., & White, G. J. (1980). Children's comprehension of causal constructions with "because" and "so." *Child Development, 51*, 565-568.

Bittetti-Capatides, J., Fiess, K., & Bloom, L. (1980). *The contexts of causality*. Paper presented at the Fifth Annual Boston University Conference on Child Language.

Bloom, L. (1970). *Language development: Form and function in emerging grammars*. Cambridge, MA: MIT Press.

Bloom, L., Lahey, M., Hood, L., Lifter, K., & Fiess, K. (1980). Complex sentences: Acquisition of syntactic connectives and the semantic relations they encode. *Journal of Child Language, 7*, 235-261.

Braine, M. D. S. (1978). On the relation between the natural logic of reasoning and standard logic. *Psychological Review, 85*, 1-21.

Braine, M. D. S., & Rumain, B. (1981). Development of comprehension of "Or": Evidence for a sequence of competencies. *Journal of Experimental Child Psychology, 31*, 46-70.

Braine, M. D. S., & Rumain, B. (1983). Logical reasoning. In P. H. Mussen (Ed.), *Carmichael's manual of child psychology: Vol. 3. Cognitive development* (pp. 263-340). New York: Wiley.

Bremner, J. G. (1982, September). *The infant's environment and development of early knowledge*. Paper presented at the Annual Conference of the Developmental Section of the British Psychological Society, Durham.

Brown, A. L. (1976). The construction of temporal succession by preoperational children. In A. D. Pick (Ed.), *Minnesota symposia on child psychology*: Vol. 10 (pp. 23-83). Minneapolis: University of Minnesota.

Brown, A. L. (1977). Development, schooling, and the acquisition of knowledge about knowledge. In R. C. Anderson, R. J. Spiro, & W. E. Montague (Eds.), *Schooling and the acquisition of knowledge*. Hillsdale, NJ: Erlbaum.

Brown, A. L., Bransford, J. D., Ferrara, R. A., & Campione, J. C. (1983). Learning, remembering, and understanding. In P. H. Mussen (Ed.), *Carmichael's manual of child psychology: Vol. 3. Cognitive development* (pp. 77-166). New York: Wiley.

Brown, A. L., & French, L. A. (1976). Construction and regeneration of logical sequences using causes or consequences as the point of departure. *Child Development, 47,* 930-940.

Brown, A. L., & Murphy, M. D. (1975). Reconstruction of arbitrary versus logical sequences by preschool children. *Journal of Experimental Child Psychology, 20,* 307-326.

Brown, R. (1973). *A first language: The early stages*. Cambridge, MA: Harvard University Press.

Bullock, M. (1981, April). *Preschoolers' understanding of causal mechanisms*. Paper presented at the Biennial Meeting of the Society for Research in Child Development, Boston.

Bullock, M., & Gelman, R. (1979). Preschool children's assumptions about cause and effect: Temporal ordering. *Child Development, 50,* 89-96.

Carey, S. (1977). Less may never mean 'more'. In R. Campbell & P. Smith (Eds.), *Recent advances in the psychology of language: Proceedings of the Stirling Conference on Psycholinguistics* (pp. 109-132). New York: Plenum.

Carey, S. (1982). Semantic development: The state of the art. In E. Wanner & L. R. Gleitman (Eds.), *Language acquisition: The state of the art* (pp. 347-389). New York: Cambridge University Press.

Carni, E., & French, L. A. (1984). *Before* and *after* reconsidered: What develops? *Journal of Experimental Child Psychology, 37,* 394-403.

Clark, E. V. (1971). On the acquisition of the meaning of "before" and "after." *Journal of Verbal Learning and Verbal Behavior, 10,* 266-275.

Clark, E. V. (1973). How children describe time and order. In C. A. Ferguson & D. I. Slobin (Eds.), *Studies of child language* (pp. 585-606). New York: Holt, Rinehart & Winston.

Clark, E. V. (1983). Meanings and concepts. In P. H. Mussen (Ed.), *Carmichael's manual of child psychology: Vol. 3. Cognitive development* (pp. 787-840). New York: Wiley.

Coker, P. L. (1978). Syntactic and semantic factors in the acquisition of *before* and *after*. *Journal of Child Language, 5,* 261-277.

Dale, P. S. (1976). *Language development: Structure and function* (2nd ed.), New York: Holt, Rinehart & Winston.

DeLoach, J. S. (1980). Naturalistic studies of memory for object location in very young children. *New Directions for Child Development, 10,* 17-32.

Donaldson, M. (1978). *Children's minds*. New York: Norton.

Eisenberg, A. R. (1980). A syntactic, semantic, and pragmatic analysis of conjunction. *Papers and Reports on Child Language Development, 19,* 70-78.

Emerson, H. F. (1979). Children's comprehension of "because" in reversible and non-reversible sentences. *Journal of Child Language, 6,* 279-300.

Emerson, H. F. (1980). Children's judgements of correct and reversed sentences with "if." *Journal of Child Language, 7*, 137-155.

Ennis, R. H. (1976). An alternative to Piaget's conceptualization of logical competence. *Child Development, 47*, 903-919.

Fiess, K., Bittetti-Capatides, J., & Bloom, L. (1979). *The origin of complex sentences in language acquisition*. Paper presented at the Biennial Meeting of the Society for Research in Child Development, San Francisco.

Ford, W. G. (1976). *The language of disjunction*. Unpublished doctoral dissertation: University of Toronto.

French, L. A. (in press). The language of events. In K. Nelson (Ed.), *Event knowledge: Structure and function in development*. Hillsdale, NJ: Erlbaum.

French, L. A. (1981, October). *But of course preschoolers understand the meaning of 'but'!*. Paper presented at the Sixth Annual Boston University Conference on Language Development.

French, L. A. (1983, April). Language in scripts. In K. Nelson (Chair), *Relations between event representations and language use*. Symposium presented at the Biennial Meeting of the Society for Research in Child Development, Detroit.

French, L. A., & Brown, A. L. (1977). Comprehension of "before" and "after" in logical and arbitrary sequences. *Journal of Child Language, 4*, 247-256.

French, L. A., & Nelson, K. (1981). Temporal knowledge expressed in preschoolers' descriptions of familiar activities. *Papers and Reports on Child Language Development, 20*, 61-69.

French, L. A., & Nelson, K. (1982). Taking away the supportive context: Preschoolers talk about the "then-and-there." *The Quarterly Newsletter of the Laboratory of Comparative Human Cognition, 4*, 1-6.

French, L. A., & Nelson, K. (1983, September). The language of event descriptions. In L. French (Chair), *The cognitive context of language use*. Symposium presented at the Meetings of the Developmental Section of the British Psychological Society, Oxford.

French, L. A., & Nelson, K. (in press). *Children's understanding of relational terms: Some ifs, ors and buts*. New York: Springer-Verlag.

Gallivan, J. (1982). *Children's understanding of "but": Evidence from spontaneous production*. Paper presented at the Annual Meeting of the Canadian Psychological Association, Montreal.

Gelman, R. (1978). Cognitive development. *Annual Review of Psychology, 29*, 297-332.

Goodz, N. S. (1978). Is before really easier to understand than after? *Child Development, 53*, 822-825.

Graves, Z. R. (1981). *The effect of context on mother-child interaction*. Unpublished doctoral dissertation: City University of New York.

Hill, S. A. (1961). *A study of logical abilities in children*. Unpublished doctoral dissertation, Stanford University, Stanford, CA.

Hood, L., & Bloom, L. (1979). What, when, and how about why: A longitudinal study of early expressions of causality. *Monographs of the Society for Research in Child Development, 44* (6, Serial No. 181).

Johannson, B. S., & Sjölin, B. (1975). Preschool children's understanding of the coordinators "and" and "or." *Journal of Experimental Child Psychology, 19*, 233-240.

Johnson, H. (1975). The meaning of *before* and *after* for preschool children. *Journal of Experimental Child Psychology, 19*, 88-99.

Kail, M. (1980). Etude génétique des présupposés de certains morphèmes grammaticaux [A developmental study of the presuppositions of particular grammatical morphemes. An example: BWT]. Un exemple: MAIS. *Approches du langage, Publications de la Sorbonne, Serie Etudes, 16,* 53-62.

Karmiloff-Smith, A. (1979). Language development after five. In P. Fletcher & M. Garman (Eds.), *Language acquisition: Studies in first language development.* Cambridge: Cambridge University Press.

Katz, E. W., & Brent, S. B. (1968). Understanding connectives. *Journal of Verbal Learning, 7,* 501-509.

Kavanaugh, R. D. (1979). Observations on the role of logically constrained sentences in the comprehension of "before" and "after." *Journal of Child Language, 6,* 353-357.

Keller-Cohen, D. (1974). Cognition and the acquisition of temporal reference. *Papers from the Tenth Regional Meeting of the Chicago Linguistic Society.*

Kun, A. (1978). Evidence for preschoolers' understanding of causal direction in extended causal sequences. *Child Development, 49,* 218-222.

Macnamara, J. (1972). Cognitive basis of language learning in infants. *Psychological Review, 79,* 1-13.

Mandler, J. M. (1983). Representation. In P. H. Mussen (Ed.), *Carmichael's manual of child psychology: Vol. 3. Cognitive development* (pp. 420-494). New York: Wiley.

Maratsos, M. (1983). Some current issues in the study of the acquisition of grammar. In P. H. Mussen (Ed.), *Carmichael's manual of child psychology: Vol. 3. Cognitive development* (pp. 707-786). New York: Wiley.

McCabe, A. E., Evely, S., Abramovitch, R., Corter, C. M., & Pepler, D. J. (1983). Conditional statements in young children's spontaneous speech. *Journal of Child Language, 10,* 253-258.

Menyuk, P. (1969). *Sentences children use.* Cambridge, MA: MIT.

Neimark, E. D. (1970). Development of comprehension of logical connectives: Understanding of "or." *Psychonomic Science, 21,* 217-219.

Neimark, E. D., & Slotnick, N. S. (1970). Development of the understanding of logical connectives. *Journal of Educational Psychology, 61,* 451-460.

Nelson, K. (1977). Cognitive development and the acquisition of concepts. In R. C. Anderson, R. J. Spiro, & W. E. Montague (Eds.), *Schooling and the acquisition of knowledge.* Hillsdale, NJ: Erlbaum.

Nelson, K., & Gruendel, J. M. (1981). Generalized event representations: Basic building blocks of cognitive development. In M. Lamb & A. L. Brown (Eds.), *Advances in developmental psychology*: Vol. 1. Hillsdale, NJ: Erlbaum.

Olson, D. R., & Nickerson, N. (1977). The contexts of comprehension: On children's understanding of the relations between active and passive sentences. *Journal of Experimental Child Psychology, 23,* 402-414.

Olson, D. R., & Nickerson, N. (1978). Language development through the school years: Learning to confine interpretation to the information in the text. In K. E. Nelson (Ed.), *Children's language*: Vol. 1. New York: Gardner Press.

Orne, M. T. (1970). Hypnosis, motivation, and the ecological validity of the psychological experiment. In W. J. Arnold & M. M. Page (Eds.), *Nebraska symposium on motivation: Vol. 18* (pp. 187-265). Lincoln, NE: University of Nebraska Press.

Paris, S. G. (1973). Comprehension of language connectives and propositional logical relationships. *Journal of Experimental Child Psychology, 16,* 278-291.

Piaget, J. (1928). *Judgment and reasoning in the child.* New York: Harcourt, Brace.

Richards, M. M. (1979). Sorting out what's in a word from what's not: Evaluating Clark's semantic features acquisition theory. *Journal of Experimental Child Psychology, 27,* 1-47.

Schmidt, C. R., & Paris, S. G. (1978). Operativity and reversibility in children's understanding of pictorial sequences. *Child Development, 49,* 1219-1222.

Shapiro, B. J., & O'Brien, T. C. (1970). Logical thinking in children ages six through thirteen. *Child Development, 41,* 823-829.

Shatz, M. (1978). The relationship between cognitive processes and the development of communication skills. In C. B. Keasey (Ed.), *Nebraska symposium on motivation*: Vol. 25 (pp. 1-43). Lincoln, NE: University of Nebraska Press.

Shultz, T. R. (1982). Rules of causal attribution. *Monographs of the Society for Research in Child Development, 47,* (1, Serial No. 194).

Siegler, R. S. (1976). The effects of simple necessity and sufficiency relationships on children's causal inferences. *Child Development, 47,* 1058-1063.

Sommerville, S. C., & Bryant, P. E. (1983, April). *Children's understanding of causal relations in domino arrays.* Paper presented at the Biennial Meeting of the Society for Research in Child Development, Detroit.

Suppes, P., & Feldman, S. (1971). Young children's comprehension of logical connectives. *Journal of Experimental Child Psychology, 12,* 304-317.

Tanz, C. (1980). *Studies in the acquisition of deictic terms.* Cambridge: Cambridge University Press.

Wason, P. C., & Johnson-Laird, P. N. (1972). *Psychology of reasoning: Structure and content.* Cambridge, MA: Harvard University Press.

Author Index

Page numbers set in italic type refer to pages on which complete reference information appears.

Abramovitch, R., 312, *337*
Abravanel, E., 244, 245, *251*
Adams, A.K., 34, 184, 188, 192, 193
Alenskas, L., *254*
Al-Issa, I., 92, *95*
Allen, R., 247, *251*
Allen, R.L., 283, *300*
Amidon, A., 307, 308, 309, *334*
Andersen, E.S., 8, 19, *34*
Anderson, E., 99, *118*
Anglin, J., 3, 4, 11, 13, 16, 17, 18, 22, 25, 30, 33, 34, *36*, 49, 51, 55n, *66*, 77, 79, *80*, 84, 86, 87, 88, 89, 90, 92, 93, *95, 96*, 104, 105, 114, 117, *119*, 139, *152*, 165, 167, 172n, *193*, 203
Antinucci, F., 288, *300*
Atkinson, M., 227, *253*
Austin, G., 89, *96*, 159, *193*
Austin, J.L., 276, *300*

Bach, K., 176, *301*
Baillargeon, R., 304, *334*

Baker, E., 5, *36*
Baldwin, P., *152*
Balfour, G., 3, *36*, 128, *152*, 206, 221
Barker, E.N., 92, *97*
Barnes, S., 191, *193*, 236, 237, *251*
Barnett, R.K., 229, *255*
Barrett, M.D., vii, viii, *x*, 2, 23, 33, *34*, 40, 45, 46n, 47, 48, 49, 50, 51, 52, 53, 55, 56, 60, 62, *66*, 85, 88, *95*, 126, 135, *151*, 164, 166, *193*, 203, 204, *220*, 295, *301*
Bartlett, E.J., 21, *34*, 138, 145, *151*, 260, *272*
Bates, E., Pref. vii, *x*, 15, *35*, 40, 47, 52, *66*, 87, 95, 161, *193*, 216, 218, *220*, 225, 226, 228, 248, 251, *255*, 293, *301*
Batterman, N., 93
Bebout, L., 310, 318, 324, 329, 331, 332, *334*, 337
Beeghly-Smith, M., 15, *35*
Benedict, H., 12, 24, *34*, 37, 85, *97*, 99, 101, *119*, 225, 228, 236, *251*
Benigni, L., vii, *x*, 40, *66*, *220*

Bennett, P., 239, *255*
Berko, J., 124, *151*
Bever, T., 125, *154*
Bierwisch, M., *34*, 122, *151*, 203, *220*
Bitetti-Capatides, J., 312, *334, 336*
Blewitt, P., 3, 18, 34, *35*, 165, 172n, 177, *193*
Bloom, L., 3, 12, 19, *35*, 39, 56, *66*, 85, *95*, 101, 103, *119*, 200, 201, 203, 208, 210, 217, 218, *220*, 226, *251*, 257, 260, 262, *272*, 277, 289, *301*, 305, 312, 330, *334, 336*
Bloor, D., 155, *193*
Bonvillian, J.D., 70, *80*, 102
Bower, T., 146, *152*, 211, *220*
Bowerman, M., 12, 13, 15, 22, 25, 26, *35*, 49, 50, 52, 57n, 58, *66*, 71, *80*, 85, 88, *95*, 104, 118, *119*, 131, *151*, 161, *193*, 200, 203, 205, *220*, *220*, 277, *301*
Boyes-Braem, P., *38*, 76, *81*, *154*, 159
Braine, M.D.S., 226, *252*, 285, 298, *301*, 304, 311, 312, *334*
Branston, M., 216, *222*
Braun-Tamesch, M.M., 139, *151*
Bremner, J.G., 322, *335*
Brent, S.B., 305, *337*
Bretherton, I., vii, *x*, 15, 26, *35*, 40, *66*, 225, 226, 228, *255*
Brewer, W.E., 21, *35*
Bridges, A., 132, 140, *151*
Broen, P., 229, *252*
Bronckart, J.P., 289, 290, 292
Brooks, L., 117, *119*
Broughton, J., 218
Brown, A.L., 304, 305, 307, 308, 315, 321, 322, 323, 325, 331, *335, 336*
Brown, R.W., 12, 16, 18, 20, *35*, 75, 79, *80*, 85, 90, *96*, 130, 131, *151*, 156, 163, 164, 165, *193*, 210, *221*, 260, 265, *272*, 281, 285, 297, 298, *301*, 304, 305, *335*
Bruner, J., 59n, *66*, 89, *96*, 130, 155, 158, 171, *193, 196*, 201, 211, 216, 218, *221*, 227, 246, *252, 254*
Bryant, P.E., 304, *338*
Budwig, N.A., *197*
Bukatko, D., 19, *36*
Bull, W.E., 278, *301*

Bullock, D., 34, *152*, 156, 157, 158, 163, 167, 175n, 180, 182, 192, 193, 194
Bullock, M., 304, *335*
Butterworth, G., 244, *252*
Bybee, J.L., 295, *301*

Callanan, M.A., 32, 34, *35*, 166, 190, *194*
Camaioni, L., vii, *x*, 40, *66*, 220
Campbell, R.N., 127, 136, 145, 146, 149, *152*
Campione, J.C., 156, 321, *335*
Canada, K., 22, *37*, 104, 117, 118, *120*, 166, *195, 196*
Cancelli, A.A., 30, 31, *37*
Caramazzo, A., 29, *36*
Carey, P., 307, 308, 309, *334*
Carey, S., 3, 33, *35*, 105, *119*, 121, 125, 127, 133, 134, 140, 142, 145, 147, 150, *152*, 305, 317, *334*
Carni, E., 307, 315, 319, 325, 331, 333, *335*
Carter, A.L., 200, 201, 209, *221*, 231, *252*
Chafe, W., 282, *301*
Chalkley, M.A., 293, 296, 297, 300, *301*
Chamberlain, A.F., 85, *96*
Chamberlain, J.C., 85, *96*
Chambers, J.C., 4, *35*
Chapman, K., 104, *119*
Chapman, R., 216, *221, 222*
Chapman, R.S., 87, *97*, 101, 103, 104, 117, 143, *154*, 230, 231, *252*
Chapman, R.W., 4, 11, 12, 23, *37*
Charney, R., 158, 184, 258, *273*
Chase, W.P., 136, *152*
Chomsky, C., 3, 35
Churcher, J., 244, *252*
Clark, E., 125, 127, 129, 146, 147, *152*, 202, 206, 207, 210, 216, *221*
Clark, E.V., vii, *x*, 1, 2, 3, 4, 13, 14, 19, 20, 21, 22, 23, (25), 28, 33, *35, 36*, Ch. 2, 50, 52, 56, *66*, 71, *80*, 85, 86, *96*, 99, 100, 101, 102, 103, 105, 115, 117, *119*, 122, *152*, 305, 306, 307, 308, 313, 314, 315, 319, 326, 327, 329, *335*

Author Index

Clark, H., 3, 20, 21, *36*, 85, 86, *96*, 117, *119*
Cochran, E., 244, *252*
Cohen, I.B., 129, *152*, 212, *221*
Coker, P.L., 307, *335*
Collis, G.M., 232, 242, *254*
Colman, M., 177, *197*
Comrie, B., 278, 280, 282, 283, *301*
Corrigan, R., 203, 215, 216, 218, *221*
Corter, C.M., 312, *337*
Cox, B., 129
Cramer, P., 31, *36*
Crawley, S., 228, 239, *255*
Crisafi, M.A., 18, *37*
Crook, C.K., 243, *254*
Cross, T.G., 158, 167, 191, *194*, 229, 239, *252, 254*
Cruse, D.A., 130, *152*
Currie-Jedermann, J., 14, *36*
Curtis, K., 126, *152*

Daehler, M.W., 19, *36*
Dale, P.S., 4, *36*, 305, *335*
Danford, J.W., 156, *194*
Danks, J.M., 3, *36*
Danziger, K., 4, *36*
Della Corte, M., 236, *252*
DeLoache, J.S., 171, *194*, 322, *335*
Dennett, D.C., *194*
Devieux, J., 229, *255*
deVos, L.F., 29, *36*
Dihoff, A., 216, *221*
Dixon, R.M., 276, *301*
Dockrell, J., 125, 127, *152*, 276, *301*
Dodd, D.H., 14, *37*
Donaldson, M., 3, *36*, 128, 139, *152*, 206, *221*, 305, 321, *335*
Dore, J., 47, 48, 52, *66*, 208, *221*, 226, *252*
Drake, D., 229, *255*

Edwards, D., 228, 249, *252*, 260, 262, 267, *273*
Eilers, R.E., 3, *36*
Eisenberg, A.R., 312, 330, *335*
Ellington, J., 3, *36*
Ellis, R., 239, *252*

Emerson, H.F., 314, 317, 324n, 327, 329, 331, 332, *335, 336*
Ennis, R.M., 304, *336*
Estes, W.K., 155, *194*
Evely, S., 312, *337*

Fagan, J.F., 212, *221*
Fantini, 146, 147
Farrar, M., 215, 216
Farwell, C., 204, 205, 207, 209, *221*, 229, *252*
Fay, D., 11, 23, 29, *36*, 87, *96*, 101, 104, *119*
Fay, W.H., 70, 79, *80*
Feifel, M., 92, 93, *96*
Feldman, S., 304, 311, 312, *338*
Fenson, L., 240, *252*
Ferguson, C.A., 131, *154*, 180, *196*, 229, 252
Fernald, A., 169n, 179, *194*
Ferrara, R.A., 156, 321, *335*
Ferrier, L., 227, *252*
Fiess, K., 312, *334, 336*
Fillmore, C., 91, *96*, 257, 259, *273*
Fischer, K., 156, 157, 158, 163, 192, *193*, 218, *221*
Folger, M., *253*
Ford, W.G., 311, 312, 314, 320, 333, *336*
Fordor, J., 203, *222*
Franklin, M.B., 47, *66*, 208, *221*
Freeman, N., 128, *152*
Fremgen, A., 11, 23, 29, *36*, 87, *96*, 101, 104, *119*
French, L.A., 304, 305, 306, 307, 308, 313, 315, 318, 319, 322, 323, 325, 327, 331, 333, *335, 336*
Friedman, C.S., 229, *255*
Fry, M.E., 102, *120*

Gallistel, C.R., 102, *119*
Gallivan, J., 313, 330, *336*
Gardner, H., 69, *80*
Gearhart, M., 158
Gelman, R., 12, *36*, 101, 102, *119*, 128, *152*, 225, *252*, 304, 305, 321, *334, 335, 336*

Gentner, D., 13, 14, 32, *36*, 89, 92, *96*, 127, *152*, 201, *221*, 226, 228, *252*
Gleitman, H., 229, *254*
Gleitman, L.R., 229, *254*
Glucksberg, S., 3, *36*
Goldin-Meadow, S., 12, *36*, 101, *119*, 225, *252*
Goodman, N., 89, *96*
Goodnow, J., 89, *96*
Goodwin, R.Q., 262, *273*
Goody, J., 192, *194*
Goodz, N.S., 307, 316, *336*
Gopnik, A., 57n, *66*, *67*, 200, 201, 204, 205, 206, 207, 209, 210, 211, 215, 216, *221*, *222*, 226, *252*
Graves, Z.R., 313, *336*
Gray, W.D., *38*, 76, *81*, *154*, 159
Greenberg, J., 50n, *67*, 104, 117, *119*, 164, 167, 179, *194*
Greenfield, P., 248, *253*, 262, 265, *273*
Grégoire, A., 101, *119*
Grieve, R., 128, *152*
Griffiths, P.D., 227, *253*
Grossberg, S., 155, *194*
Gruendel, J., 24, *37*, 49, *66*, 85, *96*, *97*, 101, 103, 158, *195*, 321, 322, 323, *337*
Guberman, S.R., 158, *196*
Guillaume, P., 158, *194*
Gutfreund, M., 191, *193*, 236, *251*

Hafitz, J., 289, *301*
Halliday, M.A.K., vii, viii, *x*, 200, 209, 218, *222*
Hamburger, H., 155, 194
Harner, L., 293, *301*
Harnish, R.M., 276, *301*
Harris, M., 239, 240, *253*
Harris, P., 120, *152*
Harris, S., 70, *80*
Haviland, S.E., 4, *36*
Hay, A., 3, *36*
Hepburn, A., 232, 241, 242, *253*
Hermelin, B., 70, *80*
Hill, S.A., 304, *336*
Hintikka, J., 156, *194*
Hood, L., 226, *251*, 277, *301*, 312, *334*, *336*

Hoogenraad, R., 128, *152*
Horton, M.S., 34, *36*, *37*, 166, *194*
Howard, D.V., 32, *36*
Howard, J.H., 32, *36*
Howe, C.J., 260, *273*
Hubley, D., 218, *222*, 241, 245, *255*
Hudson, J., 101, *119*
Hunt, J., 213, 214, *222*
Hutchinson, J., 129, 166, *195*
Huttenlocher, J., 11, *36*, 87, *96*, 101, 103, 119, 227, 241, *253*, 258, 259, 260, 261, 269, 270, *273*

Ingram, D., *222*, 226, *253*
Inhelder, B., 129, *152*

Jankowski, W., *254*
Jarret, N., 244, *252*
Johannson, B.S., 313, *336*
Johnson, D.M., 76, *81*, *154*, 159
Johnson, M., 308, *336*
Johnson-Laird, P.N., 5, 21, *37*, 89, 91, *97*, 123, 136, 276, 282, 283, *302*, 323, *338*
Joos, M., 284, *301*

Kagan, J., 240, *252*
Kail, M., 309, 317, 324n, 329, *336*
Kaplan, B., 6, *38*
Karnuloff-Smith, A., 305, *337*
Katz, E.W., 305, *337*
Katz, N., 5, *36*, 203, *222*
Kaufmann, G., 162, *194*
Kavanaugh, R.D., 245, *253*, 307, 325, *337*
Kay, D.A., 11, 16, 22, *36*, 89, *96*, 104, 114, 117, *119*, 158, *222*
Kaye, K., 156, 157, 158, 167, 184, 194, *195*, 203
Kearsley, R.B., 240, *252*
Kedesdy, J., 10, 18, *38*
Keele, S.W., 164, *196*
Keenan, J.M., 102, *119*
Keil, F.C., 93, *96*
Keller-Cohen, D., 307, *337*
Killen, M., 245, *253*

Kiparsky, P., 229, *253*
Klein, D., 236, *252*
Kosslyn, S.M., 31, *37*
Kripke, S., 212, *222*
Kuczaj, S.A., viii, *x*, 11, 22, *36*, 50n, 67, 77, *80*, 87, 88, *96*, 104, 115, 116, 117, *119*, 126, 127, 128, 129, 143, 150, *153*, 164, 167, 179, *195*, 203, *222*, 230, *253*
Kun, A., 304, *337*
Kurdek, L.A., 245, *254*

Labov, T., 11, 20, *37*
Labov, W., 11, 15, 20, *36*, *37*, 123, *153*, 284, *301*
Lahey, M., 257, *272*, 312, *334*
Lakoff, G., 187, *195*
Leech, G.N., 282, 283, 284, *301*
Lehrer, A., 123, *153*, 284, *301*
Lempers, J.D., 245, 253
Lennenberg, E., 123, *153*
Leonard, L.B., 102, 104, *119*, *120*, 229, *253*, *254*
Leopold, W.F., 49, 67, 85, *96*, 101, *120*
Leslie, A., 128, *153*
Levan-Goldschmidt, E., 244, *251*
Lewis, M.M., 6, *37*, 54n, 67, 85, *96*, 101, *120*
Lieven, E., 237, *253*
Lifter, K., 218, 289, *301*, 312, *334*
Lightbrown, P., 226, *251*, 277, *301*
Litowitz, R., 93, *96*
Lloyd, B., *120*
Lloyd, S., *152*
Lock, A., 47, *67*, 156, 157, *195*, 216, 222
Lonardo, R., 19, *36*
Lorge, I., 92, 93, *96*
Lowe, 240
Lucariello, J., 162, *195*
Lyons, J., ix, *x*, 122, 123, *153*, 278, 282, 283, *301*

Machida, S., 129, *153*
MacKain, K., 229, *255*
MacNamara, J., 5, *36*, 84, 93, *96*, 126, 217, *222*, 244, *253*, 322, *337*

MacWhinney, B., 102, *119*, 161, 169, *194*, *195*, 293, *301*
Mandler, J.M., 158, *195*, 321, *337*
Maratsos, M.P., *xx*, 296, 297, *301*, 305, 306, 313, 314, *337*
Markman, E.M., 34, *36*, *37*, 129, *153*, 162, 166, *194*
Masur, E.F., 239, *253*
Mazzie, C., 169n
McCabe, A.E., 312, 330, *337*
McCall, R.B., 245, *253*
McCarthy, D.A., 12, *37*
McCune-Nicholich, L., 200, 205, 210, 215, 216, *222*, 231, *253*
McDonald, L., 236, *253*
McGarrigle, J., 139, *152*
McLanahan, A.G., 34, *37*
McLane, J.B., *197*
McNamee, G.D., 158, *197*
McNeil, D., 209, *222*
McNeil, N., 209, *222*
McNew, S., 15, *35*
McShane, J., 48, *67*, 126, 127, *153*, 216, *222*, 248, *253*, 276, 293, 295, *301*, 302
McTaggart, J.M.E., 279, *302*
Meares, R., 239, *254*
Meck, B., *334*
Meck, E., *152*
Medin, D.L., 15, 79, *80*, 89, *97*
Meltzoff, A.N., 200, 206, 209, 210, 215, 216, *221*, *222*
Menn, L., 226, 229, *253*
Menyuk, P., 70, 79, *80*, 330, *337*
Mervis, C.A., 18, 19, *37*, 166, *195*
Mervis, C.B., 16, 18, 19, 22, *37*, *38*, 76, *81*, 104, 117, 118, *120*, 128, 130, *153*, *154*, 159, 164, 166, 167, *195*, 203, *223*
Messer, D., 230, 244, *253*
Miller, G., 5, 21, *37*, 89, 91, *97*, 117, *120*, 123, 136, *153*, 276, 278, 282, 283, *302*
Miller, J., 215, 216, *222*
Miller, R., 38, 47, *66*, 208, *221*, 280, *300*
Millikan, R.G., 156, 160, 162, *195*
Milogrom-Friedman, J., 239, *254*
Moerk, E.L., 158, 167, 191, *195*

Moore, K.C., 85, *97*, 210, *222*
Morris, J.E., 239, *252*
Mulford, R., 79, *80*, 88, *97*, 104, 117, *120*
Murphy, C.M., 244, 246, *253*
Murphy, M.D., 304, *335*
Murray, D., *152*

Neimark, E.D., 311, 329, *337*
Nelson, K., vii, viii, *x*, 1, 3, 6, 7, 8, 9, 10, 22, 23, 24, 26, 27, 28, 29, 30, 31, 32, 34, *37*, 44, 49, *67*, 70, *80*, 85, 89, 91, 92, *97*, 99, 100, 101, 102, 103, *119*, *120*, 129, 130, 133, 150, *153*, 158, 161, 168, *195*, 200, 202, 203, 213, 217, *222*, 225, 226, 228, 231, 235, 248, 249, *254*, 306, 313, 318
Newhoff, M., 102, *120*
Newport, E., 229, *254*
Nice, M.M., 99, *120*
Nickerson, N., 323, 332, *337*
Ninio, A., 131, *153*, 158, 165, 171, *196*, 247, *254*
Norlin, P.F., 90, 92, *97*
Nygren, C., 127, *153*

O'Brien, T.C., 304, *338*
O'Connor, N., 70, *80*
Oller, K.K., 3, *36*
Olsen-Fulero, L., 236, *254*
Olson, D.R., 323, 332, *337*
Orne, M.T., 313, *337*
Ortony, A., 25, *38*
Oviatt, S., 228, *254*

Palermo, D., 128, *153*
Palmer, F.R., 282, 283, *302*
Pani, J.R., 16, *37*, *153*
Paris, S.G., 311, 312, 329, *337*, *338*
Parke, R.D., 245, *253*
Patterson, P., 177, *197*
Pea, R., 209, *222*
Pepler, D.J., 312, *337*
Perlmutter, M., 14, *37*
Penman, R., 239, 240, *254*

Petersen, G., 239, *255*
Piaget, J., 3, 4, *37*, 85, 87, *97*, 129, *152*, 157, *196*, 211, 213, 214, 216, 217, *222*, *254*, 310, 314, 332, *337*
Pien, D., 236, *253*
Pollock, L.A., 225, *254*
Posner, M.L., 164, 167, *196*
Postal, P.M., 1, *37*
Prawat, R.S., 29, 30, 31, 32, *37*
Putnam, H., 84, *97*, 212, *223*
Pylyshyn, Z., 294, *302*

Ramsay, D.S., 240, 252
Ramer, A.L.H., 47, *66*, 208, *221*
Ratner, N., 158, *196*, 227
Reich, P., 3, *38*
Reich, P.A., 63, *67*
Reichele, J., 216, *222*
Rescorla, L., 3, 5, 13, 21, 23, 24, 25, 26, 28, 37, *38*, 49, 50, 53, 56, *67*, 85, 87, *97*, 99, 101, 103, *120*, 166, *196*
Rhyne, J., 70, *80*
Riccuti, M.N., 129, *153*, 213, *223*
Rice, M., 102, *120*, 145, *153*
Richards, M.M., 3, 33, *38*, 117, *120*, 128, *153*, 305, 318, *337*
Ricks, M., 14, *37*
Rips, 117
Rodgon, M.M., 245, *254*
Rogers, D., 132, 133, 135, 140, *154*
Rogoff, B., 156, *196*
Rosch, E., 16, 17, 32, 33, *37*, *38*, 72, 76, 79, *81*, 88, 90, *97*, 117, 118, *120*, 123, 128, 130, *154*, 160, 164, 165, 166, 168, 170, 172n, 188, *196*, 203, *223*
Rosenblatt, D., 225, 226, 229, 240, 250, *254*
Ross, G.S., 19, *38*, 129, 130, *154*
Rowan, L.E., 104
Rumain, B., 304, 312, *334*
Rutter, M., 70, 71, 72, *81*

Sachs, J., 167, *196*
Satterly, D., 191, *193*, 236, *251*
Saxe, G.B., *196*

Scaife, M., 244, *252*
Schaffer, H.B., 232, 241, 242, 243, *253, 254*
Schieffelin, B.B., 238, *254*
Schlesinger, J.M., 160, 161, 163, *196*, 220, *223*, 260, *273*
Schmidt, C.R., 304, *338*
Schnur, E., 232, 243, *254*
Schopler, E., 70, *81*
Schuler, A.L., 70, 79, *80*
Schwartz, R., 102, *120*, 229, 246, *253, 254*
Searle, J.R., 159, *196*, 276, *302*
Segalowitz, S.S., 310, *334*
Seiler, T.B., 71, *81*
Selfe, L., 69, 70, *81*
Seligman, M.E.P., 12, 36, 101, 225, *252*
Shapiro, B.J., 304, *338*
Shatz, M., 228, 232, 243, 247, *251, 254, 255*, 271, 272, *273*, 322, 323, *338*
Sherrod, K.B., 229, 239, *255*
Shoben, 117
Shore, C., 15, *35*
Shultz, T.R., 304, *338*
Siegler, R.S., 304, *338*
Silber, S., 271, *273*
Simon, T., 179, *194*
Simpson, C., *38*
Sinclair, H., 216, *223*, 289, 290 (table), 292, *301*
Sinha, C., *152*
Sjolin, B., 313, 336
Slobin, D., 22, *38*, 125, *154*, 217, *223*, 230, *255*, 260, *273*, 295, *301, 302*
Slotnick, N.S., 311, 329, *337*
Smiley, P., 258, *273*
Smith, 117
Smith, C.S., 293, *302*
Smith, E.E., 15, 79, *80*, 89, *97*
Smith, J., 248, *253*, 262, 265, *273*
Smith, M.E., Pref. viii, *x*
Smolak, L., 216, *223*, 248, 258
Snow, C.E., 7, *38*, 131, *154*, 167, 180, *196*, 229, 238, 239, *255*
Sommerville, S.C., 304, *338*
Spieker, S., 229, *255*
Starkey, D., 212, 213, *223*
Stern, D.N., 229, *255*
Stevenson, M.B., 244, *251*

Stone, J.B., 21, *35*
Storm, C., 190, 196
Strauss, M.S., 129, *152*, 212
Suchman, R.G., 14, *38*, 140, 154
Sugarman, S., 213, *223*
Suppes, P., 155, *194*, 304, 311, 312, *338*
Sylvester-Bradley, B., 239, *255*
Synder, L., 218, *220*, 225, 226, 228, *255*

Tager-Flusberg, H.B., 72, 73, 79, *81*
Tanz, C., 305, *338*
Tavuchis, N., 4, *35*
Templin, M.C., viii, *x*
Terrell, B.Y., 225, *254*
Thompson, J.R., 87, *97*, 101, 103, 114, 117, *120*, 143
Thomson, J., 4, 11, 12, 23, *38*, 154
Tomikawa, S.A., 14, *38*
Tomosello, M., 215, 216, *223*
Trabasso, T., 14, *38*, 140, *154*
Trevarthen, C., 218, *223*, 239, 241, 245, *255*
Tulving, E., 188, 196
Tyler, L.K., 230, *255*

Uzgiris, L., 213, 214, *223*, 245, *255*

Vendler, Z., 282, 283, 288, *302*
Volterra, V., vii, *x*, 40, *66*, 220
Vorster, J., 131, *154*
Vosniadou, S., 25, *38*
Vygotsky, L.S., 12, *38*, 129, *154*, 156, 157, 191, *196*, *197*, 220, *223*

Wales, R.J., 3, *36*, 177, 191, *197*
Wannenmacher, W., 71, *81*
Wason, P.C., 323, *338*
Watson, R., 92, 93, *97*
Weiss, A.L., 104
Wellman, H.M., 271, *273*
Wells, G., *193*, 236, 239, *251*, *255*, 260, *273*
Wells, R.S., 285, *301, 302*
Werner, H., 6, 12, *38*
Wertsch, J.V., 156, 158, 184, *197*

Wexler, K., 155, *194*
White, G.I., 310, *334*
White, T.G., 10, *38*, 132, *154*, 166, *197*
Whitehurst, G.J., 10, 18, 34, *38*
Whittaker, S., 48, 293, *302*
Wildfong, S., 29, 32, *37*
Williamson, C., 15, *35*
Winne, E., 87, *97*

Wittgenstein, L., 156, 164, *197*
Wolman, R.N., 92, *97*
Wood, D.S., *197*

Zare, S., 158, 177n, 180, *194*
Zelazo, P.R., 240, *252*
Zimmerman, B.J., *197*

Subject Index

Action words, ix, 57–58, 59–60, 62, 126, 208, 225–251, 257–272, 295–296
  see also movement words, state change words, verbs
Adjectives, 27–28, 127, 139–148, 235, 277, 278, 297, 300
  see also color terms, dimensional adjectives, spatial adjectives
Anchoring, 189–190, 191
Aspect, x, 257, 275, 278–279, 280–281, 287, 288–293, 300
Asymmetries, *see* comprehension-production asymmetries
Autism, 69–80
Auxiliary verbs, 257, 271

Basic level, 11, 16–19, 24, 30, 33, 34, 72–79, 90, 91, 92, 162–190
  see also child-basic level

Case grammar, 259–260
Category boundaries, 16, 54, 123, 160, 166, 167, 187, 188, 191

Causative verbs, 131, 261, 265
Child-basic level, 18, 166–169
Classification skills, 212–213, 218
Class inclusion, 163
Cognition-language relationship, ix, 2, 6–11, 65, 83–94, 122, 127–131, 199–220, 293–294
  see also data bases
Cognitive development, ix, 2, 9, 210–220, 303–305, 320–322, 332, 334
  see also cognition-language relationship
Collection terms, 162
Color terms, 89, 134–135, 136, 138, 144–145, 149, 150, 151
Complexive word use, 11, 12–13, 15, 19, 20, 25–26, 32
Componential theories, 1, 312, 317, 319, 320, 329, 331–332, 333, 334
  see also functional core hypothesis, semantic feature hypothesis
Comprehension-production asymmetries, ix, 11–12, 15, 19–20, 22, 28, 31, 56, 63–64, 77–78, 86–87, 101–118, 145
Constraints on actions, 228, 269, 270

Context-sensitive model, 322–331, 332, 333–334
Context-sensitive research, 305, 320–322
Contrastive features, 2, 22, 24, 54, 55, 61
  see also differentiating features, lexical contrasts
Contrastive terms, 28, 29, 33
Conversation, 228, 231–251
Cryptic representation, 149

Data bases, 124–125, 127–131, 136, 147, 148
Decontextualization, 47–49, 50, 51, 53, 57, 59, 61, 62, 63, 64, 65, 230, 306, 321
Denotation, 122, 123, 124, 126, 127, 130, 131, 132, 133, 134, 138, 140, 145, 146, 147, 148, 149, 150, 151, 275, 276
  defined, 123
Diary studies, 2, 3, 55, 83, 84–87, 89, 201, 225
Differentiating features, 3, 17
  see also contrastive features
Dimensional adjectives, 21
Disappearance words, 200–201, 204, 207, 208, 210–211, 213, 214, 215, 218, 219
  see also nonexistence words
Down Syndrome, 167
Dynamic verbs, 278, 281–293, 300

Egocentric speech, 157
Error patterns, viii, 319, 320, 329, 330, 333
  see also extensional errors, overregularization errors, phonological errors
Event-bound words, vii, 39–47, 48, 50, 51, 53, 57, 59, 60, 61, 62, 63, 64, 65
Event representations, 42–44, 45, 46, 47, 48, 49, 50, 51, 58–59, 61, 62, 63, 64, 249, 322
  see also scripts

Expressive-referential distinction, 235–236, 248
Extensional errors, 16
  see also comprehension-production asymmetries, mismatch, overextension, overlap, underextension
Extension defined, 84, 99

Family resemblance, 118, 130, 159, 168
Fast mapping, 134, 135, 143, 147, 148
Feature interdependence, 11, 15, 24, 26, 32, 33
Formats, 59
  see also routines
Functional core hypothesis, 6–11, 24–32, 33
Function words, see relational words

General purpose terms, 22, 23, 127, 271
General-Before-Specific Feature Hypothesis (GBSH), 3, 5, 10, 21, 33, 308
Grammatical role structure, 257, 258

Habituation, 19, 52, 129
Hedges, 187, 188, 190, 191
Holistic representations, 43, 50, 117, 118
Homophones, 126, 146
Hypernymy, 132, 147
Hyponymy, 126, 132

Imitation, 158, 217, 245, 246, 247, 258
Individual differences, 76, 109, 114–115, 226
  see also expressive-referential distinction, strategies of acquisition
Innate factors, 79, 294
Intension defined, 1, 84, 100
Internalization, 157
Interview studies, 83, 89–94

Kin terms, 3, 4, 5, 21

Language-games, 156, 159, 160, 161, 162, 163, 164, 165, 167, 168, 170, 171, 177, 184, 191, 192
Lexical contrasts, 21, 24, 135, 137, 139, 140, 143, 144, 145, 146, 147
 see also contrastive features
Lexical contrast theory, 21–24, 33
Lexical fields, 28
 see also semantic fields
Lexical gaps, 126, 127, 140, 141, 145, 146
Lexical selection, see name selection, word choice
Limited scope formulae, 293
Linguistic input, ix, 2, 9, 18, 22, 24, 34, 65, 131–135, 147, 228–251, 275, 295, 322–323
 articles in, 5
 prosodic features of, 229–231
 word frequency in, 229–230
 word position in, 229, 230
 see also maternal labelling, maternal speech, motherese
Locative words, 206–207, 208, 209, 213–214, 259, 262–264, 277
Logical connectives, viii, ix, 303–334

Maternal labelling, 131, 132, 155–192
 see also linguistic input, maternal speech, motherese
Maternal speech, see linguistic input, maternal labelling, motherese
 descriptive comments in, 236, 237, 238–241
 directives in, 235–236, 237, 238
  action directives in, 232–234, 238, 242, 244–249
  attention directives in, 227, 232–234, 242–244, 246
 styles, 228, 235–236
Means-ends relationships, 210, 211–212, 213, 215, 217, 218
Mental process verbs, 89, 258, 271–272
Mental retardation, 71–79
 see also Down Syndrome

Metalexical ability, 34
Metalinguistic skills, 315
 see also metalexical ability
Metaphorical extensions, 90, 91, 92
Mismatch, 203
Modifiers, 27–28, 188
Motherese, 167
 see also linguistic input, maternal labelling, maternal speech
Movement words, 258, 261

Name recall, 12, 56, 102, 104
Name recognition, 12, 102, 104
Name selection, 25
 see also word choice
Naming, vii, 159, 201–202, 293
 see also nominals, nouns, object names, proper names
Naming explosion, 203, 209, 212, 213, 218, 219
Naming games, 246–248, 249, 250
Natural kinds, 130, 165, 212
Negation, 209
Neologisms, 75
Nominal insight, 226, 250
Nominals, 225–251, 276, 278
 see also nouns, object names, proper names
Nonexistence words, 263–264
 see also disappearance words
Notice words, 201, 207, 208
Nouns, ix, 1–34, 89, 90–94, 121–151, 155–192, 277–278
 see also nominals, object names, proper names

Object concept, 210–211, 214, 215, 217, 218
 see also object permanence
Object names, ix, 47–57, 59–60, 61, 62, 63, 64, 71–79, 83–94, 99–118, 201–204, 212–213
 see also nominals, nouns, proper names
Object permanence, 12–13
 see also object concept
Onomatopoeic words, 6–7

Original word game, 20
Ostensive definition, 131, 135
Overextension, 2, 3, 4, 5, 6, 11, 14, 19, 20, 21, 22, 23, 25, 49, 51, 52, 53–57, 58, 60, 61, 63, 64, 71, 85, 86, 87, 88, 100–115, 121, 122, 125, 138, 160, 166, 203, 204, 330
  analogical, 25, 26, 31, 101
  as a communicative strategy, 19–20, 22, 23, 55–56, 57, 101–102, 103
  associative, 25, 51, 56, 75, 76
  perceptually vs. functionally based, 2, 13, 31–32, 49–50, 75–76, 85, 88
  phonological errors and, 75
  predicate statement, 25, 26, 31, 56
  processing errors and, 56, 57
  rescission of, 53–57, 58, 60, 61, 64
  wilful misnaming and, 56, 57
Overlap, 10, 85, 86, 87, 88, 100–115
Overregularization errors, 294, 295, 296, 297

Performatives, 60, 62, 265
Personal pronouns, 64
Personal-social words, *see* social-personal words
Phenic representation, 149
Phonological errors, 75
Picture-book reading, 171–191, 246–247, 250
Plans, 204–206, 208–210, 211–212, 214, 219
Play, 87, 217, 240, 249, 251
Polysemy, 28, 46
Pragmatic factors, 257–272
  see also conversation
Preemption, 125, 126, 130, 139, 144, 146, 147
Prelinguistic communication, 209, 216, 219
Preoperational concepts, 210, 211, 217
Principle of contrast, 21, 22, 23, 33
Principle of conventionality, 22, 23, 33
Procedural semantics, 276
Processing errors, 56
Proper names, 4, 5, 10, 18, 64, 89

Prototypes, ix, 50, 51, 52, 54, 56, 58, 59, 60, 61, 65, 79, 88, 103–105, 115–118, 130, 159, 164–165, 166, 168, 170, 177, 188, 203, 204, 206, 212, 213
Prototypicality, 72, 73, 75, 78
  see also typicality

Recall, *see* name recall
Recognition, *see* name recognition
Recurrence words, 205–206, 208, 209, 210, 211
Reference, 122, 124, 130, 133, 135, 148, 150, 151, 226, 257, 258, 300
  defined, 122
Referential-expressive distinction, *see* expressive-referential distinction
Refusal words, 206, 208, 209, 210, 215
Relational terms, 3, 89, 303–334
Relational words, 201–202, 204–207, 209, 214, 215, 219
Rescission of overextensions, *see* overextension, rescission of
Response strategies, 316–318, 319, 320, 333
Routines, 44, 59, 65, 169, 227, 235, 246–247, 249

Scripts, 116, 204, 249, 250, 332
  see also event representations
Semantic feature hypothesis, 1–5, 9–10, 19–21, 23–24, 33, 203, 306, 307–309, 326, 334
Semantic fields, 54, 123, 131, 135, 138, 140, 181, 183, 191
  see also lexical fields
Sense, 122, 123, 124, 126, 127, 130, 131, 132, 133, 134, 146, 147, 148, 149, 150, 151, 276
  defined, 123
Sensorimotor schemas, 204, 210, 216–217
Social-personal words, vii, 208–209, 226, 227, 241
Sorting tasks, 129, 212–213, 218
Spatial adjectives, 127
Spatial relationships, 210, 213–214

State change words, 258, 259, 261–269
Stative verbs, 278, 281–287, 297, 300
Strategies, *see* response strategies, strategies of acquisition
Strategies of acquisition, 124–127, 142–145, 148
Subordinate level, 18, 28, 33, 74, 75, 78, 92, 145, 162, 166, 168, 170, 176, 179, 181, 183, 184, 185, 189, 190
Superordinate level, 18, 19, 30, 32, 33, 34, 72–79, 90, 92, 145, 166
Symbolic processes, viii
Symbolization, 155–163
Synonymy, 3, 4, 17, 33, 126, 132, 145, 147

Temporal expression, 257, 258, 275–300
Tense, x, 257, 275, 278–280, 288–293, 294, 300
Typicality, 11, 16, 24, 26, 32, 33, 174–177
see also prototypicality

Underextension, 3, 4, 20, 49, 50, 54, 55, 58, 60, 61, 63, 71, 77, 85–86, 87, 88, 100–115, 160, 203, 204

Value hypothesis, 10–11
Verb inflections, x, 257, 275–300
Verbs, ix, x, 21, 83, 89, 90–94, 127, 139, 251, 257–258, 270–272, 275–300
  see also action words, auxiliary verbs, causative verbs, dynamic verbs, mental process verbs, stative verbs
Vocabulary growth, vii, viii, 225
  see also naming explosion

Wilful misnaming, 56, 57
Word association, 31, 34, 75, 76
Word choice, 162, 163, 174–175, 180, 184, 191
  see also name selection